Judgmental Forecasting

Judgmental Forecasting

Edited by

George Wright
Bristol Business School

and

Peter Ayton
Psychology Department,
City of London Polytechnic

JOHN WILEY & SONS
Chichester · New York · Brisbane · Toronto · Singapore

British Library Cataloguing in Publication Data:

Judgmental forecasting.
  1. Economic forecasting. 2. Judgement
  I. Wright, George II. Ayton, Peter
  338.5'442   HB3730

  ISBN 0 471 91327 8

Typeset by Acorn Bookwork, Salisbury, Wiltshire
Printed and bound in Great Britain

List of Contributors

ANDERSON-PARENTÉ, J. K.	*Psychology Department, Towson State University, Towson, Maryland 21204, USA*
ARMSTRONG, J. S.	*Wharton School, University of Pennsylvania, Philadelphia, PA 19104, USA*
AYTON, P.	*Decision Analysis Group, City of London Polytechnic, Old Castle Street, London, E1 7NT*
BARNES, V.	*Department of Psychology, University of Washington, Seattle, Washington, 98195 USA*
BEACH, L. R.	*Department of Psychology, University of Washington, Seattle, Washington, 98195 USA*
BUDESCU, D.	*Department of Psychology, University of Haifa, Haifa 31999, Israel*
BREHMER, B.	*Psykologiska Institutionen, Uppsala Universitet, Box 227, S-75104, Uppsala, Sweden*
BUNN, D.	*London Business School, Regent's Park, London, NW1 4SA*
CHRISTENSEN-SZALANSKI, J.	*College of Business Administration, University of Iowa, Iowa City, Iowa 52242, USA*
ESCHENBACH, F. G.	*School of Engineering, University of Alaska, 3211 Providence Drive, Anchorage, Alaska 99508, USA*
EVANS, J. ST. B. T.	*Department of Psychology, Plymouth Polytechnic, Drake Circus, Plymouth, Devon, PL4 8AA*
GEISTAUTS, G. A.	*School of Business and Public Affairs, University of Alaska, 3211 Providence Drive, Anchorage, Alaska 99508, USA*
JUNGERMANN, H.	*Technische Universitat Berlin, Sekr. D0303, Institut fur Psychologie, Doverstrasse 1–5/ D1000/Berlin 10/West Germany*

v

LOCK, A.   *School of Business, Kingston Polytechnic,*
                                      Penrhyn   Road,   Kingston-Upon-Thames,
                                      KT1 2EE
OTTEN, W.   *Instituut voor Experimentele Psychologie, der*
                                      Rijksuniversiteit te Groningen, pa Biologisch
                                      Centrum, Vleugal D, Kerklaan 30, 9751 NN
                                      Haren (Gn), The Netherlands
PARENTÉ, F. J.   *Psychology Department, Towson State Uni-*
                                      versity, Towson, Maryland 21204, USA
PHILLIPS, L. D.   *Decision Analysis Unit, London School of*
                                      Economics, Houghton Street, London, WC2A
                                      2AE
SAMSON, D.   *Graduate School of Management, University*
                                      of Melbourne, Parkville, Victoria 3052,
                                      Australia
THOMAS, H.   *Department of Business Administration, Uni-*
                                      versity of Illinois, 350 Commerce West, 1206
                                      S. Sixth Street, Champaign, Illinois 61820,
                                      USA
THURING, M.   *Technische Universitat Berlin, Sekr. D0303,*
                                      Institut fur Psychologie, Doverstrasse 1–5/
                                      D1000/Berlin 10/West Germany
VLEK, C.   *Institut voor Experimentele Psychologie, der*
                                      Rijksuniversiteit te Groningen, pa Biologisch
                                      Centrum, Vleugal D, Kerlaan 30, 9751 NN
                                      Haren (Gn), The Netherlands
WALLSTEN, T.   *The LL Thurstone Psychometric Laboratory,*
                                      The University of North Carolina at Chapel
                                      Hill, Davie Hall 013 A, Chapel Hall, NC
                                      27514, USA
WRIGHT, G.   *Bristol Business School, Coldharbour Lane,*
                                      Frenchay, Bristol, BS16 1QY

Contents

Contents

Preface

The idea for this book has its origins in the fourth International Symposium on Forecasting which was held at the London Business School in July 1984. At that conference we heard several papers dealing with aspects of judgment in forecasting and we were motivated to collect together a set of original chapters which would develop this theme. However, this book does not contain a subset of the conference proceedings. Rather it consists of fourteen specially commissioned papers from a mix of contributors who are based in either psychology departments or business schools. Our objective is to present an overview of judgmental forecasting in a format that is accessible to a broad-based multidisciplinary audience consisting of forecasting practitioners and academics. The chapters provide tutorial sections at appropriate points in order to allow straightforward access to the judgmental forecasting literature.

We hope that this book serves to stimulate further research on the role of judgment in forecasting so that, in the near future, more papers appear on this topic in the *Journal of Forecasting* and in the *International Journal of Forecasting*. We judge that the editors of these journals are interested in the topic since they are amongst the contributors to this book!

Judgmental Forecasting
Edited by G. Wright and P. Ayton
© 1987 John Wiley & Sons Ltd

Introduction

Judgment has been studied for many years by psychologists interested in human decision-making. Most of the research has been undertaken from the perspective of 'subjective expected utility theory', a term which has often been replaced by the simple expression, 'decision theory'. Decision theory has its roots in statistics and economics and basically proposes that two independent types of information are crucial in making good decisions: subjective probabilities attached to events occurring and subjective values or utilities attached to the outcomes of those events at some time in the future. Normative decision theory specifies how subjective probabilities and utilities should be combined in order to specify optimal decisions.

Most early studies of the human judgment of subjective probabilities showed limitations or biases in judgmental assessment. One well known, and still prevalent, example is the 'gamblers' fallacy'. Dostoevsky observed that in roulette 'after the red has come up ten times in a row, hardly anyone will persist in betting on it'. But a belief that the black is more likely to come up after a long run of red is fallacious: the roulette ball has no memory!

Paul Slovic (1982) has aptly summarized much of the research to date.

This work has led to the sobering conclusion that, in the face of uncertainty, man may be an intellectual cripple, whose intuitive judgements and decisions violate many of the fundamental principles of optimal behavior.

The purpose of this book is to take a broader look at the role of judgment in forecasting and allow you, the reader, to come to a considered view as to whether this summary of the research data is a fair or appropriate verdict. Let us say, before you begin to delve into individual chapters, that the major thrust of this book is that judgment *does* play and, indeed, *should* play a major role in the forecasting process.

Virtually all of the statistical techniques available for forecasting require a series of historical data that can be utilized in preparing the forecast. However, often such data is unavailable or irrelevant; for example, forecasting the

1

sales of a new type of product or forecasting sales of an old type of product given that another company has launched a competitive product. In such situations the manager can still apply the concept of probability but based on subjective judgments rather than historical frequencies.

However, as Makridakis and Wheelwright (1979) note, 'forecasters tend to concentrate on well-behaved situations that can be forecast with standard methodologies and to ignore the rapidly changing situation for which management may most want forecasts' (p. 339).

They also emphasize subjective components in the use of econometric models:

> most econometric forecasts incorporate a substantial subjective element, reflecting the developer's own personal opinion about the future. Thus there is some question as to how much the quantitative model contributes to better forecasting and how much the judgemental input of the developer affects the results. (p. 344)

Other textbooks have argued that judgmental forecasts are used when there is insufficient time to obtain and use a statistical forecast or when situations are changing so rapidly that a statistically based forecast would be no use, even as a guide. Makridakis and Wheelwright (1979) concluded that:

> application of quantitative approaches will continue to increase and supplement or replace many of the applications now handled through purely judgemental approaches (p. 348).

However, they also note that:

> Of course it must be remembered that just as it is impossible to say which methodology is always best, it is always impossible to conclude that quantitative methods are always better than subjective or judgementally based methods. Human forecasters can process much more information than most of the formalized quantitative methods, and such forecasters are more likely to have knowledge of specific near-term events that need to be reflected in current forecasts. (p. 348)

One instance where judgmental forecasts are routinely generated is weather-forecasting. The official forecasts issued by the National Weather Service in the United States are subjective probability forecasts. Murphy and Brown (1985) have evaluated these subjective forecasts and found that, for certain predicted categories of weather, they were more accurate than the available objective statistical techniques. In this case the forecasters have a very large amount of information available, including the output from statistical techniques. They also receive detailed feedback and have the opportunity to gain experience of making forecasts under a wide range of meteorological conditions. Furthermore they have considerable practice in quantifying their internal state of uncertainty. These circumstances may well be ideal for the relatively successful application of judgmental, as compared with quantitative, forecasting. They are certainly not the conditions available in most situations where judgment is elicited and utilized.

In discussing the possibility of combining judgmental and quantitative forecasts, Makridakis, Wheelwright and McGhee (1983) argue that:

> Whereas purely judgemental approaches may suffer from a number of biases, formal quantitative forecasting methods suffer major difficulties in situations of significant environment changes. Approaches that combine the best elements of both categories may well produce significantly improved results in comparison with those produced by using one or the other approaches alone . . . A logical conclusion is that forecasts should rely more heavily on the predictions provided by formal quantitative methods, as long as there are no major changes in the environment of organization. When such changes do occur, judgemental inputs should be given more weight. (pp. 845–862)

In a review of the use of forecasting tools within the corporate planning process, Klein and Linneman (1984) surveyed 500 of the world's largest corporations. They noted that

> The overwhelming majority of corporate planners . . . recognized the severe limitations of conventional/statistical techniques for forecasts of three or more years . . . In direct response to the turbulent environmental condition worldwide, a variety of non-analytical forecasting techniques and approaches have become accessible over the last decade. These have been variously called 'judgemental', 'speculative' or 'conjectural' techniques. . . . (p. 71)

In a companion paper, Klein and Newman (1980) point out that a turbulent environment characterized by discontinuous change may be unpredictable by statistical forecasting techniques which are dependent on the continuity of historical data.

> When dealing with radical social, political and technological change, management and planners cannot use rational analytic techniques, the very techniques with which they feel most comfortable. There is little scientific rationale for conjectured change. Consequency, such 'soft' forecasts often leave managers very nervous and sceptical. (p. 34)

In this book we hope to help those managers and planners become less nervous, less sceptical and more knowledgeable about judgmental forecasting!

The chapters in this book are grouped into four major parts which reflect, in part, differential emphasis in the research and practice of judgmental forecasting.

Part I, 'The Psychology of Individual Judgment', presents five chapters which address issues concerned with evaluation of the quality of judgment. Several themes emerge from these chapters. Do paper and pencil tests of the quality of judgment shown in the psychological laboratory have relevance to the practice of forecasting? Are there systematic biases in judgmental forecasting? If so, can they be minimized by the way in which judgment is elicited from the forecaster?

Phillips evaluates the adequacy of judgmental forecasts. He argues that given the right circumstances people can make precise, reliable and accurate judgments. He locates the assessment of subjective probability forecasts within the general axiomatic approach of decision theory and the related technology, decision analysis, and then cites studies that have shown that groups of individuals can produce accurate subjective probability forecasts. He argues that the process of judgmental forecasting should be carried out with the same degree of care as that taken when a scientist or engineer measures some physical quality.

By contrast, *Evans* draws attention to the problem of biases which may arise in the process of judgmental forecasting by reviewing laboratory research on the psychology of reasoning and judgment. He argues that people often manifest a 'confirmation bias' by testing hypotheses in a manner which is more likely to minimize rather than maximize the chances of falsification. 'Belief bias' refers to a tendency for people to generate forecasts which are consistent with their prior beliefs and subsequently to be more critical of outcomes which conflict with these beliefs. Forecasters may be prone to bias in both the generation of predictions and in the evaluation of outcomes. Finally, Evans considers how these biases may be reflected in real-world forecasting and how their effects may be minimized.

However, *Beach, Christensen-Szalanski and Barnes* argue that issues regarding the quality of human judgment are not settled and that a commonly held belief that human judgment is poor is not based on convincing data. For example, empirical studies showing poor judgmental performance tend to be cited more often than good performance results. In addition, poor performance by undergraduates on contrived paper-and-pencil tasks may not generalize to the world outside the psychological laboratory. They argue that the quality of human judgment cannot be assessed in isolation from human action. Only by assessing actions which *may* result from judgment do we focus on the *quality* of judgmental performance.

Budescu and Wallsten note that most decision-makers would probably prefer a point probability forecast over a vague estimate. However, they argue that the decision-maker would be misled if he or she gave, or was given, an estimate expressing greater precision than that warranted by the information on which the estimate was based. Precise numbers convey the *impression* of a precision which may be illusory. Budescu and Wallsten review the literature on subjective probability estimation and conclude that, in general, people are fairly reliable and coherent in their estimations. Finally, these authors evaluate numerical and non-numerical means for expressing vague uncertainties.

In the last chapter in this section, *Wright and Ayton* review research on the elicitation of consistent, coherent and valid probability forecasts. From this they develop a general model of the judgmental forecasting process showing the interdependence of consistency, coherence and validity. They describe an interactive forecasting aid and discuss research which suggests that there are consistent individual differences in forecasting ability.

Part II, 'Judgment from Groups of Individuals', presents four chapters which deal with methods of combining individual judgments to produce improved judgmental forecasts. Several themes run through these chapters in addition to those already raised in the previous part of this volume. Which form of behavioral aggregation is best? Is behavioral aggregation superior to mathematical aggregation of opinion? How should long-range forecasts be evaluated? How can problems of implementation be overcome?

Lock presents a broad-ranging review of methods of aggregating individual judgments in subjective forecasts, paying special attention to the context and process of the generation of group judgments. In the context of behavioral aggregation he compares and contrasts Delphi, the Nominal Group Technique and Brainstorming. Next he evaluates methods of mathematical aggregation and focuses on the use of linear models, the weighting of individual forecasts and the aggregation of probabilities. From his discussions he develops a seven-phase procedure to enhance group judgmental forecasting.

Parenté and Anderson-Parenté focus on the Delphi enquiry system, outlining the history and philosophical background of the technique and the defining characteristics of the method, and then differentiate it from other small-group-based forecasting techniques. Parenté and Anderson Parenté next discuss the research basis for belief in the validity of the method as a predictive technique. Early research revealed an inverse correlation between accuracy and variability of individual constituent responses in the Delphi method. However, well-controlled laboratory investigations of predictive validity are relatively uncommon because long-range scenarios are not easily verified. Indeed action may be taken to avoid or facilitate possible futures. The authors pay special attention to the role of substantive expertise in the Delphi method. They then discuss future developments with the method and focus on the role of the computer and the interface of qualitative and quantitative forecasting. Finally they suggest practical guidelines for the best use of the technique.

By contrast, *Armstrong* examines different approaches to forecasting the outcome of conflict situations. He reviews previous research and then describes his own studies. The evidence suggests that active role-playing provides more accurate predictions of outcomes than those provided by expert opinions. In seven actual situations, opinions were correct for 20 per cent of the predictions versus 70 per cent predictions for role-playing. Armstrong argues that interaction among participants may be the critical element in the superiority of role-playing and that in many situations the potential gains in accuracy should justify the costs entailed.

Geistauts and Eschenbach describe and evaluate the particular problems inherent in the implementation of judgmental forecasts. Forecasts without an impact on policy formulation or decisions are wasted and judgmental forecasts suffer from the particular disadvantage that they may appear to be non-scientific when compared with quantitative forecasting. These authors link implementation to forecast accuracy, credibility and acceptability. They then proceed to describe a case study of a large-scale Delphi application showing how credibility and acceptability can be maximized such that judgmental forecasts are implemented.

Part III, 'Use of Multiple Regression Techniques', focuses on the use of mathematical modelling in aiding or replacing judgmental forecasters. Two major themes run through these chapters in addition to the themes already introduced in the previous two parts of the book. Is it practically useful to build mathematical models of judgment when outcome data, i.e. actual values of the variable to be predicted, are not known? Are mathematical models built using known outcome data useful as forecasting aids?

Brehmer discusses the relevance and implications of Social Judgment Theory for problems of judgmental forecasting. This theory is concerned with building a mathematical model, often using multiple regression techniques, of the cognitive system employed when people make predictions on the basis of predictive cues. As such, the theory is concerned with judgments *under* uncertainty rather than judgments *about* uncertainty involving the assessment of subjective probabilities. Brehmer describes and evaluates the research findings of SJT and discusses their implications for judgmental forecasting. Finally, he introduces a computer-based cognitive aid which makes the cognitive model of the forecaster explicit and aids communication between people with different models or policies.

By contrast, *Samson and Thomas* apply multiple regression techniques to aid the insurance underwriter to relate characteristics of policyholders to the expected cost of claims in order to set realistic insurance premiums. Using a case-study they pay particular attention to the modelling of categorical explanatory variables. When outcome data, in this case cost of claims, is known, the linear model of the combination of explanatory variables can be used as the basis for forecasting cost of claims in the next forecast period. Samson and Thomas discuss whether the models, used as forecasting aids, will improve the predictions of account managers in estimating future claims and in setting appropriate premiums.

In the last chapter in this part, *Bunn* discusses statistical methods for combining forecasts. The individual forecasts may be quantitative projections or subjective opinions. Bunn differentiates two levels of linear modelling. The first level corresponds to the modelling of basic explanatory variables, such as that discussed by Samson and Thomas, and the second level is a class of linear models for combining two or more such forecasting models. Bunn makes the point that approaches to the combination of forecasts are motivated by a desire to use all the information available in an attempt to build the most accurate aggregate predictor rather than to explore causal links between variables.

Bunn discusses the relative usefulness of replacing a forecaster by a linear model of his or her cognitive processes or using outcome data, when this is known, as a basis for model estimation. Using a case study of electric load forecasting, he compares holistic expert forecasts against a variety of linear models.

Part IV, 'The Psychology of Scenarios', presents two chapters on the generation and evaluation of scenarios. This part is more speculative than previous parts in that psychological approaches to these issues are more recent and our knowledge is, at present, more limited.

Jungermann and Thüring explore psychological issues in the construction of scenarios. They first differentiate alternative conceptions of the term 'scenario' and then describe techniques that have been proposed for generating scenarios. In the main body of their chapter they present a theoretical framework of the cognitive processes involved in the construction and evaluation of scenarios. Jungermann and Thüring argue that their theoretical perspective will help the forecaster to make better use of knowledge already possessed and will highlight problem areas in the intuitive generation of scenarios.

Vlek and Otten investigate the relationship between policy decision-making and scenario evaluation and identify further weaknesses in the methodology of scenario construction. In an experimental evaluation of judgment in energy scenarios these researchers used four long-term scenarios previously utilized in the nationwide Dutch discussion of future electric power generation. In this chapter they investigate the cognitive processing of scenario information, the determinants of the judged plausibility of scenarios and the preference ordering of scenarios in terms of relative attractiveness. Vlek and Otten's empirical results add to our, at present, limited knowledge of the judgmental evaluation of scenarios.

REFERENCES

Klein, H. E. and Linneman, R. E. (1984) 'Environmental assessment: an international study of corporate practice', *Journal of Business Strategy*, **5**, 66–84.

Klein, H. E. and Newman, W. (1980) 'How to use SPIRE: a systematic procedure for identifying relevant environments for strategic planning', *Journal of Business Strategy*, **1**, 32–46.

Makridakis, S. and Wheelwright, S. C. (eds.) (1979) 'Forecasting the future and the future of forecasting. In *Studies in the Managerial Sciences: Vol. 12, Forecasting*. Amsterdam: North Holland.

Makridakis, S., Wheelwright, S. C. and McGhee, V. E. (1983) *Forecasting: Methods and Applications* (second edition). New York: Wiley.

Murphy, A. H. and Brown, B. G. (1985) 'A comparative evaluation of objective and subjective weather forecasts in the United States', in Wright, G. N. (ed.), *Behavioral Decision Making*, New York: Plenum.

Slovic, P. (1982) 'Towards understanding and improving decisions'. In W. C. Howell and E. A. Fleishmann (eds.), *Human Performance and Productivity: Vol. 12, Information Processing and Decision Making*. Hillsdale, N.J.: Erlbaum.

Part I

The psychology of individual judgment

Judgmental Forecasting
Edited by G. Wright and P. Ayton
© 1987 John Wiley & Sons Ltd

CHAPTER 1

On the Adequacy of Judgmental Forecasts

Lawrence D. Phillips
London School of Economics and Political Science

In a sense, all forecasts are 'judgmental'. Since forecasts concern future events or conditions, which cannot be predicted with certainty, there is always some element of human judgment involved in making what are essentially inductive inferences. It is an act of human judgment to accept the past as a guide to the future, to use a particular model rather than some other one to extrapolate available data, to choose appropriate premises in 'deducing' that a future state will occur. Thus, a 'non-judgmental' forecast is a contradiction, 'judgmental' forecasts a tautology. Whether they are adequate or not, 'judgmental' forecasts know no alternative.

That said, we are still entitled to ask about the adequacy of forecasts. Much recent literature has focused on assessing forecasting methods and models (Makridakis *et al.*, 1982; Huss, 1985) as if human judgment played no significant part in the forecast, other than choosing the 'best' model. Yet as Hogarth and Makridakis (1981) have argued, forecasting depends on judgmental inputs. There can be no 'objective' forecasts, in the sense of a forecast that depends solely on data. Judgment can play a direct role, as in making intuitive predictions, or an indirect role, as in using models to derive forecasts.

So, how good are people's judgments? Chapter 3 by Beach and Barnes tackles this question from a descriptive viewpoint. Drawing on research literature that reports how people actually make decisions, they conclude that it is not possible to judge the quality of human judgment. (And even if one could, then an unfavourable verdict would necessarily question the verdict itself.)

This chapter takes a different tack. It is concerned with what people *can* do, not with what they do do. Its major conclusion is that, given the right circumstances, which the chapter identifies, people can make precise, reliable and accurate judgments. The emphasis will be on intuitive predictions themselves, rather than on the more general role of judgment in forecasting.

FORECASTING AND DECISION THEORY

At first sight, it would seem that judgments can be made about almost anything: the exchange rate in six months' time between the dollar and the pound, expected market share for a particular product at the end of next year, number of hospital beds occupied next week in a given ward, total amount of rainfall next month, the party with a majority at the next national election, the winner of the men's singles at this year's Wimbledon, and so forth. Some forecasts are about future events or conditions, while others are about quantities whose specific values are currently unknown, or 'uncertain quantities', for short.

Forecasts are made, often as part of a planning process, to serve decision-making. My approach here is to embed those forecasts within the decision problem faced by the individual or organization. If an individual or group wishes to be coherent and consistent in making decisions, then there is available a theory which can be applied to ensure that consistency. A brief excursion into that theory will help to clarify the true nature of forecasts, and, in particular, the role of judgment in making forecasts.

Decision theory

Modern decision theory (Lindley, 1985) starts by presuming that a particular situation is facing an individual who wishes to make decisions that are coherent, that do not contradict one another. Put negatively, the person would not deliberately accept a 'Dutch book'. (An example of a Dutch book would be a set of bets placed on the outcome of a single horse race, such that no matter which horse won, the bettor was certain to lose money.)

The theory then proposes certain basic principles or axioms, which seem reasonable as descriptions of coherent preferences. Usually these are thought of as the preferences of a single individual, but the theory can equally be applied to a group striving to be coherent in taking actions.

The ordering principle says that it should be possible to rank the consequences that might follow from any decision in order of preference or indifference. That is, it should be possible to say that either consequence A is preferred to consequence B, or B is preferred to A, or one is indifferent between A and B. The relationship 'I don't know' is excluded, for obviously a Dutch book might be accepted by an individual choosing bets at random.

Another principle, called 'transitivity', says that if consequence A is preferred to consequence B, and B is preferred to C, then A should be preferred to C. While some people may at times violate this principle, if their violations are pointed out to them, they will most likely change their preferences so as to make them transitive. Failure to do so might result in an individual paying a sum of money, however small, to replace consequence C with the preferred consequence B, another sum to move from B to A, then another to go from A to the preferred C. But this takes the individual back to the starting point, ready for another round, thus making a 'money pump' out of him or her.

These two principles, and a few others, form the axioms of modern decision theory, and these axioms can be combined to prove theorems, as axioms in geometry can be combined by applying the laws of logic to prove theorems. The theorems, which are more useful than the axioms, are as follows:

(1) Probabilities exist. Associated with each consequence is a number between 0 and 1. These numbers represent an individual's degree of belief, such that 0 means no chance of occurring, and 1 represents certainty. These numbers combine according to the laws of probability.

(2) Utilities exist. Another set of numbers can be associated with the consequences. These numbers are a function of the subjective value and the risk associated with the consequences relative to one another.

(3) Choose the course of action with the highest expected utility. The expected utility of any course of action is obtained by weighting (i.e. multiplying) the utility of each possible consequence by its corresponding probability and adding these products.

This last theorem is a guide to action. If the individual wishes to be consistent in his or her actions, then utilities and probabilities must be determined for each consequence, the expected utility calculated for each option, and then the option with the highest expected utility chosen. Thus, we see that consequences are characterized by two components, probability and utility, both measurable, and both given a subjective interpretation. It is the product of these two components that assigns utility to options and makes possible comparisons, using the expected utility principle, of one option as against another.

Note, however, that although probabilities and utilities are given a subjective interpretation, they are constrained. In particular, probabilities are required to conform to certain laws which disallow totally arbitrary judgments and can be used to help an individual construct more satisfactory intuitive forecasts, as we shall see later.

For now, the key point is that a theory of coherent preferences logically implies that judgments need be made about only two quantities: probabilities and utilities. While the event, condition or uncertain quantity itself is the subject of judgment, it is the probabilities and utilities associated with them that are the expressions of judgment.

It is, of course, possible to ask, 'What is a best estimate for the dollar–pound exchange rate in six months?', but decision theory makes clear that the answer does not provide a sufficient basis for decision-making. Instead, a probability distribution over possible exchange rates is required, so that alternative futures are taken into consideration when formulating a decision.

In addition, it is necessary to consider utilities of possible consequences. In short, for forecasts that serve the decision-making function, an important role for judgment is assessing probabilities and utilities.

Some planners do not see it this way. They argue, correctly, that any particular scenario for the future has associated with it a vanishingly small probability of occurrence since there are a near-infinity number of possible futures. For planning it is useful to anticipate only a few of these possible futures, so assigning probabilities is irrelevant and potentially misleading. But this argument fails to recognize that the expected utility rule provides a *relative* comparison of options in light of only those futures under consideration. It is the relative magnitudes of probabilities that matter, not their absolute values. Even though the events or scenarios being considered do not form a complete list, so their absolute probabilities sum to less than one, the expected utility rule can still be applied to see which option is relatively most favoured. The relative ordering of the options will remain unchanged even if the scenario probabilities are multiplied by a constant. Thus, when it is impracticable to anticipate all possible future scenarios, assigning probabilities to those events under consideration can usefully contribute to requisite models.

Requisite decision models

By now it should be evident that I am advocating a generative use of decision theory. Statisticians often portray decision theory as a mathematical theory of optimal decisions; many operational researchers seem to think of it as a normative theory about how people should make decisions; most economists treat expected utility theory as a workable assumption about how rational people take decisions; psychologists have modified expected utility theory to explain how people actually do take decisions.

None of these approaches is taken here. Instead, decision theory, and its applied technology, decision analysis, is seen as providing a framework that can be used to help an individual or group to construct a coherent representation of a particular problem. This representation will be 'requisite' in the sense that it is just sufficient to solve the problem at hand (Phillips, 1984). The requisite model serves to clarify the thinking of an individual, and helps a group to achieve a shared understanding of the problem, sufficient in both cases for decisions to be taken.

A brief history of decision analysis

As an historical aside, the modern version of decision theory can be traced to an important paper by Frank Ramsey (1926), an Englishman who wrote his paper as a criticism of John Maynard Keynes's theory of probability.

Ramsey provided an axiomatic base for probability, interpreted as a degree of belief, and for utility, though he did not demonstrate the proofs because, as he said, 'this would, I think, be rather like working out to seven places of decimals a result only valid to two'. This was a pity, for had he shown the proofs it would have been clear how to assess the two subjective components in the theory, probability and utility.

In any event, economists were, in the 1920s, giving up the notion of measurable utility because it was not necessary for macro-economic theory (Edwards, 1954), and probability was mainly applied to repeated events whose relative frequencies could be determined by objective means. Thus, applications of Ramsey's ideas had to await further elaborations of the theory.

The first of these was contributed by von Neumann and Morgenstern (1947), whose proofs provided a method for measuring utility. Later, L. J. Savage (1954) refined and completed this work, and showed how probability could be applied to unique events. With workable methods for assessing utility and probability in place, a technology started to develop in the early 1960s, beginning with *Applied Statistical Decision Theory* (Raiffa and Schlaifer, 1961). That mathematically formidable work was followed by Raiffa's very readable blend of theory and technology (Raiffa, 1968) and Schlaifer's textbook (Schlaifer, 1969). While this work was in progress at Harvard University, Ron Howard at Stanford University combined decision theory with systems analysis to provide a technology which he called 'decision analysis' (Howard, 1966), a term that is now in general use for any systematic use of expected utility theory to help individuals or groups analyse difficult problems. The most recent major development was provided by Keeney and Raiffa (1976) who extended the theory to include decisions that must be made in the face of multiple objectives that may conflict.

UTILITY

Utilities are measures of both subjective value and risk. As an illustration of subjective value, consider how you would feel if you won £10 000 as compared to losing that same amount. Most people judge the pain of the loss to be greater than the pleasure of the win. Although the monetary amounts are the same, the subjective values associated with them are not equal.

To understand the concept of risk as it applies to utility, imagine that you have been given a wager which entitles you to a 50–50 chance to win £10 000 or nothing. This wager is itself a valuable commodity; you might be better off by £10 000, and even if you lose you will be no worse off than now. Consider, then, for how much you would be willing to sell this wager. Its expected monetary value is £5000, but many people would be willing to sell the wager for less, preferring the certainty of the sale price to the uncertainty inherent in the wager. The minimum amount of money for which you would be willing to sell the wager is your 'certainty equivalent', and the difference between this and the expected monetary value defines your risk aversion for this situation. Some readers may require selling prices above £5000. In this case, they would be referred to as 'risk seeking'. Whatever the selling price, its difference from the expected monetary value describes your risk attitude. Note, however, that the relative subjective values of £10 000, the certainty equivalent, and 0 (presumably, your current asset position) are all implicated in the judgment about risk. Thus, the notions of subjective value and risk are inextricably linked within the concept of utility.

Assessing utility

The method for assessing utility implied by von Neumann and Morgenstern's proofs is very simple. It uses a device called a 'reference wager' and requires a judgment of a probability. Imagine that you are offered a choice between a certain prize of £5000 *or* a wager that pays £10 000 if you win and nothing if you lose. What probability would have to be associated with winning in order to make you indifferent between the wager and the sure-thing? Suppose you required 0.70. Now we can compute the expected utility of the wager, recognizing that because utility is a relative measure we can arbitrarily assign a utility of 100 to the win of £10 000 and a utility of 0 to winning nothing.

$$\text{Expected utility of wager} = (0.7 \times 100) + (0.3 \times 0) = 70$$

Relative to the utilities of £10 000 or nothing, the wager is given a utility of 70. Since the wager's utility is 70, and you are indifferent between the wager and £5000, it follows that £5000 must have associated with it a utility of 70. Thus, a gift of £5000 has associated with it an increment of utility of 70, whereas a further gift of £5000 provides a utility increment of just 30. The first £5000 is slightly more than twice as desirable as the second £5000.

Most people who try to apply this process find that there is no precise indifference point, but rather an indifference region. That is, the assessor feels indifferent over a range of probabilities, and it is this range that limits the precision with which utility can be assessed. Although there are no published data on this, my experience suggests that the limits are usually about ±0.03. When those limits are exceeded, then the consequences have been inadequately described or modelled badly, in which case decomposition along the lines of multi-attribute utility theory may be called for (see Keeney and Raiffa, 1976).

This measurement method demonstrates the proof that numerical measures of utility can be determined from coherent preferences. The assessor is usually asked only for a preference between a sure-thing and a wager, and from many such preferences it is possible to locate an indifference point that gives a numerical measure of the assessor's utility. It is important to recognize that this process assigns numbers to subjective states of mind, for it is a widely held belief that a person's subjective judgments cannot be expressed in numbers. What has been demonstrated here is that reasonably precise measures can be obtained if the assessor's preferences are coherent.

The wager-based method of von Neumann and Morgenstern shows that finding the indifference point between a sure-thing and a wager is basically a process of finding a probability that causes the balance of utilities between the most and least preferred consequences to be equivalent to the utility of the sure-thing. Thus, the assessment of a utility is fundamentally a process of assessing a probability.

PROBABILITY

Probabilities are numbers between 0 and 1 that obey the addition and multiplication laws governing the 'or' and 'and' relationships, respectively, between events. Controversy arises when one attempts to associate probabilities with real-world events. In recent times, probabilities have usually been interpreted as limits of relative frequencies, applicable only to events that can in principle be repeated.

Decision theorists, on the other hand, interpret probabilities as degrees of belief about hypotheses, events or uncertain quantities. Indeed, in the preface to his two-volume work, de Finetti (1974) says PROBABILITIES DO NOT EXIST. By this he means that probabilities do not exist as properties of objects or events alone, that subjective judgment of some sort is always involved when a probability is assigned. Relative frequencies, and other data, may prove useful in assessing probabilities, but subjective judgment cannot be avoided.

The subjective view of probability does not lead to relativism, that one person's degree of belief is as good as any other person's. In the first place, probabilities must obey the probability laws; assessments must be coherent. The laws can be used generatively: to help an assessor shape his or her opinion to keep it consistent with other, related, judgments (Lindley, Tversky and Brown, 1979). In the second place, when data are available, Bayes's theorem, one of the consequences of the laws of probability, shows how probabilities should be revised to take account of these new data. It is a well known characteristic of Bayes's theorem that as more and more data are obtained, the opinions of two assessors who initially disagree, will be brought more and more into agreement. In short, the probability laws act as powerful constraints on probability assessments, and these laws can be exploited to help an individual generate a coherent set of assessments.

This is not the place to debate the relative merits of the different interpretations of probability. However, an implication for forecasting is that judgment is inescapable when uncertainty about future conditions or events is assessed.

Assessing probability

The easiest way to assess a probability is to ask a person directly for a number between 0 and 1. If each of several people is asked to state their probability that last year's winner of the mens' singles at Wimbledon will win again this year, there will be no general agreement. This reflects no flaw in the theory; rather, it illustrates the fact that probabilities are expressions of degrees of belief, and though the event in question is common to all the assessors, there are differences of opinion that are reflected in the differing probability assignments.

Determining a probability from a person's expressions of preferences requires the use of the reference wager. Imagine this event: last year's winner of the men's singles at Wimbledon will win again this year. Wager A specifies that if the same man wins, you will win a Rolls Royce, otherwise nothing. Under Wager B, you win a Rolls Royce with probability p, and nothing with probability $1 - p$. (Wager B might be played by blindly drawing a ball from an urn filled with identically shaped balls, a proportion p of which are white, and $1 - p$ are black; you win if a white ball is drawn.) There is one restriction on Wager B: the ball will not be drawn until the day of the men's singles. Thus, under either wager, the consequences for you are identical: you may or may not win a Rolls Royce on the day of the men's singles.

Depending on whether you prefer Wager A or B, the probability p is varied until you are indifferent between the wagers. At that point, you presumably believe that you have an equal chance of winning a Rolls Royce whatever wager you choose. It is obvious that the indifference probability associated with Wager B gives the probability for the event in question.

As with the wager method for assessing utility, there is rarely an exact indifference point between the two wagers, but rather an indifference region. However, for a wide variety of events, and for the great majority of assessors with whom I have worked, the indifference region is surprisingly small: usually ± 0.03, and rarely greater than ± 0.05. This finding suggests that an individual's experience of uncertainty can be translated into a number with a fair degree of precision. The notion that uncertainty can be assessed precisely may seem strange at first, but it is entirely consistent with the subjective interpretation of probability, and agrees with empirical findings.

The use of wagers in assessing probabilities demonstrates the proof that coherent preferences imply the existence of probabilities. The reference wager also provides a definition of probability: a probability p assigned to a particular event means that the assessor is indifferent between winning a prize if the event occurs and winning the same prize if a white ball is the result of a fair draw from an urn containing a proportion p of white balls. An alternative interpretation is that the assessor should be willing to bet an amount p such that if the event occurs, he or she wins 1. For example, if you give a probability of 0.4 to an event, then you should be willing to bet 0.40 to win 1.00 if the event occurs. (This latter interpretation assumes that your utility function is linear over amounts of money from 0 to 1.00.)

Summary

This section has shown that the two subjective quantities needed for effective decision-making, utilities and probabilities, can be determined from an individual's preferences through the use of reference wagers. In practice, people's preferences are not always entirely coherent, so does this invalidate the theory? From the perspective of requisite modelling, it does not. Instead of discarding expected utility theory because the premise of coherent preferences is not met, the requisite modeller uses the expected utility rule to help the individual or group to construct a coherent set of preferences. The goal is to create a model of the problem at hand which is entirely coherent within the 'small world' which it represents. Thus, coherence and consistency are the end points of requisite modelling, and are not required to begin with. Coherence is the goal, not a premise to be satisfied before the theory can be applied, and expected utility theory is used to help reach that goal.

HOW GOOD ARE PEOPLE AT ASSESSING PROBABILITIES?

By now it should be apparent that utilities and probabilities need to be assessed with care if the resulting numbers are to be taken seriously. This point must be borne in mind when the research literature is surveyed to provide an answer to the question addressed in this section, how good are people at assessing probabilities? By the mid-1970s, decision analysts had accumulated sufficient experience about assessing probabilities for some useful advice to be given (Spetzler and Stäel von Holstein, 1975), and, later, for a manual to be written (Stäel von Holstein and Matheson, 1979). The manual provides practical procedures that are designed to minimize bias and eliminate some of the more commonly observed errors of judgment that people make.

However, few published studies have used the procedures recommended by the manual. It is, therefore, difficult to determine how relevant the literature is to the question of this section. The most serious failing of the available research is that it only suggests how people perform under unrealistically restricted conditions (Phillips, 1983). Rarely do investigators see the assessment process as generative in the sense that people are often forming their judgments during the assessment process. Feelings of uncertainty are not automatically translated into numbers without some consideration on the part of the assessor. Forming a judgment is a dynamic, social process, involving interaction between the individual and his or her environment and with other people. Probabilities and utilities are not so much measured as they are generated.

Research literature

That said, it is possible to look at the research literature from this 'generative' perspective. It will be possible here to present only a representative selection.

In some early research, people were briefly presented with displays showing a large number of randomly arranged black and white counters, and were asked to judge the probability that a randomly selected counter would be white. By varying the proportion of white to black counters it was possible to obtain subjective probability judgments over a wide range of 'objective' probabilities. The results usually showed that people often over estimate low probabilities and under estimate high ones (Cohen, 1960).

Of course, that conclusion could not be reached unless the experimenter knew for certain the correct proportion of white counters. What is actually being compared in these studies is the proportions judged by two people, the experimenter with complete information, the subject with incomplete information. From the standpoint of requisite modelling, the lesson is to make maximum use of the available information. But these studies say nothing about situations in which probabilities are based on considerations other than proportions or relative frequencies, and in which nobody has complete information.

One of the most dramatic illustrations of errors people make in assessing probabilities is shown in the classic birthday problem. In a crowded room, what is the probability that two people will be born on the same day (the year can be different)?

Applying the probability laws shows that with just 35 people in the room, the probability of a coincidence is 0.80, with only 23 people, it is about 0.50. Most people are so surprised by this result, that even when the calculations are explained, they feel there is a trick somewhere. Even with simpler problems that involve combinations of events, people make mistakes (Bar-Hillel, 1973).

The lesson for requisite decision modelling is to ensure that complex events are broken down into simple ones, with judgmental assessments made only about the simple events. That is what experimenters do in these research studies, and they get the answers right. It is their behaviour, not that of their subjects who are never allowed to make calculations, which should serve as a guide in generating forecasts.

A similar conclusion can be reached in considering the many studies showing that people do not extract from available data all the information that they could (Slovic and Lichtenstein, 1971). To demonstrate this, the experimenter has to make some calculations, usually applying Bayes's theorem, for these are complex judgmental tasks. Models should be applied where they are appropriate, particularly to combine assessed probabilities or likelihoods, with experts making judgments about simpler events that are part of the models.

Recent research on probability assessment has concentrated on the rules of thumb, or heuristics, that people use in arriving at such judgments (Kahneman and Tversky, 1979). A typical line of approach is to present one group of people with a brief statement of a problem and another group with a reframed but logically identical problem, then to compare the judgments of the two groups. Usually the groups show different patterns of judgment, and this is interpreted as revealing inconsistencies, biases and violations of the probability laws or of the expected utility principle (Abelson and Levi, 1985).

Unfortunately, this research says little about how good assessments are when people make calculations, use the probability laws or the expected utility principle, or talk with other people in forming their judgments. But for requisite decision modelling there is a strong lesson here: assessors should be asked to make extra judgments so that inconsistencies can be revealed and reflected back to the assessors for reconciliation. Problems should be reframed and looked at from different perspectives to help the assessor generate a coherent set of preferences.

Once again we see an unintended consequence of the research: it shows that the practical use of the research lies in the behaviour of the experimenters rather than of the subjects. Experimenters get the answers right, and they do so by exploring alternative structural representations of the problem, by using decision theory and probability theory, by comparing intuition against model results and exploring the discrepancies. These are exactly the activities that should be pursued when formulating forecasts to ensure that the judgmental inputs are as sound as possible.

Another line of research has looked at the realism or accuracy of probability assessments made by individuals. In these experiments, people are asked questions like this one:

> Which is longer?   probability that
>   (a) Panama Canal   you are correct
>   (b) Suez Canal   _____

Respondents are asked to tick the answer they think is correct, and then to write next to the question a probability that indicates how sure they are that the correct answer has been selected.

The answer to this question is 'Suez Canal', but unless you ticked the wrong answer and said you were 100 per cent sure, in which case your probability assessment is wrong, it is not possible to tell how good that single probability judgment was. However, it would be possible to characterize your ability at assessing probabilities in general if you had answered more questions, at least 200. By grouping together all questions for which you had assessed the same probability, we could determine the percentage of questions you answered correctly in the group. A graph of these two variables, percentage correct and assessed probability, for all groups, is known as a calibration curve. An example of some experimental results is shown in Figure 1. The diagonal line represents perfect calibration: when people say they are 0.80 certain, they are correct 80 per cent of the time. But most calibration curves lie below the diagonal, as here: when these people say they are 0.80 certain, they are right about 65 per cent of the time. A review of studies in this area can be found in Lichtenstein, Fischhoff and Phillips (1980).

The implications of this research for forecasting are, in my judgment, dubious (though Fischhoff and MacGregor, 1982, disagree). Consider the calibration curve shown in Figure 2. It represents the probabilities assessed by

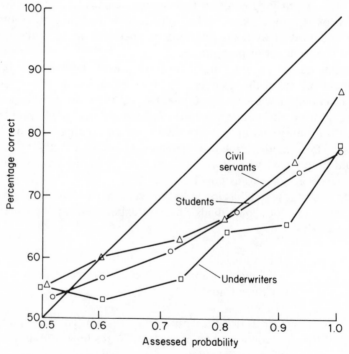

Figure 1. Calibration curves using general-knowledge questions

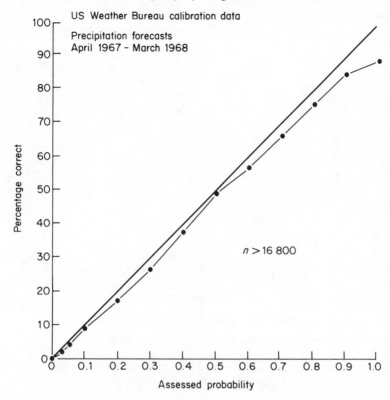

Figure 2. Calibration curves for precipitation forecasts

many different meteorologists for precipitation at locations all over the United States. Forecasts for the time period immediately following the forecast are shown, but calibration deteriorated only slightly as the lag between forecast and subsequent event occurred. Note that the 1967–68 results (taken from United States Weather Bureau, 1969) show good calibration; more recent results (e.g., Murphy and Winkler, 1977) are even better.

Good calibration has been observed in several applied studies. Consensus judgments of probabilities that R&D projects would succeed show reasonable calibration (Balthasar, Boschi and Menke, 1978), while probability distributions generated by groups of banking experts about future interest rates turned out to be nearly well-calibrated, with some tendency toward underconfidence (Kabus, 1976). Fischhoff and Beyth (1975) asked a number of people to make probability assessments for 25 possible consequences of President Nixon's trip to China. The probabilities were given before the trip was made, but after the trip the assessments were shown to be calibrated.

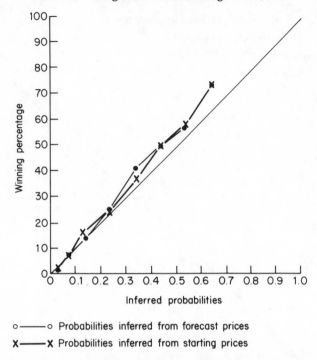

Figure 3. Calibration curve for probabilities inferred from
bets for the 1973 flat season

Probabilities inferred from bets on horse races show excellent calibration
(Hoerl and Fallin, 1974). Both bookies and punters appeared to be well-
calibrated when I used data provided in a study by Dowie (1976) to construct
the calibration curves shown in Figure 3. (The forecast prices are those made
by the bookies before the betting starts, while the starting prices are the result
of betting by the punters up to the point where the race starts.) Common to
both these studies is a slight tendency to undervalue the favourite (the
probability of winning is higher than the inferred probability), and perhaps a
slight inclination to overvalue the long-shot, the opposite to Cohen's (1960)
results.

Together, these studies provide what Wallsten and Budescu (1983) call an
'existence demonstration—there do exist conditions under which experts can
provide subjective probabilities which are relatively free of bias, are well
calibrated, and score well'. In short, people *can* be well-calibrated.

What are the conditions under which good calibration can be expected? No
definitive answers can be found in research to date, but several conditions can
be identified in the studies of good calibration.

First, calibration is usually better for future events than for general-knowledge questions (Wright and Ayton, 1986). Certainly, the usual finding of over-confidence that characterizes studies using general knowledge questions cannot be generalized with confidence to forecasting future events.

Second, most of the studies showing good calibration were done with experts. Experiments using general-knowledge questions have shown no difference in calibration between experts and novices (Lichtenstein, Fischhoff and Phillips, 1980), but no studies comparing the calibration of experts with that of non-experts have been done using future-event questions. Nevertheless, it is rare for non-experts to show calibration as good as experts, so it is likely that expertise matters.

Third, several studies were conducted with groups of assessors. I have obtained probability assessments from several groups of people who had differing perspectives on the uncertain quantity or event in question. For all of these groups, individuals used their own experience to influence others. In general, the practitioner has the 'hands on' experience that makes the assessment process meaningful, the researcher with field experience extends the practitioner's knowledge, while the scientist (who is sometimes reluctant to assess probabilities) identifies and questions assumptions that others may be making. Although research is lacking on this topic, it appears that by sharing knowledge and experience, groups can generate better assessments of probabilities than any individual working alone.

Fourth, training helps. A study by Lichtenstein and Fischhoff (1980) showed that feedback improves calibration, and that most improvement occurs early in the training session. Weather forecasters in The Netherlands began making probability forecasts in October 1980, and by the end of the second year, calibration had improved substantially. Murphy and Daan (1984) attribute this to feedback given to the forecasters in October 1981 about their calibration during the first year, and to experience in probability forecasting gained during the first year.

Fifth, certain assessment techniques consistently yield better calibration than others. Asking for a best guess about an uncertain quantity, then assessing the values that lie at the 0.05 and 0.95 fractiles (or any other fractiles), gives a probability distribution that is 'too-tight': the true value of the uncertain quantity will too frequently fall in the tails of the distribution. A better approach is to specify possible values of the uncertain quantity and for each value to obtain an assessment of the probability that the true value will be less (or more, if that is easier for the assessor). This approach, the 'probability method', gives better-calibrated distributions than the 'fractile method' (Seaver, von Winterfeldt and Edwards, 1978). To establish the range of possible values of the uncertain quantity, the assessor should be asked to imagine different scenarios that could lead to very high or very low values of the uncertain quantity (Stäel von Holstein and Matheson, 1979). When assessments are being obtained for specific future events, rather than uncertain quantities, listing reasons why the event may *not* occur will improve calibration (Koriat, Lichtenstein and Fischhoff, 1980). One reason why these techniques help is that by encouraging the assessor to think of alternative futures, they increase the mental availability of plausible scenarios, thus counteracting the 'anchoring effect' of a 'best guess' on probability assessments (Tversky and Kahneman, 1973).

One more area of research bears on the question of how good people can be at assessing probabilities. When Phillips and Wright (1977) carried out a calibration study in Hong Kong, with Chinese students, nurses and businessmen as participants, they obtained a near-horizontal curve. No matter how sure these people said they were, they were correct only about 50 per cent of the time. These results have been replicated in Malaysia and Indonesia (Wright *et al.*, 1978) in a programme of research that has examined cultural and individual differences in probabilistic thinking.

One of the experiments in the programme asked participants to write a response to questions like 'Will you catch a head cold in the next three months?' We wanted to see whether people would, without any prompting, use probability words or phrases in their responses. We found that about 10 to 15 per cent of our participants never used any probability expressions at all; they usually wrote 'Yes', 'No' or 'Don't know'. In assessing probabilities, these people more frequently said they were 100 per cent sure, and were more frequently wrong when they said that, than participants who used at least some probability words or phrases. In summary, this research has shown that about 1 person in 10 in the West (and more in the East) is not a probabilistic thinker.

That said, it is important to distinguish between a person's inclination to think probabilistically or otherwise, as distinct from his or her ability to do so. It appears that many people, especially in the East, do not think in terms of probabilities when faced with general-knowledge questions, for Wright and Phillips (1980) found that cultural differences in calibration disappear when future events are substituted for general-knowledge items. Apart from a tendency to say they are 100 per cent sure too often, people who are not inclined to use probability phrases are still quite capable of thinking probabilistically (Wright and Phillips, 1979). It is more a matter of turning them on to this mode of thinking. But the general lesson is clear: some people are not disposed to think about uncertainty, so they may not be able to provide good probability assessments.

CONCLUSIONS

Now it is possible to answer more directly the question about the adequacy of judgmental forecasts. Interest has focused on discovering what people can do under favourable conditions, while the research literature has mostly been concerned with describing what people actually do, usually without help, guidance or training. Our approach has been action-oriented: we presume forecasts are being made to help decision-makers, and we assumed that the decision-makers are at least striving to be coherent in their approach to a particular problem.

From this perspective, forecasts become a part of 'requisite' models, which in turn are only as complex as is needed to solve a particular problem. An important goal, then, is to generate forecasts that are themselves 'requisite'. When judgmental forecasts are needed, coherence implies that alternative futures should be considered, and that judgments should be expressed as utilities and probabilities of possible consequences. Since the assessment of a utility can be carried out by finding a probability that makes the assessor indifferent between a sure-thing and a wager, it is probability assessment that is fundamental.

So, how adequate are judgmental assessments of probabilities? We can answer that question in terms of precision, reliability and accuracy. Precision refers to the error with which a person can express with a number his or her feeling of uncertainty. When reference gambles are used properly, it is possible to define a region of indifference that is about ±0.03. Thus, people can express their uncertainty as probabilities with considerable precision.

Reliability refers to the internal consistency with which probability assessments are made. Only a few experiments are available on this, but they suggest that around ±0.05 is about right (reviewed in Wallsten and Budescu, 1983). That is, if people were asked to assess probabilities for so many events that they could not, a week later, remember their answers, they would give new assessments that are within 5 percentage points of the original assessments. Experience suggests that this degree of reliability occurs even when the assessor claims to be 'pulling numbers out of the air'.

Finally, accuracy. This refers to the degree of calibration characteristic of probability assessments. The previous section showed that, if the person is inclined to think in probabilities, an individual can be well-calibrated for future events. But this depends on establishing the right conditions for the assessment process.

From the perspective of requisite models, our concern should be with getting the conditions right so that it will be possible for assessors to generate precise, reliable and accurate assessments of probability. Getting these right should include at least the following:

(1) If the assessor is unfamiliar with probabilistic thinking, some training should be given (a training session is given in Appendix B of Hogarth, 1987). At the very least, some brief familiarization using reference wagers should be provided. If the assessor continues to experience great

difficulty in making probability judgments, the assessment should be abandoned and another assessor sought.

(2) Only experts in the substantive area should be asked for assessments. This is particularly important where probabilities for complex events are needed.

(3) Groups of experts should be used where possible.

(4) Proper assessment procedures should be used (see the manual by Stäel von Holstein and Matheson (1979) for practical procedures).

(5) Whenever possible, complex events should be broken down into simple events, and assessments given only for the latter. This includes using Bayes's theorem, not unaided judgement, to aggregate data.

(6) Assessment procedures should always exploit coherence. More assessments should be obtained than are needed so that coherence can be checked. It may even be necessary to introduce extra events, to 'extend the conversation', thus ensuring that at least some of the probabilities will be redundant.

(7) The assessment process should be iterative, not 'once-off'. Incoherence should be brought to the attention of the assessor, who can then work toward providing a coherent set of probabilities.

(8) Difficulties in obtaining a probability assessment are frequently a sign that the problem is structured differently from the assessor's internal model of the problem. Restructuring so as to provide more direct access to the assessor's experience may help.

By now it should be clear that the assessments required in making judgmental forecasts have to be carried out with the same care that a scientist or engineer would exercise in measuring some physical quantity. But with care, it is possible to obtain precise, reliable and accurate judgmental forecasts.

REFERENCES

Abelson, R. P. and Levi, A. (1985) 'Decision-making and decision theory', in G. Lindzey and E. Aronson (eds.), *Handbook of Social Psychology*, New York: Random House.

Balthasar, H. U., Boschi, R. A. A. and Menke, M. M. (1978) 'Calling the shots in R&D', *Havard Business Review*, May–June, 151–160.

Bar-Hillel, M. (1973) 'Compounding subjective probabilities', *Organizational Behavior and Human Performance*, 9, 396–406.

Cohen, J. (1960) *Chance, Skill and Luck*, Harmondsworth: Penguin.

Dowie, J. (1976) 'On the efficiency and equity of betting markets', *Economica*, 43, 139–150.

Edwards, W. (1954) 'The theory of decision making', *Psychological Bulletin*, 51, 380–417.

de Finetti, B. (1974) *Theory of Probability: A Critical Introductory Treatment*, New York: Wiley.

Fischhoff, B. and Beyth, R. (1975) '"I knew it would happen"—remembered probabilities of once-future things', *Organizational Behavior and Human Performance*, **13**, 1–16.

Fischhoff, B. and MacGregor, D. (1982) 'Subjective confidence in forecasts', *Journal of Forecasting*, **1**(2), 155–172.

Hoerl, A. E. and Fallin, H. K. (1974) 'Reliability of subjective evaluations in a high incentive situation', *Journal of the Royal Statistical Society*, **137**, 227–230.

Hogarth, R. M. (1987) *Judgement and Choice: The Psychology of Decision*, 2nd edn, Chichester: Wiley.

Hogarth, R. M. and Makridakis, S. (1981) 'Forecasting and planning: An evaluation', *Management Science*, **27**(2), 115–138.

Howard, R. A. (1966) 'Decision analysis: Applied decision theory', in D. B. Hertz and J. Melese (eds.), *Proceedings of the Fourth International Conference on Operational Methods*, New York: Wiley-Interscience, pp. 55–71.

Huss, W. R. (1985) 'Comparative analysis of load forecasting techniques at a southern utility', *Journal of Forecasting*, **4**, 99–107.

Kabus, I. (1976) 'You can bank on uncertainty', *Havard Business Review*, May–June, 95–105.

Kahneman, D. and Tversky, A. (1979) 'Prospect theory: An analysis of decision under risk', *Econometrica*, **47**, 263–291.

Keeney, R. L. and Raiffa, H. (1976) *Decisions with Multiple Objectives*, New York: Wiley.

Koriat, A., Lichtenstein, S. and Fischhoff, B. (1980) 'Reasons for confidence', *Journal of Experimental Psychology: Human Learning and Memory*, **6**, 107–118.

Lichtenstein, S. and Fischhoff, B. (1980) 'Training for calibration', *Organizational Behavior and Human Performance*, **28**, 149–171.

Lichtenstein, S., Fischhoff, B. and Phillips, L. D. (1981) 'Calibration of probabilities: State of the art to 1980', in D. Kahneman, P. Slovic and A. Tversky (eds.), *Judgment under Uncertainty: Heuristics and Biases*, New York: Cambridge University Press.

Lindley, D. V. (1985) *Making Decisions*, 2nd edn, London: Wiley.

Lindley, D. V., Tversky, A. and Brown, R. V. (1979) 'On the reconciliation of probability assessments', *Journal of the Royal Statistical Society A*, **142**, 146–162.

Makridakis, S., Anderson, A., Carbone, R., Fildes, R., Hibons, M., Lewandowski, R., Newton, H., Parzen, E. and Winkler, R. (1982) 'The accuracy of extrapolation (time series) methods: Results of a forecasting competition', *Journal of Forecasting*, **1**, 111–153.

Murphy, A. H. and Daan, H. (1984) 'Impacts of feedback and experience on the quality of subjective probability forecasts: Comparison of results from the first and second years of the Zierikyce Experiment', *Monthly Weather Review*, **112**(3), 413–423.

Murphy, A. H. and Winkler, R. L. (1977) 'Reliability of subjective probability forecasts of precipitation and temperature', *Journal of the Royal Statistical Society Ser.C*, **26**, 41–47.

von Neumann, J. and Morgenstern, O. (1947) *Theory of Games and Economic Behavior*, 2nd edn, Princeton, N.J.: Princeton University Press, 1947.

Phillips, L. D. (1983) 'Theoretical perspective on heuristics and biases in probabilistic thinking', in P. C. Humphreys, O. Svenson and A. Vari (eds.), *Analysing and Aiding Decision Processes*, Amsterdam: North Holland.

Phillips, L. D. (1984) 'A theory of requisite decision models', *Acta Psychologica*, **56**, 29–48.

Phillips, L. D. and Wright, G. N. (1977) 'Cultural differences in viewing uncertainty and assessing probabilities', in H. Jungermann and G. de Zeeus (eds.), *Decision Making and Change in Human Affairs*, Dordrecht, Holland: Reidel.

Raiffa, H. (1968) *Decision Analysis*, Reading, Mass.: Addison-Wesley.

Raiffa, H. and Schlaifer, R. (1961) *Applied Statistical Decision Theory*, Boston, Mass.: Harvard Business School Division of Research.

Ramsey, F. P. (1926) 'Truth and probability', in F. P. Ramsey, *The Foundations of Mathematics and other Logical Essays*. New York: Harcourt Brace, 1931. Reprinted in H. E. Kyburg, Jr, and H. E. Smokler (eds.), *Studies in Subjective Probability*, New York: Wiley, 1964.

Savage, L. J. (1954) *The Foundations of Statistics*, New York: Wiley.

Schlaifer, R. (1969) *Analysis of Decisions under Uncertainty*, New York: McGraw-Hill.

Seaver, D. A., von Winterfeldt, D. and Edwards, W. (1978) 'Eliciting subjective probability distributions on continuous variables', *Organizational Behavior and Human Performance*, **29**, 379–391.

Slovic, P. and Lichtenstein, S. (1971) 'Comparison of Bayesian and regression approaches to the study of information processing in judgment', *Organizational Behavior and Human Performance*, **6**, 649–744.

Spetzler, C. S. and Stäel von Holstein, C.-A. S. (1975) 'Probability encoding in decision analysis', *Management Science*, **22**, 340–58.

Stäel von Holstein, C.-A. S. and Matheson, J. (1979) *A Manual for Encoding Probability Distributions*, SRI International, Menlo Park, CA.

Tversky, A. and Kahneman, D. (1973) 'Availability: a heuristic for judging frequency and probability, *Cognitive Psychology*, **5**, 207–232.

United States Weather Bureau (1969) *Report on Weather Bureau Forecast Performance 1967–8 and Comparison with Previous Years*, Technical Memorandum WBTM FCST, 11, Silver Spring, Maryland: Office of Meteorological Operations, Weather Analysis and Prediction Division.

Wallsten, T. S. and Budescu, D. V. (1983) 'Encoding subjective probabilities: A psychological and psychometric review', *Management Science*, **29**, 151–173.

Wright, G. and Ayton, P. (1986) 'Subjective confidence in forecasts: A response to Fischhoff and MacGregor', *Journal of Forecasting*, **5**, 117–123.

Wright, G. N. and Phillips, L. D. (1979) 'Personality and probabilistic thinking: An exploratory study', *British Journal of Psychology*, **70**, 295–303.

Wright, G. N. and Phillips, L. D. (1980) 'Cultural variation in probabilistic thinking: Alternative ways of dealing with uncertainty', *International Journal of Psychology*, **15**, 239–257.

Wright, G. N., Phillips, L. D., Whalley, P. C., Choo, G. T. G., Ng, K.-O., Tan, I. and Wisudha, A. (1978) 'Cultural differences in probabilistic thinking', *Journal of Cross-cultural Psychology*, **9**, 285–299.

Judgmental Forecasting
Edited by G. Wright and P. Ayton
© 1987 John Wiley & Sons Ltd

CHAPTER 2

Beliefs and Expectations as Causes of Judgmental Bias

Jonathan St. B. T. Evans
Plymouth Polytechnic

It is natural to think of forecasting as a rather specialized exercise conducted by trained professionals in a variety of fields ranging from meteorology to economics. However, the prediction of future events is fundamental to many processes that the human brain is required to carry out in everyday actions such as perceiving objects, enjoying music, understanding speech or driving a car. If the brain were unable to exploit the predictability of real world events such actions would be impossible.

While the brain is, in this sense, an habitual generator and tester of forecasts, the processes involved—as in speech perception—are generally not consciously accessible to the individual. While professional forecasting would seem to involve a more explicit level of thought, I would argue that high level cognitive processes also have a substantial element of automaticity. The reason that this is important is that such automatic or 'intuitive' processes may lead people, including expert judges, to exhibit subtle biases of which they are unaware. In this chapter, I will focus upon the problem of biases which may arise from the way in which forecasts are generated, and evidence evaluated, in the context of the knowledge we already possess about a topic and the expectations which such beliefs generate. It is of course, appropriate for prior beliefs to influence our judgments to an extent—as prescribed, for example, in Bayesian decision theory—but we shall see that the natural human tendency to maintain beliefs may result in important errors.

Forecasting involves both reasoning and judgment, two aspects of human thinking that have been extensively studied by experimental psychologists. A number of recent books have appeared which provide specialist reviews and/or collections of papers on the psychology of deductive reasoning (Evans, 1982), inductive and scientific reasoning (Tweney, Doherty and Mynatt,

1981), statistical inference and social judgment (Nisbett and Ross, 1980; Kahneman, Slovic and Tversky, 1982) and general coverage of all these topics (Johnson-Laird and Wason, 1977; Evans, 1983). This chapter will provide selective discussion of relevant aspects of these literatures.

In general, research on the psychology of reasoning and judgment has identified many types of mistakes and biases, despite the prevalent use of subject populations of above-average intelligence (undergraduate students). The practical relevance of reasoning research in the present discussion revolves mostly around the questions of which aspects of professional fore-casting are most prone to bias, and the conditions under which forecasters are more or less likely to make mistakes. I should point out that reports of biases in the literature have engendered some quite heated controversy among philosophers and psychologists about the implications for human rationality (see, for example, Cohen (1981), and associated commentaries). However, the question of whether or not subjects' behaviour in these experiments should be described as irrational leads one into philosophical debate about the definition of rationality, the adequacy of normative theories of logic and so on. It would be a distraction from my main purpose to engage in a discussion of the rationality issue here, though the accuracy of various claims of bias in the reasoning studies considered will be carefully examined.

There are three main stages in forecasting which I will consider here:

(i)   Formation of theories and assumptions upon which forecasts are based.
(ii) Generation of hypotheses and predictions.
(iii) Search for evidence and empirical evaluation of the success of forecasts.

Psychological study of the process of forecasting and scientific reasoning has been heavily influenced (perhaps disproportionately so) by the philosophy of science propounded by Popper (e.g. 1959). Studies which have concerned themselves directly with simulations of scientific hypothesis testing have consequently focused upon the issue of whether people are sufficiently concerned with falsification or disconfirmation of their hypotheses. A strong claim made by a number of authors is that people manifest a 'confirmation bias', i.e. that contrary to Popper's recommendations, people test their hypotheses in a manner likely to minimize rather than maximise their chance of falsification. If this claim is sound, it would appear to point to a serious potential source of bias in professional forecasting. Consequently, I shall devote a section to fairly detailed discussion of this literature.

One of the ambiguities in the claims of confirmation bias, as we shall see, concerns the question of whether people test their hypotheses adequately or whether they formulate the correct hypotheses to test. The process of generating predictions from well-formed theories is (or, rather, ought to be) one of deductive reasoning. That is, a forecast is a logical deduction or necessary consequence of a theory, and if the forecast is falsified then logically the theory cannot, in its entirety, be correct. Thus potential for mistakes and biases are provided by the mental processes involved in deducing conclusions and evaluating evidence. (Forecasts generated by formal procedures such as computer models are less vulnerable in this regard, though biases may still arise in the construction of the model.) Hence, we shall look also at work on deductive reasoning with especial reference to claims of 'belief bias'. This refers to a tendency for people to generate conclusions (forecasts) which conform to their prior beliefs and to be more critical in their evaluation of conclusions which conflict with their beliefs.

Confirmation and belief bias are related phenomena in that both involve the notion that people's thinking is channelled and biased by prior beliefs and expectations which inhibit logical reasoning. We will consider the evidence for each in turn. We will also look briefly at some general evidence which supports the view that such biases are liable to be persistent and difficult to eradicate since people lack awareness of the thought processes underlying their judgments, and are prone to overconfidence. A final section will provide detailed consideration of the conclusions which may be drawn from the work discussed and its application to professional forecasting.

CONFIRMATION BIAS

The tasks discussed here are not based on examining people's reasoning in the real world, but rather are simple laboratory tasks, designed to simulate the demands of hypothesis-testing in science and other contexts. The advantage of using such artificial tasks is the degree of control of experimental conditions which is possible, and the consequent ability to make inferences about the nature of people's thought processes. Before examining such experiments it is important to make a logical distinction between *necessary* and *sufficient* conditions. Consider the assertion:

If an integer is prime then it is odd.

A conditional rule of this sort specifies that the antecedent is sufficient for the consequent and that the consequent is necessary for the antecedent. (The rule can also be expressed as a universal statement, 'All prime numbers are odd'.) In this example, the claim is that being prime is a sufficient condition for a number to be odd, whilst oddness is a necessary condition for being prime. Hence the rule asserts that a number which is prime must also be odd and that a number which is not odd (even) cannot be prime.

This rule is an example of what might be called a practical certainty. Logically, the rule is false, of course, since there exists an exception to it—the number 2. On the other hand since there is only one such exception among the infinite set of integers, the rule will nearly always be true. This example illustrates a problem for the claim of Popper (1959) that all scientific theories

should be phrased as strict universal claims to ensure their potential falsifi-
ability. Firstly, it might well be argued that the discovery of laws of nature which
are practical certainties would be a very useful scientific objective. Secondly,
it can be argued that rules with no exceptions occur so rarely in real life that it
is unreasonable to expect people to have developed natural reasoning systems
based upon strict universality.

Many psychological experiments have been conducted to investigate
people's ability to reason with sentences phrased as conditionals or universals
(for a review see Evans, 1982). These experiments show that people make a
number of mistakes on such problems and interpret rules differently according to the context in which they are presented. There is also some direct
evidence that people interpret universal statements as asserting a fuzzy rather
than strictly universal relationship (Newstead and Griggs, 1984). i.e. to take
the claim 'All A are B' to mean, in practice, 'Nearly all A are B'.

One finding in the literature on conditional reasoning has led to the
supposition that people exhibit a confirmation bias, or verification bias as it is
sometimes known. It appears that while people can recognize the conditions
which falsify a conditional rule, they are not inclined to seek such falsifying
evidence themselves. For example, suppose you tell subjects that a set of
cards have a capital letter on one side and a number on the other, and then
present them with the following claim:

If a card has a D on one side then it has a 4 on the other side.

This rule is clearly falsified by any card which has a D on one side but does not
have a 4 on the other. If subjects are shown a card with a D and a 6 then they
will nearly always say that this contradicts the rule. Similarly if the subject is
asked what a card with a 6 on could have on the back they will normally
recognize that it cannot be a D, if the rule is true. Performance on these tasks
is, however, at striking odds with subjects' responses to a problem originally
devised by Wason (1966) and known as the four-card selection task. Suppose
subjects are given the above rule and then shown four cards lying on a table,
which display on their facing sides the following symbols:

D   R   4   6

The subject is then asked to decide which cards would need to be turned over
in order to find out whether the rule is true or false. This task differs from the
ones described above in that subjects are required to seek evidence to
investigate the truth of the rule, rather than simply to evaluate evidence which
is presented. Since only a D without a 4 can falsify the rule, subjects should
specify the D (in case there is not a 4 on the back) and the 6 (i.e. not-4) in case
there is a D on the back.

In fact, only a small minority of subjects choose this correct combination of
cards. Most say either that only the D must be turned, or else the D and the 4.

Turning the 4 is actually irrelevant since the rule would allow any letter to be on the back (there is no assertion that a 4 must have a D).

We thus have an apparently simple task on which most subjects fail to exhibit an appropriate hypothesis-testing strategy. We know from other experiments that they understand the conditions which would falsify the rule, yet they do not choose the card 6 which could well demonstrate its falsity. Wason's original explanation was that subjects have a confirmation bias. That is to say they are not seeking evidence that the rule is false (D and not-4) but rather looking for evidence that it is true, i.e. to find cards with a D on one side and a 4 on the other.

Wason's early theory seemed to imply a motivational bias, i.e. that people somehow prefer to confirm rather than disconfirm hypotheses. However, later evidence has shown that the error is due to cognitive limitations. For example, Evans and Lynch (1973) showed that performance on the task could be facilitated enormously if a negative was added to the rule as follows:

If a card has a D on one side then it does not have a 4 on the other side.

The negative means that rule is now falsified by the presence of a card with a D on one side and a 4 on the other, hence the correct selections are D and 4, which most people choose. Evans and Lynch suggested that subjects were exhibiting a 'matching bias', i.e. tending to investigate the cards named in the rule, regardless of the presence of negatives which reverse the logical status of such choices. The matching bias hypothesis has received support in a number of experiments (see Evans, 1982).

It has also been shown that performance on the selection task can be greatly facilitated without the introduction of negatives, if a realistic context of the right sort is used (for a review see Griggs (1983). It appears that the context must be one in which people have had some real life experience (or closely analogous experience) which alerts them to the conditions which violate the rule. For example, Griggs and Cox (1982) presented subjects with the rule:

If a person is drinking beer then the person must be over 18 years of age.

Each of the four cards had the age of the person written on one side and the beverage they were drinking written on the other. The visible sides were labelled DRINKING BEER, DRINKING COKE, 22 YEARS OF AGE and 16 YEARS OF AGE. Seventy-four per cent of subjects correctly said that they would need to turn over the first and last cards while not one subject made the correct choices in a control condition using the letters and numbers form of the task. Subjects were students at the University of Florida where the rule corresponds to a state law and all were familiar with the condition which violates the law in real life (drinking under age).

The finding that realistic materials can reduce the difficulty of the selection task might alleviate worries that it indicates any serious bias of thinking that might arise in real life, and some authors have attacked it on these grounds (e.g. Cohen, 1981). However, the fact the subjects can show a strong non-logical matching bias when testing hypotheses should cause some concern, especially since realistic materials only seem to facilitate when the subject already knows the falsifying contingency. Moreover, another reasoning task invented by Wason (1960) has been seen as providing clearer evidence of a confirmation bias.

This problem is known to aficionados as the '2 4 6' problem. The subject is told that the experimenter has a rule in mind which classifies sets of three integers, which we will call triples. The subject is then told that an example of a triple which conforms to the experimenter's rule is 2 4 6. The subject is then instructed to try to discover the rule by generating triples for testing. The experimenter provides feedback, telling the subject in each case whether the triple conforms or not. Subjects are instructed not to announce the rule until they are quite certain they know it.

The experimenter's rule, is in fact 'any ascending sequence', but the example chosen is deliberately biased to suggest a much more specific rule. What typically happens is that subjects formulate a hypotheses such as 'ascending in equal intervals' and test triples like: 1 2 3; 4 8 12; 101 103 105; 20 40 60; 1000 2000 3000—and so on. In every case, of course, the experimenter replies that the triple conforms to his rule. Eventually subjects announce their rule, convinced of its correctness and are puzzled, sometimes even angry when told it is incorrect. Subjects will even sometimes announce several alternative verbalizations of the same rule. For example, a subject who is told that the rule 'ascending in equal intervals' is wrong, may announce a few trials later that the rule is 'adding a number, always the same, to make the next number' (see Wason and Johnson-Laird (1972) for an interesting discussion of such protocols).

What is happening here is that the subject is forming a hypothesis which is a subset of the experimenter's rule. Hence the subject has discovered a sufficient condition for generating correct triples, but not a necessary one. This means that as long as subjects formulate positive tests, i.e. instances which conform to their own hypotheses, they can never be falsified. What subjects fail to do is to make negative predictions. They think, in effect, 'If my hypothesis is right then 10 20 30 should conform', but *don't* think, 'If my rule is correct then 10 15 30 should not conform'. If the latter, negative prediction was tested then the hypothesis would be immediately falsified since the experimenter would say that it conformed to his rule.

Before I discuss interpretations of this finding I should point out that the basic result has been widely replicated on a number of different tasks, and is not specific to the 2 4 6 formulation. Thus Miller (1967) discovered a very similar effect when subjects were instructed to discover the rules of an artificial grammar by typing strings of letters into an on-line computer.

Mynatt, Doherty and Tweney (1977), worried that the 2 4 6 might be too artificial a simulation of scientific hypothesis-testing, created a physical environment simulated in computer graphics and required subjects to 'fire particles' and discover the rules which led to them being 'absorbed'. Exactly the same pattern emerged in these alternative tasks. Subjects discovered partially correct rules which were sufficient but not necessary to produce the effects of interest, tested them exclusively by positive predictions, and failed to eliminate their hypotheses.

Several authors (e.g. Pollard, 1982) have noted a similarity between the characteristic error on the 2 4 6 and related tasks, to the matching bias exhibited on the four-card selection task. Both would seem to result from some sort of positivity bias: on the selection task subjects concentrate on the cards named in the rules and give insufficient attention to those not named. On the 2 4 6 task, subjects concentrate on what should occur if their hypotheses are correct, to the neglect of considering what should *not* occur. As with the selection task, however, it is arguable whether subjects are bad Popperians in a motivational sense. In other words the failure to eliminate hypotheses may be due not to a desire to confirm but to a failure to think of the means by which disconfirmation may be achieved.

An interesting finding reported by Tweney *et al.* (1980) in the final experiment of their paper, is that performance can be substantially facilitated when the method of feedback is changed. Instead of the usual right/wrong feedback subjects were told that the triples fell into two categories, arbitrarily labelled DAX and MED, and that 2 4 6 was an example of a MED. The instance of correct announcements of the rule increased dramatically, while inspection of subjects' protocols showed that subjects were still testing positive predictions. The reason for this improvement is that subjects tested hypotheses about DAX as well as MED. Suppose the subject forms the hypothesis that MEDs are triples which ascend at equal intervals. At the same time they form the complementary hypothesis that DAXs are triples which do *not* increase with equal intervals. In testing the sufficiency of the DAX hypothesis they accidentally test the necessity of the MED hypothesis. Hence, they are led to test triples which do not increase in equal intervals and thus receive feedback which eliminates their false hypotheses.

What this shows is the importance of how a problem is represented in the mind of the subject to its ease of solution. A different reasoning problem invented by Wason (see Wason and Brooks, 1979) called the THOG problem, which I do not have space to describe here, also produces a characteristic error akin to matching bias. Griggs and Newstead (1982) have shown that performance on this task is facilitated also when the problem presentation induces subjects to attach positive labels to part of the problem structure normally defined negatively—a closely analogous finding to that of Tweney *et al.*

The experiments discussed in this section do not prove that people are bad Popperians, in the sense that they are bent on confirming hypotheses. What they do show is that subjects can fall prey to biases which severely restrict their imagination of the ways in which hypotheses may be tested. In consequence subjects may consistently fail to eliminate false hypotheses and instead become convinced of their truth. Once this has occurred subjects may then become strongly fixated on their belief and resistant to subsequent demonstrations of its falsity. Wason and Johnson-Laird (1972) provide a number of case studies of such fixation on both the 2 4 6 and selection task (see also Wason (1977) for a discussion of self-contradiction in reasoning).

In a sense, the experiments discussed in this section may well underestimate any motivational component in confirmation bias, because the hypotheses subjects test are artificial and hence not related to any strongly held prior beliefs. Scientists and other professional forecasters, on the other hand, are likely to have strong motivational commitment to their theories arising from years of effort expended, professional status derived from published work and so on. In the next section I will consider studies concerned with distortions of reasoning arising from real world beliefs, the so-called 'belief bias' effect.

BELIEF BIAS

In a deductive reasoning task subjects are usually presented with the premises of a logical argument and then asked to evaluate the validity of a conclusion, or choose the correct conclusion from a list of alternatives. Logically an argument is valid if the conclusion must be true whenever all the premises are true. An invalid argument is one whose premises do not *necessarily* entail the truth of the conclusion.

The relationship between truth and validity is easily confused by those not trained in logic, and the onus is on experimenters to make the task requirements clear in the instructions for the task. In a study by Evans, Barston and Pollard (1983) which will be considered in some detail here, the relevant passages in the instructions was as follows:

> This is an experiment to test people's reasoning ability. You will be given four problems. In each case, you will be given a prose passage to read and asked if a certain conclusion may be logically deduced from it. You should answer this question on the assumption that all the information given in the passage is, in fact, true. If you judge that the conclusion necessarily follows from the statements in the passage, you should answer 'yes', otherwise 'no'.

Note that these instructions clearly define the task as a judgment of the validity of the conclusion which should not be affected by any *a priori* beliefs that the subject may hold about its truth. Valid conclusions may, of course, be false (provided at least one premise is false). The belief bias effect is a tendency for subjects to judge believable conclusions to be valid and unbelievable conclusions to be invalid, regardless of the logical validity.

A number of papers have reported claims of belief biases in reasoning, dating back to Wilkins (1928), although many of these are open to methodological criticism (see Evans, 1982, Chapter 6; Revlin *et al.*, 1980). The Evans *et al.* (1983) study involved three experiments in which subjects had four types of problem to solve which can be described by the type of conclusion: Valid–Believable, Valid–Unbelievable, Invalid–Believable and Invalid–Unbelievable. Believability of conclusions was determined by ratings of the statements by a separate group of subjects. An example of a Valid–Unbelievable argument is:

> No addictive things are inexpensive.
> Some cigarettes are inexpensive.
> Therefore, some cigarettes are not addictive.

The percentage of decisions to accept arguments as valid over the three experiments is shown in Table 1. It will be seen that both logic and belief exert powerful effects on the decisions. Thus subjects accept more valid than invalid arguments, demonstrating ability to understand the logic of the arguments. They also demonstrate a marked non-logical bias to accept more believable conclusions—whether or not they are logically valid. There is also a significant interaction, i.e. more belief bias is exhibited on invalid than valid arguments. The cause of this interaction is obscure and it will not be discussed here.

Evans *et al.* also report analyses of verbal protocols produced by some subjects who were instructed to 'think aloud' whilst solving the problems. It was found that the more often and earlier that subjects made reference to the premises of the argument, the less likely they were to exhibit belief bias. Conversely, most belief bias in responding was associated with those protocols in which subjects appeared to be concentrating on the conclusion. Hence, attention to premises appears to be correlated with better reasoning, while focus on the conclusion is associated with more belief bias.

Table 1 Percentage of subjects accepting conclusions in Evans, Barston and Pollard (1983) (Combined data of three experiments, *n* = 120.)

	Believable	Unbelievable
Valid	89	56
Invalid	71	13

Examination of individual subjects' data revealed a surprising pattern. One might well assume from the protocol analyses that there are two types of subjects: those who reason from the premises and those who make direct truth judgments about the conclusions. In fact this is not so. Most subjects show a mixture of problems in which their responses are logical or belief biased, with a corresponding mixture of protocol classifications. This shows an important connection with a point made about conditional reasoning experiments earlier in the chapter. The fact that people *can* reason well does not mean that they will necessarily do so; nor does it mean that they can avoid biases. This general finding in reasoning research must make us pessimistic about the prospects of expert judges being resistant to biases.

The significance of the belief bias effect is that people seem to be prone to accept evidence uncritically if the conclusion favours their prior beliefs and (to a lesser extent) liable to disregard evidence which leads to conclusions incompatible with such beliefs. Whilst the evidence of confirmation bias suggests that forecasters may be liable to generate predictions which are less likely to falsify their theories, the belief bias work suggests that they may well be biased in their evaluation of evidence as well.

Evidence to support this extrapolation from the research on belief biases in reasoning comes from other tasks presented by psychologists. For example, Lord, Ross and Lepper (1979) presented student subjects with the method and results of two empirical studies one of which supported the view that capital punishment deters potential murderers and the other of which led to the opposite conclusion. Subjects tended to be more convinced by the study which supported their beliefs and more likely to criticize the design and methodology of the one which led to a less congenial conclusion. In fact the materials were rigged so that for half the subjects one type of research design was associated with one type of outcome and for the other half design and outcomes were matched in reverse fashion.

Another related phenomenon is that of 'illusory correlation' (for a review see Nisbett and Ross (1980, Chapter 5)). Some of the most significant work on this topic has been conducted by Chapman and Chapman (e.g. 1971). What happens is that people see correlations or associations in data which are not statistically present, but which are expected to occur on the basis of theories which they hold. They have demonstrated this type of bias in expert judges. It appears that many well-qualified clinicians retain a faith in projective personality tests, such as the Rorschach inkblot test, as means of diagnosing mental disorders, in spite of the lack of good objective evidence of their validity. The clinicians report that they find such tests a good diagnostic tool in practice. That this belief is maintained by the perception of illusory correlations is supported by laboratory studies in which subjects are shown a number of case details in which the test results and diagnoses are given. Although the materials are constructed to show no correlations, the subjects report the associations that they expect to find.

The studies discussed in this section indicate that people's perception and critical evaluation of evidence is likely to be biased by prior beliefs, with the consequence that such theories will be unreasonably maintained. There is recent evidence that such bias may also occur in the spontaneous production of inferences, where no conclusion is provided for evaluation (Oakhill and Johnson-Laird, 1985). In terms of forecasting, such a bias would entail selectively generating predictions that confirm *a priori* beliefs and ignoring others which may equally be deduced from the available evidence.

SELF-KNOWLEDGE

We have now examined quite a lot of evidence which, by extrapolation from laboratory findings, suggests that forecasters may be prone to bias in both the generation of predictions and the evaluation of evidence for the correctness of their theories. In this section, I will look briefly at some more general evidence which should make us cautious about the exercise of intuitive judgment in human experts. The problem is: how well do people understand their own thought processes? Are people (a) aware of the basis upon which their judgments are made, and (b) realistically apprised of the accuracy with which they can make such judgments? If the answer to these questions were affirmative we could be more optimistic about the likelihood of error occurring and the chance of correcting it.

Unfortunately, there is quite a lot of evidence to suggest the answers to both these questions are negative. One study which looked directly at self-awareness in logical reasoning was that of Wason and Evans (1975). In the discussion of research on the Wason selection task earlier in the chapter it was pointed out that correct responding may be induced by introducing a negative consequent into the conditional rule, so that matching (the dominant bias) and logic coincide. Wason and Evans gave subjects both the affirmative (hard) and negative (easy) form of the task, with half the subjects receiving the tasks in one order and half in the reverse order. In both cases subjects were asked to explain the reasons for their choices.

As expected subjects demonstrated a large matching bias in their selections and solved the negative version of the problem far more often. The interesting finding was that when subjects gave the correct solution, they also gave very logical-sounding explanations of their choices—demonstrating apparent insight into the task. Those who performed the easy task first, however, showed no transfer in performance to the second, hard, task and the apparent insight into the logical nature of the task disappeared in both the responses and explanations given on the second task. Wason and Evans concluded that subjects' choices were unconsciously determined and that the verbal explanations offered were rationalizations rather than accounts of mental processes.

A subsequent, highly influential theoretical paper by Nisbett and Wilson (1977) reviewed a considerable body of evidence from the work of both cognitive and social psychologists supporting similar conclusions about people's introspective abilities. Nisbett and Wilson argued that when people are asked to explain their behaviour they do so by constructing theories to account for what they have done, and in no sense have any direct access to their own mental processes. In fairness, it should be pointed out that these views have caused considerable controversy. Ericsson and Simon (1980, 1984) among others have challenged the arguments of Nisbett and Wilson, and Morris (1981) has criticized the conclusions of Wason and Evans.

If people are not conscious of the thought processes underlying their decisions and actions, as many psychologists believe, then the opportunity to reduce error by self-criticism is evidently limited. Moreover, the evidence of rationalization suggests that people not only are unaware of their thought processes, but also construct explanations to convince themselves and others. It is evident that these processes could be combined with the sort of biases described earlier in the chapter to permit people not only to generate biased judgments but also to maintain an illusion of rationality through self-deception.

The second question raised in this section is that of whether people are aware of the limitations of the accuracy of their judgments. The answer would seem to be negative, since there exists a large amount of evidence that overconfidence is a very prevalent feature of human intuitive judgment (see Kahneman, Slovic and Tversky, 1982, part VI). For example, if people are given a general knowledge test and asked to estimate the likelihood that their answers are correct, then their estimates are consistently overconfident when compared with the objective probability of success. This overconfidence in intuitive judgment applies equally to judgments about future events, i.e. forecasts. In one such study, Fischhoff and MacGreggor (1982) asked subjects to predict events which would be consummated within 30 days of the experiment, e.g. results of local elections and popular sporting events. The proportion of correct predictions was 0.618 whereas the mean confidence in predictions was 0.722.

These sorts of finding might seem a little surprising since one would expect people to learn from mistakes made in the past and realize their limitations as forecasters. In fact, related research reveals that people are quite poor at learning from past mistakes and display a phenomenon known as hindsight bias or the 'knew-it-all-along-effect' (see Fischhoff (1982) for a review). It has been demonstrated in a number of studies that people will overestimate the likelihood that they could have predicted an event, if they are provided with outcome knowledge. If asked to recall earlier predictions after outcomes are known people will also remember more accurate predictions than they actually made. This self-flattery is not conscious but based on genuine internalized beliefs.

CONCLUSIONS AND IMPLICATIONS FOR FORECASTING

Many of the studies discussed in this chapter have utilized relatively artificial reasoning or judgment tasks performed in the laboratory. However, they have been deliberately selected to illustrate phenomena which have been widely replicated over a range of laboratory tasks and can therefore be assumed to reflect rather general tendencies in human thinking. Several studies which confirm these kinds of finding with expert judges or in more naturalistic contexts have also been cited.

I will assume the validity of the general phenomena discussed and consider here how these biases are likely to be reflected in professional forecasting and what steps can be taken to minimize their effects. It seems reasonable to assume that forecasters will often hold strong attachment to particular theories and beliefs, and would prefer to be right rather than wrong with their predictions. Hence, we would expect both confirmation and belief biases to operate, with the result that rival theories will tend to be maintained even when the objective evidence available ought to discriminate one from another.

The perseveration of theories in the face of conflicting evidence is, of course, a commonplace observation in science and in social science. It has always struck me, for example, that the genius of Einstein in developing the theory of relativity was due in part to his peculiar resistance to the psychological factors which maintain beliefs. At the time, the overwhelming majority of experimental evidence supported Newtonian mechanics. Indeed, a number of the predictions that Einstein formulated to discriminate his theory from Newton's could not be tested until much later, when appropriate technologies were developed, such as highly accurate nuclear clocks. Inventive genius requires more than great powers of reasoning—it involves the ability to question aessumptions so fundamental that others take them for granted. Incidentally, a fascinating case study of Einstein's thought processes leading up to his theory of relativity is provided by Wertheimer (1961).

Although I do not claim any particular expertise in economics, this would seem to be an interesting area for consideration in the psychology of forecasting. To an outsider it would appear that (a) a characteristic feature of economics is that forecasts of real world events are often generated, (b) such forecasts are frequently wrong and (c) rival theories are persistently maintained in the face of all evidence. I believe that economic forecasting is extremely difficult, but I also think that it is in an area which is especially vulnerable to the factors which lead to belief maintenance, for several reasons.

Firstly, economics is a true social science which means that the processes it studies are a function of human culture and the structure of society. Hence, it is possible to confuse what one thinks the way of the world is and how one thinks it ought to be—more easily than in physics, say. It seems fairly apparent that the intellectual theory of the economy held by certain individuals is related to their political convictions. When academic theories are linked with personal and political beliefs then the likelihood of belief maintenance becomes much greater.

A second relevant factor in economic forecasting is the fact that theories are generally tested against real world events rather than laboratory simulations. This has the consequence that objective and clear-cut evidence is harder to obtain. In the absence of experimental controls one is invariably looking at the effects of factors through correlations, with causes being hard to identify. For example, one cannot run an experiment where two identical versions of the British economy are managed under monetarist and Keynesian principles. Comparisons between periods of government adopting either approach are, of course, confounded by a whole host of changing historical variables. Also, predictions which fail can invariably be explained away as being due to some unforeseen real world event exerting an effect. The inaccuracy of recent forecasts by the British Treasury have, for example, been explained by reference to the outbreak of the Falklands War in 1982 and the miners' strike in 1984. My point is not to dispute the claim that such factors confound the forecast nor the contention that they are unforeseeable. My point is that significant effects of unanticipated events will occur so frequently in practice, that it is hard to see how clear falsifying evidence for theories can be obtained. The world inevitably provides excuses for the failures of forecasts.

Forecasting of real world events is, of course, fraught with difficulties. I have mentioned that forecasters may be able to justify maintaining theories in the face of failed predictions, but the converse holds also. Confirmation of a prediction does not necessarily verify the theory on which it is based. For example, opponents of the abolition of capital punishment in Britain forecast an increase in the rate of murders and violent crime, which in fact occurred. Abolitionists, however, do not concede this as evidence for the deterrent effect of capital punishment and point to a variety of other changing factors which could account for the crime rate statistics.

Another difficulty with real world forecasting is that decisions frequently have to be made on the basis of the forecasts. For example, a company's investment strategy will depend upon forecasts of the state of future markets or a government's defence spending upon its assessment of likely developments in the world's political climate. This means that one may not find out whether a forecast is good until it is too late. From the point of view of testing the underlying theories it also has the unfortunate consequence that the decision taken may affect the outcome of the forecast. For example, one could argue that a forecast of cold East–West relations by one of the superpowers would be a self-fulfilling prophecy if it led to a major armament programme.

A different example, familiar to psychologists, is that of validating assessment tests to select people for particular occupations. Few organizations are keen to take on an equal number of people who do badly and do well on the test to compare their subsequent performance—the only scientific way to assess the predictive validity of the test.

The evidence of confirmation and belief biases suggests that scientists as well as social scientists will be vulnerable. Nevertheless, I contend that the greater the involvement of personal and political beliefs in theories and the more intrinsic difficulties that are presented in the collection of relevant evidence then the more powerful will be the tendency towards belief maintenance. Let us finally consider what may be done to offset such biases.

First of all it is important for forecasters to be aware of the sort of psychological evidence discussed in this chapter, particularly the limited extent of knowledge that people have directly available about their own thought processes. It may be unpalatable to be told that you will be over-confident, unaware of the thought process underlying your judgments and adept at rationalizing outcomes. The evidence is strong, however, and we should all accept that we are prey to such human frailties—not just our colleagues and rivals! The problem, of course, is not one of integrity—for example, the subjects in the illusory correlation studies honestly believe that the patterns they expect to see are present.

Secondly, we should demand high standards in the construction and presentation of theories. Karl Popper (1959) has made a number of recommendations about the means of maximizing testability. For example, he points out that the more general a theory's assumptions, and the more specific its predictions, the more susceptible it is to falsification. It is also important to try to generate risky predictions—i.e. ones which would not be generated on other grounds if the theory were not held.

Thirdly, in view of the vulnerability of intuitive reasoning and judgment to bias, we should be careful to specify all assumptions explicitly and to test the accuracy of the process of inference leading to predictions. Some twenty years ago a movement towards mathematical modelling in psychology hoped to achieve such clarification of theory construction and testing, but this approach proved very restrictive on the range of psychological ideas and experimental tasks which could be dealt with. The current fashion for cognitive science has led many psychologists to propose that theories of human cognition and intelligence can best be formalized by computer simulations, though this approach also has its critics. It must also be noted that the tradition of mathematical and computer modelling in economics does not appear to have produced a convergence of theoretical views.

Controversy in science has, of course, a healthy aspect and the adversarial pursuit of rival theories by enthusiastic supporters doubtless provides much necessary human motivation for the process of discovery. Nevertheless, the evidence of bias in generating and evaluating forecasts and the tendency towards unreasonable maintenance of beliefs should be cause for concern. Whilst I do not pretend that there are any easy solutions, I do believe that more general awareness of the psychological factors which contribute to error in forecasting is of great importance.

REFERENCES

Chapman, L. J. and Chapman, J. (1971) 'Test results are not what you think they are', *Psychology Today*, November, 18–22 and 106–110.

Cohen, L. J. (1981) 'Can human irrationality be experimentally demonstrated?', *The Behavioral and Brain Sciences*, **4**, 317–370.

Ericsson, K. A. and Simon, H. A. (1980) 'Verbal reports as data', *Psychological Review*, **87**, 215–251.

Ericsson, K. A. and Simon, H. A. (1984) 'Protocol Analysis: Verbal reports as data', Cambridge, Mass.: MIT Press.

Evans, J. St.B. T. (1982) *The Psychology of Deductive Reasoning*, London: Routledge & Kegan Paul.

Evans, J. St.B. T. (ed.) (1983) *Thinking and Reasoning: Psychological Approaches*, London: Routledge & Kegan Paul.

Evans, J. St.B. T., Barston, J. L., and Pollard, P. (1983) 'On the conflict between logic and belief in syllogistic reasoning', *Memory and Cognition*, **11**, 295–306.

Evans, J. St.B. T. and Lynch, J. S. (1973) 'Matching bias in the selection task', *British Journal of Psychology*, **64**, 391–397.

Fischhoff, B. (1982) 'For those condemned to study the past: Heuristics and biases in hindisight', in Kahneman, D. Slovic, P. and Tversky, A. *Judgment under Uncertainty: Heuristics and Biases*, Cambridge: Cambridge University Press.

Fischhoff, B. and McGreggor, D. (1982) 'Subjective confidence in forecasts', *Journal of Forecasting*, **1**, 155–172.

Griggs, R. A. (1983) 'The role of problem content in the selection task and in the THOG problem', in J. St.B. T. Evans (ed.), *Thinking and Reasoning: Psychological Approaches*, London: Routledge & Kegan Paul.

Griggs, R. A. and Cox, J. R. (1982) 'The elusive thematic materials effect in the Wason selection task', *British Journal of Psychology*, **73**, 407–420.

Griggs, R. A. and Newstead, S. E. (1982) 'The role of problem structure in a deductive reasoning task', *Journal of Experimental Psychology: Learning, Memory and Cognition*, **8**, 297–307.

Johnson-Laird, P. N. and Wason, P. C. (1977) *Thinking: Readings in Cognitive Science*, Cambridge: Cambridge University Press.

Kahneman, D., Slovic, P. and Tversky, A. (1982) *Judgment under Uncertainty: Heuristics and Biases*, Cambridge: Cambridge University Press.

Lord, C., Ross, L. and Lepper, M. R. (1979) 'Biased assimilation and attitude polarisation: The effect of prior theories on subsequently considered evidence', *Journal of Personality and Social Psychology*, **37**, 2098–2109.

Miller, G. A. (1967) *The Psychology of Communication*, New York: Basic Books.

Morris, P. E. (1981) 'Why Evans is wrong in criticising introspective reports of subject strategies', *British Journal of Psychology*, **72**, 465–468.

Mynatt, C. R., Doherty, M. E. and Tweney, R. D. (1977) 'Confirmation bias in a simulated research environment: an experimental study of scientific inference', *Quarterly Journal of Experimental Psychology*, **29**, 85–96.

Newstead, S. E. and Griggs, R. A. (1984) 'Fuzzy quantifiers as an explanation of set inclusion performance', *Psychological Research*, **46**, 377–388.

Nisbett, R. E. and Ross, L. (1980) *Human Inference: Strategies and Shortcomings of Social Judgment*, Englewood Cliffs, N.J.: Prentice-Hall.

Nisbett, R. E. and Wilson, T. D. (1977) 'Telling more than we can know: Verbal reports on mental processes', *Psychological Review*, **84**, 231–295.

Oakhill, J. and Johnson-Laird, P. N. (1985) 'The effects of belief on the spontaneous production of syllogistic conclusions', *Quarterly Journal of Experimental Psychology*, **37A**, 553–570.

Pollard, P. (1982) 'Human reasoning: Some possible effects of availability', *Cognition*, **12**, 65–96.

Popper, K. (1959) *The Logic of Scientific Discovery*, London: Hutchinson.

Revlin, R., Leirer, V., Yopp, H. and Yopp, R. (1980) 'The belief bias effect in formal reasoning: The influence of knowledge on logic', *Memory and Cognition*, **8**, 584–592.

Tweney, R. D., Doherty, M. E., Warner, W. J., Pliske, D. B., Mynatt, C. R., Gross, K. A. and Arkkezin, D. L. (1980) 'Strategies of rule discovery in an inference task', *Quarterly Journal of Experimental Psychology*, **32**, 109–24.

Tweney, R. D., Doherty, M. E. and Mynatt, C. R. (eds.) (1981) *On Scientific Thinking*, New York: Columbia University Press.

Wason, P. C. (1960) 'On the failure to eliminate hypotheses in a conceptual task', *Quarterly Journal of Experimental Psychology*, **12**, 129–149.

Wason, P. C. (1966) 'Reasoning', in B. M. Foss (ed.), *New Horizons in Psychology I*, Harmondsworth: Penguin.

Wason, P. C. (1977) in Johnson-Laird and Wason (1977).

Wason, P. C. and Brooks, P. G. (1979) 'THOG: the anatomy of a problem', *Psychological Research*, **41**, 79–90.

Wason, P. C. and Evans, J. St.B. T. (1975) 'Dual processes in reasoning?', *Cognition*, **3**, 141–154.

Wason, P. C. and Johnson-Laird, P. N. (1972) *Psychology of Reasoning: Structure and Content*, London: Batsford.

Wertheimer, M. (1961) *Productive Thinking*, London: Tavistock.

Wilkins, M. C. (1928) 'The effect of changed material on the ability to do formal syllogistic reasoning', *Archives of Psychology*, *New York*, No. 102.

Judgmental Forecasting
Edited by G. Wright and P. Ayton
© 1987 John Wiley & Sons Ltd

CHAPTER 3

Assessing Human Judgment: Has it Been Done, Can it Be Done, Should it Be Done?

Lee Roy Beach
University of Washington

Jay Christensen-Szalanski
University of Iowa

and

Valerie Barnes
Battelle Seattle Research Center

The purpose of this chapter is to describe an alternative perspective on a topic that has received considerable attention of late: the quality of human judgment. The most broadly accepted view is that, in general, human judgment is seriously biased, and that this results from judges' reliance upon inappropriate or irrational procedures to arrive at their judgments. Given this view, it follows that the use of judgments as input to forecasting models is fraught with risk (e.g. Armstrong, 1985).

We do not question that having reservations about the adequacy of human judgment is justified to some degree. Everyone rues erroneous past judgments and knows that someday they will rue judgments that they have not yet even made. There is no doubt that human judgment, and human reasoning in general, is imperfect—why else would explicit, and often elaborate logical systems have been devised to clarify and help it?

On the other hand, demonstrations of judgmental fallibility need careful interpretation lest they be seen as broad indictments of reasoning in general. In particular, it must be recognized that many of these demonstrations rely upon a narrow range of conditions that purposely are designed to highlight fallibility, and that their success in doing this does not necessarily mean that the demonstrated errors will occur in less contrived circumstances. What actually is at issue is whether the results of these demonstrations are indictments of human judgment in general. If it is decided that they are, then the next issue is whether the problems are sufficiently serious to recommend relinquishment of the use of judgment and reasoning in workaday tasks, such as forecasting.

What follows is an overview of the viewpoint that runs counter to the one that has just been described. The argument is that the major issues concerning the quality of human judgment and reasoning are far from settled, and that many of the most widely accepted negative conclusions are, in fact, not supported by convincing data. Support for this argument comes from closer examination of four areas: (1) the 'Citation Bias', (2) the Research Tasks, (3) the Problem of 'Framing' and (4) the Criterion Problem.

THE 'CITATION BIAS'

If a reader who is unfamiliar with the literature on judgment and reasoning were to pick up a recent review or read the introduction to a current article, he or she would receive the distinct impression that few, if any, studies have ever obtained evidence of good performance. However, this impression would be quite wrong. The problem is that studies showing good performance seldom are cited or discussed, a 'phenomenon' that has been called the 'citation bias' (Christensen-Szalanski and Beach, 1984).

Christensen-Szalanski and Beach (1984) reviewed more than 3500 abstracts of articles on judgment and reasoning published between 1972 and 1981. Of these there were 84 empirical studies (that is, only 84/3500 = 2.4 per cent of the literature consists of empirical work, showing that, in this area at least, when all is said and done, more is said than done). Of these 84 studies, 47 obtained poor performance and 37 obtained good performance; a ratio of about 1.3 to 1. However, examination of the Social Sciences Citation Index showed that on the average the ratio of subsequent citations of poor performance results to good performance results was 6 to 1. That is, poor performance results were cited an average of six times more often than were good performance results. Moreover, this ratio progressively got more lopsided over the ten years from 1971 to 1981, starting at about 1 to 1 and going to about 9 to 1. (The quality of the journals in which the articles were published was held equal so this cannot account for the difference.)

Further, Christensen-Szalanski and Beach (1984) polled the United States members of the Judgment and Decision Making Society to see what their views were on the quality of human judgment, and also asked them to recall examples of both poor and good performance. It was found that experienced researchers (i.e. more than 15 publications in the area) had a far higher opinion of the quality of human judgment than did less experienced researchers (i.e. fewer than 5 publications)—perhaps the latter got their education during the recent emphasis on poor performance and believed what they read (or alternatively, maybe the former are not keeping up with the literature). For all respondents, the number of recalled examples of poor performance exceeded those of good performance (median = 4 vs. 1, $p < 0.001$). However, of the examples given by at least 10 per cent of the respondents, all of those for poor performance were from a very limited set of laboratory studies, almost all of which used undergraduates as subjects. In contrast, 58 per cent of the examples of good performance were from a fairly wide variety of studies in applied settings and/or using experts as subjects (e.g. livestock judges, weather-forecasters, accountants, physicians). In a moment we will return to the question of laboratory materials and undergraduates vs. applied settings and experts.

It has been argued (Armstrong, 1985; Evans, 1984; Kahneman and Tversky, 1982; but see Amabile, 1983) that the emphasis upon poor performance is informative in the same sense that perceptual errors are informative and that such an emphasis is to be expected because researchers must focus upon problems in order to solve them. This is true, as long as it is kept in perspective (see Jungermann, 1983). However, it also has been argued (e.g. Lopes and Ekberg, 1980; Rachlin *et al.*, 1981) that good performance also can be informative about how judgments take place and how reasoning proceeds. Moreover, ignoring good performance (e.g. Nisbett and Ross, 1980) can unduly discolour our view of human judgment and reasoning— witness the negative view held by the less experienced members of the Judgment and Decision Making Society, even though 44 per cent of the empirical studies report good judgment and reasoning.

In summary, it appears that reports of good performance virtually have been ignored and that it is possible that this has had an undue negative influence upon people's views about the quality of judgment and reasoning.

THE RESEARCH TASKS

The generalizability of research results to workaday uses of judgment and reasoning heavily depends upon the degree to which the research conditions and tasks are analogous to and applicable to those workaday conditions and tasks (e.g. Kruglanski, Friedland and FarKash, 1984). Identity is not necessary but at a minimum a clear parallel is required. In the vast majority of the most famous judgment and reasoning studies, the task requires the subjects, usually undergraduate students, to supply answers to problems of the following sort, called 'word problems':

(1) A cab was involved in a hit-and-run accident at night. Two cab companies, the green and the blue, operate in the city. A witness reports that the offending cab was blue, and legal action is brought against the blue

cab company. The court learns that 85 per cent of the city's cabs are green and 15 per cent are blue. Further, the court learns that on a test of ability to identify cabs under appropriate visibility conditions, the witness is correct on 80 per cent of the identifications and incorrect on 20 per cent. What is the probability that the responsible cab was in fact a blue cab? (The 'correct' answer is 0.41 but subjects favour 0.80; Kahneman and Tversky, 1972.)

(2) Consider the following two-stage game. In the first stage, there is a 75 per cent chance to end the game without winning anything, and a 25 per cent chance to move into the second stage. If you reach the second stage you have a choice between: (1) a sure win of $30 or (2) 80 per cent chance to win $45. Your choice must be made before the game starts, i.e. before the outcome of the first stage is known. Please indicate the option you prefer. (The 'correct' answer is the second choice but subjects prefer the first; Tversky and Kahneman, 1981.)

There has been a good deal of discussion about whether results deriving from such abstract word problems are or are not generalizable to much workaday judgment and reasoning (e.g. Berkeley and Humphreys, 1982; Beyth-Marom and Arkes, 1983; Christensen-Szalanski and Beach, 1983; Ebbesen and Konecni, 1980; Fiedler, 1983; Groner, Groner and Bischof, 1983; Kahneman and Tversky, 1982; Wallsten, 1983). This is especially confusing because in some cases the errors subjects make can be reduced by rephrasing or otherwise altering the problems (Fischoff, 1982; Nisbett *et al*., 1983; Tversky and Kahneman, 1981) or by making the frequencies in the problem concrete by having the subjects actually experience them (Beach, 1966; Christensen-Szalanski and Beach, 1982; Wheeler and Beach, 1968). Moreover, performance that is poor by laboratory standards may not be poor outside the laboratory; Hogarth (1981) has pointed out that laboratory tasks usually are static but that non-laboratory, real-world tasks seldom are, and Evans and Pollard (1982) and Pollard (1982) argue that so-called biases and heuristics often produce quite satisfactory results outside the laboratory. Christensen-Szalanski (1986) explores this point in some detail and gives examples in which judgmental errors in fact have no negative implications for the action that is based upon them.

Interpretations of results for word problems often are weakened further by the lack of unanimity among the subjects about the answers, correct or otherwise. Many subjects seem mostly to be confused. Indeed, in one study (Christensen-Szalanski and Beach, 1982), around 20 per cent of the subjects refused to give an answer at all, claiming that they simply did not know— subjects such as these usually are not included in the data analyses (e.g. Bar-Hillel, 1980, p. 219), so it is difficult to know how common such non-responding is.

In summary, observed poor performance in laboratory studies using very selected problems may not generalize to workaday judgment and reasoning and may not have the implications that it appears to have for the quality of action based upon that judgment and reasoning.

THE PROBLEM OF 'FRAMING'

The way in which a problem is understood, classified, or the like is called 'framing'. In their studies of framing, Tversky and Kahneman (1981) have shown that apparently minor changes in how a problem is presented can strongly influence the answers that groups of judges give to it. Indeed, this lability of frames can be regarded as yet another example of the generally low quality of human judgment and reasoning, and part and parcel of the poor performance observed in so many studies. Indeed, many researchers agree that framing is a big problem and that it is the source of many supposedly poor judgments and much supposedly poor reasoning (Bazerman, 1984; Fischhoff and MacGregor, 1983).

Alternatively, framing can be seen as having very strong implications for those studies that report poor performance. That is, if many subjects are misframing the problems (from the experimenter's viewpoint at least), then what on earth do the results mean? Does it make sense to infer from their answers that subjects as a group fell victim to the so-and-so bias on some problem if, in fact, they did not see themselves as working on that problem at all?

In an examination of this question, Barnes (1984) presented 10 subjects with a series of the word problems that are commonly used in judgment studies and that are framed by most experimenters as 'sample size problems', 'conjunction problems', and 'prior probability problems'. When subjects were asked to divide the problems into groups of similar problems, unlike the experimenters, their groups were based on concepts like 'math problems', 'problems about people', and 'other'. That is, problems that experimenters frame as being of a specific type got distributed among several of the subjects' groups indicating that the subjects' frames were very different from the experimenters' frames.

When subjects were asked to describe what they were doing as they worked on each problem, they sometimes appeared to grasp the feature that experimenters would regard as essential and their answers were fairly similar to what experimenters would regard as accurate. In other cases their approach was substantially different from what experimenters would do and their answers were correspondingly different. However, of most importance is the observation that subjects' approaches were appropriate to *their own frames* and in most instances their answers were a reasonable product of their approaches. That is, granting their approach, their answers were justifiable.

It is reasonable to think that how subjects frame a problem depends upon who they are—upon their familiarity and experience with the problem as well as their interest in it. In light of this it is instructive to note that most of the evidence for poor performance has been obtained from studies that use undergraduates as subjects. In contrast, good performance often has been found when experts make judgments within the sphere of their expertise. Of course, a major aspect of being an expert is the ability to recognize that a particular problem is an example of a specific problem class, and therefore is solved using specific techniques. Researchers must use caution when basing conclusions about the quality of human judgment upon the behavior of non-experts, i.e. undergraduates, who appear prone to use frames other than the one that the experimenter assumes to be appropriate and who, therefore, are likely to give the answers that are incorrect from the experimenter's point of view.

Problems stemming from using non-experts as subjects are exacerbated by the use of word problems as the experimental apparatus. Many of these problems are difficult for even sophisticated people to understand. Phillips (1983) reports an exercise undertaken by one of his advanced classes in decision analysis in which the task was to frame the second of the two example problems given above, the one about the two-stage gamble. Specifically, the goal was to diagram the logical structure of the problem. Phillips found that the different analysts produced different structures and only were able to arrive at the one the original experimenters apparently had assumed was correct by reasoning backward from the answer that the experimenters had designated as correct. While these student analysts may not have been true experts, they certainly were fairly sophisticated and they had the tools for analysing and framing problems, and even at that they had difficulties. Small wonder that untrained undergraduates find such problems opaque.

In summary, insofar as subjects differ in how they frame a problem, they are applying their judgment and reasoning skills to different problems, and to problems that are not the problem upon which the experimenter thinks they are working. Moreover, while expertise consists of recognizing the appropriate frame, some problems are elusive even to experts.

THE CRITERION PROBLEM

In most reports of poor judgmental or reasoning performance the argument is that to do anything other than what is prescribed by the experimenter's frame for the problem is to behave contrary to logical considerations with which the subject clearly would agree. For example, in 'conjunction problems' most judges will agree that if one event is unlikely to occur and a second also is unlikely, that it is *very* unlikely that they both will occur [i.e. $P(a$ and $b)$ is less than either $P(a)$ or $P(b)$]. However when faced with problems involving this consideration, judgments sometimes reflect it (Barclay and Beach, 1972) and sometimes they do not (Tversky and Kahneman, 1983).

Notice that for this particular problem, as is true for a large proportion of the problems in this literature, the experimenter's frame, called the *normative model*, is formal probability theory, which is a very special kind of logic. Hacking (1975), among others (e.g. Hammond, 1982) calls this logic aleatory—which derives from the Greek word *aleator*, which is a dice player. In short, aleatory logic is the logic of gambling, whence much of modern probability theory derives. A major feature of this logic is the Principle of Extensionality which, in essence, states that all elements in a particular set are mutually intersubstitutable. That is, the interest is in the set and not in the individual elements—just as the unemployment rate refers to the problem for the aggregate rather than the plight of the individual. In gambling this means that knowledge about individual elements is irrelevant—a five on this throw of a die, for example, is the same as a five on any other throw. Element-specific knowledge explicitly must be ignored.

In contrast to the logic of aleatory probability is the logic (or logics—there may be many) of epistemic probability (e.g. Hacking, 1975). Epistemic logic means that the appraisal of probabilities derives from knowledge about the elements, that is, from what the assessor (judge) knows about the causal network in which the event in question is embedded, upon the weight of evidence, etc. This logic requires that element-specific knowledge *not* be ignored; it is central to the assessment and set membership is merely one aspect of it.

Barnes (1984), building upon a suggestion by Kahnemann and Tversky (1982), examined the possibility that some of the observed poor performance in judgment and reasoning tasks results from subjects using epistemic logic on what 'properly' are aleatory problems. She also explored how the way in which a problem is presented can induce the subjects to use this epistemic logic instead of the desired aleatory logic. That this approach has substance is shown by the observation that if problems are presented in a manner that makes the intersubstitutability of events clear ('Imagine you were to walk down the street and chanced to see . . .') they apparently elicit aleatory framing and logic (e.g. Barclay and Beach, 1972), while problem presentation that emphasizes the uniqueness of the event ('Jack is a 45-year-old man . . .') does not (e.g. Kahneman and Tversky, 1973).

While in most discussions it is assumed that aleatory rather than epistemic logic is appropriate, this assumption is not necessarily justified from the subject's point of view. Consider this hypothetical experiment:

Suppose that an experimenter were to *randomly* select a church in the United States and visit it one Sunday afternoon in June, the traditional month for American weddings. He stands outside and waits for the wedding party to merge. Then he approaches the Best Man and asks the following question: 'If I were to randomly select an American couple getting married this afternoon, what is the probability that they would still be married to each other ten years from now?'

Assuming that he knows the American divorce rate, the Best Man probably would give it, in probability form, as his answer. However, what if the experimenter asked:

What is the probability that the newly married couple for whom you just were Best Man still will be married to each other ten years from now?

For the experimenter, the change in question does not change the problem—he randomly selected this couple and he knows absolutely nothing about them as individuals; for him they are mutually intersubstitutable with any other American couples getting married on that day, or on any other day for that matter. But, for the Best Man, the subject of this experiment, the change of question reflects a substantial change in the problem. The base rate (the prior probability of divorce) may influence his answer, but only if he is particularly cynical. (Indeed if he really thought the base rate accurately described his friends' chances of success, he might well have declined to serve as Best Man on the grounds that it would be a poor investment of his time and effort.) Rather, his answer to the second question, the one that is specific to his friends as individuals, properly is based upon his knowledge about them and his theories about what leads to successful and unsuccessful marriages.

It perhaps is presumptuous to condemn the Best Man for abandoning aleatory logic when answering the second question. It perhaps is unreasonable to insist that the frame that is appropriate from the experimenter's point of view is the only admissible frame, and that use of any alternative is an instance of poor judgment or irrationality. It perhaps would be more to the point to undertake an investigation of (1) the circumstances that justify use of the aleatory frame or the epistemic frame, (2) the conditions that promote judges to adopt the one frame or the other, (3) the differences between framing when the subject is or is not working in areas about which he or she is particularly knowledgeable, (4) the degree to which answers follow in a justifiable manner from the frame that is adopted, and (5) the degree to which imprecision in answers makes any difference in the subsequent course of things.

We think it is particularly important to consider the last of these five points; whether or not imprecision makes any difference. Much of the justification for all the research and all the concern about the quality of judgment and reasoning derives from uneasiness about what might result from such errors. Fuelled by recognition of errors that we ourselves have made, and by observations of errors made by others (particularly our leaders), and by fears about the future, we seem to have assumed that any and all error necessarily is dangerous.

There are three kinds of error. The first kind may result from misframing—if a particular frame in fact is *the* correct one, then even excellent performance using a different one is apt to produce an inappropriate answer, with whatever ramifications that may have. The second kind of error may result from lack of an adequate 'answer-generating process'—the subject may frame the problem correctly but not know how to solve it, or he or she may 'know' an incorrect method of solving it. The third kind of error may result from inadequate precision in the answer-generating process—reliance upon faulty input, 'noise' in the process itself, or problem demands that exceed the subject's selected level of processing precision.

So far as we know, with the exception of misframing, little has been done to examine these different sources of error. However, the review by Christensen-Szalanski (1986) demonstrates the importance of looking at them. Thus, the quality of judgment and reasoning cannot be assessed in isolation from the outcome. The judgment seldom is an end in itself. It is a guide to subsequent action and that action, and what happens as a result of it, is the ultimate criterion for assessing quality (Brehmer, 1984; Brunswik, 1952).

In summary, the experimenter's frame is not necessarily the only correct one and, because of this, it often is not clear upon what basis to evaluate the quality of judgment and reasoning.

CONCLUSION

The arguments that question the validity of the prevailing negative view about the quality of judgment and reasoning are, (1) that reports of good performance are given too little attention, (2) that the tasks used to evaluate judgment and reasoning often are contrived and unrepresentative of the tasks to which the results are generalized, and that the subjects tend to be unrepresentative of the people one commonly regards as qualified judges, (3) that subjects often frame the problems differently than experimenters do and therefore are working at a different task than the experimenter assumes they are, and (4) that it often is unclear what frame is appropriate for a given problem and therefore it is unclear what the criterion is for evaluating performance.

In light of this, the reader has every right to be perplexed about just how the allegedly pervasive fallibility of judgment and reasoning became so broadly accepted as established fact. This stems, in part, from the way in which this area of research has developed. Much of the early research was motivated by the desire to demonstrate that people's judgment and reasoning processes do not correspond to the prescriptions of the various normative models to which they were compared, and that the models were inappropriate evaluative criteria and inadequate descriptions of judgment and reasoning (e.g. Barclay, Beach and Braithwaite, 1971). However, and this is somewhat ironic, somewhere along the line things got reversed; in later studies the models were affirmed as prescriptive of the sole legitimate processes by which the problems in question could be solved, and, when behaviour did not correspond to a specific model, the behaviour rather than the model was judged inappropriate and inadequate. This switch meant that a rather minor question about tactics for studying judgment and reasoning became a major question, of interest to far more than a few cognitive psychologists, about the general quality of judgment and reasoning.

A prime example of this reversal occurred in the 1960s and 1970s in the study of 'conservatism'. Here subjects' revisions of their opinions were compared to the revisions prescribed by Bayes's theorem; opinion revision appeared to be consistently less than the prescribed amount and this was labelled 'conservatism'. That the Bayesian prescription was not labelled 'extreme' and the theorem rejected as a model of opinion revision, which now is generally recognized to be the case, is an early symptom of the aforementioned logical reversal and well may have been the beginning of much of the difficulty (Edwards, 1983).

However it all got started, there has developed a bewildering array of 'Biases', 'Heuristics', and 'Fallacies' that serves to justify the prevailing negative view of judgment and reasoning. Fortunately, in the past few years there has been a change in the tone, if not the methodology, of the work in this area (e.g. Kahneman, 1981; Kahneman and Tversky, 1984; Tversky and Kahneman, 1983). This change emphasizes that the models' inadequacy is the issue of interest rather than the inadequacy of the behaviour. However, this change may have come a bit late; the general fallibility of judgment has been widely accepted and continues to be a major theme (e.g. Slovic, Lichtenstein and Fischhoff, 1985).

Consider what happens if one turns the present state of affairs around and takes the judgment and reasoning processes as the given, the thing to be understood, and rejects the models on the basis of all the research that shows that they are not descriptive of what people are doing. The result is that one is left with two options. The first is to re-examine the normative models and see if they can be reformulated to be both descriptive and logically acceptable from a formal perspective (Cohen, 1977; Goldsmith, 1978; Shafer, 1976). Or one can abandon them in favour of some drastically different model (e.g. Anderson, 1986). Originally, this was what was supposed to be done to normative models when they proved to be inadequate descriptions (Barclay, Beach and Braithwaite, 1971), but for the most part this aspect of their use somehow got forgotten.

The second option is to educate judgment and reasoning to make it more like the normative models (Edwards, 1983, 1984). This of course assumes that one thinks that the normative models are in fact the best way to make the judgments or to reason. If one does, then this option allows one to produce experts by training them to do what they ought to do rather than merely passing verdict upon what they spontaneously do using whatever knowledge they have acquired genetically, by revelation, or through the vagaries of experience.

This second option is of particular appeal to those who have an interest in procuring high quality, serviceable judgments and reasoning, such as forecasters. It is of less appeal to those psychologists who want to get at the 'pure essence' of judgment and reasoning, and who think that laboratory studies can provide such access while somehow avoiding the contaminating influences of prior education. Admittedly, some studies suggest, rather uncharitably perhaps, that undergraduates provide such an opportunity, but in general this seems to us (and to Edwards, 1983, 1984) to be a doomed enterprise. It seems futile to think that the high-level, abstract tasks that usually are used in such studies can offer a glimpse of 'the Natural Mind' unfettered by acquired knowledge. It is better to study experts explicitly doing what experts do and to abandon the naive search for the grail of 'pure', 'natural' mental processes.

Adopting this change in research strategy would mean that evaluation of quality would be solely in terms of how well the products of judgment and reasoning served the functions for which they were produced. That is, the question of general quality would become meaningless, because it *is* meaningless. This in turn would allow us to forget about the inflammatory issue of how good or bad our minds are, and get down to work on the less flashy, but more substantive, problem of how to properly integrate human judgment and reasoning into the advanced technologies that rapidly are becoming the furniture of our lives. In short, the question of the *general* quality of judgment and reasoning not only is not settled, it probably never will be, and it probably never need be—the sole issue is how well the products of judgment and reasoning work in particular contexts or how well they can be made to work given appropriate training.

ACKNOWLEDGMENT

This work was supported by Office of Naval Research Contract No. ONR N00014-82-K-0657

REFERENCES

Amabile, T. M. (1983) 'Brilliant but cruel: Perceptions of negative evaluators', *Journal of Experimental Psychology*, **19**, 146–156.

Judgmental Forecasting

Anderson, N. H. (1986) 'A cognitive theory of judgment and decision', in B. Brehmer, H. Jungermann, P. Lourens, and G. Sevon (eds.), *New Directions in Research on Decision-making*, New York: North-Holland.

Armstrong, J. S. (1985) *Longrange forecasting: From crystall ball to computers*, 2nd edition, New York: Wiley.

Bar-Hillel, M. (1980) 'The base rate fallacy in probability judgment', *Acta Psychologica*, 44, 211–233.

Barclay, S. and Beach, L. R. (1972) 'Combinatorial properties of personal probabilities', *Organizational Behavior and Human Performance*, 8, 176–183.

Barclay, S., Beach, L. R. and Braithwaite, W. P. (1971) 'Normative models in the study of cognition', *Organizational Behavior and Human Performance*, 6, 389–413.

Barnes, V. (1984) 'The quality of human judgment: An alternative perspective', unpublished Ph.D. dissertation, University of Washington, Seattle, Washington.

Bazerman, M. H. (1984) 'The relevance of Kahneman and Tversky's concept of framing to organizational behavior', *Journal of Management*, 10, 333–343.

Beach, L. R. (1966) 'Accuracy and consistency in the revision of subjective probabilities', *IEEE Transactions on Human Factors in Electronics*, HFE-7, 29–37.

Berkeley, D. and Humphreys, P. (1982) 'Structuring decision problems and the "bias heuristic" ', *Acta Psychologica*, 50, 201–252.

Beyth-Marom, R. and Arkes, H. R. (1983) 'Being accurate but not necessarily Bayesian: Comments on Christensen-Szalanski and Beach', *Organizational Behavior and Human Performance*, 31, 255–257.

Brehmer, B. (1984) 'Brunswikian psychology for the 1990's', in K. M. J. Lagerspetz and P. Niemi (eds.), *Psychology in the 1990's*, New York: Elsevier.

Brunswik, E. (1952) *Conceptual framework of psychology*, Chicago: University of Chicago.

Christensen-Szalanski, J. J. J. (1986) 'Improving the practical utility of judgment research', in B. Brehmer, H. Jungermann, P. Lourens and G. Sevon (eds.), *New Directions in Research on Decision-making*, New York: North-Holland.

Christensen-Szalanski, J. J. J. and Beach, L. R. (1982) 'Experience and the base-rate fallacy', *Organizational Behavior and Human Performance*, 29, 270–278.

Christensen-Szalanski, J. J. J. and Beach, L. R. (1983) 'Believing is not the same as testing: A reply to Beyth-Marom and Arkes', *Organizational Behavior and Human Performance*, 31, 258–261.

Christensen-Szalanski, J. J. J. and Beach, L. R. (1984) The Citation Bias: Fad and fashion in the judgment and decision literature', *American Psychologist*, 39, 75–78.

Cohen, L. J. (1977) *The probable and the Provable*, Oxford: Clarendon Press.

Ebbesen, E. B. and Konecni, V. J. (1980) 'On the external validity of decision making research: What do we know about decisions in the real world?', in T. S. Wallsten (ed.), *Cognitive Processes in Choice and Decision Making*, Hillsdale, N.J.: Erlbaum.

Edwards, W. (1983) 'Human cognitive capabilities, representativeness, and ground rules for research', in P. Humphreys, O. Svenson and A. Vari (eds.), *Analysing and Aiding Decision Processes*, New York: North-Holland.

Edwards, W. (1984) 'Decision analysis: A nonpsychological psychotechnology, in V. Sarris and A. Parducci (eds.), *Perspectives in Psychological Experimentation: Toward the Year 2000*, Hillsdale, N.J.: Lawrence Erlbaum.

Evans, J. St.B. T. (1984) 'In defense of the citation bias in the judgment literature', *American Psychologist*, 39, 1500–1501.

Evans, J. St.B. T. and Pollard, P. (1982) 'Statistical judgment: A further test of the representativeness construct', *Acta Psychologica*, 51, 91–103.

Fiedler, K. (1983) 'On the testability of the availability heuristic', in R. W. Scholz (ed.), *Decision Making under Uncertainty*, New York: North-Holland.

Fischhoff, B. (1982) 'Debiasing', in D. Kahneman, P. Slovic and A. Tversky (eds.), *Judgment under Uncertainty: Heuristics and Biases*, New York: Cambridge University Press.

Fischhoff, B. and MacGregor, D. (1983) 'Judged lethality: How much people seem to know depends upon how they are asked', *Risk Analysis*, 3, 229–236.

Goldsmith, R. W. (1978) 'Assessing probabilities of compound events in a judicial context', *Scandinavian Journal of Psychology*, 19, 103–110.

Groner, R., Groner, M. and Bischof, W. F. (1983) 'The role of heuristics in models of decision', in R. W. Scholz (ed.), *Decision Making under Uncertainty*, New York: North-Holland.

Hacking, I. (1975) *The Emergence of Probability*, Cambridge: Cambridge University Press.

Hammond, K. (1982) 'To whom does the future belong: Is you is or is you ain't my baby?', paper presented at the third annual meeting of the Judgment and Decision Making Society, Minneapolis, Minnesota, November, 1982.

Hogarth, R. (1981) 'Beyond discrete biases: Functional and dysfunctional aspects of judgmental heuristics', *Psychological Bulletin*, 90, 197–217.

Jungermann, H. (1983) 'The two rationality camps', in R. W. Scholz (ed.), *Decision Making under Uncertainty*, New York: North-Holland.

Kahneman, D. (1981) 'Who shall be the arbiter of our intuitions?', *Behavioral and Brain Sciences*, 4, 339.

Kahneman, D. and Tversky, A. (1972) 'Subjective probability: A judgment of representativeness', *Cognitive Psychology*, 3, 430–454.

Kahneman, D. and Tversky, A. (1973) 'On the psychology of prediction', *Psychological Review*, 80, 237–251.

Kahneman, D. and Tversky, A. (1982) 'On the study of statistical intuitions', *Cognition*, 11, 123–141.

Kahneman, D. and Tversky, A. (1984) 'The psychology of decision making', *Naval Research Reviews*, 36, 20–24.

Kruglanski, A. W., Friedland, N. and Farkash, E. (1984) 'Lay persons' sensitivity to statistical information: The case of high perceived applicability', *Journal of Personality and Social Psychology*, 46, 503–518.

Lopes, L. L. and Ekberg, P. H. (1980) 'Test of an ordering hypothesis of risky decision making', *Acta Psychologica*, 45, 161–167.

Nisbett, R. E., Krantz, D. H., Jepson, C. and Kunda, Z. (1983) 'The use of statistical heuristics in everyday inductive reasoning', *Psychological Review*, 90, 339–363.

Nisbett, R. E. and Ross, L. (1980) *Human Inference: Strategies and Shortcomings of Social Judgment*, Englewood Cliffs, N.J.: Prentice-Hall.

Phillips, L. (1983) 'A theoretical perspective on heuristics and biases in probabilistic thinking', in P. Humphreys, O. Svenson and A. Vari (eds.), *Analysing and Aiding Decision Processes*, New York: North-Holland.

Pollard, P. (1982) 'Human reasoning: Some possible effects of availability', *Cognition*, 12, 65–96.

Rachlin, H., Battalio, R., Kagel, J., and Green, L. (1981) 'Maximization theory in behavioral psychology', *Behavioral and Brain Sciences*, 4, 371–388.

Shafer, G. (1976) *A Mathematical Theory of Evidence*, Princeton, N.J.: Princeton University Press.

Slovic, P., Lichtenstein, S. and Fischhoff, B. (1985) 'Decision making', in R. C. Atkinson, R. J. Herrnstein, G. Lindzey and R. D. Luce (eds.), *Stevens' Handbook of Experimental Psychology*, New York: Wiley.

Tversky, A. and Kahneman, D. (1981) 'The framing of decisions and the psychology of choice', *Science*, 211, 453–458.

Tversky, A. and Kahneman, D. (1983) 'Extensional versus intuitive reasoning: The conjunction fallacy in probability judgment', *Psychological Review*, **90**, 293–315.
Wallsten, T. S. (1983) 'The theoretical status of judgmental heuristics', in R. W. Scholz (ed.), *Decision Making under Uncertainty*, New York: North-Holland.
Wheeler, G. and Beach, L. R. (1968) 'Subjective sampling distributions and conservatism', *Organizational Behavior and Human Performance*, **3**, 36–46.

Judgmental Forecasting
Edited by G. Wright and P. Ayton
© 1987 John Wiley & Sons Ltd

CHAPTER 4

Subjective Estimation of Precise and Vague Uncertainties

David V. Budescu
University of Haifa

and

Thomas S. Wallsten
University of North Carolina at Chapel Hill

OVERVIEW

The purpose of this chapter is to distinguish precise from vague uncertainties, and to review the literature on subjective risk estimation with respect to each type. In the first section precise uncertainties are defined as those that are expressible in terms of probability theory; vague uncertainties are those that are not. It is argued that the decision-maker is poorly served when provided with forecasts that are more precise than is warranted by the available information. The research on subjective probability estimation, which is relevant to precise uncertainties, is reviewed in the second section. The third section first discusses some recent approaches to vague uncertainties, and then reviews the sparse empirical literature on the topic. The chapter is summarized in the fourth and final section.

PRECISE VS. VAGUE UNCERTAINTIES

The basic distinction between qualitatively different types of uncertainty can be traced back to the seminal works of Knight (1921) and Keynes (1921). Knight (1921) distinguished measurable risk from unmeasurable uncertainty. The category of risk includes situations for which probability distributions of outcomes are known either on the basis of *a priori* calculations or statistics of past experience. The category of uncertainty includes those unique situations to which calculations and past experiences do not apply.

In a closely argued treatise, Keynes (1921) distinguished three kinds of uncertainty. Arguing in part from an analogy to the construct of similarity, and in part from an analysis of the relation between a proposition and the relevant evidence, he maintained that there are some pairs of events for which an individual cannot judge which of the two is more probable or whether they are equally probable, that for other pairs of events, the individual can judge which is more probable, but not how much more so, and, finally, 'that in a very special type of case . . . a meaning can be given to a numerical comparison of magnitude' (Keynes, 1921, p. 34).

Keynes clearly believed that this last case was the least frequently encountered. Furthermore, although some probabilities could be ranked from impossible to certain, not all could be put in the same ordering, so the result was what we now call a partial order (Roberts, 1979).[1] Finally, in anticipation of the axiomatic development by Koopman (1940), Keynes noted that in some instances it might be possible by means of suitable comparisons to determine that the numerical probability of an event lies between two values. In this case, he argued, the probability is known only vaguely.

To summarize, both Knight (1921) and Keynes (1921) distinguished measurable from unmeasurable uncertainty, while Keynes (1921) also maintained that some uncertainties were non-comparable. Both men, of course, acknowledged the special extreme cases of certainty and impossibility.

Despite this auspicious beginning, with a few notable exceptions (e.g. Ellsberg, 1961), the distinctions among types of uncertainty have had little impact on modern economics, decision theory, or decision analysis, at least until recently. Indeed, in an introduction written for a new printing of Knight's (1921) book, Stigler wrote, 'modern analysis no longer views the two classes (of uncertainty) as different in kind' (Stigler, 1971, p. xiv). Although referring only to economics, Stigler's assessment could as well have applied to decision analysis and to decision theory more generally. This is truly unfortunate, however, because most real-world uncertainties, on the basis of which decisions must be made, are precisely ones for which probabilities can be at best only vaguely estimated.

To illustrate, consider the following example, adapted from Wallsten and Forsyth (1985). Imagine that you are about to undergo a serious operation and the surgeon tells you that she judges the probability to be 0.90 that you will survive the operation. You ask how precise that estimate is. In scenario one, she tells you that she has performed this operation in this hospital and with this staff on about 100 people of whom 90 per cent have survived. Thus, 0.90 is a very solid estimate based on this history.

In scenario two, she says the operation is relatively new, it has been done close to 100 times on a variety of people throughout the world, of whom 90 per cent have survived. Neither she nor anyone in her hospital has done the operation before. Her hospital's overall survival rate is much better than average, but on the other hand this operation requires procedures with which they have had little experience. As a result, your survival probability may be better or worse than 0.90, but 0.90 is the best judgment she can give. You ask if she can provide a probability distribution over survival probability. She replies that possibly she could, but she would not have much confidence in it. Indeed, on further questioning, she is willing to state confidently that in her judgment your survival probability is greater than 0.60 and less than 1.0, but beyond that she cannot state whether a broad, left-skewed distribution, a symmetric distribution peaked at 0.90, or any of a great many other possibilities is a more accurate subjective probability distribution over survival probability.

This example illustrates two related points. One is that the firmness of the estimate is relevant to the decision. Although in both cases, the expected survival probability is 0.90, you might be more inclined to undergo the operation under scenario one, where the estimate is firm, than scenario two, where it is not, which is, of course, what Ellsberg (1961) showed.

The second point is the more subtle, and currently the more controversial. This is that the softness of the estimate in scenario two is not well represented by a particular second order distribution (i.e. a probability distribution over a probability value). Many distributions seem equally justifiable, or alternatively, none is justifiable.[2] The estimate is therefore vague. Alternatively, if the available information justifies a particular second order distribution over survival probability, then the estimate may not be firm, but it is also not vague.

To be specific, we define a precise uncertainty as one that can be justifiably expressed in terms of either a point probability estimate or a second order distribution over probability values; all other uncertainties are vague. The use of probabilities is certainly justifiable when there is a history of relative frequencies from which they can be estimated. For present purposes, focusing on subjective forecasts, we will also consider the use of probabilities to be justifiable if (a) the person who is estimating the uncertainty feels that the nature of the information base warrants their use, and (b) the estimated values satisfy the requisite probability axioms.

In attempting to characterize situations in which an expert is likely to consider the uncertainty to be properly represented by a probability distribution, it is important first to discuss linguistic ambiguity. Examples of such ambiguity occur when forecasters are asked to predict the probability of a very severe thunderstorm, the likelihood of a sharp drop in the interest rate, or the chances of a close ball game. In each case the events are only vaguely defined, leaving considerable room for individual interpretation, and obviously inducing uncertainty in the forecaster's mind (see also Murphy and Brown, 1983). Tamburrini and Termini (1982) point out correctly that this source of vagueness is not in the state of the world, but in language and the nature of the representation it provides for describing the various states. Russell wrote, 'Apart from representation, whether cognitive or mechanical, there can be no such things as vagueness or precision; things are what they are' (Russell, 1923, p. 85). Thus, in principle, this source of uncertainty can be completely eliminated by precise and detailed definitions over the domain of discourse, but in practice such elimination may be difficult to achieve.

Vesely and Rasmuson (1984) usefully distinguish two other sources of uncertainty. One is physical uncertainty, which is generally due to stochastic variability, or to measurement or sampling error, and which is certainly expressible by means of probability distributions. However, elaborate forecasting is not necessary (although elaborate experimentation may be) if what is desired is a probability distribution or a confidence interval over a parameter estimatable from data.

The other source of uncertainty is that which is due to lack of knowledge. This source becomes important as soon as one goes beyond the data in any way. If the extrapolation from the data to other events, populations, or situations is based on a precisely formulated, well-accepted model, then the uncertainty is minimal. The less firm is the basis for extrapolation, the greater is the uncertainty, and virtually always the uncertainty is of a judgmental nature. It is, further, a matter of judgment as to whether the uncertainty is expressible by means of a single probability distribution, or is better expressed in some other fashion. We are not prepared to suggest rules by which the judgment should be made, but simply point out the importance of explicitly making it when a subjective forecast is based on indirect data.

We offer Levi's (1980, pp. 431–444) analysis of the Reactor Safety Study (Nuclear Regulatory Commission, 1975) as a single illustration of the importance of the problem. The Nuclear Regulatory Commission used a fault-tree analysis to assess the probabilities of serious accidents in commercial nuclear reactors. Limited data were available for some nodes of the tree, but procedures vary over plants sufficiently that a single probability estimate of failure at a node could not be applied throughout the industry; a distribution was required instead. Also, simplifications were introduced whenever the computations would have otherwise become too unwieldy. For these reasons, assumptions and distributions were invoked throughout the analysis with very little data against which to check them, but they were justified on *a priori* and pragmatic grounds. The analysis, naturally, resulted in numerical probability estimates with respect to system failures. Levi demonstrated that alternative, equally justifiable assumptions may lead to very different probability estimates.

> The moral of the story is that we should learn to suspend judgment. We should, in the case under consideration, learn to acknowledge that the data justifies and, indeed, obligates us to suspend judgment concerning the objective chance distribution over failure rates within a given range of values. We should be prepared to adopt credal states for hypotheses about failure rates in specific cases which are indeterminate and which allow many diverse distributions to be permissible. (Levi, 1980, pp. 441–442)

Although couched in the context of model-bound risk calculations, Levi's example applies equally well to subjective estimates of risk. If particular probability distributions are not justified, then specifying one may be misleading. Thus, we argue that a forecaster should employ point probability estimates or second order probability distributions when he or she thinks they are justified by the available information, but should estimate the uncertainty more vaguely otherwise.

Further, we argue that although most decision makers would probably prefer a point estimate over a precise second order distribution, and prefer both to a vague estimate, they would feel misled if they were given an estimate of greater precision than was warranted by the information. For example, commenting that numbers denote authority and a precise understanding of relationships, a committee of the U.S. National Research Council wrote that there is an

> important responsibility not to use numbers, which convey the impression of precision, when the understanding of relationships is indeed less secure. Thus, while quantitative risk assessment facilitates comparison, such comparison may be illusory or misleading if the use of precise numbers is unjustified. (National Research Council Governing Board Committee on the Assessment of Risk, 1981, p. 15)

In a similar vein, when Ruckelshaus was the Administrator of the U.S. Environmental Protection Agency (EPA), he said, 'If I am going to propose controls that may have serious economic and social effects, I need to have some idea how much confidence should be placed in the estimates of risk that prompted these controls' (Ruckelshaus, 1984, p. 158).

The reason that decision-makers want to know how firm the estimates are, of course, is that they lose a measure of control if forced to make decisions without full knowledge of all the dimensions of uncertainty.[3] Recall in this context the results of Becker and Brownson (1964), Curley and Yates (1985), Einhorn and Hogarth (1985), Ellsberg (1961), and Yates and Zukowski (1976), all of which demonstrate that people make different decisions when the probabilistic information is vague than when it is precise. Similarly, Slovic, Fischhoff, and Lichtenstein (1980) have shown that peoples' reactions to risky events depend dramatically on how much is known about them. Because the degree of vagueness about an uncertainty affects the decision that is made, vagueness must be considered an important dimension of uncertainty. Hence, knowledge of it should not be denied to the decision-maker. From this perspective, it is the job of forecasters to estimate the uncertainty of future events as accurately and precisely as possible, but not to give the illusion of more precision than justified by the interpretation of the data.

Maintaining the distinction between precise and vague uncertainties, we now review the literature on subjective probability estimation, which is relevant to precise uncertainties. We then discuss some alternative methods for representing vague uncertainties and the available evidence on how and how well people use them.

SUBJECTIVE PROBABILITY ESTIMATION

This section is based primarily on our recent comprehensive review of the probability estimation literature (Wallsten and Budescu, 1983). In that review we claimed that subjective probability is an unobservable individualized theoretical construct and that it must be evaluated by the same criteria that are usually applied to such psychometric and psychological constructs. Further, it is necessary that subjective probabilities satisfy the requisite probability axioms.

Two types of axiom systems led to a strictly additive probability distribution over states of the world. One class is likelihood-based and specifies necessary and sufficient conditions for a set of states to be (weakly) ordered by the relation 'is not more likely than'. The other class is preference-based and specifies conditions to be met by a set of gambles (weakly) ordered according to the relation 'is not preferred to'. The latter class of axioms leads to joint establishment of probabilities of states and utilities of outcomes. Corresponding to the two types of axiom systems are two classes of methods for eliciting, or encoding, subjective probabilities. Direct methods focus exclusively on the likelihood of the various states, while indirect methods utilize choices among lotteries to infer subjective probabilities (and utilities). Extensive descriptions of the numerous subjective probability encoding methods can be found in various sources, some of which also include recommendations concerning their relative advantages (see references in Wallsten and Budescu (1983).

Our original review considered separately the probability encoding research employing non-expert participants in psychological studies and that employing substantive experts such as physicians, military intelligence analysts, or meteorologists. The review focused on five criteria of goodness: reliability, internal consistency, calibration, external validity, and construct validity. The internal consistency and construct validity properties arise primarily from consideration of the axioms, while the other criteria represent additional desirable and necessary features of encoding procedures. We present here a summary of our original view. Readers interested in a more detailed discussion of these matters and a bibliography of the research should consult the more complete discussion by Wallsten and Budescu (1983).

Reliability

The results of any scaling or encoding procedure are said to be reliable to the degree that they are free of random error. Reliability is a *sine qua non* of any measurement technique, and is usually assessed by means of correlations between two independent scalings of the same events. In general reliability is high for all subjective probability encoding methods. However, high correlations do not establish the uniqueness of subjective probability values. Uniqueness implies identical encoded values on two or more occasions, or in other words, that the regression equation relating two independent encodings have zero intercept and unit slope. Only two studies of which we are aware have evaluated reliability from this perspective. Goodman (1973) reported small mean signed deviations between two separate encodings. Using a regression analysis, Wallsten, Forsyth, and Budescu (1983), demonstrated systematic changes from the first to the second encoding.

Internal consistency

This criterion compares encoded probabilities of mutually exclusive events combined according to the laws of probability theory with encodings of the resulting compound events. Typically, subjective probabilities of mutually exclusive and exhaustive events tend to be subadditive (i.e. their sum is less than unity). Estimated probabilities of unions and intersections are highly correlated with predictions based on probability calculus, yet some systematic discrepancies are evident, especially when results are based on indirect judgments. Bar-Hillel (1973) suggests that intersection probabilities are overestimated and union probabilities are underestimated, probably as a result of an 'anchoring and adjustment' strategy.

Calibration

This is generally considered to be the most important criterion for a forecaster since it directly compares his or her performance with empirical reality. A forecaster is well-calibrated if for all events assigned a given probability, p, the proportion that occurs is in fact close (ideally equal) to p. The bivariate plot of the proportion of events occurring vs. the forecaster's probability assigned to the events defines a 'calibration curve'. The curve for a perfectly calibrated forecaster is linear with unit slope and zero intercept. Statistical measures of goodness of probability estimation are described by Lichtenstein, Fischhoff, and Phillips (1977, 1982), Yates (1982), and Yates and Curley (1985).

Lichtenstein, Fischhoff and Phillips (1977, 1982) have reviewed the literature on calibration and have concluded that generally people tend to be overconfident, i.e. events assigned probability p occur with proportion less than p. Most of the laboratory research is somewhat artificial in the sense that it depends on answers and confidence ratings to almanac questions. Thus, the probability assessed is rather special (the probability of answering the items correctly), and systematic effects of item difficulty and subject ability are found routinely. The most encouraging results in this area are the excellent levels of calibration obtained by weather forecasters, particularly (but not exclusively) when predicting precipitation, the reasonable levels of calibration obtained in several medical experiments and some positive effects of training in reducing overconfidence (Lichtenstein, Fischhoff, and Phillips, 1982).

External validity

External validity is established when subjectively estimated probabilities correlate highly with relative frequency counterparts. Indeed, the two sets of values are highly correlated in laboratory experiments, but systematic biases are found. These biases have usually been explained in terms of the heuristics of representativeness and availability (e.g. Tversky and Kahneman, 1974), and can be eliminated to some degree by training.

Construct validity

Construct validity is established when encodings obtained by two or more distinct techniques are highly correlated, as well as when encoded values correctly predict independent behaviour, such as choices. Correlations between results of various elicitation methods are generally very high, especially among the direct methods. Further, these inter-method correlations are higher than are correlations with external objective distributions, and in some cases they are as high as can be expected given the magnitudes of the reliability correlations. Unfortunately, there has been little research using encoded probability values to predict choices.

To summarize, encoded subjective probabilities are generally reliable. To a first order of approximation they satisfy the basic requirements of probability theory while nevertheless violating certain axioms in specific ways. Encoded judgments tend to correlate highly with external criteria when the latter are available. Further, when judgments are elicited by different techniques, they are more similar to each other than either is to external criteria. No single method of elicitation yields systematically better or worse results than the others. Finally, experienced experts are highly calibrated, and calibration can be improved through training.

In seeking to understand the generally positive results in combination with certain systematic violations of the axioms, we suggested in our original review that,

> subjective certainty is not precisely determined internally, but rather itself has some variability, vagueness, or fuzziness (Freeling, 1980, 1981; Wallsten, Forsyth, and Budescu, 1983; Watson, Weiss, and Donnell,

1979), the representation of which depends on the encoding method. (Wallsten and Budescu, 1983, p. 167)

To continue the line of reasoning from the first section of this paper, recall our argument that decision-makers' best interests are served when uncertainty is expressed only as precisely as is warranted by the information. We may hypothesize, now, that in fact the less precise is the forecaster's subjective uncertainty, the more poorly is it represented as a probability distribution. To our knowledge, this interesting conjecture has not been empirically tested, although Einhorn and Hogarth (1985) test and verify a related prediction.

The notion that subjective probability is not precisely defined has been recognized by those researchers who have presented process models for probability assessment. For example, in an attempt to explain overconfidence, Pitz (1974) suggested that probabilities of complex events are assessed in a serial process in which uncertainties related to previous stages are discarded and ignored in order to facilitate integration at later stages. The level of uncertainty can be indexed by the number of serial processes necessary to reach the final assessment; the larger their number, the greater the level of uncertainty. Koriat, Lichtenstein and Fischhoff (1980) described a three-stage model for assessment of probabilities that included memory search for relevant evidence, assessment of evidence to generate an internal representation of uncertainty, and conversion of this feeling to a number of means of a response mechanism. Support for some of the model's predictions regarding the first two stages was provided by Koriat, Lichtenstein and Fischhoff (1980), and some of the characteristics of the supposed response mechanism were examined by Ferrell and McGoey (1980).

Recently, Einhorn and Hogarth (1985) offered a process model, expressed in quantitative form, for assessment of subjective probabilities when the probability information is ambiguous. In this model, people first anchor their judgments on an initial estimate based on their prior experience or provided by an external source, and then adjust the initial value by imagining other values that the probability could take. The degree of adjustment depends on two factors, the level of ambiguity, and the relative importance of adjusting up or down from the original estimate. Einhorn and Hogarth (1985) and Hogarth and Kunreuther (1985) report data from a wide assortment of experiments that are consistent with the predictions of their model.

REPRESENTING VAGUE UNCERTAINTIES

We now consider means for expressing vague uncertainties. If, as argued previously, decision-makers generally need to know how precise a probability estimate is, and furthermore, probability estimation suffers when information is vague, ambiguous, or indirect, then methods should be developed that simultaneously better serve the decision-maker's needs and allow a more veridical expression of the forecaster's judgment.

Relevant theoretical and empirical work is sparse, but developing. This research may be dichotomized according to whether the representation of uncertainty is numerical or non-numerical. We consider numerical representations first.

Shafer (1976, 1981) has developed a mathematical theory of evidence, within which belief measures are assigned to events in accordance with both the direction and the weight of the evidence. If very little evidence is available with respect to a hypothesis H, then belief in H, $B(H)$, and belief in not-H, $B(\text{not-}H)$, are both very low, so that $B(H) + B(\text{not-}H) < 1$. As evidence accumulates, $B(H) + B(\text{not-}H)$ approaches 1, and in the limit belief measures are identical to additive probabilities. Thus, the amount of evidence, or in our terminology the vagueness of judgment, is indicated by the degree to which the sum of the belief in an event and the belief in its complement differs from one.

Shafer and Breipohl (1979) demonstrate the usefulness of belief measures for risk assessment, but Shafer (1981) explicitly states that his theory is not posed as a descriptive model of judgment. Nevertheless, Krantz (1982) has investigated the axiomatic conditions necessary for Shafer's model to hold descriptively. As of now, however, there are no data on the matter.

From a different perspective, Levi (1980) has developed an epistemological theory in which, subject to certain constraints, notably credal convexity,[4] credence should be maintained in all probability distributions about an outcome or hypothesis that are consistent with one's body of knowledge. It was on the basis of his carefully worked out system that he produced the analysis of the Reactor Safety Study that we presented in the first section of this chapter. In contrasting his development with that of the 'intervalists' (Levi's term), who propose the assignment of upper and lower probabilities to events, Levi suggests that the convex set of credal distributions might be represented by its envelope. Although Levi does not suggest this, a measure of the width of the envelope might be an indicator of the vagueness of judgment. Gärdenfors and Sahlin (1982, 1983) suggest further that possible probability distributions can be ordered according to a measure of epistemic reliability r. No explicit form is assumed for r nor are its properties specified.

The empirical work of Becker and Brownson (1964), Curley and Yates (1985), Ellsberg (1961), Goldsmith and Sahlin (1983), Larson (1980), Slovic and Tversky (1974), and Yates and Zukowski (1976) supports the notion that preferences and decisions are influenced by the firmness of the probabilities involved. However, most attempts to clarify, describe and predict the relationships between the nature of the ambiguity and the subjects' choices have been less than successful so far.

'Intervalists' include Dempster (1967), Keynes (1921), Koopman (1940), Kyburg (1961), and Suppes (1974), all of whom have discussed systems in which upper and lower probabilities are assigned to events or hypotheses. Generally, these systems do not preserve additive probability measures. For example, Koopman (1940) provided a set of axioms for a 'theory of intuitive probability', in which the likelihood ordering of events need not be complete. That is, for any two events A and B, the person either judges $A \geq B$, $B \geq A$, or declines to judge, where $\geq$ means 'is at least as likely as'. If the axioms are satisfied, then it is possible to derive for each event A, two numbers, $P_*(A)$ and $P^*(A)$, such that $0 \leq P_*(A) \leq P^*(A) \leq 1$. If all event pairs in the set are judged so that the events are totally ordered, then $P_*(A) = P^*(A)$, and the usual additive probability results. Feagans and Biller (1981) have suggested that a person's willingness and ability to judge the relative likelihood of pairs of events will depend on the information available to support the judgments; the more information there is, the greater the number of pairs of events that can be judged, and the closer together are $P^*(A)$ and $P_*(A)$. Thus, the difference between $P^*(A)$ and $P_*(A)$ can be taken as a measure of vagueness.

A risk assessment study based on Koopman's (1940) system was carried out, in which eight health experts encoded their uncertainty regarding dose–response functions (Wallsten, Forsyth, and Budescu, 1983). Various dose–response events were compared to canonical probability events in a manner that allowed the judges to express either precise or upper and lower probabilities regarding them. No judge provided precise subjective probabilities. Analysis of the judgments at the level of individual subjects demonstrated that the upper and lower probabilities were reliable over time, and that they satisfied very stringent consistency requirements for seven out of eight judges. Although this is only a single study, it suggests the feasibility of the procedure.

Despite the availability of some elegant numerical methods for communicating vague uncertainties, it appears, at least anecdotally, that many people prefer to use more 'natural' probability expressions, such as 'doubtful', 'probable', 'slight chance', and so forth. There are at least three reasons why this apparent preference might exist. First, frequently the information on which the forecasts or evaluations are based is itself not sufficiently precise or numerical that there is any natural way to translate it into probabilistic or numerical statements. Thus, linguistic terms are used to reflect the nonnumerical nature of the data.

Second, translation of this information into numerical form may suggest to the user of the information a level of precision and confidence that is inappropriate. Related to this second point is the third, which is that many people feel they understand and can respond to information better when it is in verbal rather than a numerical form. Indeed, as Zimmer (1983) has pointed out, it was not until the seventeenth century that probability concepts were formally developed, yet expressions for different degrees of uncertainty existed in many languages long before then. Zimmer (1984) suggested that people generally handle uncertainty by means of verbal expressions and their associated rules of conversation, rather than by means of numbers. Also, at the individual level, the ability to understand and properly use language develops prior to mastering and understanding the intricate numerical system.

At least two important classes of questions arise when considering the use of non-numerical probability expressions for communicating uncertainty. One concerns factors that affect or determine the meanings of such phrases to an individual, and the other concerns the degree to which different people agree on the interpretations of the phrases.

A common experimental approach has been to have subjects give numerical equivalents to various probability phrases. The overwhelming result has been that there is great inter-subject variability in the numerical values assigned to probability terms and great overlap among terms (Bass, Cascio, and O'Connor, 1974; Beyth-Marom, 1982; Budescu and Wallsten, 1985; Foley, 1959; Johnson, 1973; Lichtenstein and Newman, 1967; Simpson, 1944, 1963). Within-subject variability in the assignment of numbers to probabilistic terms is not minor, but is considerably less than between-subject variability (Beyth-Marom, 1982; Budescu and Wallsten, 1985; Johnson, 1973). Indeed, when asked to rank order 11 probability terms, subjects did so consistently over four replications, but the ranks assigned to terms differed reliably over subjects (Budescu and Wallsten, 1985). Needless to say, subsets of suitably spaced expressions are ranked similarly by most people.

Interesting as these results are, they are only partially relevant to each class of questions. Specifically, the fact that different people assign unequal numerical equivalents to words, or that the same people do so at different times, tells us little about the meanings of the expressions to individuals or the disparity of meanings over individuals. That is because a particular expression might have a commonly understood vague meaning which, however, is differentially translated into point estimates. Investigation of this possibility requires alternative models and procedures from those described thus far.

Models for formally representing the vague meanings of verbal expressions have been developed within fuzzy set theory, beginning with the pioneering paper by Zadeh (1965). The work applies quite broadly, but for the present our interest is only in the suggestion by Watson, Weiss, and Donnell (1979), Zadeh (1975), Zimmer (1983, 1984) and others that the theory is useful in describing and working with the vague meanings of non-numerical probability phrases. Accordingly, probability expressions are conceived as 'linguistic variables' (e.g. Zadeh, 1975), and are formally represented by functions over the [0,1] probability interval, such as the hypothetical ones shown in Figure 1. For each function, the ordinate denotes membership values representing the degree to which the probabilities on the abscissa are members of the vague concept denoted by the expression. Alternatively, for an expression W, the ordinate can be thought of as the truth value of the statement 'the probability *p* is described by *W'*. The function generally ranges from 0, absolutely false, to 1, absolutely true.

This approach raises numerous empirical questions. The first is whether functions of the sort depicted in Figure 1 can be established reliably? If so, many other questions follow. For example, are the functions valid by any reasonable criteria, do most people show the same function for a phrase, do the functions vary over contexts, and do the function shapes predict how expressions are selected to communicate the level and vagueness of uncertainty? Our colleagues and we have begun to investigate some of these questions.

Wallsten, Budescu, Rapoport, Zwick, and Forsyth (1986) recently developed and successfully tested a modified pair-comparison procedure for establishing membership functions of probability terms. The judgments obtained from our subjects were highly reliable, satisfied a set of necessary conditions required for measurement of membership, and were fitted well by the scale values extracted by appropriate algebraic models. Finally, the membership functions were validated through prediction of an independent set of judgments involving pairs of expressions. In a subsequent study (Rapoport, Wallsten, and Cox, in press) the construct of membership was further validated, by showing consistent similarity between the results obtained from the modified pair-comparison, direct estimation, and ranking procedures.

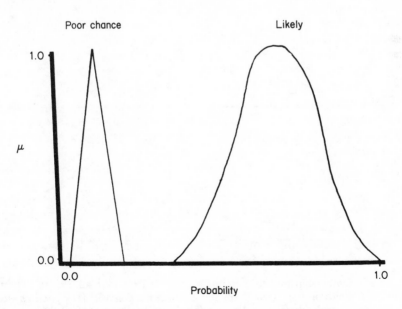

Figure 1. Hypothetical membership functions for two terms. From Wallsten *et al.* (1986)

Having established that the vague meanings of probability terms can be quantified in terms of membership functions, one must identify those features of the results that are unique to this representation and could not be deduced from other, simpler methods (e.g. associating each word with a range of numerical values). The novelty and specific information of this methodology can be best understood by examining visually some of the empirically derived functions. Figure 2 from Wallsten *et al.* (1986) shows membership functions from four subjects to illustrate the range of results obtained.

The four functions displayed for each subject describe the phrases for *doubtful* (D), *tossup* (T), *good chance* (GC), and *probable* (Pr). The functions are relatively similar for tossup, but otherwise no two subjects demonstrate the same understanding of a given expression. Some functions are monotonic, which means that the expression spans a range of probabilities, and the probability best described by the expression is at one end of the range. Other functions are single peaked, which again indicates a range of meaning, but now with the best probability somewhere in the centre of the range.

We have utilized these procedures now on well over 50 subjects to derive a few hundred membership functions, with the result that slightly over half the time they are monotonic, slightly less than half the time they are single peaked, and very occasionally they are point, flat, or multipeaked functions (this latter may represent nothing more than unreliable measurement).

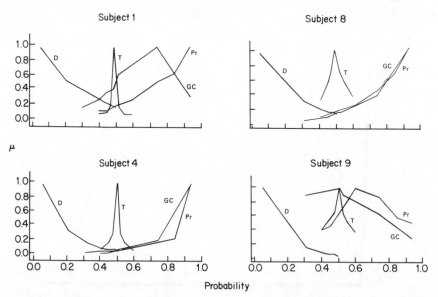

Figure 2. Membership functions empirically derived for four subjects in Experiment 2 of Wallsten *et al.* (1986) for the expressions *doubtful* (D), *good chance* (GC), *probable* (Pr), and *tossup* (T). From Wallsten *et al.* (1986)

Obviously, this richness of meanings (shapes) within and between individuals could not be deduced from individual or group ranges of values for terms (e.g. Beyth-Marom, 1982). We caution, however, that our measurement procedure has thus far been limited to the simple context of uncertainty associated with a probability spinner, i.e. a circle radially divided into two coloured sectors over which a pointer is randomly spun. It is reasonable to expect that individual differences in interpreting probability expressions will be even greater when the uncertainty is ill-defined rather than represented by a precise proportion.

We have not yet attempted to relate function shape or location to choice of expression for communicating uncertainty. However, preliminary results from a direct verbal estimation task point to a surprising richness of the subjective lexicon of uncertainty (20 subjects generated 113 different phrases to describe 11 distinct probabilities), and to a relatively consistent use of language by each person. On the average, individuals used exactly the same expression for two replications of a given event (represented by a probability spinner) in 67 per cent of the cases, which compares with a 77 per cent replication rate for numerical estimates under similar circumstances (Budescu, Weinberg, and Wallsten, 1986). Data from the same study indicate that the subjects' performance is very similar when rating or bidding for bets in which the probabilities are displayed numerically, graphically, or verbally.

It appears that the interpretations of probability expressions vary over contexts. For example, in two experiments, including one utilizing meteorologists, Wallsten, Fillenbaum, and Cox (1986) demonstrated that the interpretations of forecasts using neutral probability terms (e.g. *possible*) and terms above neutral (e.g. *usually*) were strong, positive functions of the generally perceived probability, or base rate, of the predicted event, while the interpretations of forecasts using terms below neutral (e.g. *rarely*) were much less affected by the base rate. Indeed, the interpretations of the forecasts appeared to represent some kind of weighted average of the meaning of the expression and the base rate. Similar base rate effects were obtained by Pepper and Prytulak (1974). From another perspective, Zimmer (1984) demonstrated systematic effects on the shapes of membership functions as a function of domain of discourse (e.g. natural versus social science).

The research summarized thus far would appear to suggest that use of probability expressions may not be an effective means of communicating vague uncertainties from one person to another, although there may be the illusion of communication. This would occur because both the forecaster and the decision-maker have a clear, consistent understanding of the verbal expressions, but the two understandings do not necessarily coincide.

However, the opposite is also possible. Namely, that people process information more optimally in a verbal than a numerical form, and therefore that communication is enhanced. The possibility that verbal information processing is superior to numerical was suggested by Zimmer (1983, 1984), who offers data (Zimmer, 1983) indicating that people's judgments are well-calibrated when they are made verbally.

There is currently no research directly comparing decisions made on the basis of verbal and numerical expressions of uncertainty. Preliminary analyses of our data (Budescu, Weinberg, and Wallsten, 1986) suggest, however, that in the spinner context, in which probabilities are well-defined, there are only small differences between the two types of decisions. Whether this result should be attributed to the optimality of verbal communication, as Zimmer implies, or to suboptimality in processing probabilistic information (e.g. Kahneman, Slovic, and Tversky, 1982), and whether it would apply in more natural situations in which the uncertainty is vague, are still open questions that remain to be investigated in the future.

SUMMARY

The main points of this chapter are easily summarized. It is argued that the decision-making process is best served when uncertainty is communicated as precisely as possible, but no more precisely that warranted. When probability estimates are justified by the information, people are capable of providing them in a reliable manner that generally conforms to the axioms of probability theory. However, the more vague is the individual's opinion, the less well is it represented by means of unique probabilities. There exist both numerical and non-numerical means for expressing vague uncertainties. Each class of methods appears to have advantages and disadvantages, but much research remains to be done with respect to both.

ACKNOWLEDGMENT

Preparation of this chapter was supported by Grant No. 8203394 from the US–Israel Binational Science Foundation, a Hugo Bergman Award to Budescu, and by Contract No. 903-83-K-0347 from the US Army Research Institute. The views, opinions, and findings contained in this paper are those of the authors and should not be construed as official US Department of the Army position, policy, or decision. We thank Robin Hogarth, George Loewenstein, Ian McEwin, and Amnon Rapoport for comments on a previous draft.

NOTES

1. A partial order is one that is reflexive, transitive, and antisymmetric (but not necessarily connected). For example, it might be known or judged that $A > B = C > D > F$, and also that $C > E > F$, but with no order relation established (or establishable) between D and E.

2. Levi (1980) and Gärdenfors and Sahlin (1982, 1983) develop this and related issues at length.
3. This notion of control is similar to one discussed by Feagans and Biller (1981).
4. The requirement of credal convexity, roughly, is that if two probability distributions are consistent with one's knowledge, then so are all mixtures of the distributions.

REFERENCES

Bar-Hillel, M. (1973) 'On the subjective probability of compound events', *Organizational Behavior and Human Performance*, **9**, 396–406.

Bass, B. M., Cascio, W. F. and O'Connor (1974) 'Magnitude estimation of expressions of frequency and amount', *Journal of Applied Psychology*, **59**, 313–320.

Becker, S. W. and Brownson, F. O. (1964) 'What price ambiguity? Or the role of ambiguity in decision making', *Journal of Political Economy*, **72**, 62–73.

Beyth-Marom, R. (1982) 'How probable is probable? Numerical translation of verbal probability expressions', *Journal of Forecasting*, **1**, 257–269.

Budescu, D. V. and Wallsten, T. S. (1985) 'Consistency in interpretation of probabilistic phrases', *Organizational Behavior and Human Decision Processes*, **36**, 391–405.

Budescu, D. V., Weinberg, S. and Wallsten, T. S. (1986) 'Decisions based on numerical, graphical and verbal probabilities'. IPDM Report No. 39, Haifa: the University of Haifa Institute of Information Processing and Decision Making.

Curley, S. P. and Yates, J. F. (1985) 'The center and range of the probability interval as factors affecting ambiguity preferences', *Organizational Behavior and Human Decision Processes*, **36**, 273–287.

Dempster, A. P. (1967) 'Upper and lower probabilities induced by a multivalued mapping', *Annals of Mathematical Statistics*, **38**, 325–339.

Einhorn, H. J. and Hogarth, R. M. (1985) 'Ambiguity and uncertainty in probabilistic inference', *Psychological Review*, **92**, 433–461.

Ellsberg, D. (1961) 'Risk, ambiguity, and the Savage axioms', *Quarterly Journal of Economics*, **75**, 643–669.

Feagans, T. B. and Biller, W. F. (1981) 'Assessing the health risks associated with air quality standards', *The Environmental Professional*, **3**, 235–247.

Ferrell, W. R. and McGoey, P. J. (1980) 'A model of calibration for subjective probabilities', *Organizational Behavior and Human Performance*, **26**, 32–53.

Freeling, A. N. S. (1980) 'Fuzzy sets and decision analysis', *IEEE Transactions on Systems, Man, and Cybernetics*, **SMC-10** 341–354.

Freeling, A. N. S. (1981) 'Reconciliation of multiple probability assessments', *Organizational Behavior and Human Performance*, **28**, 395–414.

Foley, B. J. (1959) 'The expression of certainty', *American Journal of Psychology*, **72**, 614–615.

Gärdenfors, P. and Sahlin, N. E. (1982) 'Unreliable probabilities, risk taking, and decision making', *Synthese*, **53**, 361–386.

Gärdenfors, P. and Sahlin, N. E. (1983) 'Decision making with unreliable probabilities', *British Journal of Mathematical and Statistical Psychology*, **36**, 240–251.

Goldsmith, R. W. and Sahlin, N. E. (1983) 'The role of second-order probabilities in decision making', in P. Humphreys, O. Svenson, and A. Vari (eds.), *Analyzing and aiding decision processes*, Budapest: Hungarian Academy of Sciences.

Goodman, B. C. (1973) 'Direct estimation procedures for eliciting judgments about uncertain events', Technical Report, Ann Arbor: University of Michigan Office of Research Administration.

Hogarth, R. M. and Kunreuther, H. (1985) 'Risk, ambiguity and insurance', Chicago: Center for decision research, Graduate School of Business, University of Chicago.

Johnson, E. M. (1973) 'Encoding of qualitative expressions of uncertainty', Technical Paper 250, Arlington, Va.: US Army Research Institute for the Behavioral and Social Sciences.

Kahneman, D., Slovic, P. and Tversky, P. (1982) *Judgment under Uncertainty: Heuristics and Biases*, Cambridge: Cambridge University Press.

Keynes, J. M. (1921) *A Treatise on Probability*, London: Macmillan. (Reprinted 1962 with an introduction by N. R. Hanson, New York: Harper & Row.)

Knight, F. H. (1921) *Risk, Uncertainty, and Profit*. (Reprinted with an introduction by George Stigler, 1971.) Chicago: University of Chicago Press.

Koopman, B. O. (1940) 'The axioms and algebra of intuitive probability', *Annals of Mathematics*, **41**, 269–292.

Koriat, A., Lichtenstein, S. and Fischhoff, B. (1980) 'Reasons for confidence', *Journal of Experimental Psychology: Human Learning and Memory*, **6**, 107–118.

Krantz, D. H. (1982) 'Foundations of the theory of evidence', paper presented at the Annual Meeting of the Society for Mathematical Psychology, Princeton, N.J.

Kyburg, H. E. (1961) *Probability and the Logic of Rational Belief*, Middletown, Conn.: Wesleyan University Press.

Larson, J. R. (1980) 'Exploring the external validity of a subjectively weighted utility model of decision making', *Organizational Behavior and Human Performance*, **26**, 293–304.

Levi, I. (1980) *The Enterprise of Knowledge*. Cambridge, Mass.: MIT Press.

Lichtenstein, S., Fischhoff, B. and Phillips, L. D. (1977) 'Calibration of probabilities: The state of the art', in H. Jungermann and G. deZeeuw (eds.), *Decision Making and Change in Human Affairs*, Amsterdam: D. Reidel.

Lichtenstein, S., Fischhoff, B. and Phillips, L. D. (1982) 'Calibration of probabilities: The state of the art to 1980', in D. Kahneman, P. Slovic and A. Tversky (eds.), *Judgment under Uncertainty: Heuristics and Biases*, Cambridge: Cambridge University Press.

Lichtenstein, S. and Newman, J. R. (1967) 'Empirical scaling of common verbal phrases associated with numerical probabilities', *Psychonomic Science*, **9**, 563–564.

Murphy, A. H. and Brown, B. G. (1983) 'Forecast terminology: Composition and interpretation of public weather forecasts', *Bulletin of the American Meteorological Society*, **64**, 13–22.

National Research Council Governing Board Committee on the Assessment of Risk (1981) *The Handling of Risk Assessments in NRC Reports*, Washington, DC: US National Research Council.

Nuclear Regulatory Commission (1975) *Reactor Safety Study: An Assessment of Accident Risks in U.S. Commercial Nuclear Power Plants*, Washington, DC: National Research Council.

Pepper, S., and Prytulak, L. S. (1974) 'Sometimes frequently means seldom: Context effects in the interpretations of quantitative expressions', *Journal of Research in Personality*, **8**, 95–101.

Pitz, G. F. (1974) 'Subjective probability distributions for imperfectly known quantities', in L. W. Gregg (ed.), *Knowledge and Cognition*, New York: Wiley.

Rapoport, A., Wallsten, T. S. and Cox, J. A. (in press) 'Direct and indirect scaling of membership functions of probability phrases', *Mathematical Modeling*.

Roberts, F. S. (1979) *Measurement Theory with Applications to Decision Making, Utility, and the Social Sciences*, Reading, Mass.: Addison-Wesley.

Ruckelshaus, W. D. (1984) 'Risk in a free society', *Risk Analysis*, **4**, 157–162.

Russell, B. (1923) 'Vagueness', *Australasian Journal of Psychology and Philosophy*, **1**, 84–92.

Shafer, G. (1976) *A Mathematical Theory of Evidence*, Princeton, N.J.: Princeton University Press.

Shafer, G. (1981) 'Constructive probability', *Synthese*, **48**, 1–60.

Shafer, G. and Breipohl, A. M. (1979) 'Reliability described by belief functions', *Proceedings of the 1979 Annual Reliability and Maintainability Symposium*, pp. 23–27. New York, NY: IEEE.

Simpson, R. H. (1944) 'The specific meanings of certain terms indicating differing degrees of frequency', *Quarterly Journal of Speech*, **30**, 328–330.

Simpson, R. H. (1963) 'Stability in meanings for quantitative terms: A comparison over 20 years', *Quarterly Journal of Speech*, **49**, 146–151.

Slovic, P. (1972) 'From Shakespeare to Simon: Speculations—and some evidence—about man's ability to process information', Eugene, Or.: Oregon Research Institute Research Bulletin, 12.

Slovic, P., Fischhoff, B. and Lichtenstein, S. (1980) 'Perceived risk', in R. Schwing and W. A. Albers, Jr (eds.), *Societal Risk Assessment: How Safe is Safe Enough?* New York: Plenum.

Slovic, P. and Tversky, A. (1974) 'Who accepts Savage's axiom?', *Behavioral Science*, **19**, 368–373.

Stigler, G. (1971) 'Introduction', in F. H. Knight, *Risk, Uncertainty, and Profit*, Chicago: University of Chicago Press.

Suppes, P. (1974) 'The measurement of belief', *Journal of the Royal Statistical Society, Ser. B*, **36**, 160–175.

Tamburrini, G. and Termini, S. (1982) 'Some foundational problems in the formalization of vagueness', in M. M. Gupta and E. Sanchez (eds.), *Fuzzy Information and Decision Processes*, Amsterdam: North-Holland.

Tversky, A. and Kahneman, D. (1974) 'Judgment under uncertainty: Heuristics and biases', *Science*, **185**, 1124–1131.

Vesely, W. E. and Rasmuson, D. M. (1984) 'Uncertainties in nuclear probabilistic risk analyses', *Risk Analysis*, **4**, 313–322.

Wallsten, T. S. and Budescu, D. V. (1983) 'Encoding subjective probabilities: A psychological and psychometric review', *Management Science*, **29**, 151–173.

Wallsten, T. S., Fillenbaum, S. and Cox, J. A. (1986) 'Base rate effects on the interpretations of probability and frequency expressions', *Journal of Memory and Language*, **25**, 571–587.

Wallsten, T. S. and Forsyth, B. H. (1985) 'On the usefulness, representation, and validation of non-additive probability judgments for risk assessment', unpublished manuscript.

Wallsten, T. S., Forsyth, B. H. and Budescu, D. V. (1983) 'Stability and coherence of health experts' upper and lower subjective probabilities about dose–response functions', *Organizational Behavior and Human Performance*, **31**, 277–302.

Wallsten, T. S., Budescu, D. V., Rapoport, A., Zwick, R. and Forsyth, B. (1986) 'Measuring vague meanings of probability terms', *Journal of Experimental Psychology: General*, **115**, 348–365.

Watson, S. R., Weiss, J. J. and Donnell, M. L. (1979) 'Fuzzy decision analysis', *IEEE Transactions on Systems, Man, & Cybernetics*, **SMC-9**, 1–9.

Yates, J. F. (1982) 'External correspondence: Decompositions of the mean probability score', *Organizational Behavior and Human Performance*, **30**, 132–156.

Yates, J. F. and Curley, S. P. (1985) 'Conditional distribution analyses of probabilistic forecasts', *Journal of Forecasting*, **4**, 61–73.

Yates, J. F. and Zukowski, L. G. (1976) 'Characterization of ambiguity in decision making', *Behavioral Science*, **21**, 19–25.

Zadeh, L. A. (1965) 'Fuzzy sets', *Information and Control*, **8**, 338–353.
Zadeh, L. A. (1975) 'The concept of a linguistic variable and its application to approximate reasoning (II)', *Information Sciences*, **8**, 301–357.
Zimmer, A. C. (1983) 'Verbal vs. numerical processing of subjective probabilities', in R. W. Scholz (ed.), *Decision Making under Uncertainty*, Amsterdam: North-Holland.
Zimmer, A. C. (1984) 'A model for the interpretation of verbal predictions', *International Journal of Man–Machine Studies*, **20**, 121–134.

Judgmental Forecasting
Edited by G. Wright and P. Ayton
© 1987 John Wiley & Sons Ltd

CHAPTER 5

The Psychology of Forecasting

George Wright
Bristol Business School

and

Peter Ayton
City of London Polytechnic

In this chapter we describe and evaluate recent work on judgmental forecasting. We will be concerned with problems of structuring planning decisions and with the evaluation of probabilistic forecasts. We will focus on problems of eliciting reliable and valid judgmental forecasts and we will describe the ways in which forecasting might be improved—either by aiding forecasters to make improved forecasts or by selection of those people with an ability to make realistic forecasts of the future. Figure 1 sets out the way we will organize our discussion of judgmental forecasting. It reflects a view that three relatively distinct, but interacting, stages in the judgmental forecasting process can usefully be separated and described.

RESEARCH ON HUMAN JUDGMENT

In this review we focus on human judgment of subjective probability. Evans (1982) has described a number of psychological phenomena which suggest that the process of judgmental forecasting might be expected to be rather vulnerable to error. Yet, *subjective* probabilities are the prime numerical inputs to decision analysis (cf. Raiffa, 1968), cross-impact analysis (Dalkey, 1972), fault-tree analysis (Fischhoff, Slovic and Lichtenstein, 1978) and many other management technologies. Often actuarial or relative frequency-based data are unavailable or are believed to be unreliable for direct input as a probability forecast. At other times the decision-maker may realize that unique changes in the world will have a causal impact on the likelihood of an event to be forecast and so invalidate regression and time-series predictions based on averaging techniques. Economists have termed such discontinuous changes in time series, 'turning points'. In such cases the forecaster can only rely on judgment. But how good are judgmental forecasts?

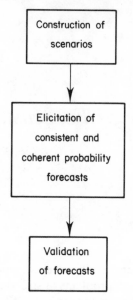

Figure 1. The judgmental forecasting process

Arguably, a broad range of psychological research is relevant to this issue. Here we will concentrate on those findings that have specific applicability to judgmental forecasting.

Problems of structuring forecast scenarios

Some studies have shown that the decision-maker's estimates, judgments and choices are affected by the way knowledge is elicited. Fischhoff, Slovic and Lichtenstein (1978) investigated estimation of failure probabilities in decision problem representation called fault trees. Figure 2 gives a fault-tree representation for the event 'a car fails to start'. This is the full version of a fault tree produced from the use of several car-repair reference tests.

In several experiments members of the public were presented with various 'full' and 'pruned' fault trees. For example, three of the first six sub-events in Figure 2 would be omitted from the presentation to be implicitly included under the seventh sub-event 'all other problems'. The subjects were asked:

For every 100 times that a trip is delayed due to a 'starting failure' estimate, on average, how many of the delays are caused by the 7(4) factors?

It was found that the amount of probability placed on 'all other problems' did not increase significantly when it contained three of the other main sub-

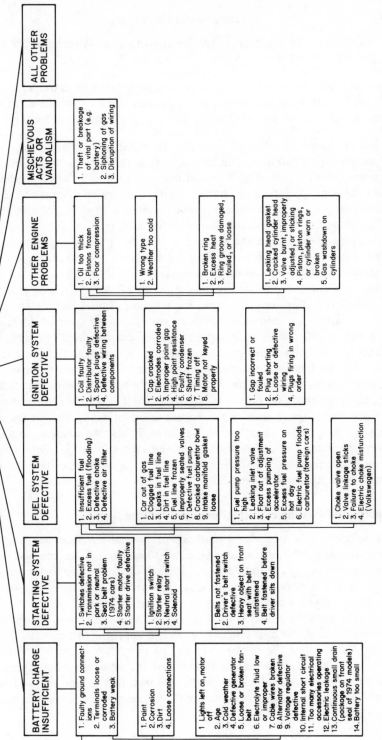

Figure 2. A possible fault tree for discovering why a car won't start (Fischhoff, Slovic and Lichtenstein, 1978)

events. In a subsequent experiment the importance of 'all other problems' was emphasized by asking subjects:

> In particular we would like you to consider its [the fault tree's] complete-ness. That is, what proportion of the possible reasons for a car not starting are left out, to be included in the category, 'all other problems'?

However, focusing subjects' attention on what was missing only partially improved their awareness. This insensitivity to the incompleteness of the fault tree was labelled 'out of sight out of mind'. This finding was confirmed with technical experts, garage mechanics. Neither self-rated degree of knowledge nor actual garage experience had any significant association with subjects' ability to detect what was missing from the fault tree.

Another finding from the study was that the perceived importance of a particular sub-event of branch of the fault tree was increased by presenting it in pieces (i.e. as two separate branches).

The implications of this study for the growing fields of decision analysis and scenario evaluation are, we think, far-reaching. Initial incomplete problem representations or scenarios may lead the decision-maker or forecaster to have unwarranted confidence in the stated representation of a possible future.

This is because complex problems are often so intricate that their structure is not well-understood. Technical analysts may construct provisional problem representations based on their client's descriptions or on the analysts' own intuitions and past experience. However, as these researchers have shown, the decision-maker may have little appreciation of when the structure of a scenario or plan is complete or realistic. Fault-tree analysis and related diagnostic aids give no indication as to when the knowledge elicited from the client is adequate or when ignorance should encourage hesitation and con-tinued information gathering.

Problems of eliciting consistent probability forecasts

Two commonly used *direct* methods for probability assessment are point estimates and odds estimates. One well-known *indirect* method used in decision analysis is the indifference method. Consider wager A presented in Figure 3. If it does rain at 11 a.m. tomorrow outside your home you win £100; if it does not you win nothing.

Now consider wager B, which refers to the 'spinner bet' consisting of a pointer which is free to rotate over a circle comprising two colours, black and white. I can adjust the relative amount of these two colours. If the pointer lands in the black you win £100; if it lands in the white you win nothing. Given that the proportion of black and white sectors is that in Figure 1, which wager would you prefer, wager A or wager B? Or are you indifferent between the wagers?

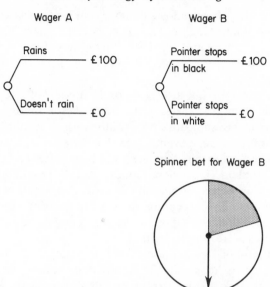

Figure 3. Indirect measurement of probability

If you preferred wager A to wager B then I would increase the proportion of black to white until you prefer wager B to wager A. I would then reduce the proportion of black until you are indifferent between the two wagers. The relative proportion of black to white would then be equivalent to your subjective probability that it will rain tomorrow. This indifference bet method allows *me* to measure your subjective probability without requiring *you* to state any numbers to describe your degree of belief. The only restriction in this method is that the utilities of the outcomes in the two wagers must be strictly identical. In this instance wager B must be played at, or shortly after, 11 a.m. tomorrow, when we know whether it has actually rained or not. If the result of wager B was to be paid out now, your utility for an 'instant' £100 may be higher than that for a 'delayed' £100 and so the two wagers would not be strictly identical.

Notice that although people may differ in their utility for £100, this amount is similar in both wagers and therefore has no bearing on the measurement of subjective probability.

Which of these three methods is the best for elicitation of subjective probability? The empirical evidence is, unfortunately, contradictory. Sometimes the indirect methods are inconsistent with direct methods and sometimes they are not. Beach and Phillips (1967) demonstrated consistency between probability estimates inferred from wagers and direct estimates. However, Winkler (1967) showed that statistically naive subjects were inconsistent between direct and indirect assessment methods, whereas statisticians were not. Generally, direct odds estimates, perhaps because they have no upper or lower limit, tend to be more extreme than direct probability estimates. If probability estimates derived by different methods for the same event are inconsistent, which method should be taken as the true index of degree of belief?

One way to answer this question is to use the method of assessing subjective probability that is most consistent. In other words there should be high agreement between the subjective probabilities, assessed at different times by a single assessor for the same event, given that the assessor's knowledge of the event is unchanged. Unfortunately, there has been relatively little research on this important problem. In a review, Goodman (1973) evaluated the results of several studies using direct estimation methods. Test–retest correlations were all above 0.88 with the exception of one study using students assessing odds—here the reliability was 0.66. It was concluded that most of the subjects in all experiments were very consistent.

The implications of this research for forecasting and planning are not clear-cut. The forecaster should be aware that different assessment techniques are likely to lead to different probability forecasts when these are converted to a common metric. The last section of this paper discusses the operation of a computer aid to judgmental forecasting that we have developed to monitor inconsistencies between assessment methods.

Problems of eliciting coherent probabilities

Consider a single throw of a dice which has six sides. The probability of a *named* single side, say a 4, landing face up is one-sixth. The probability of *any* one side landing face up is 1, i.e. certainty. More formally the additivity axiom states that the probabilities of a set of mutually exclusive and exhaustive events *must* sum to one.

However, subjective probabilities attached to sets of mutually exclusive and exhaustive events have been shown to sum to less than or more than one. For example, in a probability revision task, involving the updating of opinion in the light of new information, Phillips, Hays and Edwards (1966) found four out of five subjects assessed probabilities that were greater than unity. These four subjects increased their probability estimates for likely hypotheses but failed to decrease probabilities attached to unlikely hypotheses. In another probability revision study, Marks and Clarkson (1972) found that 49 out of 62 subjects gave probability estimates for complementary events that summed to more than unity. Conversely, Alberoni (1962) asked subjects to estimate sampling distributions from binomial populations on the basis of small samples and found that in most cases subjective probabilities summed to less than unity.

In a study addressed directly to the descriptive relevance of the additivity axiom, Wright and Whalley (1983) found that most untrained probability assessors followed the additivity axiom in simple two-outcome assessments, involving the probabilities of an event happening and not happening. However, as the number of mutually exclusive and exhaustive events in a set was increased, more subjects, and to a greater extent became supra-additive in that their assessed probabilities tended to add to more than one. With the number of mutually exclusive and exhaustive events in a set held constant, more subjects were supra-additive, and supra-additive to a greater degree, in the assessment of probabilities for an event set containing *individuating* information. In this study the individuating background information was associated with the possible success of a racehorse in a race that was about to start. It consisted simply of a record of that horse's previous performances. It seems intuitively reasonable that most probabilistic predictions are based, in the main, on one's knowledge and not to any large extent on abstract notions such as additivity. Individuating information about the likelihood of an event's occurrence may psychologically dis-associate an event from its event set. A similar phenomenon has been noted by Kahneman and Tversky (1972) and the term 'representativeness' was coined to refer to the dominance of individuating information in intuitive prediction. One of their tasks illustrating the phenomenon asked subjects individually to judge the likelihood that an individual is a graduate student in a particular field of specialization.

Consider the following problem adapted from Tversky and Kahneman.

This is a brief description of Tom W. written by a psychologist when Tom was in his senior year at high school:

Tom W. is of high intelligence, although lacking in true creativity. He has a need for order and clarity and for neat and tidy systems in which every detail finds its appropriate place. His writing is rather dull and mechanical, occasionally enlivened by somewhat corny puns and flashes of imagination of the sci-fi type. He seems to have little feel and little sympathy for other people and does not enjoy interacting with others. Self-centred, he nonetheless has a deep moral sense. This personality description has been chosen, at random, from those of 30 engineers and 70 social scientists. What is your probability that Tom W. is an engineer?

You have probably answered that Tom W. is more likely to be an engineer than a social scientist. However, Tversky and Kahneman argue that the base-rate should have had predominance over the low-reliability personality sketch, such that your probability response should be little different, if at all, from the base-rate probability of a 0.7 chance that Tom W. is a social scientist. Using similar problems, Tversky and Kahneman found that when no individuating information is given, base rates are properly utilized, but when worthless information is given, as in the above example, base-rates are ignored. Tversky and Kahneman coined the term *representativeness* to refer to the dominance of individuating information in intuitive prediction.

Clearly, judgmental forecasts should be monitored for additivity and incoherence should be resolved. Also, if relevant base-rate information exists it should be utilized as a major input to judgment.

However, a simple normalization may not be a quick and easy solution to incoherence. Lindley, Tversky and Brown (1979) outlined a major problem:

> Suppose that I assess the probabilities of a set of mutually exclusive and exhaustive events to be
>
> $$0.001, 0.250, 0.200, 0.100, 0.279 \ldots$$
>
> It is then pointed out to me that these probabilities sum to 0.830 and hence that the assessment is incoherent. If we use the method ... with the probability metric, we have to adjust the probabilities by adding 0.034 to each $[= (1/5)(1 - 0.830)]$ to give
>
> $$0.035, 0.284, 0.234, 0.134, 0.313$$
>
> The problem is with the first event, which I originally regarded as very unlikely, has had its probability increased by a factor of 35! Though still small it is no longer smaller than the others by two orders of magnitude. (p. 168)

The last section of this paper shows how our computer-aid monitors probability forecasts for additivity and suggests possible normalizations to the forecaster in order to achieve additivity in judgmental forecasts.

Incoherence of time period forecasting

Wheelwright and Makridakis (1980), in their review of forecasting methods and their applications, have differentiated time horizon as the one most useful criteria for matching a specific forecasting situation with the most appropriate forecasting technique. These authors differentiate immediate-term, short-term, medium-term and long-term horizons. By immediate-term they mean those forecasts that are prepared for one month or less in advance. Short-term refers to a one-to-three-month horizon whilst medium-term refers to three months to two years and long-term to a horizon greater than two years. Only the distinction between immediate-term and short-term need concern us here. For immediate-term forecasting the techniques most appropriate are smoothing techniques. Smoothing methods are often not appropriate for short-term situations and decomposition, control and other more complex techniques are often used. Until now the role of judgment in immediate and short-term forecasting has not been systematically evaluated.

In a recent study, we (Wright and Ayton, 1984) asked respondents to give a probability forecast of a named event, such as the pound falling to value of less than $1.30, occurring at least once in (1) the month of November, 1983, (2) in the month of December, 1983, and (3) in *both* of the months in the two-month period. This analysis revealed that subjects showed marked incoherence when their assessments were compared to the probability laws.

For example, the probability forecast of the event happening at least once in both months should be equal to the probability forecast of the event happening at least once in November multiplied by the probability forecast of the event happening at least once in December assuming that the event has occurred at least once in November.

Formally, by the probability laws:

$$P(A \text{ and } B) = P(A)P(B \backslash A)$$

For the event happening at least once in either (but not both) of the months:

$$P(A \text{ or } B) = P(A)P[1 - (B \backslash A)] + P(1 - A)P(B \backslash \bar{A})$$

For the event happening in either or both of the months:

$$P(A \text{ and/or } B) = P(A)P(B \backslash A) + P(A)P[1 - (B \backslash A)] + P(1 - A)P(B \backslash \bar{A})$$

As you might expect, as far as human judgments are concerned the two halves of the equation seldom balance! Which forecasts are best? *Intuitive* 'secondary' forecasts of $P(A \text{ and } B)$, $P(A \text{ or } B)$ and $P(A \text{ and/or } B)$ or *normative* 'secondary' forecasts calculated by the probability laws on the basis of the less complex intuitive 'primary' forecasts of $P(A)$, $P(B)$, $P(B \backslash A)$ and $P(B \backslash \bar{A})$?

On the basis of previous research and theory on the psychology of judgment the normative 'secondary' forecast should be better than the intuitive 'secondary' forecasts. Why should this be so?

The rationale for this assertion is similar to the rationale supporting the use of subjective expected utility theory (SEU), multi-attributed utility theory (MAUT) and Bayes's theorem as ways of improving decision-making (see Wright, 1984). These three theories are used to improve decision-making not by giving the decision-maker any extra information but my making the best use of the information the decision-maker already possesses. In the field of decision analysis (which is based on SEU) the rationale for the validity of the decision aid is that of 'divide and conquer'. The decision-maker assesses primary inputs of subjective probabilities and utilities and SEU recomposes these to specify the 'optimal' decision. Similarly, in a MAUT analysis the decision-maker assesses subjective attribute weightings and scales each object under consideration on each attribute in turn. MAUT then recomposes these assessments to specify the object with the highest overall utility.

In applications of Bayes's theorem the decision-maker assesses subjective prior probabilities of the hypotheses about the world being correct and also likelihood of these hypotheses being correct, given updated information about the world. Bayes's theorem combines these subjective priors and likelihoods to produce optimal posterior opinions.

In summary, human decision-makers are able to supply *simple* intuitive inputs to decision theories which utilize these inputs to specifying more complex overall judgments or decisions.

Some authors (Hogarth, 1975; Slovic, 1982) have marshalled the evidence for suboptimality in human judgment in support of the notion that man's limited capacity in terms of memory, attention and reasoning capabilities leads the decision-maker to be suboptimal. In other words, human decision-makers simply cannot do all the mathematics required for holistic decisions whilst they are able to provide the simpler primary inputs required by the normative decision theories. Of course, these primary inputs may not be perfect but at least the mathematical manipulations can be performed reliably!

We would also invoke a similar rationale for the use of normative secondary forecasts instead of intuitive secondary forecasts.

However, there are limits to the principle of decomposition as a viable procedure for improving judgmental forecasting. In terms of the time period forecasts discussed above one could, in theory, recompose judgments made about infinitesimally small periods of time. But the probability of a major increase in the price of oil in the next year is plainly not usefully assessed by recombining probabilities elicited for each component hour. Yet it may well be useful to ask an expert to evaluate probabilities for each component month and to reflect on any inconsistencies with respect to the basic probability laws. Determination of the optimal level of specificity for judgmental input into a forecast aiding system is, at present, a rather intuitive ad hoc judgment in itself.

Similar problems have confronted the development of cross-impact analysis (Duperrin and Godet, 1975; Mitchell and Tydeman, 1976; Godet, 1976; Kelly, 1976; McLean, 1976). This technique aims to take advantage of experts' intuitive understanding of the domain of their expertise by asking them to judge conditional probabilities. Real-world events are rarely independent in the sense of being uninfluenced by the occurrence or non-occurrence of any other events. The cross-impact method effectively asks experts to translate their understanding of the causality underlying a set of events into appropriate conditional probabilities that indicate the influence of events on each other. These probabilities are then mathematically corrected so that they conform to the laws of probability theory.

Recent developments and practical implementations of the cross-impact technique reveal difficulties in resolving the inconsistencies in the subjective judgments of experts. Kirkwood and Pollock (1982), utilizing both simple and conditional probabilistic forecasts, chose to omit some of the judgments altogether in order to find a fit for judgments corrected with the probability axioms. For two out of three expert subjects all the conditional probability estimates had to be discarded. As the conditional judgments reflect the underlying causal models of the experts, and as such may be seen as important inputs to the forecast, this is a serious problem. Furthermore, when judgmental data are omitted in this way the range of resulting forecasts output by the technique for the set of scenarios under consideration are less disciminatory. Thus, although this study listed forecast probabilities to five decimal places in some cases, one of the experts produced judgments which, when resolved by a best-fit technique, sorted the nineteen different scenarios into only five different categories of probability. One other of the two remaining experts produced only six different categories.

Other versions of the cross-impact technique have aimed to mathematically minimize inter-expert inconsistencies which clearly takes no account of the *reasons* experts may have for differing; averaging the outputs of two different causal models may produce forecasts inconsistent with either or indeed any plausible model of events. Given that the assumptions of experts in generating the judgments remain unstated it is difficult to resolve any differences between them in a manner that preserves the integrity of their expertise. Essentially the use of cross-impact analysis relies on knowledge being tapped from experts. Demonstrations of the technique have shown that even apparently simple event scenarios can have complex systems of relevant antecedents underpinning the likelihood of their occurrence. There is, however, a danger that the knowledge implicit in the forecast judgments will be corrupted rather than correctly extrapolated by the mathematical corrections performed.

Problems of eliciting valid probability forecasts

Interestingly, no attempts have been made to assess the *validity* of the forecasts resulting from this method by, for example, validating them with the true probabilities of the events being forecast. Such a procedure allows different forecasting aids and individual differences in forecasting ability to be evaluated. Validation of forecast probabilities is discussed in the next-but-one section of this chapter. In the next section we discuss possible influences on the validity of judgmental forecasts.

Influences on the elicitation of valid probability forecasts

An experiment relevant to long-term judgmental forecasting was conducted by Milburn (1978) who investigated the *imminence* of a forecast period by eliciting forecasts of an event occurring in each of four successive decades in the future. Half of the events had what were classified as 'positive' outcomes (e.g. 'hunger and poverty are no longer problems in the US') and the other half had 'negative' outcomes (e.g. 'I have to spend some time in the hospital because of a serious illness'). It was found that subjects perceived *desirable* events as becoming increasingly more likely to occur in each of the four successive decades in the future. By contrast, *undesirable* events were perceived as becoming less likely in each of the four successive decades.

However, in a complementary experiment where each subject only gave forecasts for one of the decades, there was a significant downward trend in perceived likelihood for both types of event across time in the future. These results are difficult to interpret. One explanation involves the availability heuristic (Tversky and Kahneman, 1974) which refers to the finding that we often judge the probability of an event by the ease with which relevant information of that event is imagined. Instances of frequent events are typically easier to recall than instances of less frequent events, thus availability is often a valid one for the assessment of frequency and probability. However, since availability is also influenced by factors unrelated to likelihood, such as familiarity, recency and emotional saliency, reliance on it may result in systematic biases. Availability would predict that the subjects will feel that the world may change more and become progressively less like the present in successive decades. Thus it should be harder to imagine what the world will be like and events should be seen as less probable. Desirable events may increase in probability over time because desirability has a greater effect in more ambiguous circumstances. Owing to the time periods involved, there was no attempt to assess the validity of the forecasts. Perhaps the most significant result from this research is that when subjects do not have to produce a number of forecasts for successive time periods the pattern of results changes. The influence of imminence does not seem to be straightforward. It interacts with the desirability of the events to be forecast and changes as a function of the method of elicitation of the forecasts.

Zakay (1983) has investigated the *desirability* of an event on probability forecasting in a way that controls for alternative explanations of changes in subjective probabilities. Subjects were asked to assess probabilities that positive value events (e.g. win a lottery) and negative value events (e.g. be hurt in a road accident) will happen to themselves and also to someone who the probability assessor did not know but who is 'of the same population as yours in terms of age, origin, income, social status and personality'. It was found that subjects perceived desirable life events as being more likely to occur to themselves than to another person similar to themselves. Undesirable life events showed the opposite effect. This pattern of responding can be termed an optimistic bias. It may be that operation of the availability heuristic would tend to retrieve many instances of undesirable events occurring to others from news reports, but not to oneself. The availability heuristic does not explain the findings for desirable events, however.

Snyder's (1978) real-life study of the effect of the value of outcomes on forecasting investigated public betting on horse racing and found that punters attempted to recoup losses by selecting even longer odds horses than usual on the last race of the day. This result replicates an earlier study by McGlothlin (1956) and also suggests an interaction between subjective probability and utility.

Weinstein (1980) found that perceived controllability of events correlated positively with the amount of optimistic bias. Controllability was measured on a five-point subjective rating scale ranging from 'there is nothing that we can do that will change the likelihood that the event will take place' to 'completely controllable'. Indeed, perceived controllability, whether real or imaginary, may have a strong influence on judgments of the likelihood of outcomes (Langer, 1982).

The way in which forecast probabilities vary as a junction of the *time duration* of a forecast period has received little attention. Howell and Burnett (1978) suggested that short time spans will be influenced to a greater degree by local context effects and less by knowledge of the past frequency of events. Thus subjects may believe in 'luck' playing a bigger part in the short term and be prone to unstable ephemeral influences. The gambler's fallacy (e.g. the belief that a coin which has come up heads many times in a row will be more likely to come tails on the next throw) is cited as an illustration of this view. In a follow-up study (Howell and Kerkar, 1982) subjects participated in a task where they served as emergency vehicle despatchers for a hypothetical city. Each subject gained experience with events (types of emergency calls) generated from different parts of the city by a stationary stochastic process. Subjects then had to answer a series of questions concerning either the observed frequency of specified kinds of events or the probability that those same events would occur on future occasions. However, despite subjects' ability to make good judgments of observed historic frequency, future forecasts of subsequent events appeared to depend more heavily on less appropriate transient information.

In summary it is clear that forecast probabilities will vary as a function of the desirability, imminence, time period and perceived controllability of the event to be forecast.

Measurement of the validity of probability forecasts

Our own research has focused on people's ability to produce well-calibrated forecasts. Calibration is one measure of the validity of subjective probability assessments. For a person to be perfectly calibrated, assessed probability should equal percentage correct over a number of assessments of equal probability. For example, if you assign a probability of 0.7 as the likelihood for each of ten events occurring, seven of those ten events should occur. Similarly, all events that you assess as being certain to occur (1.0 probability assessments) should occur.

Using calibration and related measures our research aim has been to investigate the relative influence of the person, the forecasting situation or an interaction of the two on forecasting performance.

Previously some individual differences in forecasting ability had been reported, although relating these to specific personality variables has proved difficult. In a study investigating economic forecasting, O'Carroll (1977) found substantial differences between individuals' performances, as evaluated by a scoring rule, that were consistent over the five forecasting tasks being analysed. These tasks involved predicting each week for eighteen weeks, the *Financial Times* share index, the dollar–sterling rate, etc. Borges *et al.* (1980) attempted to relate subjects' accuracy of prediction of their own academic performance to the personality/cognitive measures of self-esteem and locus of control. Although some significant correlations were found the picture is not clear since age and gender of the subjects moderated the correlations. In personality psychology, *three* main theoretical positions describe the individual and his interaction with the environment. Personologism advocates that stable intraorganismic constants such as traits or cognitive styles are the main determinants of behavioural variation. Situationism emphasizes environmental (situational) factors as the main sources of behavioural variation. Interactionism, a synthesis of personologism and situationism, implies that the interaction between these two factors is the main source of behavioural variance (cf. Furnham and Jaspars, 1983; Ayton and Wright, 1985; 1986).

We (Wright and Ayton, 1984) found strong evidence for personologism in judgmental forecasting across differing forecasting periods and for events sets differing in subjective desirability. These periods differed both in imminence and in time duration. This result, based on response and performance measures of judgmental forecasting suggests that it may well be possible to select people for their forecasting ability. Conversely, the effects of situationism, measured in terms of the variations in imminence, time duration, and desirability of the events to be forecast had a minimal influence on judgmental forecasting. In general, with the forecasting tasks we used, there was little evidence for task contingency on this aspect of decision-making. Forecasting behaviour seems to be more of a personal characteristic, the aetiology of which has yet to be explored. Whether there are separable cognitive styles that can describe individual differences in judgmental forecasting is another issue that as yet is unanswered. The number of dimensions along which forecasting ability may be distributed is not known.

However, one significant situational finding was that people are more sure of specified events happening in the month subsequent to the imminent one. This effect is independent of the subjective desirability of the events, and contradicts Milburn's (1978) finding of an interactive effect of desirability and imminence upon forecast probabilities. But recall that Milburn's study concerned forecasts for four successive *decades*. One explanation of the contradiction between the two studies may be that in longer-term forecasting, ambiguity and lack of information may result in a stronger interaction between the utility of an outcome and the judged likelihood of its occurrence. Nevertheless it is unclear why people should be more sure, in general, of events happening in the less-imminent future than in the imminent future.

In our study the effect of increasing the time duration of a forecast period from one month to two months had no effect on forecasting response and peformance. Clearly, the possibility that shorter-term forecasts will be more prone to unstable ephemeral influences discussed by Howell and Burnett (1978) does not hold true for immediate-term and short-term forecasts.

In general, across and within our three forecasting periods the subjective desirability of events had no effect on their perceived likelihood of occurrence, measured as mean full-range probability forecasts. However, a correlational analysis did reveal that people who used more 100 per cent responses tended to find the events to be forecast subjectively more desirable. Users of 100 per cent responses did not, however, find the events to be forecast subjectively more desirable than non-users. Clearly the effect of desirability in forecasting is negligible in the context studied here. This result contrasts with Zakay's (1983) study, discussed earlier, which found a strong desirability effect. However, the events utilized by Zakay were of a much more personal nature than those used in our study. Zakay's subjects were asked to assess probabilities that positive value events (e.g. win a lottery) and negative value events (e.g. be hurt in a road accident) will happen to themselves and to others. One inference to be drawn is that if the event to be forecast does not have a personal impact on the forecaster then the effect of the subjective desirability of the event on its perceived likelihood will be minimal. The subjective desirability of a 'desirable' personal event may be relatively much higher than the subjective desirability of a 'desirable' non-personal event.

Our measures of individual coherence in probability assessment had few significant correlations or associations with our other means of forecasting response and performance, with the exception that people who were more coherent on our additivity measures tended to rate the task of producing probability forecasts easier than less coherent people. The lack of significant relations between coherence and forecasting performance surprised us since the two ways of assessing the adequacy of a forecaster are logically interrelated. If a forecaster is inconsistent or incoherent he cannot be well-calibrated. It does not follow, however, that consistency or coherence necessarily produces good calibration. The issue is similar to the distinction between reliability and validity in questionnaire design (see Wallsten and Budescu, 1983 and Wright and Fowler, 1986). One explanation of our results may be that we used a subset of our questions to measure coherence and tried to relate this analysis to forecasting performance over a wider range of questions. However, we could not measure an individual's forecasting performance solely on the basis of the subset of coherence questions owing to the small size of this subset. There is also some doubt as to whether measures of calibration are an appropriate index of the validity of probabilistic judgment. Yates (1982) argues that too much emphasis has been placed on calibration as a measure of probabilistic judgment and that resolution is perhaps a more appropriate measure. Resolution as Yates (1982, p. 150) notes, refers to: 'the ability of the forecaster to discriminate individual occasions on which the event of interest will and will not take place'. Yates documents the considerable misunderstanding that has often accompanied the use of this measure and points out that a measure of resolution can be computed and interpreted even if the subjective responses are completely non-numerical. In fact, as resolution reflects the ability of the assessor to sort events into categories for which the hit rates are either 1 or 0, a well-calibrated forecaster who used probabilistic responses of other than 1 or 0 would not be well resolved. Thus, for example, judgments of 0.6 and 0.7, if well-calibrated will have hit rates of 0.6 and 0.7 and so will be poorly resolved. However, if judgments of 0.6 and 0.7 had hit rates of 0 and 1 they would be perfectly resolved but, because the numerical labels do not accurately reflect the hit rate, they would be miscalibrated.

Yates argues that the appeal of calibration is largely aesthetic and that resolution pertains to a much more fundamental skill. We have some sympathy for this argument particularly in view of the fact that it is possible to be perfectly calibrated merely by locating the base-rate probability for a whole set of judgments and that, in a good deal of reported research, the base-rate is easily detectable as 0.5. Though, of course, in many real-world contexts, accurate identification of the base-rate would reflect considerable skill.

However, as can be seen from the above example, resolution measures are rather deterministic assessments and do not reward forecasters for the accuracy of their probabilistic responses and, of course, for many practical purposes, this is a desirable quality of judgment.

The number of different categories of probability that can validly be distinguished—what we might term acuity—is also clearly an important characteristic and this is not reflected in either calibration or resolution measures.

Which measure to attend to rather depends on which particular characteristic of a set of forecasts one is interested in assessing. Plainly there is no simple measure of the validity of a set of probabilistic judgments and arguably there is a need for further statistical measures to be developed.

The large number of questions a subject needs to answer in order to produce a stable individual measure of calibration is a major problem in studying judgmental forecasting. A minimum of seventy questions is usually taken as a rule-of-thumb baseline but if further more systematic studies are to be made of the effects of desirability, imminence, time period, perceived controllability and coherence, the task for both the experimenter and subject is enormous. Nevertheless, given the primacy of judgmental forecasts as inputs to decision-aiding technologies, further systematic investigations of judgmental forecasting are of major importance.

'FORECAST': A COMPUTER AID TO JUDGMENTAL FORECASTING

On the basis of our belief in the importance of eliciting consistent and coherent probability forecasts as a baseline for valid or well-calibrated judgments we have developed an interactive computer decision aid called 'Forecast'. 'Forecast' aids three types of forecasting. First, it aids the forecasting of the *time period* or date when a specified event may happen. This type of judgmental forecasting can be used as an input to network analysis and the logic can easily be extended using different events rather than different time periods. Second, it aids the forecasting of the possible outcomes of an event when these can be expressed in numerical terms as *outcomes on a single continuous scale*. Third, it aids the forecasting of the possible outcomes of an event when these can be expressed as *discrete or discontinuous outcomes*. The user selects from a menu which type of forecast he or she wishes to make and the program then interactively elicits forecast probabilities.

Time period forecasting

For time period forecasting, the program elicits from the user the beginning and end of the time period of interest. We will call this time period, time period B. Next the program elicits a point probability estimate and an odds estimate for the event happening at least once in the forecast period, for example, the pound sterling falling to a value of less than \$1.30. These formally equivalent estimates are compared by the program and inconsistencies are reported to the user for resolution. This procedure gives $P(B)$. Next, the program attempts to extend the time period of the forecast by a *subsequent* time interval consisting of the same number of days as the main time period of interest. We will call this time period, time period C. The program then elicits $P(C)$. Following this the program investigates the possibility of the event occurring at least once in a similar length time period *prior* to the main time period of interest. We will call this time period, time period A. The program elicits $P(A)$ and then *subdivides* the main time period of interest, period B, and elicits two further forecasts, $P(D)$ and $P(E)$.

At the next stage, the program investigates if the perceived likelihood of the event occurring in each of the subsequent time periods is independent or

P(A and B)	P(A)P(B\A)
P(B and C)	P(B)P(C\B)
P(D and E)	P(D)P(E\D)
P(A or B)	P(A)P[1 − (B\A)] + P(1 − A)P(B\Ā)
P(B or C)	P(B)P[1 − (C\B)] + P(1 − B)P(C\B̄)
P(D or E)	P(D)P[1 − (E\D)] + P(1 − D)P(E\D̄)
P(A and or B)	P(B)P(C\B) + P(B)P[1 − (C\B)] + P(1 − B)P(C\B̄)
P(A and or B)	P(A)P(B\A) + P(A)P[1 − (B\A)] + P(1 − A)P(B\Ā)
P(B)	P(D)P(E\D) + P(D)P[1 − (E\D)] + P(1 − D)P(E\D̄)

Figure 4. Summary of program output for time period forecasting

dependent on whether or not the event occurred in the prior time period. If the assessments are seen as conditional the program elicits the conditional probabilities, $P(B\backslash A)$, $P(B\backslash\bar{A})$, $P(C\backslash B)$, $P(C\backslash\bar{B})$, $P(E\backslash D)$ and $P(E\backslash\bar{D})$.

The program subsequently elicits a forecast of the event happening at least once in *each* of the paired time periods, i.e. $P(A$ and $B)$, $P(B$ and $C)$ and $P(D$ and $E)$. Next the program elicits forecasts of the event happening in one *or* both of the combined time periods B and C and in combined periods A and B, i.e. $P(B$ and/or $C)$ and $P(A$ and/or $B)$. Finally the program elicits forecasts of the event happening at least once in one (but not both) of two time intervals, i.e. $P(A$ or $B)$, $P(B$ or $C)$ and $P(D$ or $E)$.

Figure 4 gives a summary of the program's output. The first probability of each pair is an intuitive holistic forecast whilst the second probability expression is the 'equivalent' normative probability forecast recomposed from the user's input to the program.

Continuous variable forecasting

After the main menu the program elicits the minimum and maximum values of the range of outcomes. The program also checks that the user's minima and maxima are as defined by asking for probability estimates for outcomes outside of this interval. Next, the program interactively subdivides this range into an acceptable number of divisions. Following this the program proceeds to elicit forecasts for the sub-ranges. Next the program reports assessed probabilities to the user *and*, if the assessments are not additive, presents two normalizations, $N1$ and $N2$. $N1$ simply allocates the computed amount of non-additivity equally among the sub-range forecasts. Normalization $N2$ shares any non-additivity proportionally according to the value of the original sub-range forecasts.

The program goes on to enquire if either of the normalizations are acceptable or if the user wishes to change his own forecasts to achieve additivity.

Finally the program reports cumulative forecasts to the user.

Discrete variable forecasting

After the main menu the program asks for an event name and a list of all possible outcomes. The program adds a 'catch-all' outcome to the user's outcome listing and goes on to elicit assessment for the likelihood of the outcomes, initially using both point probabilities and odds as response modes. If any probability above 0.01 is placed in the 'catch-all' outcome the program prompts for further decomposition into specified possible outcomes.

As with the continuous forecasting option, the program next presents assessed probabilities *and*, if the assessments are not additive, presents normalizations $N1$ and $N2$ to the user for evaluation.

Figure 5 sets out the essential logic of the procedures underlying 'Forecast'.

The program decomposes holistic forecasts and recomposes these by means of the normative probability laws. Recomposed coherent forecasts are then presented to the forecaster together with his or her holistic forecasts and, if there are discrepancies, the forecaster is given the opportunity to reflect on these discrepancies.

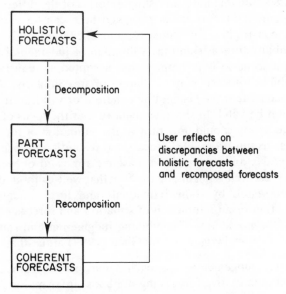

Figure 5. The essential logic of the 'Forecast' program

On reflection, the user may decide to accept the recomposed forecasts, provided by the program, retain the original holistic forecasts or 'adjust' the holistic forecasts in the light of presented recompositions.

We would argue that the user should accept the coherent recomposed forecasts for the forecasts must be at least as 'well-calibrated' as the holistic forecasts.

The program is similar to cross-impact analysis in that it prompts consideration of conditional probabilities; users consider the impact of an event on the probability of its own re-occurrence. However, there are some important differences between the two techniques. Our program can be seen as an improvement on cross-impact methodology inasmuch as it utilizes probability axioms to alert the user rather than to directly amend the user's judgment. Thus the user may re-enter judgments that conform to his or her own view of causality as well as the probability laws. As such it may be seen as a consciousness-raising device rather than a strict corrective. Contemplation of inconsistent and incoherent forecasts requires the user to re-evaluate his or her expressions of uncertainty and prompts consideration of the realism of implicit scenarios, or causal models, responsible for the initial generation of likelihoods. Consequently we suggest that stage 1 of Figure 1, our view of the forecast process, is affected and, we hope, improved by interaction with the program.

CONCLUSION

We have discussed judgmental forecasting in terms of the different stages we identified in Figure 1. The research reviewed here can be seen to address separately the construction of scenarios, the elicitation of consistent and coherent probability forecasts and the validation of judgmental forecasts.

However, if a scenario is incomplete but accepted as realistic, then subsequent probability forecasts may be inappropriate. Similarly, if probability forecasts are inconsistent they cannot be coherent or valid. In turn, coherent forecasts may not be valid. In short, we believe that the focus of research on judgmental forecasting should now turn to the validation of forecasts. Forecasting aids such as our program 'Forecast' aid resolution of inconsistent and incoherent forecasts and so provide a baseline for valid or well-calibrated judgments. Our research is beginning to show that well-calibrated forecasting is an ability possessed by some individuals and little influenced by the forecasting situation or an interaction of situation and forecaster.

In discussing the possibility of combining judgmental and statistical forecasts, Makridakis, Wheelwright and McGhee (1983) argue that:

> Whereas purely judgemental approaches may suffer from a number if biases, formal quantitative forecasting methods suffer major difficulties in situations of significant environmental changes. Approaches that combine

the best elements of both categories may well produce significantly improved results in comparison with those produced by using one or the other approaches alone . . . A logical conclusion is that forecasts should rely more heavily on the predictions provided by formal quantitative methods, as long as there are no major changes in the environment or organization. When such changes do occur, judgemental inputs should be given more weight. (p. 862)

We hope that our discussions have provided an underpinning for this development. However, in order to see if our general view of the judgmental forecasting process (Figure 1) is valid psychologically many questions have yet to be answered. Scenario generation requires identification of a *plausible* set of events and so the output of stages two and three can be seen to influence stage one. Thus the processes labelled in our sequential description of the forecasting process are not entirely independent. Quite how these stages might interact remains a matter for speculation at present but our judgmental forecast is that these problems will become a subject of future research.

ACKNOWLEDGMENT

This research was supported by Economic and Social Research Council project grant no. C00232037 entitled 'Judging the likelihood of future events'. This chapter is a revised and amended version of a paper of the same title that appeared in *Futures* in 1986.

REFERENCES

Alberoni, F. (1966) 'Contribution to the study of subjective probability', *Journal of General Psychology*, **66**, 421–464.

Ayton, P. and Wright, G. (1985) 'The evidence for interactionism in psychology: a reply to Furnham and Jaspars', *Personality and Individual Differences*, **6**, 509–512.

Ayton, P. and Wright, G. (1986) 'Persons, situations, interactions and error: consistency, variability and confusion', *Personality and Individual Differences*, **7**, 233–235.

Beach, L. R. and Phillips, L. D. (1967) 'Subjective probabilities inferred from estimates and bets', *Journal of Experimental Psychology*, **75**, 354–359.

Borges, M. A., Roth, A., Nichols, T. and Nichols, B. S. (1980) 'Effects of gender, age, locus of control and self-esteem in estimates of college grades', *Psychological Reports*, **47**, 831–837.

Dalkey, N. (1972) 'An elementary cross-impact model', *Technological Forecasting and Social Change*, **3**, 341–351.

Duperrin, J. C. and Godet, M. (1975) 'A method for constructing and ranking scenarios', *Futures*, **7**, 302–312.

Evans, J. St.B. T. (1982) 'Psychological pitfalls in forecasting', *Futures*, **14**, 258–265.

Fischhoff, B., Slovic, P. and Lichtenstein, S. (1978) 'Fault trees: sensitivity of estimated failure probabilities to problem representation', *Journal of Experimental Psychology: Human Perception and Performance*, **4**, 330–344.

Furnham, A. and Jaspars, J. (1983) 'The evidence for interactionism in psychology: a critical analysis of the situation-response inventories', *Personality and Individual Differences*, **4**, 627–644.

Gilchrist, W. (1976) *Statistical Forecasting*, Chichester: Wiley.

Godet, M. (1976) 'SMIC 74: a reply from the authors', *Futures*, **8**, 336–340.

Goodman, B. C. (1973) 'Direct estimation procedures for eliciting judgement about uncertain events', Engineering Psychology/Technical Report 001313-S-T, University of Michigan.

Hogarth, R. (1975) 'Cognitive processes and the assessment of subjective probability distributions', *Journal of the American Statistical Association*, **70**, 271–294.

Howell, W. C. and Burnett, S. A. (1978) 'Uncertainty measurement: a cognitive taxonomy', *Organizational Behavior and Human Performance*, **22**, 45–68.

Howell, W. C. and Kerkar, S. P. (1982) 'A test of task influence in uncertainty measurement', *Organizational Behavior and Human Performance*, **30**, 365–390.

Kahneman, D. and Tversky, A. (1972) 'Subjective probability: a judgement of representativeness', *Cognitive Psychology*, **3**, 430–454.

Kelly, P. (1976) 'Further comments on cross-impact analysis', *Futures*, **8**, 341–345.

Kirkwood, C. W. and Pollock, S. M. (1982) 'Multiple attribute scenarios, bounded probabilities, and threats of nuclear theft', *Futures*, **14**, 545–553.

Langer, E. J. (1982) *The Psychology of Control*, Beverly Hills: Sage.

Lindley, D. V., Tversky, A. and Brown, R. V. (1979) 'On the reconciliation of probability assessments', *Journal of the Royal Statistical Society*, **142**, 146–180.

Makridakis, S., Wheelwright, S. C. and McGhee, V. E. (1983) *Forecasting: Methods and Applications*. Chichester: Wiley.

Marks, D. F. and Clarkson, J. K. (1972) 'An explanation of conservatism in the book-bag-and-poker-chips situation', *Acta Psychologica*, **36**, 145–160.

McGlothlin, W. H. (1965) 'Stability of choices among uncertain alternatives', *American Journal of Psychology*, **69**, 604–615.

McLean, M. (1976) 'Does cross-impact analysis have a future?', *Futures*, **8**, 345–349.

Milburn, M. A. (1978) 'Sources of bias in the prediction of future events', *Organizational Behaviour and Human Performance*, **21**, 17–26.

Mitchell, R. B. and Tydeman, J. (1976) 'A note on SMIC 74', *Futures*, **8**, 64–67.

Murphy, A. H. and Brown, B. G. (1985) 'A comparative evaluation of objective and subjective weather forecasts in the United States', in G. N. Wright (ed.), *Behavioral Decision Making*, New York: Plenum.

O'Carroll, J. M. (1977) 'Subjective probabilities and short-term economic forecasts: An empirical investigation', *Applied Statistics*, **26**, 269–278.

Phillips, L. D., Hays, W. L. and Edwards, W. (1966) 'Conservatism in complex-probabilistic inferences', *IEEE Transactions on Human Factors in Electronics*, **7**, 7–18.

Raiffa, H. (1968) *Decision Analysis—Introductory Lectures on Choices under Uncertainty*, Reading, Mass.: Addison-Wesley.

Slovic, P. (1982) 'Towards understanding and improving decisions', in W. C. Howell and E. A. Fleishmann (eds.), *Human Performance and Productivity: Vol. 2, Information Processing and Decision Making*, Hillsdale, N.J.: Erlbaum.

Snyder, W. (1978) 'Decision making with risk and uncertainty: The case of horse-racing', *American Journal of Psychology*, **91**, 201–209.

Tversky, A. and Kahneman, D. (1974) 'Judgment under uncertainty: Heuristics and biases', *Science*, **185**, 1124–1131.

Wallsten, T. S. and Budescu, D. V. (1983) 'Encoding subjective probabilities: A psychological and psychometric review', *Management Science*, **29**, 151–173.

Weinstein, N. D. (1980) 'Unrealistic optimism about future life events', *Journal of Personality and Social Psychology*, **39**, 806–820.

Weist, J. D. and Levy, F. K. (1977) *A Management Guide to PERT/CPM*, Englewood Cliffs, N.J.: Prentice-Hall.

Wheelwright, S. C. and Makridakis, S. (1980) *Forecasting Methods for Management* (third edition), New York: Wiley.

Winkler, R. L. (1967) 'The assessment of prior distributions in Bayesian analysis', *Journal of the American Statistical Association*, **62**, 776–800.

Wright, G. (1984) *Behavioral Decision Theory*, Harmondsworth: Penguin; and Beverly Hills: Sage.

Wright, G. and Ayton, P. (1984) 'Judgemental forecasting: personologism, situationism or interactionism?', paper presented to the Second European Conference on Personality, Bielefeld, FRG.

Wright, G. and Fowler, C. (1986) *Investigative Design and Statistics in Psychology*, Harmondsworth: Penguin.

Wright, G. and Whalley, P. (1983) 'The supra-additivity of subjective probability', in B. P. Stigum and F. Wenstop (eds.), *Foundations of Utility and Risk Theory*, Dordrecht: Reidel.

Yates, J. F. (1982) 'External correspondence: Decompositions of the mean probability score', *Organizational Behavior and Human Performance*, **30**, 132–156.

Zakay, D. (1983) 'The relationship between the probability assessor and the outcomes of an event as a determiner of subjective probability', *Acta Psychologica*, **53**, 271–280.

Part II

Judgment from groups of individuals

Judgmental Forecasting
Edited by G. Wright and P. Ayton
© 1987 John Wiley & Sons Ltd

CHAPTER 6

Integrating Group Judgments in Subjective Forecasts

Andy Lock
Business School, Kingston-upon-Thames

INTRODUCTION

The aggregation of forecasts, whether across formal quantitative methods or individual judgmental forecasts, has been shown to yield improved forecasts in terms of mean average percentage error (MAPE) given quite innocuous conditions, such as positive validity of judges. This paper examines both the approaches to aggregating forecasts and the context and process of generating group judgments. It attempts to combine contributions from a variety of separate literatures which are relevant to the problem of group judgmental forecasting. Care needs to be taken with some of the empirical work in the fields of group processes and group judgments as experimental groups are usually synthetic and frequently unfamiliar with the basic task. Familiarity with the task, and the context in which it takes place appear to be important determinants of performance.

The chapter begins with consideration of the context of group judgments, specifically the purpose for which the forecast is required and the reasons for using multiple forecasts. It considers the positive and negative aspects of group processes and discusses the range of possible tasks and the impact of specific task characteristics. The section on behavioural aggregation covers what is possibly the best-known subjective forecasting technique, Delphi, together with Nominal Group Technique (NGT) and brainstorming. The use of linear models, the weighting of individual forecasts and the aggregation of probabilities are analysed and some conclusions drawn about methods of methematical aggregation. The topic of Inquiry Systems is introduced because of its insights into the specification of the forecasting task and the creative approaches it has stimulated to developing group processes. Finally a general approach to group judgmental forecasting is proposed.

THE SOCIAL AND OPERATIONAL CONTEXT OF FORECASTS, JUDGMENTS AND DECISIONS

For the purpose of this discussion, we are primarily concerned with forecasts and judgments that take place in an organizational context, usually a commercial or governmental one. Here forecasting is closely related to decision-making, and such decision-making will normally involve multiple individuals as influences if not actual participants in the decision-making process. Whilst it may be desirable to separate the initial forecasting process from decision-making (see Hammond and Adelman, 1976), because one's preferred course of action might bias the forecast, there are likely to be a multiplicity of viewpoints and a need to revise and aggregate the initial estimates in the light of the subsequent interaction. Divorcing the treatment of forecasting from its context not merely has the potential result of it being ignored, but also separates it from a rich source of material, particularly important in the context of subjective forecasting.

The probable gains are not entirely costless, however; Nisbett and Ross (1980) observe that there is likely to be a trade-off between correctness and consensus. Makridakis and Wheelwright (1977) identify what they call 'organizational roadblocks' to improved forecasting performance, which occur particularly when the benefits from improved forecasts do not accrue to the organizational unit that is supposed to provide them. Those with experience of sales forecasting by the sales team will be familiar with the problem, because of the perceived impact of the forecast on sales targets. As will be seen later, some of the negative effects can be attenuated by modifying the nature of the tasks or the degree and manner of interaction.

REASONS FOR USING GROUP JUDGMENTS

The usual reason put forward for using group judgments, rather than a single individual one, to construct a forecast is couched in terms of improved forecasting accuracy, primarily the deviations of single point estimates from the actual resultant values. We might also be concerned, however, with gaining more information about the possible range of outcome values (giving some insight into the risk involved in any consequent decision). There is considerable evidence that human judges seriously underestimate the ranges of possible values for variables in subjective probability tasks (Lichtenstein, Fischhoff and Phillips, 1982). The use of group judgments of ranges is of potential use in constructing broader ranges for the estimated variable.

Other reasons for using group judgments in subjective forecasting relate to the end purpose of the forecasts. If they are to be used as inputs to a decision model or process, the sensitivity of the chosen decision to alternative forecasts is of interest (for example, the impact of alternative forecast sales distributions in the decision whether or not to launch a new product—e.g. NEWFOOD A. in Eskin and Montgomery (1977)). The final reason is behavioural in terms of the likely improvement in commitment of a group responsible for implementation of a decision resulting from involvement in the processes leading to the decision (cf. Salancik, 1977).

THE POSITIVE IMPACT OF GROUP JUDGMENTS

There is some literature on the effectiveness of groups versus individuals in problem-solving tasks (see, for example, Kelley and Thibaut, 1954; Davis, 1969 and 1973; Steiner, 1972; Hackman and Morris, 1978). Nisbett and Ross (1980, p. 267) conclude that group solutions are generally better. Gettys *et al.* (1980) report that groups produce more hypotheses in problem-solving tasks than individuals and are more likely to find the 'correct' one (given the nature of tasks). However, not surprisingly, marginal information diminishes with group size, and social interaction inhibits performance (see next section), though it is still better than individual.

Other studies have shown that composites formed of individual judgments out-perform the individuals and even 'bootstrapped' models of their judgments (Goldberg, 1970; Camerer, 1981). 'Bootstrapping'—constructing linear models of individuals' judgments of an outcome based on several cues to replace the individual—is based throughout on the idea that the gain in using models is due to the elimination of the random component in judgment. Even if there is still a consistent bias, if we are prepared to assume that the random components are not perfectly correlated, then aggregation reduces the impact of random individual forecasting errors resulting in an improved forecast.

The final point can be either a positive aspect or a pitfall. Group choices exhibit shifts in risk taking from individual ones (Janis and Mann, 1977) either in the direction of caution or the 'risky shift', where the group is prepared to adopt a riskier alternative than they would as individuals.

PITFALLS OF GROUP PROCESSES

Unstructured group processes (often referred to as interacting groups to distinguish them from certain formalized group techniques) have a number of well-documented shortcomings.

(1) 'Group think' (Janis and Mann, 1977)
   This emerges as a restriction on the range of ideas or views generated by a group. In individual meetings it is reflected in the way one idea is pursued for a considerable time and how thinking falls into a rut. It reflects a desire for and encouragement of conformity not merely within the

context of the single meeting but in the larger organizational one. It often also reflects a common information base.

(2) Inhibition of contributions

Frequently caused by status incongruities, many participating individuals are reluctant to express opinions. This can reflect the level of self-evaluation, unwillingness to express contrary opinions to those already put forward, and pressures by dominant individuals.

(3) Premature closure

This is the tendency to adopt the first feasible or apparently satisfactory alternative, rather than to fully explore the problem.

In practice, it is clear that there are groups whose composition or context makes interaction difficult and inhibits the performance of judgmental tasks. Specifically, the results are a reduction in the range of ideas or estimates generated and the direction that the integration of ideas takes. In other contexts, the development of Devil's Advocate and Dialectical Inquiry methods (Mason and Mitroff, 1981) is an attempt to overcome some of these problems. Other approaches could involve modifying the group task, the group composition or the group procedure. Some common approaches to this form of behavioural aggregation are discussed later.

It is possible, however, that we have to accept the political difficulties because these are associated with the broader context and are not directly eradicable (and, in particular, not directly eradicable without strong commitment from key individuals)—the art of the possible. Indeed there may be a tension between the forces leading to effective cohesive groups and those that lead to the expression of a variety of viewpoints. We do need to note the importance of consensus in promoting group interaction which may be important for the implementation of whatever decision hangs upon the judgmental task.

TASKS AND TASK CHARACTERISTICS

It might be argued that the costs involved in using group judgments for subjective forecasts perhaps restrict their use to larger-scale problems. The evidence based on direct comparisons between quantitative and subjective forecasts (for example, salespeople's estimates of sales and time-series as causal models), leads one to conclude that subjective methods are most appropriate in situations where formal quantitative models are not particularly suitable, either where little or no past data exists, or where the basis of the model may change. For example, Delphi is frequently discussed in the context of technological forecasting and group subjective judgments are of considerable use for long-range forecasting and the construction of scenarios. The benefits that properly managed group processes can bring to these areas lie primarily in the richness of information available.

Elsewhere in the book the matter of the individual judgmental forecasting task is discussed, though one should mention Wagenaar and Timmers (1978) result that people perform better at forecasting over longer periods with fewer data points. It is worth considering a number of residual task characteristics, relating to groups.

Hogarth (1981b) identifies three task characteristics which he saw as affecting decision performance in an organizational context:

(1) the level of commitment involved in a particular choice,
(2) the extent of redundant information in the environment,
(3) the availability and form of feedback.

Hogarth (1981a) also observes that real life judgmental processes are continuous and adaptive for coping with a dynamic environment. Task environments are therefore likely to be unstable.

It is worth reinforcing the points about feedback and redundant information. The main exceptions to the generally dismal picture of the quality of human judgment when faced with estimation tasks have been in situations where the feedback is deliberately monitored. The best-known studies relate to US weather forecasters (see Murphy and Winkler 1977; Murphy and Daan, 1984), who are shown to produce well-calibrated estimates of subjective probabilities of climatic phenomena. Usually feedback is not deliberately monitored and is also confused with much other extraneous information. We are all familiar with the human ability to post-rationalize and inability to learn from experience (Argyris, 1976). Where judgmental forecasts are performed on a repetitive and sequential basis the collection and clear provision of relevant past data is likely to have a positive effect on performance.

The second aspect of the task in the context of group subjective forecasts relates to causality—the individual and collective beliefs about the generating processes involved in the phenomenon to be forecast. The influence of context and beliefs about causality on inference is familiar from a number of literatures (see Einhorn and Hogarth, 1981; Blumer, 1969). It is proposed here that processes that explicitly discuss and treat different models of causality are likely to improve group and individual forecasting performance particularly in stimulating learning through successive estimates. A possible method is to elicit individual's estimates of the quantities to be forecast and showing them to the group, asking each individual to outline the reasoning behind an estimate and then reviewing the estimates. It will be seen later that this resembles the Nominal Group Technique. We now move on to explicitly consider methods of aggregating forecasts.

BEHAVIORAL AGGREGATION

Armstrong (1978) suggests that group discussion has some usefulness in the construction of a subjective forecast. The notion that participants can share their views and arrive at a consensus is appealing and the implied process fits in with the concepts of using it to develop group cohesion and commitment to the subsequent course of action. It is, of course, subject to the dangers of 'groupthink' and the problems associated with the concomitant political processes.

True behavioral aggregation would require the group itself to reach a consensus. This process is particularly prone to the biases and pitfalls outlined before. Ferrell (1985, pp. 138–139) usefully summarizes aspects of behavioural aggregation. It is, however, important to discuss three methods that involve different levels of controlled transmission of information between participants, Delphi, NGT and brainstorming. Some comparative empirical work has been done, but relatively little with real groups and real problems. This is understandable, given the problems of designing experiments under such conditions, but must lead one to be wary of some of the research claims.

Delphi (Dalkey, 1969)

Delphi is perhaps the best-known method of using group judgments in forecasting. It was developed at the RAND Corporation by Dalkey, Helmer and others primarily for technological forecasting, but has seen a wide variety of applications. The basic principles of the multistage method are the elimination of direct social contact providing unattributed contributions, the provision of feedback, and the opportunity for the revision of opinions.

The participants are asked individually, usually by mailed questionnaires but more recently by interactive computer contact, for their estimates of the variable in question. These are then collated and summarized in such a way as to conceal the origin of individual estimates. The results are then circulated and the participants are asked if they wish to revise their earlier forecasts. These rounds can continue until the estimates stabilize, though in practice the procedure rarely goes beyond a second round.

The method has the benefit of reducing or avoiding any attenuation of performance that may accompany social interaction. In particular, it overcomes the problem of the dominant individual and the influence of who speaks first. However, as Hogarth (1975) points out, Delphi is hard to pin down precisely. It is not clear from the discussions of Delphi whether the reasoning behind estimates is to be collated and synthesized. If not, a lot of information which could be of benefit, if pooled, goes to waste. Armstrong (1978) similarly takes a somewhat sceptical view of Delphi, but suggests a possible role for such methods in scenario construction. For some relatively recent positive perspectives on Delphi, one may refer to Linstone and Turoff (1975) and Sackman (1975). Dalkey (in Dalkey *et al.*, 1972) presents some results about the revision of estimate from first to second rounds together with the impact of the provision of further factual information which seems to support the point about gains from pooling of information on which forecasts are based. A range of evaluative studies of Delphi forecasts can be seen in Bardecki (1984), Parenté *et al*. (1984) and Rohrbaugh (1979).

It appears from a range of other studies that Delphi is not as effective as a mixed interaction and controlled feedback process, though these studies were not done with stable decision-making units. The method is useful in structuring communication, though it is vulnerable to variation in problem definition, as it is hard to revise the question in the course of the procedure. There is also a lack of definition of a consistent process of aggregation of the individual estimates.

Nominal Group Technique (NGT) (Delbecq, Van de Ven and Gustafson, 1975; Van de Ven and Delbecq, 1971)

Delbecq, Van de Ven and Gustafson (1975) emphasize that their specific concern is with judgmental decision-making and pooled judgments, not with routine meetings or with negotiation and bargaining processes. A meeting using NGT starts without any interaction. The individuals (up to about ten) commence by writing ideas related to the problem down on a pad of paper. Then each individual in turn briefly presents one of the ideas. These are recorded on a flip chart. Discussion does not take place until all the ideas are recorded. Then each one is discussed. Finally each individual writes down his/her evaluation of the priorities of the ideas, by rank ordering or rating. These are then mathematically aggregated to yield a group decision.

The prime difference between NGT and the Delphi technique is that communication does take place between the participating individuals. It separates out the processes of independent idea generation, structured feedback, evaluation and aggregation of opinions. It increases individual participation. The technique has been used in experimental circumstances to estimate subjective probabilities. The results (Gustafson *et al*., 1973) showed NGT to be superior to Delphi, a conventional group and independent individuals in terms of error percentage and variability of estimations. One should record the normal caveat about experimental groups' results holding for functioning organizational groups. One should also note the importance of the leader role. It is likely that this is best performed by someone outside the judgmental group. In many ways the more recent decision conference bears a considerable resemblance to NGT. In practical terms, like Delphi, the framing of the question(s) is critical to the functioning of the procedure.

Brainstorming

Brainstorming seems now a very dated word, yet the idea of encouraging offbeat or outrageous ideas in response to a problem has its attractions. Does it have a lot to do with forecasting? Well, not directly, but what is useful is the notion of suspending critical comment until the idea-generation phase is over. Participants, of course, may be still inhibited by what people might say afterwards, but the right atmosphere encourages creativity and unorthodox thinking. This may be particularly productive when the variable to be forecast is some way in the future and surrounded by considerable environmental uncertainty. However, Bender *et al.* (1969) point out the problems of bringing a lot of experts together in one place, and also take a negative view of the likely impact of group dynamics. The experimental work on brainstorming (especially Osborn, 1957) does show that brainstorming groups performed better than brainstorming individuals and out-performed conventional interacting groups in problem-solving. It was very much the positive content in brainstorming that inspired the development of NGT, for example.

MATHEMATICAL AGGREGATION

An excellent survey and review of the literature on the combination of individual judgments is due to Ferrell (1985). It is intended that this section should complement rather than rehearse that review.

A number of literatures converge to give us both pragmatic and theoretical insights. There has been some interest in the conventional forecasting literature for more than 15 years (most authors start their references with Bates and Granger (1969)) in the effectiveness of combining forecasts, usually where different methods have been used (a range of references are included in the bibliography). Another literature has been concerned with the aggregation of individual subjective probability distributions (sometimes called the Multi-Bayesian problem) (see for example, Genest (1984) and Weerahandi and Zidek (1981)). The studies of empirical models of human judgment, sometimes referred to as 'bootstrapping', examined, in a number of cases, the performance of a composite of the judgments of the individual subjects (Goldberg, 1970). It is also worth briefly noting two related literatures— voting, nicely summarized by Chechile (in Swap, 1984, pp. 97–114) (also note Arrow's classic (1951) work); and the game theoretic/bargaining literature (see Murnighan in Guzzo (1982), and Shubik (1982)).

Linear models

The majority of authors, particularly in the literature on the combination of forecasts, have primarily discussed the performance of a linear sum of the individual forecasts. (A notable exception is the pari-mutuel method for aggregating subjective probabilities proposed by Eisenberg and Gale (1959), though Hogarth (1975) was unable to find any examples of its actual application.) There has been an extensive debate on the merits of differential weighting (to be discussed in the next section), but rather less about the principles of a linear aggregation, though the discussion of Newbold and Granger's (1974) paper at the Royal Statistical Society evidences some disquiet at the brute empiricism of the procedures.

Newbold and Granger were concerned with comparing forecasting performances of Box–Jenkins, Holt–Winters and stepwise autoregression over a large number of time-series and considered methods of combining them. They, like Bates and Granger (1969) concluded that combining forecasts offered improvements over the individual methods at relatively little cost (if the other forecasts had been produced already). A similar but more extensive study is reported by Makridakis and Winkler (1983, and Winkler and Makridakis, 1983) using ten different forecasting methods and Makridakis's 1001 time-series database. Performance was compared in terms of Mean Average Percentage Error (MAPE). They found that the specific methods selected for inclusion in a combined forecast had little effect on its accuracy and that accuracy increased (and its variability decreased) as additional methods were added to the forecast, though the gains tailed off after about four or five were combined. Combined forecasts generally had an advantage over the individual methods, though rarely over all the methods simultaneously (see also Bopp, 1985). Similarly a simple average performed well, but not as well as the best of the weighting procedures. Moriarty and Adams (1984) emphasize the general performance improvement of composite forecasts and argue that it has not been given the attention it deserves in applied literature (in this case, a marketing one). Ashton and Ashton (1985) report similar results for the aggregation of subjective forecasts, again finding that gains tailed off after the inclusion of the fourth forecast. The impact of the number of judges is also explicitly considered in Libby and Blashfield (1978).

To weight or not to weight?

Bates and Granger (1969) showed that if errors in two forecasts are uncorrelated then the optimum weight k is given by $\sigma_2^2/(\sigma_1^2 + \sigma_2^2)$. Newbold and Granger (1974) outline five different methods of computing differential weights. Winkler (1981), considering the problem of dependence (correlation between different estimator errors), arrived at a similar result to Newbold and Granger showing that if the covariance matrix Σ is known then the vector of optimal weights (w) is given by the equation:

$$w = (\Sigma^{-1} . 1)/(1' . \Sigma^{-1} . 1)$$

where 1 is the unit summation vector $(1,1,1,\ldots,1)$. He also shows that the prior for Σ, Σ_0, can be substituted and revised for subsequent data, given assumptions of an underlying normal process for the forecast errors. In a similar spirit is Bunn's (1975, 1977, 1978) work on Bayesian models for combining forecasts.

One of the difficulties with using differential weights for combining fore-casts is the requirement for relevant prior knowledge of a method's (or judge's) forecast accuracy. Gwilym Jenkins (in the discussion of Newbold and Granger, 1974) expressed concern that the weights for forecast combinations were chosen from the same series—an obvious source of bias.

For the combination of individual judgments a number of other weighting methods have been proposed. Dalkey suggested using self-ratings as weights. De Groot (1974) considered processes of revision of individual judgments in the light of others' judgment by assessing relative expertise. However, Einhorn and Hogarth (1975) note that differential weighting schemes in group decision-making often reflect selective status rather than relative expertise. Equal weighting avoids arguments about relative weighting and performs remarkably well compared with differential weighting (Winkler and Makridakis, 1983; Ashton and Ashton, 1985). They state that if all the judges have positive validity and reasonably similar variability, then equal weighting will work well. This reflects the general consensus in the judgment and decision literature about the performance of equal weighting of participants' judgments (see Wainer (1976), Dawes (1979), Dawes and Corrigan (1974), amongst others). The difficulties with differential weighting based on past peformances are that

(a) the task might not be the same—the specific quantity to be forecast may be more or less familiar to the judge than those previously estimated;
(b) learning may have taken place—judges who performed poorly in previ-ous tasks may be able to improve their performance.

However, the special case of differential weighting to reflect additional information is discussed later.

Aggregating probabilities

Probabilities pose particular problems of aggregation, that are not resolved by simple averaging. Dickey and Freeman (1975) proposed modelling per-sonal priors over a large population with a Dirichlet distribution. One should also point out Morris's (1974, 1977, 1983) contribution to the field. Dalkey (1972) proves what he calls an 'impossibility theorem' apparently showing that no aggregation function exists that satisfies the rules of probability and has a contribution from each of the individual estimates. Bordley and Wolff (1981) claim to resolve the problem by focusing on what appears to be a 'context-free' assumption—that the aggregation rule would be the same whatever the context.

Winkler and Sarin (1981) propose as a practical procedure the conversion of assessed probabilities to log odds and assuming the vector of log odds for the experts to be normally distributed. Following Winkler (1981), the covariance matrix has to be estimated, where the diagonal elements (variances) represent the 'shakiness' of each expert's assessment and the off-diagonal elements (covariance) are estimates of the interrelationships between the experts. Winkler and Sarin also observe that it is helpful to have some rationale behind the responses in terms of verbal explanations to avoid losing sight of the real goals of the procedure.

Bordley (1982b) arrives at a formula similarly based on the log odds of an event

$$O_G = \left(\prod_{k=1}^{n} (O_k)^{w_k} \right)(O_0)^{(1 - \sum_{k=1}^{n} w_k)}$$

where O_0 may be viewed as a prior odds assessment, making the form of the function dependent upon the event being assessed. Whilst this begs the question of who assesses O_0 and the weights w_k (a real prior expert or some synthesis of the individual views) it has some interesting consequences.

—if $\Sigma w_k > 1$ the expert (DM) is more certain than the group—a 'risky' shift.
—if $\Sigma w_k < 1$ the DM is more cautious.

Weerahandi and Zidek's (1981) work looks at the frequently quoted requirement that assessments should be internally and externally Bayesian and they observe that one should use a geometric rather than an arithmetic mean to achieve this result. Genest (1984) shows that certain of the assumptions made in Morris (1983) and Bordley (1982b) and others lead to the perverse 'dictatorship' result (the group estimate based on a single opinion). He proposed the following function

$$G(f_1, \ldots, f_i, \ldots, f_n) = \prod_{i=1}^{n} f_i^{w_i} \bigg/ \int \prod_{i=1}^{n} f_i^{w_i} \, d\mu$$

where the weights w_i are non-negative and sum to unity.

Some issues and a conclusion

To a large extent, the approach one adopts to aggregation reflects one's overall goals in constructing a judgmental forecast, in particular whether one is trying to get a single estimate of central tendency or a reflection of the range of possible values. In the latter case one might wish to adopt a non-linear aggregation model that gave greater weight to extremal estimates. Whatever the model adopted one has in some sense to rely on the good faith of the forecasters, because it is really quite easy to introduce deliberate bias to the results.

A specific concern relating to the weighting issue and also affecting equal weights stems from the 'groupthink' notion discussed earlier. In an organizational setting, a significant proportion of the judges might share the same information base and intuitive models of the phenomenon under discussion.

(a) Does a judge add information to the base? Note the special case (considered by Hogarth (1978), where one forecaster could have provided a number of forecasts, possibly at different times.
(b) What happens if x out of n judges have identical subjective probability distributions?

In both these cases, taking them to an extreme there can be a similarity to the practice of stuffing ballot boxes. It raises the issue for the individual, who, as convener, arbitrator or aggregator, has to decide on which judges to include, what functional form to use and what weights to apply. Whilst one has the option of using a non-linear function to aggregate the forecasts, a more satisfactory pragmatic solution is to try and ensure a panel of experts who represent a broad range of opinion and are not dominated by any particular group and to use an equal-weighted linear model to aggregate their opinions (or a long-odds model to aggregate probabilities). If it is critical to estimate the distribution tails accurately, some pragmatic adjustment might be made to reflect the tendency to estimate overly tight distributions.

INQUIRY SYSTEMS (CHURCHMAN, 1972)

Inquiry Systems (IS) are simply philosophical systems that underlie different approaches to analysing or investigating particular phenomena. They are of interest here because the notions have stimulated a number of creative approaches to group processes, particularly in the policy formulation area (see Mason and Mitroff, 1981). There are five different categories, almost arranged in increasing hierarchical order (see Mitroff and Turoff, in Linstone and Turoff (1975)). In this context there is a key theme attached to each:

(1) Leibnizian IS
    Is it possible to construct a rational model of the phenomenon?
(2) Lockean IS
    How good are the estimates? To what extent is there a consensus about them?
(3) Kantian IS
    What alternative combinations of models and estimates exist? Which best satisfies the requirements of the task?
(4) Hegelian IS
    Is it possible to take sharply differing views of the phenomenon? Is a synthesis possible?

(5) Singer–Churchman IS
Have we asked the right questions? Does the breadth of perspective match that of the complete problem? How can we learn about our own perspectives?

The fifth is perhaps the hardest to capture and describe. The main approaches that Churchman's ideas have stimulated are those of Devil's Advocate and Dialectical Inquiry (though of course these ideas are much older). To counter tendencies towards 'groupthink' particularly for strategic management problems, individuals or small groups are explicitly charged with either playing the Devil's Advocate role or using the dialectical approach to present an alternative view (or counter-plan). From the empirical evidence presented by Schwenk and Cosier (1980), the latter seems to be more effective in the context of strategic planning. It is suggested here that the explicit allocation of these roles would improve group performance in forecasting tasks.

A GENERAL APPROACH TO GROUP JUDGMENTAL FORECASTING

It would appear from the material presented that there are benefits to be gained from communication between members of the group of judges. The procedure proposed draws upon the ideas in Nominal Group Technique and Inquiry Systems already discussed. It consists of seven phases:

(1) Problem/task definition.
(2) Pre-collection of estimates of the variable of interest and the reasoning behind the estimate.
(3) Sharing of the estimates and clarification of the underlying reasoning behind them.
(4) Discussion of the underlying reasoning.
(5) Encouragement of multiple advocacy (dialectic inquiry).
(6) Individual revision of estimates.
(7) Synthesis of estimates.

A number of key issues need to be considered.

The role of the leader

Delbecq, Van de Ven and Gustafson (1975, pp. 80–81) briefly discussed the role of the leader (or convener) in the context of NGT and emphasized the importance of understanding the process, being self-confident enough to lead the group through the process, and being seen as legitimate. They do not really discuss whether the leader should or should not be an organization member. The success of an insider would appear to depend on the leadership style and the role played normally by the leader. A consultative or participative style would seem to be more conducive to effective group performance for this kind of task. Significant benefits are likely to accrue from the use of an external leader or convener, in terms of perceived independence, status and legitimacy (with the right individual), potential catalytic function, importation of an outside viewpoint, and as an outsider the ability to draw further information from the group. There is considerable similarity with the function of the leader in the decision conference (cf. Phillips, 1984).

Defining the task

The forecasting task presented to the group has, obviously, to relate to the purpose for which the forecast is required. Unless it is thought likely that the information will contaminate responses, it is worth outlining the context of the problem. Also time and resources permitting, it is worth piloting some possible definitions of the problem. Finally, though the pre-collection of estimates might take place at the actual meeting, notification of the problem or task to stimulate advance thinking is desirable, though with cautions about importing 'groupthink' beforehand.

Dialogue and multiple advocacy

The importance of internalizing the reasoning behind a forecast, the intuitive models of the phenomenon, together with attempts to represent the broader context of the problem (the reasons why the forecasts are required) has been emphasized already. The processes aid the sharing of information relevant to the problem and form the basis of an effective dialogue between the participants (cf. Lock and Thomas, 1983). The use of models that command some agreement can reduce debate where it can be shown that it has little impact on the final outcome, can focus on areas of genuine disagreement and can provide the basis for learning.

The function of multiple advocacy of the Devil's Advocate or dialectical type is to counter effects of the 'groupthink' variety. It legitimizes alternative viewpoints, particularly where they might be otherwise difficult to adopt in a corporate situation. It is suggested that the dialectical approach of presenting an alternative viewpoint may be more effective in most contexts than that of the Devil's Advocate. The effectiveness of the approach is likely to depend on the ability of the leader to bring them out and experience elsewhere suggests that the roles have to an extent to be set up beforehand.

Synthesis of estimates

In the procedure proposed, both the initial and revised estimates are made individually. It was suggested earlier in the chapter that, once one had decided who would participate, a linear equally weighted combination of forecasts would perform perfectly adequately. On this basis one has two forecasts, the initial one and the revised one. As a good Bayesian, the author will argue that the critical question is whether it affects any decision that is subsequently made. In slightly different contexts, such as sales forecasts for budgeting purposes, it is desirable to have a range of forecasts (akin to the idea of flexible budgets) to stimulate organisational thinking about the consequences of different outcomes. The goal is not necessarily the provision of a single point forecast, though such a forecast may be desirable to serve as a subsequent target, in technological forecasts, for example.

ADVANTAGES OF THE APPROACH

The ideas behind the approach have been drawn from a range of literatures. Sets of stages and issues are identified. This should aid preliminary thinking about a forecasting process as well as its actual execution. It combines the benefits of communication of ideas and beliefs about causal structures and their consequent discussion with some controls to attenuate the negative aspects of interaction, in particular 'groupthink' and the inhibition of contributions. Throughout the chapter there has been an emphasis on displaying ranges of estimates to assist with analysis of the sensitivity of the final decision. Proper recording of the stages of the process and the explicit combination with environmental feedback may form the basis for enhanced organizational learning.

POSTSCRIPT

In some ways, the general conclusions of the chapter seem rather humdrum. There are benefits to communication and discussion between group members, so long as these are structured as in nominal group approaches. For most purposes linear models are perfectly adequate for aggregation, and differential weights do not offer real advantages in practical terms. More is to be gained by using the possibilities of sharing information and enhancing understanding of the generating processes of the variable under consideration and the wider problem, so long as suitable measures are taken to counter 'groupthink' and to stifle overpowering personalities. There do appear to be gains from externalizing the aggregation process and doing it on a mathematical basis, thus separating it from the controlled interaction. More attention needs to be given to the potential of groups for giving insights into the possible variability of outcomes rather than the provision of single point estimates.

ACKNOWLEDGMENT

I would like to thank Rick Hough for his assistance with the collection of material for this chapter.

REFERENCES

Argyris, C. (1976) 'Theories of action that inhibit learning', *Amer. Psychologist*, **31**, 638–654.

Armstrong, J. S. (1978) *Long Range Forecasting*, New York: Wiley–Interscience.

Arrow, K. J. (1951) Social Choice and Individual Values, New York: Wiley.

Ashton, A. H. and Ashton, R. H. (1985) 'Aggregating subjective forecasts: some empirical results', *Man. Sci.*, **31**, 12, 1499–1508.

Bardecki, M. J. (1984) 'Participants' response to the Delphi method. An attitudinal perspective', *Technology Forecasting and Social Change*, **25**, 3, 281–292.

Bates, J. M. and Granger, C. W. J. (1969) 'The combination of forecasts', *Opl. Res. Qtrly.*, **20**, 451–468.

Bender, A. D., Strack, A. E., Ebright, G. W. and von Haunalter, G. (1969) 'Delphic study examines developments in medicine', *Futures*, **1**, 289–303.

Blumer, H. (1969) *Symbolic Interactionism: Perspective and Method*, Englewood Cliffs, N.J.: Prentice-Hall.

Boje, D. M. and Murnighan, J. K. (1982) 'Group confidence pressures in internal decisions', *Manag. Sci.*, **28**, 10, 1187–1196.

Bopp, A. E. (1985) 'On combining forecasts: some extensions and results', *Man. Sci.*, **31**, 12, 1492–1498.

Bordley, R. F. (1982a) 'The combination of forecasts: a Bayesian approach', *Jnl. of the O.R. Soc.*, **33**, 171–174.

Bordley, R. F. (1982b) 'A multiplicative formula for aggregating probability assessments', *Manag. Sci.*, **28**, 10, 1137–1148.

Bordley, R. F. and Wolff, R. W. (1981) 'On the aggregation of individual probability estimates', *Manag. Sci.*, **27**, 8, 959–964.

Brown, L. D. and Rozeff, M. S. (1978) 'The superiority of analyst forecasts as measures of expectations: evidence from earnings', *Jnl. Fin.*, **33**, 1–16.

Bunn, D. W. (1975) 'A Bayesian approach to the linear combination of forecasts', *Opl. Res. Qtrly.*, **26**, 325–329.

Bunn, D. W. (1977) 'A comparative evaluation of the outperformance and minimum variance procedures for the linear synthesis of forecasts', *Opl. Res. Qtrly.*, **28**, 653–662.

Bunn, D. W. (1978) 'A simplification of the matrix Beta distribution for combining estimators', *Jnl. O.R. Soc.*, **29**, 1013–1016.

Bunn, D. W. and French, S. (1980) 'Outranking probabilities and the synthesis of forecasts', *Jnl. O.R. Soc.*, **31**, 454–551.

Camerer, C. (1981) 'General conditions for the success of bootstrapping models', *Org. Behav. and Hum. Perf.*, **27**, 411–422.

Churchman, C. W. (1972) *The Design of Inquiring Systems*, New York: Basic Books.

Cummings, L. L., Huber, G. P. and Arendt, E. (1974) 'Effect of size and spatial arrangement on group decision making', *Acad. Man. Jnl.*, **17**, 460–475.

Dalkey, N. C. (1969) *The Delphi Method: An Experimental Study of Group Opinion*, Santa Monica, Cal.: RAND Corporation.

Dalkey, N. C. (1972) *An Impossibility Theorem for Group Probability Functions*, (P-4862), Santa Monica, Cal.: RAND Corporation.

Dalkey, N. C., Rourke, D. L., Lewis, R. and Snyder, D. (1972) *Studies in the Quality of Life*, Lexington, Mass.: Lexington Books.

Davis, J. H. (1969) *Group Performance*, Reading, Mass.: Addison-Wesley.

Davis, J. H. (1973) 'Group decision and social interaction: a theory of social decision schemes', *Psych. Rev.*, **80**, 97–125.

Dawes, R. M. (1979) 'The robust beauty of improper linear models in decision making', *Amer. Psychologist*, **34**, 571–582.

Dawes, R. M. and Corrigan, B. (1974) 'Linear models in decision making', *Psych. Bull.*, **81**, 95–106.

De Groot, M. H. (1974) 'Reaching a consensus', *Jnl. Am. Stat. Ass.*, **69**, 118–121.

Delbecq, A. L., Van de Ven, A. H. and Gustafson, D. H. (1975) *Group Techniques for Program Planning*, Glenview, Ill.: Scott Foresman.

Dickey, J. and Freeman, P. (1975) 'Population-distributed personal probabilities', *Jnl. Am. Stat. Assoc.*, **70**, 362–364.

Dickinson, J. P. (1973) 'Some statistical results in the combination of forecasts', *Opl. Res. Qtrly.*, **24**, 253–260.

Dickinson, J. P. (1975) 'Some comments on the combination of forecasts', *Opl. Res. Qtrly.*, **26**, 205–210.

Einhorn, H. J. (1972) 'Expert measurement and mechanical combination', *Org. Behav. and Hum. Perf.*, **7**, 86–106.

Einhorn, H. J. and Hogarth, R. M. (1975) 'Unit weighting schemes for decision making', *Org. Behav. and Hum. Perf.*, **13**, 171–192.

Einhorn, H. J. and Hogarth, R. M. (1981) 'Behavioural decision theory: processes of judgement and choice', *Ann. Rev. of Psych.*, **32**, 53–88.

Einhorn, H. J. and Hogarth, R. M. (1983) 'Prediction, diagnosis and causal thinking in forecasting', *Jnl. Forecasting*, **1**, 23–36.

Einhorn, H. J., Hogarth, R. M. and Klempner, E. (1977) 'Quality of group judgement', *Psych. Bull.*, **84**, 158–172.

Eisenberg, E. and Gale, D. (1959) 'Consensus of subjective probabilities', *Ann. Math. Stat.*, **30**, 165–168.

Eliashberg, J. and Winkler, R. L. (1981) 'Risk sharing and group decision making', *Manag. Sci.*, **27**, 1221–1235.

Eskin, G. J. and Montgomery, D. B. (1977) *Cases in Computer and Model Assisted Marketing: Data Analysis*, Palo Alto, Cal.: Scientific Press.

Ferrell, W. R. (1985) 'Combining individual judgements', in G. Wright (ed.), *Behavioural Decision Making*, New York: Plenum Press, pp. 111–145.

Fischer, G. W. (1981) 'When oracles fail—a comparison of four procedures for aggregating subjective probability forecasts', *Org. Behav. and Hum. Perf.*, **28**, 96–110.

Genest, C. (1984) 'A conflict between two axioms for combining subjective distributions', *Jnl. Reg. Stat. Soc.*, **B**, **46**, 3, 403–405.

Gettys, C. F., Manning, C., Mehle, T. and Fisher, S. (1980) 'Hypothesis Generation: a final report of three years of research', Technical Report no. TR 15-10-80, Decision Processes Laboratory, University of Oklahoma, Norman, OK 73019.

Goldberg, L. R. (1970) 'Man versus model of man', *Psych. Bull.*, **73**, 6, 422–432.

Gray, P. and Nilles, J. M. (1983) 'Evaluating a Delphi forecast on personal computers', *IEEE Transactions on systems, Man and Cybernetics*, **SMC-13**, 2, 222–223.

Gustafson, D. H., Shulka, R. K., Delbecq, A. L., and Webster, G. W. (1973) 'A comparative study of differences in subjective likelihood estimates made by individuals, interacting groups, Delphi groups and nominal groups', *Org. Behav. and Hum. Perf.*, **9**, 280–291.

Guzzo, R. A. (ed.) (1982) *Improving Group Decision Making in Organizations*, New York: Academic Press.

Hackman, J. R. and Morris, C. G. (1975) 'Group tasks, group interaction process and group performance effectiveness. A review and proposal integration', in L. Berkowitz (ed.), *Advances in Experimental Social Psychology*, Vol. X., New York: Academic Press.

Hackman, J. R. and Vidmar, N. (1970) 'Effect of size and task type on group performance and member reactions', *Sociometry*, **33**, 37–54.

Hammond, K. R. and Adelman, L. (1976) 'Science, values and human judgment', *Science*, **194**, 389–396.

Hogarth, R. M. (1975) 'Cognitive processes and the assessment of subjective probability distributions', *Jnl. Am. Stat. Ass.*, **70**, 271–286.

Hogarth, R. M. (1978) 'A note on aggregating opinions', *Org. Behav. and Hum. Perf.*, **21**, 40–46.

Hogarth, R. M. (1981a) 'Beyond discrete biases: functional and dysfunctional aspects of judgemental heuristics', *Psych. Bull.*, **90**, 2, 197–217.

Hogarth, R. M. (1981b) 'Decision making in organizations and the organization of decision making', paper presented by Eighth research Conference on Subjective Probability, Utility and Decision Making, Budapest, August, 1981.

Huber, G. P. (1980) *Managerial Decision Making*, Glenview, Ill.: Scott, Foresman.

Janis, I. L. and Mann, L. (1977) *Decision Making*, New York: The Free Press.

Jenkins, G. M. (1982) 'Some practical aspects of forecasting', *Jnl. Forecasting*, **1**, 3–21.

Kadane, J. B., Dickey, J. M., Winkler, R. L., Smith, W. S. and Peters, S. C. (1980) 'Interactive elicitation of opinion for a normal linear model', *Jnl. Am. Stat. Ass.*, **75**, 845–854.

Kelley, H. H. and Thibaut, J. W. (1954) 'Experimental studies of group problem solving and process', in G. Lindzey (ed.), *Handbook of Social Psychology*, Vol. II, Cambridge, Mass.: Addison-Wesley.

Libby, R. and Blashfield, R. K. (1978) 'Performance of a composite as a function of the number of judges', *Org. Behav. and Hum. Perf.*, **21**, 121–129.

Lichtenstein, S., Fischhoff, B. and Phillips, L. D. (1982) 'Calibration of probabilities: the state of the art to 1980', in D. Kahneman, P. Slovic and A. Tversky (eds.), *Judgement under Uncertainty*, Cambridge: Cambridge University Press.

Linstone, H. A. and Turoff, M. (1975) *The Delphi Method: Techniques and Applications*, Reading, Mass.: Addison-Wesley.

Lock, A. R. and Thomas, H. (1983) 'Making policy analysis palatable in organizations: the policy dialogue paradigm', working paper, University of Illinois, Urbana-Champaign.

Mabert, V. A. (1976) 'Statistical vs. Sales Force—executive opinion short range forecasts: a time series analysis case study', *Decision Sciences*, **7**, 310–318.

Makridakis, S. and Wheelwright, S. C. (1977) 'Forecasting: issues and challenges for marketing management', *Jnl. Marketing*, **41**, 24–38.

Makridakis, S. and Winkler, R. L. (1983) 'Averages of forecasts: some empirical results', *Man. Sci.*, **29**, 987–996.

Mason, R. O. and Mitroff, I. I. (1981) *Challenging Strategic Planning Assumptions*, New York: Wiley.

Moriarity, M. M. and Adams, A. J. (1984) 'Management judgement forecasts, composite forecasting models and conditional efficiency', *Jnl. Mark. Res.*, **21**, 3, 239–250.

Morris, P. A. (1974) 'Decision analysis expert use', *Man. Sci.*, **20**, 9, 1233–1241.

Morris, P. A. (1977) 'Combining expert judgements: A Bayesian approach', *Man. Sci.*, **23**, 7, 679–692.

Morris, P. A. (1983) 'An axiomatic approach to expert resolution', *Man. Sci.*, **29**, 1, 24–32.

Murphy, A. and Daan, H. (1984) 'Impact of feedback and experience on the quality of subjective probability forecasts', *Monthly Weather Rev.*, **112**, 3, 413–423.

Murphy, A. H. and Winkler, R. L. (1977) 'Can weather forecasters make reliable probability forecasts of precipitation and temperatures?', *Nat. Weather Digest*, **2**, 2–9.

Newbold, P. and Granger, C. W. J. (1974) 'Experience with forecasting univariate time series and combination of forecasts', *Jnl. Roy. Stat. Soc., A,* **137,** 2, 131–165.

Nisbett, R. and Ross, R. L. (1980) *Human Inference: Strategies and Shortcomings of Social Judgement,* Englewood Cliffs, N.J.: Prentice-Hall.

Osborn, A. F. (1957) *Applied Imagination,* New York: Scribners.

Parente, F. J., Anderson, J. K., Myers, P. and O'Brien, T. (1984) 'An examination of factors contributing to Delphi accuracy', *Jnl. Forecasting,* **3,** 2, 173–182.

Phillips, L. D. (1984) 'A theory of requisite decision models', *Acta Psychologica,* **56,** 29–48.

Pyke, D. L. (1970) 'A practical approach to Delphi', *Futures,* **2,** 143–152.

Rohrbaugh, J. (1979) 'Improving the quality of group judgements: social judgement analysis and the Delphi technique', *Org. Behav. and Hum. Perf.,* **24,** 73–92.

Sackman, H. (1975) *Delphi Critique,* Lexington, Mass.: Lexington Books.

Salancik, G. R. (1977) 'Commitment and the control of organizational behaviour and belief', in B. M. Staw and G. R. Salancik (eds.), *New Directions in Organizational Behaviour,* Chicago: St. Clair Press.

Sarin, R. K. (1982) 'Strength of preference and risky choice', *Op. Res.,* **30,** 982–997.

Schwenk, R. C. and Cosier, R. A. (1980) 'Effects of the Expert, Devil's Advocate and Dialectical Enquiry methods of prediction performance', *Org. Behav. and Hum. Perf.,* **26,** 409–424.

Shubik, M. (1982) *Game Theory in the Social Sciences,* Cambridge, Mass.: MIT Press.

Sjöberg, L. (1982) 'Aided and unaided decision making: improving intuitive judgement', *Jnl. Forecasting,* **1,** 349–363.

Steiner, I. D. (1972) *Group Process and Productivity,* New York: Academic Press.

Swap, W. C. (ed.) (1984) *Group Decision Making,* Beverly Hills, Cal.: Sage.

Van de Ven, A. H. and Delbecq, A. L. (1971) 'Nominal versus interacting group processes for committee decision making effectiveness', *Acad. Man. Jnl.,* **14,** 203–213.

Vinokur, A. and Burstein, E. (1978) 'Depolarization of attitudes in groups', *Jnl. Pers. and Soc. Psych.,* **36,** 872–885.

Wagenaar, W. A. and Timmers, H. (1978) 'Intuitive prediction of growth', in D. F. Burckhardt and W. H. Ittelson (eds.), *Environmental Assessment of Socioeconomic Systems,* New York: Plenum.

Wainer, H. (1976) 'Estimating coefficients in linear models: it don't make no never mind', *Psych. Bull.,* **83,** 312–317.

Weerahandi, S. and Zidek, J. V. (1981) 'Multi-Bayesian statistical decision theory', *Jnl. Roy. Stat. Soc., A,* **144,** 85–93.

Winkler, R. L. (1981) 'Combining probability distributions from dependent information sources', *Man. Sci.,* **27,** 479–488.

Winkler, R. L. and Makridakis, S. (1983) 'The combination of forecasts', *Jnl. Roy. Stat. Soc., A,* **146,** 2, 150–157.

Winkler, R. L. and Sarin, R. K. (1981) 'Risk assessment: consulting the experts', *The Environmental Professional,* **3,** 265–276.

Wright, G. (ed.) (1985) *Behavioral Decision Making,* New York: Plenum.

Judgmental Forecasting
Edited by G. Wright and P. Ayton
© 1987 John Wiley & Sons Ltd

CHAPTER 7

Delphi Inquiry Systems

Frederick J. Parenté *and* **Janet K. Anderson-Parenté**
Towson State University, Maryland

HISTORY AND DEFINING CHARACTERISTICS OF THE DELPHI METHOD

'Project Delphi' was an Air Force-funded RAND Corporation project designed to determine ways to extract reliable consensus opinion from groups of experts through the use of questionnaires and controlled opinion feedback (Dalkey, 1969, 1968, 1967; Dalkey and Helmer, 1963). In the early studies, groups of experts were asked to assume the role of a Soviet strategic planner and to estimate the bombing requirements necessary to cripple munitions output from US industrial targets. Since the mid-1950s, the Delphi method's principal application has been in technological forecasting (predicting when technologies will emerge), although it has been used in a variety of contexts in which judgmental information is indispensable or empirical data would be too costly or otherwise impossible to obtain (Preble, 1983; Schoenman and Mahayan, 1977). For example, Delphi methods might be used to estimate the content value of information (Brockhoff, 1984), quality of life under different conditions (Dalkey, 1972), or to assess the effects of establishing policy (Turoff, 1975; Resher, 1981).

Regardless of the type of prediction, Delphi inquiries usually consist of four distinct phases. First, the subject matter is explored. Either the pollster or the panellists may determine the topics. It is necessary to define the goals of the Delphi and to evaluate possible reasons for differences of opinions about the relevance of issues. Second, the issues are summarized into 'scenarios', or possible future events. Third, the panellists are asked to provide their opinions concerning the likelihood that the events will occur, when the events will occur, or, perhaps, the impact of the event given that it is likely to occur. Fourth, the results of the polling are tallied, and this statistical feedback is provided to the panellists before they are repolled. At this stage, anonymous discussion may occur to air dissenting opinion.

The yield from a Delphi inquiry is a quantified group consensus, usually expressed in terms of the median responses of the group to the various scenarios (Brown, Cochran, and Dalkey, 1969; Brown, 1968). Repeated polling has the effect of reducing the variability of the group response thus increasing consensus (Helmer, 1964; Brown and Helmer, 1964). It is generally assumed that the decrease in variability that occurs over successive rounds is correlated with accuracy of the group prediction. Consequently, iterative polling continues until variability has stabilized (Chaffin and Talley, 1980; Dajani, Sincoff, and Talley, 1979). The characteristic phenomenon of Delphi is that the group response is typically more accurate than the average panellist's projections, and it is frequently more accurate than the most accurate panellist, if that individual could have been identified *a priori* (Parenté *et al.*, 1984).

The fact that Delphi forecasts will be correct more often than not is one reason for the method's widespread use as a technological forecasting tool. In addition, its appearance in the open literature coincided with the explosive development of aerospace, defence, and computer research/development projects over the past 30 years (Platt, 1981; Balachandra, 1980; Martino, 1980). Delphi forecasts have been widely used in project planning, to predict emerging technologies, and to determine the impact of new technologies where historical data is unavailable. The technique has also been used to determine future budget allocations, urban and regional planning, campus and curriculum development, educational technology, and medical planning, and to predict complex consumer behaviour (Zarnowitz, 1984; Kruuse, 1983; Wissema, 1982; Turner, 1981; Leblanc, Rigaud, and Schreiber, 1979; Connors, 1978; Johnson, 1976; Glenn, 1973; Amara and Salancik, 1972; Judd, 1972; Helmer, 1966).

The most distinguishing features of Delphi are its goal (to aggregate expert opinion about the future) and its procedure (iterated polling of experts with feedback of consensus opinion between polls). Several other techniques are widely used to collect expert opinion but are not strictly Delphi and should not be confused with it (Hill, 1982). For example, the traditional group meeting may be the most common approach to forecasting but is not a Delphic poll (Pokempner and Bailey, 1970). Group meetings usually involve pressure to conform, which the Delphi group structure is designed to avoid. They seldom require iterated polling and feedback procedures, and there may be no monitor group to structure the discussion. Opinion polls are similar to the Delphi mail survey in format. However, they are not designed to predict the future, but are more generally used to survey intentions (e.g. voter preferences). Developmental discussion groups are similar to Delphi because they are structured by a 'facilitator' who encourages minority opinion (Maier and Maier, 1957). However, the technique is usually used for problem-solving rather than forecasting, and quantitative feedback of the group's consensus may not be provided.

Other procedures are more easily confused with Delphi. Estimation–Talk–Estimation (ETE) meetings (Gustafson *et al.*, 1973) are very similar to Delphi because they require group estimations before and after group discussion of the issues. Like Delphi, discussion of dissensus is encouraged (Maier and Solem, 1952). However, ETE usually involves more face-to-face interaction among the panellists which is not the case in conventional Delphic polls (Dressler, 1972). Focus groups (Goldman, 1962) are commonly used to combine panellists' opinion on narrowly defined issues. They are often used for predicting consumer behaviour or changes in a market. Unlike Delphi, however, anonymous responding may not be encouraged and the group may not receive structured feedback. Role-playing is a group exercise in which the panellists act out a scenario. The panellists responses are therefore studied to predict how a person would behave in a 'real-life' situation. For example, groups may be asked to role-play opposing military strategies. Sometimes props are used to make the situation realistic. Feedback is available since the group can immediately evaluate the effect of its decisions and the resulting alterations in their opponents' strategies. Although role-playing has been used by the military to study the behaviour of strategists commanding armies in mock wars (Goldhamer and Speir, 1959), it has not been extensively used in technological forecasting (Busch, 1961; Cyert, March, and Starbuck, 1961). Moreover, the paradigm of role-playing differs from Delphi in that there is no attempt to force consensus of opinion prior to making a decision.

Regardless of the application, Delphi techniques can be roughly divided into three categories:

Conventional Delphi. Most applications of Delphi are a combination of a polling procedure and a conference. Responsibility for communication among the conference panellists is delegated to a smaller monitor team (Delbecq and Gustafson, 1975). Although experts are in the same physical location, anonymity is preserved because they are not face-to-face. The first round is unstructured. Panellists generate the scenarios and monitors summarize these into a single set. In round 2, the consolidated list of scenarios is returned to the panellists who estimate the date of occurrence for each event. The monitors then prepares a statistical summary of each scenario which usually includes the median date and the interquartile range of dates. A new survey is presented in round 3 along with the statistical summaries. Therefore, panellists are given at least one opportunity to re-evaluate their original answers based on examination of the group response. If their new ratings fall outside of the interquartile ranges, they are asked to provide reasons why they are correct and the group is wrong. In round 4, panellists are provided with a new statistical summary and a list of justifications for dissenting opinions prior to repolling with the same scenarios.

Paper-and-pencil Delphic polls. This is similar to a conventional Delphi although the poll is usually conducted by mail (e.g. Anderson *et al.*, 1981). After the first round, the survey results are analysed and shared with the experts, who are then asked to complete the survey again, this time knowing how they and their peers rated the scenarios before. The researcher typically determines the scenarios, often without the assistance of the panellists. Paper-and-pencil Delphis are especially relevant when the issues are well-defined. However, because the poll is usually conducted by mail, successive rounds may be delayed, and the final results may not be available for several months.

'Real-time' Delphi. This is an expert polling system whereby the results of successive rounds are immediately tallied and the respondents are presented with feedback by computer (Johansen and Schuyler, 1975). Opportunity for discussion may or may not be available since the panellists may be in different parts of the world during the Delphi. The advantages are that responding is anonymous, feedback to the panellists is immediate, and the final results are usually available at the end of the session.

VARIATIONS OF DELPHI

Philosophical Differences

Although theory development has been conspicuously absent from the literature on Delphi, the methodology and philosophical basis have been adequately documented and will be briefly described (Mitroff and Turoff, 1975; Helmer, 1967a, 1967b; Helmer and Rescher, 1959). Delphi philosophy has been heavily influenced by John Locke although other types of inquiry systems have appeared in the literature.

Lockean inquiries are based on the assumption that knowledge follows from data and that the accuracy of perception is highly correlated with consensus among the perceivers. The conference and paper-and-pencil Delphic poll are, perhaps, pure examples of Lockean systems in that perceptions of the future are gleaned entirely from the consensus of the individual panellists; it is assumed that the measure of consensus (variance of the panellists predictions) is an index of the accuracy of the prediction. However, this assumption has not been consistently validated (Armstrong, 1978).

The philosophy of Gottfried Wilhelm Leibnitz has also influenced some Delphi inquiries. The basic assumption of this approach is the reverse of the

Lockean inquiry. That is to say, knowledge exists independently of data and is analytic (Boring, 1950). Therefore, foresight is assumed to transcend data and effective modelling of the future depends upon the forecaster's ability to abstract relationships that may not be directly testable with the available data. The widely cited *Limits to Growth* (Meadows, 1972) is a good example of Leibnitzian inquiry since the model was derived prior to any data verification. Kane's (1973) model for cross-impact simulation (KSIM) also has Leibnitzian components because a model of a system is constructed by a panel of experts which is assumed to represent the system on purely logical grounds, independently of any data analytic component.

Inquiry systems based on Immanuel Kant's philosophy assume that knowledge is synthetic, that is, it has both theoretical and empirical components. Theoretical speculations about the future are useless without empirical verification. Likewise, purely empirical descriptions are equally inadequate if they do not lead to a unifying theory. Kantian inquiry systems are especially relevant when the goal is to integrate an area that is poorly structured or where there are several competing philosophies or potential means to an end. For example, the goal of cost–benefit analysis is to identify several different approaches to a problem and to evaluate each empirically or by simulation. By examining the various courses of action, it is assumed that one will emerge as the most feasible for future application.

Dialectic inquiries are based on the assumption that knowledge about the future emerges from the conflict of plan and counterplan. Opposing concepts are pitted against each other with the goal of producing a revised system that is best suited to the problem at hand. Dialectic systems are applicable to poorly structured situations in which there is no better tool than the opinion of experts, that is, the future is 99 per cent speculation, assumption, or opinion (Mason, 1969). Unlike the Lockean system, where validity of the forecast is measured by consensus, the dialectic method assumes that intense conflict will expose illogical arguments which may be camouflaged by consensus (Mitroff, 1971). The Policy Delphi may include dialectic features designed to produce plan-counterplan arguments concerning policy or resource allocation alternatives (Schnieder, 1972).

Application differences

Delphi applications can also be distinguished in terms of their purpose (Kendall, 1977). Although Delphi has been traditionally used to predict if or when an event will occur (Parenté *et al.*, 1984), other forecasting problems cannot be easily classified into 'if' and 'when'. For example, if one is relatively sure an event will occur (e.g. industrialization of space), then a 'how much' prediction may be relevant. In the same vein, one might wish to predict 'how good', e.g. quality of life (Dalkey, 1972).

The goal of Delphi may be to define alternative futures (Mitchell, Tydeman, and Georgiades, 1977; Vanston *et al.*, 1977; Adelson and Aroni, 1975; Sutherland, 1975). These Delphis are usually accompanied by a suggested plan of action either to implement or to avoid a certain future. In this case, we are not predicting 'if', 'when', 'how much', or 'how good'. Rather, the goal is to identify alternative scenarios along with corresponding action plans or fall-back positions. The purpose is to ensure that desirable scenarios occur or that plans are available in the event of disaster. For example, a Policy Delphi may be undertaken to anticipate liabilities associated with a new product or job function, then to generate protective policy statements for the company.

There are several procedural variations of Delphi (Martino, 1983). In the conventional Delphi, if the issues are well-defined, scenarios may be developed by the monitor team rather than by the panellists in round 1. Political and economic forecasts may be presented to the panellists along with the scenarios. This is especially useful in an industrial context where the experts are technical specialists who may not be cognizant of political or economic considerations. Panellists may be required to estimate dates of 'possible', 'likely', or 'virtually certain' occurrence of each event. Sometimes probability statements may be required indicating 10, 50, or 90 per cent certainty. Delphi has also been used with face-to-face group interaction. Panellists discuss the events and register their votes anonymously via electronic devices that feed into a small computer (called a 'consensor'). The computer immediately displays the distribution of votes on a television monitor. The consensor permits voting at any point in the discussion. Panellists can terminate the meeting when consensus has been reached.

CHARACTERISTIC DELPHI PHENOMENA

Perhaps the best research and development of the Delphi method was performed at the RAND Corporation in the 1960s (Dalkey, 1969; Helmer, 1964; Dalkey and Helmer, 1963). Unfortunately, most of these findings were presented in technical reports and were not widely cited until the 1970s. Although literally hundreds of practical applications of Delphi have since been published, few were designed to investigate the validity of the method itself. We will begin by describing the original research paradigm (Brown, Cochran, and Dalkey, 1969) to convey the context from which experimental conclusions were derived.

Many of the first studies used questions of the almanac sort (Dalkey, 1968), for example: 'How many million board feet of lumber were produced in the United States in 1962?'; 'What was the total tonnage, in millions shipped through the port of New York in 1962?'; 'What is the specified operational gross weight in pounds, of the Gemini capsule (exclusive of occupants)? This type of question was chosen because correct responses to them could be immediately verified. Also, subjects typically did not know the answers but had enough general information relevant to the answers so they could make an educated guess. After the initial estimation (and on subsequent rounds), each subject was informed of the median of the group's answers on the preceding round and/or the limits within which 50 per cent of the group's answers lay. The general procedure was repeated for several rounds with feedback and reassessment. A typical experiment would study thirty subjects, a control group of 15 who underwent the basic procedure, and an experimental group who performed some variant of it.

Individual first round answers for the experimental groups were lognormally distributed (Martino, 1970b). Consequently, most subsequent analyses were performed on logarithmic transformations of the data rather than on raw data *per se*. The range of answers was impressively large (often differing by a factor of 10 to the fourth power). The second-round repsonses indicated a decided shift toward the group median, that is, a convergence of answers toward the group's consensus (Helmer, 1964). Although the convergence was significant, the range of estimates was still large and the distribution was still best described as lognormal.

The most striking effect was that, on the opening round, there was a wide spread of answers. On succeeding rounds, the answers converged. However, there was never complete convergence even after three or more rounds. The tendency for individual panellists to change their answers was related to the distance of the answer from the median of the group. Those individuals whose answers were furthest from the central tendency were more likely to change their opinion on subsequent rounds. These individuals were labelled 'swingers'. A second type of panellist resisted changing their answers. These 'holdouts' were usually more confident of their answers although their predictions were typically less accurate than the median of the total group.

The group median tended to become more accurate with iteration. Specifically, about 2/3 of group medians shifted toward the correct answer on the second poll. However, the group median was a strong attraction for the swingers and they tended to change their answers in the direction of the median on later rounds, which decreased the variability. The fact that with iteration, accuracy of the group responses increased, and at the same time variability of the group responses decreased, revealed an inverse correlation between accuracy and variability of responses in the Delphi method.

Convergence of responses in progressive rounds could be predicted from how far away the panellists' answers were from the feedback median. The further away the answer, the more likely that change would occur, usually in the direction of the median. However, two centres of attraction were discovered: the group's median (M), and also the true answer (T). Some part of the decision to change one's mind in subsequent rounds was due to evaluation of information that had not been considered or digested during the first round. In general, controlled feedback was thought to improve accuracy so long as the pull of the M did not overshadow the pull of T. Indeed, in some experiments, additional facts were provided between the first and second round to enhance the reconsideration process. This manipulation caused significant improvements in accuracy (Dalkey, Brown, and Cochran, 1970b).

CAUTIONS IN THE USE OF DELPHI

Scientific evaluations of Delphi have been secondary to the use of the technique for answering practical questions. Consequently, well-controlled laboratory investigations are uncommon in the literature (Hill and Fowles, 1975). Whether or not the Delphi method produces accurate results has been especially difficult to evaluate because long-range scenarios are not easily verified (Linstone and Turoff, 1975). Frequently, some action was taken to avoid a predicted catastrophe or to actuate a desirable future. Although the scientific merits of Delphi have been discussed (Anderson, 1973), tests of competing theories have not been published. Only a handful of controlled studies on the effects of polling and feedback have been published (Parenté *et al.*, 1984; Riggs, 1983). In general, Delphi methods are quite popular, but they have not escaped the critic's eye. When viewed from the standards of psychological test development, severe problems have been noted (Sackman, 1974; Weaver, 1972, 1970).

Validity

Sackman argues that the Delphi technique simply measures a small sample of attitudes toward future events but seldom measures the events themselves. It then leaps from opinion to description of the future with no empirical verification of opinion. The assumption is that consensus will ensure accuracy of the projections. Again, it is difficult to demonstrate Delphi's validity because the outcomes may not occur for 10–20 years. In addition, forecasts are often worded in broad generalizations such as 'quality of life' or 'technological advances' that cannot be easily verified. Content validity is also a problem because it may be impossible to determine whether selected items that comprise the questionnaire represent a systematic sampling of key elements of the future.

Reliability

Sackman's critique of Delphi goes on to discuss considerations of test-item and test–retest reliability. Dalkey (1968) indicated increasing reliability of group medians that varied as a function of sample size. However, Sackman points out that this would be expected for purely statistical reasons since the standard error of measurement is known to vary inversely with the square root of the sample size. Martino (1970d) assessed the test-item reliability of Delphi by listing analogous items in independent studies that resulted in similar predictions. He also cited a high degree of consistency in McLoughlin's (1969) study where groups of experts provided independent forecasts for over 50 identical questionnaire items. However, Sackman points out that Martino did not report any correlation coefficients or descriptive statistics and, further, the 'high degree of consistency' also resulted in a 14-year spread of opinion for events that were expected to occur in 20 years. Thus, neither study can be interpreted as convincing evidence of test-item reliability.

Test–retest reliability refers to consistency of results obtained from repeated use of the same questionnaire. Presumably, similar results should be obtained if the questionnaire is reliable. This concept is crucial to the Delphi method because opinions about the future will change with the times, especially in an age of rapid technological advance. Reliability may also change with the composition of the panel. Sackman points out that no convincing tests of Delphi reliability are available in the literature, even for short-term forecasts. If Delphi methods yield unstable predictions in the short run, because of attitude fluctuations over time, then their value as a prognostic tool would be worthless in the long run.

Standards for the use of experts

Sackman goes on to point out that rarely are expert panels selected according to a premeditated sampling procedure. Indeed, with the exception of our own research (Anderson, Parenté, and Gordon, 1981), the authors have not found any published Delphic poll that has stated its specific standards for selection of panellists (e.g. college degree and so many years of experience). Dropout of participants between the first and second polling are seldom reported. Moreover, there is no body of literature that speaks to the issue of how best to define the composition of the panel. Often, these individuals may be a group of friends or, worse still, a special interest group with obvious bias.

The larger issue of whether or not it is necessary to use experts at all in Delphic polling has been examined. Armstrong (1978) surveyed the literature and found that although minimal expertise in a given field would improve the accuracy of problem solutions, clinical diagnosis, and economic forecasts, higher levels of expertise resulted in diminishing returns. This led to his popular quotation, 'Don't hire the best expert you can—or even close to the best. Hire the cheapest'. Welty (1974, 1972) also argues that using expert panellists is probably unnecessary to improve accuracy in Delphic polling. In summary, there are no published guidelines defining expertise, and no evidence that using prestigious experts improves Delphi accuracy.

Several rebuttals of Sackman's scathing critique have been published (Coats, 1975; Scheele, 1975; Goldschmidt, 1975). These authors pointed out that poorly designed instruments, inadequate sampling, and poor selection of respondents are not unique to Delphi methods but are common to mediocre research in every field. Moreover, Delphi was never intended to be used as a scientific tool nor to be considered a sicentific activity. It was developed to elicit opinion on issues that were difficult to analyse with scientific methods. The method itself was merely adopted to overcome the problems of the face-to-face conference format and to ensure airing of diverse views.

Linstone (1975) pointed out that Sackman's standards for evaluating Delphi were actually intended for psychological test development. They apply to personality questionnaires given to individuals and may not be applicable to instruments designed to elicit group opinion about the future. He admits that there are problems with Delphi applications but, these are the result of misunderstanding the technique and its intent. Linstone has categorized these problems into eight areas, many of which Sackman failed to mention. The value of Linstone's review is that it is not a critique *per se*. It provides guidelines for identifying common 'pitfalls' in future Delphi applications. Where possible, we have made suggestions for avoiding the problems that Linstone outlines.

Linstone notes a tendency of many panellists to discount the future. That is to say, some panellists fear the future and consequently, their predictions may not deviate from the established norm. Those that do are discounted or ignored. The problem is especially difficult when panellists with specialized expertise are used. For example, Linstone notes that after the Second World War, reciprocating engine experts predicted that the propeller aircraft would be standard up through the 1980s. Other military experts failed to see the advent of rocketry and predicted that manned bombers would remain the primary weapon system.

'The prediction urge' refers to a tendency to misinterpret the results of Delphic polls as patent statements such as 'event A will occur by year B' or 'there is a 75 per cent chance that event A will occur'. One of the strengths of the Delphi method is its ability to expose uncertainty. The prediction urge is detrimental because it tends to stress prediction and to discount uncertainty. Results that exhibit convergence of opinion are accepted whereas those that indicate wide divergence are considered unusable. To overcome the prediction urge, users of the Delphi method must be certain to qualify their results, perhaps avoid using probability estimates, and to stress interpretation of dissensus as well as the panellists' certainties.

Most panellists display a tendency towards simplistic judgment, ignoring the 'big picture'. For example, logical scenarios may be judged more likely to occur because the panellist can easily understand them. Illogical scenarios may be judged less likely because the panellist cannot conceive of the events easily. The English language exacerbates the problem because scenario statements often fail to communicate the complexities of hypothetical future events. Moreover, panellists usually have difficulty abstracting interactions among a system of variables, so they tend to make isolated predictions. One way to obviate the problem is to combine Delphi with a technique that forces the panellist to consider interacting events. Cross-impact analysis (discussed later) is a step in this direction.

The fact that experts may not provide accurate predictions is difficult to accept. However, experts may have a tendency to focus on the part (simplification urge) and to ignore the whole. Groups of experts, each knowledgeable about one aspect of a complex system, do not constitute expertise about the entire system. It may be argued that any technique used to elicit group judgments from experts systematically reproduces error. The problems of illusory expertise can be handled in several ways. First, the field of relevant experts must be adequately sampled with a systematic and well-documented procedure. Second, journals could require a statement of criteria for panellist selection in Delphi publications. In addition, researchers should discuss the dropout rate and resulting limitations to the results.

'Sloppy execution' refers to a vast array of problems resulting from poor interaction among the monitor team and the participants. Receiving a paper-and-pencil Delphic poll in the mail may give the impression of 'just another survey'. Excessive specification or vague statments reduces the information content of the scenarios, resulting in equally vague predictions. Reporting only statistical medians can cause excessive response bias towards the group's central tendency. Several steps can be taken to contain the problem. Salancik, Wenger, and Helfer (1971) provide guidelines for scenario-writing. The pole should be designed so that differing, or even opposing scenarios are apparent. When possible, written justifications should be provided, in addition to statistical feedback. Panellists must be made to feel that the task is important. Perhaps monetary incentives for correct predictions could be used to improve the amount of cognitive effort the panellists invest in the scenarios.

Bias towards optimism in short-range forecasts or pessimism in long-range studies is a common occurrence in Delphi (Martino, 1970c). In the long run, panellists may fail to envision technological advances that will overcome seemingly unsolvable problems. In the short term, panellists discount the magnitude of stumbling blocks that seem like trivial problems when a technology is about to emerge. Panellists should be made aware of the tendency before the first poll. Cross-impact analysis should be used to force panellists to attend to the interactions among the different events in the system. It may also be possible to predict and correct for optimism/pessimism bias using well-developed theories of adaptation level (Helson, 1964).

The tendency to misuse a trendy or faddish technique is also a problem for Delphi applications. Delphi tends to 'oversell' itself leading some corporations to adopt the technique because they assume that it is superior to existing methods (e.g. the group meeting). Individuals in the organization may not accept the fact that consensus-based goals or policies do not coincide with their own. They may only accept Delphi outcomes that reflect the consensus of their own 'bailiwick'. In many institutions, overselling Delphi may create more problems than it solves. As a first step, the organization must decide if they need a Delphi inquiry system and can accept its results.

False feedback can distort responding on subsequent rounds (Scheibe, Skutsch, and Schofer (1975). Therefore, seemingly valid results could be used for deception or manipulative purpose, or to sway legislative opinion prior to a major governmental decision. Perhaps the only way around this problem is to insist that the panellists take an active role in the monitoring and staff activities. The use of computers for 'real-time' Delphis may provide some solution to the problem so long as computer programs are thoroughly checked before the Delphi begins.

Evaluation

We assert that the Delphi technique is a valuable technological forecasting tool despite seemingly devastating criticisms. Problems with Delphi procedures are not unsolvable; it would be premature to throw out the oracle with the holy water. The intent and purpose of Delphi are frequently misunderstood. Delphi was designed as a tool to overcome the biasing effects of face-to-face discussion. It was never proposed as a scientific activity and it would be inappropriate to evaluate it with strict scientific criteria. A major criticism of Delphi is that its predictions are difficult to test because they are long-range (e.g. 20 years or more). However, it is unreasonable to prejudge the efficacy of Delphi just because we must wait to validate its predictions. Indeed, we may not have to wait much longer since many long-range forecasts of the 1950s and 1960s could be evaluated before the end of the decade.

A purely scientific evaluation of Delphi fails to provide reasonable alternatives for long-range forecasting. To reiterate, Delphi may be the only way to predict emerging technologies when there is no empirical database. Even if conventional quantitative methods could be used in lieu of Delphi, there is little evidence that these procedures provide more accurate long-range forecasts.

THE QUESTION OF ACCURACY: THEORY AND DATA

Although probabilistic, and axiomatic explanations of Delphi have been proposed, the most widely accepted is 'the theory of errors' (Dalkey, 1975). The basic assumption of the theory is that N heads are better than one. This principle has been useful for centuries. Juries, councils, task forces

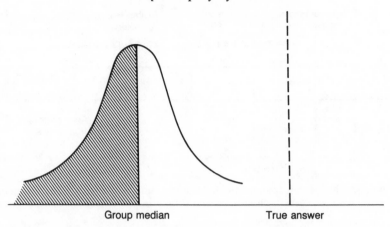

Figure 1. The group median is more accurate than half of the group

all depend on it. Likewise, the Delphi method assumes that the aggregate response will reflect the collective cognition of the group, thus providing a forecast that is generally superior to that of most individuals in the group (Loye, 1978). The median response of the group (M) will be at least as close to the true answer as one-half of the group (Figure 1). Moreover, if the range of individual answers includes the true answer, then M will be more accurate than more than half of the group (Figure 2). Therefore, regardless of where the true answer falls, the median response of the group will be more accurate than a majority of individual panellists. However, it may not be more

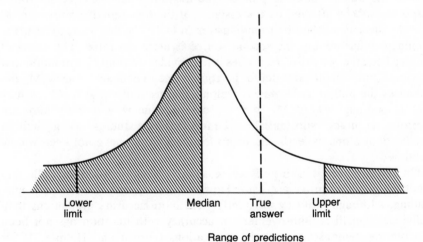

Figure 2. The range of estimates contains the true answer. The group estimate is more accurate than a majority of panellists

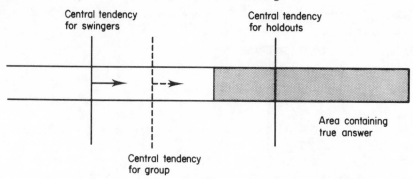

Figure 3. Change in responding with iterated polling and feedback for swingers, holdouts, and total group

accurate than the most accurate panellist. Dalkey (1975) has outlined the mathematics of this phenomenon. Although he has labelled it a 'theory of errors', he describes it as more of an analogy than a formal theory.

The reasons why accuracy would improve with iterated polling and feedback have not been well defined. Improvement with iteration is thought to result from the relationship between the 'swingers' and the 'holdouts' outlined in Figure 3. It is clear from the diagram that the mean of the group will usually fall between the mean of the holdouts and swingers. The holdouts are assumed to be more accurate than the swingers and the total group on the first round. With iteration, however, the mean of the swingers moves toward the mean of the total group. Two forces operate in the convergence process, the pull of the median and the pull of true answer. Change in second round responses will be affected by the distance of the first-round answer from M plus the distance of the first round answer from T. The first source exerts the dominant influence but the second source is more desirable. The effect of feeding back the panellists' responses is to provide additional information that may not have been considered in round one. Feedback damps M and enhances the pull of T. However, Delphis that use only M as feedback may bias responding toward M. In these cases, reducing variability may not improve accuracy substantially. Unfortunately, studies using written justifications alone as feedback, or no feedback at all, have not been widely published.

On the surface, it is intuitively reasonable that iteration of polls and feedback would improve accuracy. However, the appeal of intuition is misleading. Although groups consistently yield more accurate predictions than individual panellists, improvement in accuracy with iteration has not been consistently demonstrated. Early publications (Brown and Helmer, 1964; Dalkey and Brown, 1971), noted that convergence of responses correlated with a more accurate group prediction. However, Parenté *et al.* (1984) found no consistent relation between accuracy and variability of responses in a two-round Delphi poll. Parenté *et al.* (1984), experimentally separated the effects of feedback and iteration on accuracy. One group of 50 college students answered a poll which was later given again along with feedback on their previous responses. A second group answered a poll which was later given again with no feedback. Two types of accuracy were investigated, 'if' accuracy—how accurate the groups were in predicting whether or not the events would occur—and 'when' accuracy—how accurate a group was in predicting the time courses for the events. Relative to individual panellists, the group 'if' and 'when' predictions were significantly more accurate. Significant improvement in 'when' accuracy occurred over rounds. However, the result was due to iteration rather than feedback. Although both groups' 'if' accuracy was significantly better than chance (70 per cent correct predictions), it was unaffected by iteration or feedback. Similar results have been reported by Boje and Murnighan (1982). In general, these results support the 'theory of errors'; they do not, however, indicate that feedback facilitates Delphi accuracy.

Earlier research concerning the accuracy/feedback issue produced mixed results. Hample and Hilpert (1975) found that with no feedback, subsequent rounds were more accurate on 47 per cent of comparisons. With feedback this percentage jumped to 58 per cent. Best (1974) reported a slight gain in accuracy when feedback was provided in a two-question study. Similar results were reported by Jolson and Rossow (1971). However, a slight decrease in accuracy was reported by Gustafson *et al.* (1973). Although feedback may improve accuracy slightly, it is questionable whether the benefits of repeated polling outweight the costs. It is also possible that feedback can reduce accuracy. Feedback is probably most useful when the issues are well defined and the panellists or group can routinely evaluate the accuracy of their predictions (Armstrong, 1978).

In several of Dalkey's experiments, subjects were asked to rate either their confidence in their responses or their perceived competence (Dalkey, Brown, and Cochran, 1970a). The goal was to identify the most knowledgeable individuals by their self-ratings. Intuitively, this subgroup would be more accurate than the total group. The correlation between accuracy and confidence was variable among the groups, ranging from 0.07 to 0.65. Nevertheless, the authors concluded that there was an overall 'meaningful' relationship. Dalkey and Brown (1971), using 'real-world' scenarios, found that self-ratings were significantly correlated with accuracy. In addition, Best (1974) asked university faculty members to estimate demand for a business magazine and also to estimate current student enrollment in their college of business. This study also revealed a significant relationship between accuracy and self-rated expertise. Similar results were reported by Jolson and Rossow (1971). Accuracy of short-range forecasts of weather bureau forecasters are significantly correlated with self-rated expertise (Williams, 1951). However, Winkler (1971) found little relation between self-ratings and accuracy in predictions of football scores. Results of earlier studies indicate either null findings or small positive relations (Holtzman and Sells, 1954; Kaplan, Skogstad, and Girshick, 1950; Thorndike, 1938).

Garretson (1984) systematically evaluated the relationship among self-ratings, accuracy, and variability in short-term Delphic polling. Fifty groups of college students (10 per group) responded to 20 scenarios describing possible outcomes of events of public interest. Timely scenarios such as 'The United States invades Grenada?' were used. These events had not yet occurred but could be evaluated within the succeeding 2 months. Beneath each scenario was a space for subjects to check whether or not they thought the event would occur within 60 days from the time of the test. Under this was a 60-day time scale on which subjects marked when they thought the scenarios would occur (see also Parenté *et al.*, 1984). Subjects were instructed to decide whether they thought the scenario would occur within the 60-day period. If so, they were to check off the approximate date of occurrence along the 2-month time line.

Half the groups were asked to predict all scenarios regardless of how much they felt they knew about the topic. The other groups were told to respond only if they felt competent to make an educated guess, otherwise, not to respond.

Both group's 'if' accuracy was significantly better than chance. The group's 'if' and 'when' predictions were significantly more accurate than the average individual panellists. However, it was assumed that instructing certain groups to select scenarios on the basis of their perceived knowledge about the events would enhance accuracy. Actually, the reverse effect was obtained. Those groups who were forced to respond to all of the scenarios were significantly more accurate in their predictions of time course. That is, instructions to selectively predict the scenarios reduced 'when' accuracy. There was no difference between the groups with respect to probability of occurrence predictions ('if'). It should also be noted that Garretson (1984) did not find a significant relation between the variability of the groups' responses and either type of accuracy.

Some additional research findings are noteworthy. The role of sex in determining the group accuracy was also evaluated in Dalkey's (1969) study. In general, women were less accurate than men and were also more likely to change their responses than men. Women majoring in the physical and biological sciences were more accurate than those majoring in the social sciences and humanities. However, the reverse was true for men, contrary to expectation. It was also discovered that first impressions were more accurate than lengthy considerations. The quickest responses were usually the most accurate. This effect was attributed to the tendency of some subjects to over-refine their answers or to over-consider the issues. Curiously, the intelligence level of the group members was unrelated to accuracy in Dalkey's studies; however, Loye (1980) indicated that certain personality factors are related to prediction accuracy.

Hogath (1978) has answered the question, 'How many experts should be included in the panel?', in order to maximize accuracy. Under a wide range of circumstances, the most accurate forecasts will be obtained when the inter-correlation of panellists' opinions is higher than 0.30, and the average validity of the panellists does not exceed the mean correlation. Validity is somewhat difficult to define. Ideally, it is computed as a correlation between the individual panellist's past predictions and verified outcomes (i.e. their track record for accuracy). In the absence of this information, presumably some measure of expertise could be substituted. Adding members to the panels will improve accuracy so long as this relationship holds. However, regardless of how many participants are included, accuracy may decrease if the panel's mean validity exceeds its consensus.

Loye (1983) proposed a neuropsychological model of decision-making in forecasting that is applicable to the problem of selecting Delphi panellists. Drawing heavily on Luria's (1973, 1966) theory of functional brain systems, Loye asserts that the hemispheres of the brain analyse the future differently. The left hemisphere is logical. It processes serial, linear, temporal, and verbal characteristics of information. The right hemisphere is responsible for visual/spatial processing. It may be described as holistic, intuitive, analogic, and subjective. The forebrain is responsible for integrating these two analytic sources and evaluating the consequences of future action. When the problem involves predicting the future, the two hemispheres may present either a consensus or conflict prediction to the mediating forebrain. To the extent that one side of the brain dominates, then the panellist's predictions are biased by their logic (left) or intuition (right). Loye has shown that the most accurate forecasters depend on the use of both right- and left-brain functions. He has developed a Hemispheric Consensus Prediction Profile test to measure hemispheric dominance. His data show that individuals whose scores indicate mixed dominance are significantly better at foreign affairs and economics predictions relative to right- or left-brain-dominant panellists.

Evaluation

The undeniable advantage of the Delphi inquiry is that group's predictions will be right significantly more often than they are wrong. In practically all studies we have reviewed, Delphi group predictions were more accurate than chance and/or individual panellists' predictions. However, the use of iteration and feedback procedures to improve accuracy should be investigated further since the underlying assumption (consensus is related to accuracy) has not been consistently verified. Although modified polling and feedback procedures have been shown to significantly increase Delphi accuracy (Ford, 1975), in general, there is a dearth of well-controlled experimentation to determine effective variations of the Delphi method.

Using self-ratings to isolate expert opinion is of questionable utility. It is probably safe to say that self-ratings are useful for screening panellists to eliminate those with limited knowledge. Conventional intelligence measures are probably not useful measures of expertise. However, the panellist's track record of accuracy on previous polls is an obvious selection criteria that has not been systematically investigated. Significant improvement in Delphi accuracy may result if neuropsychological screening tests are used to select 'mixed dominant' panellists or panels with a balance of left- and right-hemisphere-dominant participants.

THE FUTURE OF DELPHI

The role of the computer

Computerized conferencing is a system of communication in which panellists can use a computer terminal to give their opinions on a topic and read those of other panellists. In essence, it is the typewriter version of the telephone conversation with several extension terminals. When combined with the Delphi technique, the qualities of anonymity and controlled opinion feedback are preserved by asking the panellist to provide code names. The computer keeps track of the discussion comments and the group's predictions. The system is 'real-time' because simultaneous human interaction is facilitated by electronic interface. When the system is shut off, the final polling, data analysis, and perhaps, the interpretation of results, can be immediately available. Aside from obvious speed and accuracy considerations, there are additional advantages that the computer conference Delphi has over paper-and-pencil polls or traditional Delphis (Johansen and Schuyler, 1975).

Computer conferencing allows panellists to speak or listen when they wish. No one person can dominate the conversation as would be true with an extended phone communication system where only one person could speak at a time. Participants can read the wealth of input at their own speed. Moreover, since the computer stores the discussion, participants do not have to become involved concurrently. Real-time Delphis are usually terminated when the computer is turned off; however, some systems may be ongoing. Participants can choose a convenient time to go to the terminal, review the statistical summary and written opinions, then respond with their own comments (Rauch and Randolf, 1979).

Linstone and Turoff (1975) have pointed out several additional advantages of computer conferencing that would be available with sophisticated systems.

The computer may establish a common discussion file which permits each panellist to develop or expand upon a portion of the discussion (e.g. a subset of scenarios). The computer can keep track of the justifications for the various scenario votes so that panellists can review those from other individuals or groups. The computer may also be programmed to accept conditional messages. These are: (1) private messages to only one individual or to a subgroup at the conference; (2) messages that do not enter the discussion until a specified future date and time; (3) messages that do not enter unless someone else writes a message that contains a certain key word; (4) messages that enter anonymously. The computer can also chart and present feedback of responses in a variety of different ways, rapidly.

The computerized Delphi conference is an attractive alternative to conventional Delphis when time is an issue, the cost of assembling panellists would be prohibitive, frequent meetings would be necessary, or the issues are complex and would require study and contemplation before meaningful group opinion could be obtained. It may also be used when large groups are surveyed. It is desirable when the issues generate heated debate and strict anonymity is necessary to promote unbiased discussion. However, computer conferencing is not without problems. Computer systems may be less useful to some panellists (e.g. the blind or those who cannot type, etc.). It may be expensive to implement a real-time system in most companies, or the costs may outweigh the benefits. The system's feedback could be tampered with to produce bias. Such systems are subject to 'crashes' and other electronic inconveniences that may discourage their use. At the present time, the potential of the computer for automating the Delphic polling process is the most attractive characteristic of computer conferencing. However, it is unlikely that shortcomings in the theory and development of the Delphi method are going to be solved by computer conferencing. Indeed, the introduction of an electronic medium into the Delphi method may create unforeseen problems not unlike those that emerged when the discipline of psychology began doing personality testing by computer (Canoune and Leyhe, 1985).

Interfacing qualitative and quantitative forecasting

Cross-impact analysis is not a Delphi Method *per se*, but a technique designed to determine the underlying relations among possible future events (Kane, 1973; Dalkey, 1975; Turoff, 1975). The initial steps in a cross-impact analysis involve identifying the variables that determine the future, then formulating a table of interrelations among them. At this stage, the Delphi method may be used to aggregate anonymous input concerning the variables and their probabilities. The term 'interrelation' refers to the increase or decrease in the likelihood of occurrence for a future event produced by the occurrence or non-occurrence of all predecessor events in the set. However, the task of evaluating the implications of these interactions rapidly gets out of hand, and some computational aid (e.g. cross-impact analysis) is necessary to organize the large number of interdependencies.

Most cross-impact models have four distinct phases. Again, the Delphi method may be used to facilitate the first 2 phases. (1) preliminary identification of relevant variables plus estimating the probability that these events would occur during the time period being investigated, (2) estimating the interdependency among the events (i.e. a quantitative description of the effect of the occurrence, or non-occurrence, of one event on the likelihood of occurrence of each of the others in the set), (3) some form of mathematical–statistical manipulation whereby the probability of each event in the system is modified in terms of the number and magnitude of other impacting events in the system, (4) re-estimating the probability of future occurrence for the events in the system. These final probabilities represent the average likelihood of occurrence for each event considering the accumulated impacts of the other events in the set.

During the first phase, the initial probabilities and impact weights may be collected by the Delphi technique (Enzer, 1971). A range of opinion can therefore be used to estimate the uncertainty of the variables' impact. Judges may also be asked to rate the importance of each event before cross-impact analysis is applied. This combination of Delphi panel ratings and mathematical analysis is especially useful for identifying sensitive events. Sensitive means that the event can be modified by indirect action (e.g. manipulating other variables in the system). Likewise, the analysis also identifies events that are likely to be insensitive to the others in the set, thereby necessitating direct action if they are to be strongly influenced.

A novel variation of cross-impact analysis has been proposed by Myers (1984) and Gur (1979). It is essentially the reverse of the KSIM procedure proposed by Kane (1973). Rather than relying on panels of experts to develop impact matrices that are subsequently used to predict the future, this technique analyses empirical time-series data, then derives impact matrices that are capable of reproducing the original measurements. Myers has developed a computer program to perform the calculations. The program may yield several matrices that can mathematically reproduce the original measurements. However, some of the impact relations may be logically impossible. Myers suggests a modified Delphi procedure to decide which of the alternative matrices is the most feasible explanation of the system.

The major advantage of cross-impact analysis is its focus on understanding a system of variables holistically and dynamically. It attempts to organize data describing a large number of possible outcomes so that a relatively small number of inputs are sufficient to account for the behaviour of the system. The technique also forces the researcher (or Delphi panel) to discern reasons why certain changes are likely to occur. Finally, once a satisfactory impact table is generated, 'what-would-happen-if' questions can be easily evaluated by changing the impact values and noting the effect of the change on the entire system.

Suggestions for future applications of Delphi

How can the Delphi method be best used? In light of the considerations presented in this chapter, we suggest the following guidelines (see also Martino, 1983; Jillson, 1975). The researcher should keep in mind, however, that applications of Delphi will differ greatly in terms of their intent and purpose. All of our suggestions may not be appropriate for variations of Delphi.

Selection of panellists

(1) Criteria for inclusion of panellists in Delphi studies should be clearly stated (e.g. educational level, years of experience, and cross-disciplinary experience). The researcher should remember that using prominent experts may not increase accuracy. It will be necessary, however, to use panellists who are capable of understanding the issues and making educated guesses. Self-ratings may be useful for screening out uninformed panellists but should not be relied on to produce high levels of accuracy.

(2) The method of sampling panellists should be clearly stated. The goal should be to define the population of individuals most likely to affect change in the scenarios and then to construct a representative sample of panellists composed of members from each cohort.

(3) There is no upper limit on the panel size so long as the participants are adequately sampled. At a minimum however, the panel should be composed of 10 participants after dropout.

(4) Agreement to serve on the panel should be obtained before the poll begins. If the scenarios are simply mailed to a list of prospective panellists, the moderator may not get enough panellists and control of sampling will be severely limited.

Formulation of scenarios

(1) The content validity of the scenarios (i.e. the ability of the poll to adequately sample the issues) is as important as the representativeness of the sample. Perhaps the best way to ensure content validity is to adequately survey the literature (and experts) prior to developing a tentative list of relevant scenarios. For large paper-and-pencil Delphi

surveys, preliminary polling of panellists to clarify wording of the scenarios or to generate additional scenarios prior to constructing the final poll is highly recommended.

(2) Scenario statements should be no longer than 20 words and should be stated in such a way that they can be easily verified (e.g. Grain sales to the Soviet Union will increase by 50 per cent by 1990). Excessive use of jargon should be avoided. Phrases such as 'in widespread use', 'becomes a reality', 'normal', 'generally available', should be avoided.

(3) Twenty-five scenarios should be considered the upper limit. Alternative forms of the polling instrument should be constructed with different orderings of scenario statements to eliminate fatigue effects for the latter items (Huckfeldt and Judd, 1974).

(4) The polling questionnaire should be constructed for the convenience of the panellist. Check-the-box or fill-in-the-blank statements are preferred. Instructions should be short and, preferably, printed at the top of the questionnaire for easy reference while filling out the poll.

(5) Compound statements of the form, 'Method X achieves capacity Y by the year _____', should be avoided since panellists may believe that Y will be achieved but not necessarily by X.

(6) When the purpose of the Delphi is to generate scenarios, instructions to the panellists should include examples of well-written and poorly written scenarios.

Execution

(1) There is no one best way to execute a Delphi inquiry. If speed is an issue, then the traditional or computer conference methods are most appropriate. If cost is an issue, then the paper-and-pencil method is preferable.

(2) Regardless of the approach, the principle of anonymity must be ensured and expression of dissenting opinion must be encouraged. Moderators must avoid injecting their opinions into the feedback.

(3) It is not clear whether the gains in accuracy that result from iteration of polls with feedback are larger than one might get by adding additional panellists rather than adding rounds. The decision to iterate polls will be affected by factors such as increases in the non-response rate that may occur on the second and third rounds. In many cases, the cost of repeating the poll will outweigh the benefits of reduced error on the latter polls. If feedback is provided, the researcher should consider feeding back written justifications and/or the range of estimates along with the group medians.

(4) Self-ratings may be used to screen outlying panellists who admit total lack of knowledge on the topic. However, they should not be used to define expert panels.

(5) Panellists should be acquainted with the various problems of Delphi methodology (e.g. Linstone's pitfalls) prior to filling out the poll, and encouraged to avoid them. If the poll is iterated, it is especially important that panellists understand the purpose of successive rounds and how to interpret feedback.

Reporting results

(1) Delphi publications should include a statement concerning the content validity of the scenarios and a discussion of the sampling procedure for panellists. In general, the goal should be to provide all necessary information for systematic replication of the findings.
(2) Presentation of response distributions for each scenario is desirable. Discussion of the results should focus upon two types of findings: (a) those scenarios for which there was consensus across groups, and (b) those scenarios on which there was lack of agreement among the panellists.
(3) Short-range forecasts tend to be optimistic and long-range tend to be pessimistic (Martino, 1970c). The range of estimation may also vary as a function of the remoteness of the estimate (Asher, 1979). It may be necessary to adjust the estimates accordingly.
(4) Because of a tendency to oversimplify predictions, interpretation of isolated scenarios should be avoided. If possible, a clustering procedure such as multidimensional scaling (Carroll and Wish, 1975) should be used to group the scenarios.

REFERENCES

Adelson, M. and Aroni, S. (1975) 'Differential images of the future', in H. Linstone and M. Turoff (eds.), *The Delphi Method: Techniques and Applications*, London: Addison-Wesley, pp. 433–462.
Amara, R. C. and Salancik, G. R. (1972) 'Forecasting: from conjectural art toward science', *Technological Forecasting and Social Change*, 3, 420–426.
Anderson, G. (1973) 'Methods in futures studies: a view from the theory of science', *Technological Forecasting and Social Change*, 5, 305–320.
Anderson, J. K., Parenté, F. J. and Gordon, C. (1981) 'A forecast of the future for the mental health profession', *American Psychologist*, 36, 845–855.
Armstrong, J. S. (1978) *Long-range Planning: From Crystal Ball to Computer*, New York: Wiley.
Asher, W. (1979) *Forecasting: An Appraisal for Policy-Makers and Planners*, Baltimore: The Johns-Hopkins Press.
Balachandra, R. (1980) 'Technological forecasting—who does it and how useful is it?', *Technological Forecasting and Social Change*, 1, 75–85.
Balachandra, R. (1980) 'Perceived usefulness of technological forecasting techniques', *Technological Forecasting and Social Change*, 2, 155–160.
Best, R. J. (1974) 'An experiment in Delphi estimation in marketing decision making', *Journal of Marketing Research*, 11, 448–452.

Boje, D. M. and Murnighan, J. K. (1982) 'Group confidence pressures in iterative decisions', *Management Science*, **28**, 1187–1196.

Boring, E. (1950) *A History of Experimental Psychology*, New York: Appleton-Century-Crofts.

Brockhoff, K. (1984) 'Forecasting quality and information', *Journal of Forecasting*, **3**, (4), 417–428.

Brown, B. (1968) 'The delphi process: a methodology used for elicitation of opinions of experts', The RAND Corporation, P-3925.

Brown, B., Cochran, S. and Dalkey, N. C. (1969) 'The Delphi Method II: structure of experiments', The RAND Corporation, RM-5967-PR.

Brown, B. and Helmer, O. (1964) 'Improving the reliability of estimates obtained from the consensus of experts', The RAND Corporation, P-2986.

Busch, G. A. (1961) 'Prudent manager forecasting', *Harvard Business Review*, **39**, 57–64.

Canoune, H. L. and Leyhe, E. W. (1985) 'Human versus computer interviewing', *Journal of Personality Assessment*, **49**(1), 103–106.

Carroll, J. D. and Wish, M. (1975) 'Multidimensional scaling: models, methods, and relations to Delphi', in H. Linstone and M. Turoff (eds.), *The Delphi Method: Techniques and Applications*, London: Addison-Wesley, pp. 402–431.

Chaffin, W. W. and Talley, W. K. (1980) 'Individual stability in Delphi studies', *Technological Forecasting and Social Change*, **16**, 67–73.

Coats, J. F. (1975) 'In defense of Delphi: a review of delphi assessment, expert opinion, forecasting and group process by H. Sackman', *Technological Forecasting and Social Change*, **7**, 193–194.

Connors, E. T. (1978) 'Technological forecasting—an overview for educators', *Educational Technology*, **8**(2), 32–35.

Cyert, R. M., March, J. G. and Starbuck, W. H. (1961) 'Two experiments on bias and conflict in organizational estimation', *Management Science*, **7**, 254–264.

Dajani, J. S., Sincoff, M. Z. and Talley, W. K. (1979) 'Stability and agreement criteria for the termination of Delphi studies', *Technological Forecasting and Social Change*, **13**, 83–90.

Dalkey, N. C. (1967) 'Delphi', The RAND Corporation, P-3704.

Dalkey, N. C. (1968) 'Predicting the future', The RAND Corporation, P-3948.

Dalkey, N. C. (1969) 'The Delphi Method: An experimental study of group opinion', The RAND Corporation, RM-5888-PR.

Dalkey, N. C. (1972). *Studies in the Quality of Life: Delphi and Decision Making*, Lexington, Mass.: Lexington Books.

Dalkey, N. C. (1975) 'Toward a theory of group estimation', in H. Linstone and M. Turoff (eds.), *The Delphi Method: Techniques and Applications*, London: Addison-Wesley, pp. 236–261.

Dalkey, N. C. and Brown, B. (1971) 'Comparison of group judgement techniques with short-range predictions and almanac questions', The RAND Corporation, R-678-ARPA.

Dalkey, N. C. and Helmer, O. (1963) 'An experimental application of the Delphi Method to the use of experts', *Management Science*, **9**, 458–467.

Dalkey, N., Brown, B. and Cochran, S. (1970a) 'The Delphi Method III: Use of self-ratings to improve group estimates', *Technological Forecasting*, **1**, 283–291.

Dalkey, N. C., Brown, B. and Cochran, S. W. (1970b) 'The Delphi Method IV: effect of percentile feedback and feed-in of relevant facts', The RAND Corporation, RM-6118-PR.

Delbecq, A. L. and Gustafson, D. H. (1975) *Group Techniques For Project Planning: A Guide to Nominal Group and Delphi Processes*, Glenview, Ill.: Scott Foresman.

Dressler, F. F. S. (1972) 'Subjective methodology in forecasting', *Technological Forecasting and Social Change*, 3, 427–439.

Enzer, S. (1971) 'Delphi and cross-impact techniques: an effective combination for systematic futures analysis', *Futures*, March, 48–61.

Ford, D. A. (1975) 'Shang inquiry as an alternative to Delphi: some experimental findings', *Technological Forecasting and Social Change*, 7, 139–164.

Garretson, G. (1984) 'Relationship between delphi accuracy, variability, and self-ratings of group predictions', *Cognition, Artificial Intelligence, and Simulation Monographs*, (1)10, State University of Maryland—Towson, Towson, Md. 21204.

Glenn, J. (1973) 'Forecasting techniques as teaching methods', *Technological Forecasting and Social Change*, 5, 95–102.

Goldhamer, H. and Speir, H. (1959) 'Some observations of political gaming', *World Politics*, 12, 71–83.

Goldman, A. E. (1962) 'The group in-depth interview', *Journal of Marketing*, 26, 61–68.

Goldschmidt, P. G. (1975) 'Scientific inquiry or political critique?: remarks on Delphi assessment, expert opinion, forecasting, and group process by H. Sackman', *Technological Forecasting and Social Change*, 7, 195–213.

Gur, Y. (1979) 'An extension of structural modeling', *Technological Forecasting and Social Change*, 14, 399–408.

Gustafson, D. H., Shukla, R. K., Delbecq, A. and Walster, G. W. (1973) 'A comparison study of differences in subjective likelihood estimates made by individuals, interacting groups, Delphi groups, and nominal groups', *Organizational Behaviour and Human Performance*, 9, 280–291.

Hample, D. J. and Hilpert, F. P. (1975) 'A symmetry effect in delphi feedback', paper presented at the International Communication Association convention, Chicago.

Helmer, O. (1964) 'Convergence of expert consensus through feedback', The RAND Corporation, P-2973.

Helmer, O. (1966) 'The use of the delphi technique in problems of educational innovations', The RAND Corporation, P-3499.

Helmer, O. (1967a) 'Analysis of the future: The Delphi Method', The RAND Corporation, P-3558.

Helmer, O. (1967b) 'Systematic use of expert opinions', The RAND Corporation, P-3821.

Helmer, O. and Rescher, N. (1959) 'On the epistemology of the inexact sciences', *Management Science*, 6, 25–52.

Helson, H. (1964) *Adaptation Level Theory*, New York: Harper & Row.

Hill, G. W. (1982) 'Group versus individual performance: are $N + 1$ heads better than one?', *Psychological Bulletin*, 91(3), 517–539.

Hill, K. Q. and Fowles, J. (1975) 'The methodological worth of the Delphi forecasting technique', *Technological Forecasting and Social Change*, 7, 179–192.

Hogarth, R. M. (1978) 'A note on aggregating opinions', *Organizational Behavior and Human Performance*, 21, 40–46.

Holtzman, W. H. and Sells, S. B. (1954) 'Prediction of flying success by clinical analysis of test protocols', *Journal of Abnormal and Social Psychology*, 49, 459–490.

Huckfeldt, V. E. and Judd, R. C. (1974) 'Issues in large scale Delphi studies', *Technological Forecasting and Social Change*, 6, 75–88.

Jillson, I. A. (1975) 'Developing guidelines for the Delphi Method', *Technological Forecasting and Social Change*, 7, 211–222.

Johnson, J. L. (1976) 'A ten-year Delphi forecast in the electronics industry', *Management Review*, 65(8), 45–55.

Johansen, R. and Schuyler, J. (1975) 'Computerized conferencing in an educational system: A short-range scenario', in H. Linstone and M. Turoff (eds.), *The Delphi Method: Techniques and Applications*, London: Addison-Wesley, pp. 550–562.

Jolson, M. A. and Rossow, G. (1971) 'The Delphi process in marketing decision making', *Journal of Marketing Research*, **8**, 443–448.

Judd, R. C. (1972) 'Delphi in Educational Planning', *Technological Forecasting and Social Change*, **4**, 173–486.

Kane, J. (1973) 'A primer for a new cross-impact language', *Technological Forecasting and Social Change*, **5**, 95–102.

Kaplan, A., Skogstad, A. L. and Girshick, M. A. (1950) 'The prediction of social and technological events', *Public Opinion Quarterly*, **14**(1), 13–110.

Kendall, J. (1977) 'Variations of Delphi', *Technological Forecasting and Social Change*, **4**, 75–85.

Kruuse, P. (1983) 'Utilization of Delphi methods for university planning', *Technological Forecasting and Social Change*, **24**, 269–275.

Leblanc, D., Rigaud, M. R. and Schreiber, H. R. (1979) 'Technological forecasting and planning exercises in engineering curricula', *Technological Forecasting and Social Change*, **14**(2), 153–168.

Linstone, H. (1975) 'Eight basic pitfalls: a checklist, in H. Linstone and M. Turoff (eds.), *The Delphi Method: Techniques and Applications*, London: Addison-Wesley, pp. 573–586.

Linstone, H. and Turoff, M. (1975) *The Delphi Method: Techniques and Applications*, London: Addison-Wesley.

Loye, D. (1978) *The Knowable Future: A Psychology of Forecasting and Prophecy*, New York: Wiley.

Loye, D. (1980) 'Personality and prediction', *Technological Forecasting and Social Change*, **16**, 93–104.

Loye, D. (1983) 'The brain, the mind, and the future', *Technological Forecasting and Social Change*, **23**, 267–280.

Luria, A. R. (1966) *Higher Cortical Functions in Man*, New York: Basic Books.

Luria, A. R. (1973) *The Working Brain*, New York: Basic Books.

Maier, N. R. F. and Maier, R. A. (1957) 'An experimental test of the effects of developmental versus free discussions on the quality of group discussion', *Journal of Applied Psychology*, **41**, 320–323.

Maier, N. R. F. and Solem, A. R. (1952) 'The contribution of a discussion leader to the quality of group thinking: The effective use of minority opinions', *Human Relations*, **5**, 277–288.

Martino, J. (1970a) 'The precision of Delphi estimates', *Technological Forecasting and Social Change*, **1**, 293–299.

Martino, J. (1970b) 'The lognormality of Delphi estimates', *Technological Forecasting*, **1**, 355–358.

Martino, J. (1970c) 'The optimism/pessimism consistency of Delphi panelists', *Technological Forecasting and Social Change*, **2**, 221–224.

Martino, J. (1970d) 'The consistency of Delphi forecasts', *The Futurist*, 63–64.

Martino, J. (1980) 'Technological forecasting—an overview', *Management Science*, **26**(1), 28–33.

Martino, J. (1983) *Technological Forecasting for Decision-Making* 2nd edn, New York: American Elsevier.

Mason, R. (1969) 'A dialectic approach to strategic planning', *Management Science*, **15**, 8.

McLoughlin, W. G. (1969) 'Product cycle planning', paper presented at the Technological Forecasting Conference, Lake Placid, New York.

Meadows, D. (1972) *Limits to Growth*, New York: Universal Books.

Mitchell, R. B., Tydeman, J. T. and Georgiades, J. (1977) 'Structuring the future—applications of a scenario-generation procedure', *Technological Forecasting and Social Change*, **14**(4), 409–428.

Mitroff, I. and Turoff, M. (1975) 'Philosophical and methodological foundations of Delphi', in H. Linstone and M. Turoff (eds.), *The Delphi Method: Techniques and Applications*, London: Addison-Wesley, pp. 17–36.

Mitroff, I. (1971) 'A communication model of dialectical inquiring systems—a strategy for strategic planning', *Management Science*, **17**(10), 634–648.

Myers, P. (1984) 'Empirical solution to a cross-impact analysis as a method of quantifying the component interactions of an intact complex system', *Cognition, Artificial Intelligence, and Simulation Monographs*, (10)4, State University of Maryland—Towson, Towson, Md. 21204.

Parenté, F. J., Anderson, J. K., Myers, P. and O'Brien, T. (1984) 'An examination of factors contributing to delphi accuracy', *Journal of Forecasting*, **3**(2), 173–182.

Platt, J. (1981) 'The acceleration of evolution', *Futurist*, **15**(1), 14–23.

Pokempner, S. J. and Bailey, E. (1970) *Sales Forecasting Practices*, New York: Conference Board.

Preble, J. F. (1983) 'Public sector use of the Delphi technique', *Technological Forecasting and Social Change*, **23**, 27–88.

Rauch, W. D. and Randolf, R. H. (1979) 'Computer assisted panel sessions (CAPS): Review of an experiment in accelerated international teleconferencing', *Technological Forecasting and Social Change*, **13**, 235–258.

Resher, W. (1981) 'Methodological issues in science and technology forecasting: uses and limitations in public policy deliberations', *Technological Forecasting and Social Change*, **20**(2), 101–112.

Riggs, W. E. (1983) 'The Delphi Method: An experimental evaluation', *Technological Forecasting and Social Change*, **23**, 89–94.

Sackman, H. (1974) 'Delphi assessment', The RAND Corporation, RM-1283-PR.

Salancik, J. R., Wenger, W. and Helfer, E. (1971) 'The construction of delphic event statements', *Technological Forecasting and Social Change*, **3**, 65–73.

Scheele, D. S. (1975) 'Consumerism comes to Delphi: comments on Delphi assessment, expert opinion, forecasting and the group process by H. Sackman', *Technological Forecasting and Social Change*, **7**, 215–219.

Scheibe, M., Skutsch, M. and Schofer, J. (1975) 'Experiments in Delphi methodology', in H. Linstone and M. Turoff (eds.), *The Delphi Method: Techniques and Applications*, London: Addison-Wesley, pp. 262–282.

Schnieder, J. B. (1972) 'The policy Delphi: a regional planning application', *Technological Forecasting and Social Change*, **5**, 481–487.

Schoenman, M. E. F. and Mahayan, V. (1977) 'Using Delphi to assess community health needs', *Technological Forecasting and Social Change*, **10**, 203–210.

Sutherland, J. W. (1975) 'Architecting the future: A Delphi-based paradigm for normative system-building', in H. Linstone and M. Turoff (eds.), *The Delphi Method: Techniques and Applications*, London: Addison-Wesley, pp. 463–486.

Thorndike, R. L. (1938) 'The effect of discussion upon the correctness of group decision when the factor of a majority influence is allowed for', *Journal of Social Psychology*, **9**, 343–362.

Turner, P. (1981) 'A 1969 Delphi on medicine', *Futures*, June, 221–223.

Turoff, M. (1975) 'An alternative approach to Cross-Impact Analysis', in H. Linstone and M. Turoff (eds.), *The Delphi Method: Techniques and Applications*, London: Addison-Wesley, pp. 338–365.

Turoff, M. (1975) 'The policy Delphi', in H. Linstone and M. Turoff (eds.), *The Delphi Method, Techniques and Applications*, London: Addison-Wesley, pp. 84–100.

Vanston, J. H. Jr, Parker-Frisbie, W., Cook-Lopreato, S. and Poston, D. L. Jr (1977) 'Alternative scenario planning', *Technological Forecasting and Social Change*, **10**, 159–180.

Weaver, W. T. (1970) 'Delphi as a method for structuring the future: testing some underlying assumptions', Educational Policy Research Center, Syracuse, New York.

Weaver, W. T. (1972) 'Delphi: a critical review', Syracuse University Research Corporation, RR-7.

Welty, G. (1972) 'Problems of selecting experts for Delphi exercises', *Academy of Management Journal*, **15**, 121–124.

Welty, G. (1974) 'The necessity, sufficiency, and desirability or exports as value forecasters', in Leinfellner, W. and Kohler, E. (eds.), *Developments in Methodology of Social Science*, Boston: Reidel, pp. 363–379.

Williams, P. Jr (1951) 'The use of confidence factors in forecasting', *Bulletin of the American Meteorological Society*, **39**, 279–281.

Winkler, R. (1971) 'Probabilistic prediction, some experimental results', *Journal of the American Statistical Association*, **66**, 675–685.

Wissema, J. G. (1982) 'Trends in technological forecasting', *Research and Development Management*, **21**(1), 27–36.

Zarnowitz, V. (1984) 'The accuracy of individual and group forecasts from business outlook surveys, *Journal of Forecasting*, **3**, 11–26.

Judgmental Forecasting
Edited by G. Wright and P. Ayton
© 1987 John Wiley & Sons Ltd

CHAPTER 8

Forecasting Methods for Conflict Situations

J. Scott Armstrong
University of Pennsylvania, Philadelphia

In 1975, a consortium sponsored by the Argentine government tried to purchase the stock of the British-owned Falkland Islands Company, a monopoly that owned 43 percent of the land in the Falklands, employed 51 percent of the labour force, had a monopoly on all wool exports, and operated the steamship run to South America. The stockholders were willing to sell, especially because the Argentine consortium was reportedly willing to pay 'almost any price'. But the British government stepped in to prevent the sale (Murray N. Rothbard, as quoted in *The Wall Street Journal*, 8 April 1982). In my opinion, the actual solution in the Falklands War left both sides worse off than before. In contrast, a sale of the Falklands would have benefited both sides in the short run, and, as companies seldom wage shooting wars, this would probably have been a good long-range solution. Apparently, Britain did not predict how the Argentine generals would act when it blocked the sale, and the Argentine generals did not predict how Britain would respond when they occupied the islands. Accurate forecasting by each side in this situation might have led to a superior solution.

This study examines the evidence on alternative procedures that can be used to forecast outcomes in conflict situations. I first define what is meant here by conflict situations. Next, I describe alternative forecasting methods. This is followed by a presentation of hypotheses on which method is most appropriate. The evidence is reviewed in two stages—first the prior research, then research that we have done.

CONFLICT SITUATIONS

In this study, conflict situations are those where two or more parties have opposing objectives, differing strategies, or competing claims to a given resource. Differences in objectives occur, for example, when the seller is trying to get a high price for a product while the buyer wants a low price. An example involving different strategies would be the conflict involved among groups in New Zealand over the issue of whether the All Blacks rugby team should have been allowed to play in South Africa; all of the parties were in favour of freedom and dignity, but they disagreed about strategies to achieve these objectives. Examples of conflict over resources include that between Britain and Argentina over the Falklands, between competitors such as Hertz and Avis, between labour and management, between parties involved in attempts to take over a company, or between buyer and seller.

The situation becomes more difficult to predict when large changes or unusual events occur. These could be due to changes in the environment or they could be brought about by actions of one of the parties. In such cases, it is difficult to learn from experience. This chapter is concerned with predictions in situations with large changes.

FORECASTING METHODS

A variety of methods can be used to forecast in conflict situations. Brief descriptions are provided here for some of the more important methods.

Expert opinion

People who have had relevant experience in similar situations should be able to make useful predictions. Therefore, Argentine generals might be expected to make accurate predictions about the actions by Britain. Avis executives can forecast actions by Hertz. Expert opinion is especially relevant for small changes and for changes well within the experience of the experts.

Experts in human behaviour could make predictions about the outcomes of situations. For this, they would draw upon the empirical studies that have been done on conflict resolution. Especially qualified would be those experts who specialize in negotiation processes.

Game theory

In contrast to expertise on the situation, one might use experts in game theory. These experts could try to translate information about actual situations into a game theory framework in order to predict the outcome. A key issue here is whether the game theorist can obtain sufficient relevant information for practical situations.

Intentions surveys

One possibility is to ask participants how they will act in a given situation. The advantage here is that in addition to having information about the environment, they also understand their own motivation. On the negative side, they may be unwilling to reveal their true intentions. Projective tests (What would your friend do in such a case?) might be considered, but the chief difficulty would arise in getting participants to respond to the survey. Furthermore, participants may lack insight as to how they would behave when large changes occur.

Extrapolation by analogies

By examining analogous situations, one may be able to predict for a new situation. For example, the issue of fluoridation of water supplies has led to conflict in many communities in the USA, so the outcome of a new case could be predicted by examining similar cases (e.g. 'In what percentage of these similar cases did the proponents of fluoridation win?'). Analogous situations also allow one to assess alternative strategies. Gamson (1975) examined violence as a strategy of social protest in a variety of situations (e.g. women's suffrage). Regrettably, violence generally proved to be a good strategy for protesters. Extrapolation by analogies is less relevant, however, for large changes, new strategies, or new situations.

Laboratory experiments

Key features of a conflict situation might be translated into a laboratory experiment. The greater degree of control in the laboratory must be weighed against the loss of realism. The laboratory experiment is common in marketing research, for example, as seen in the use of simulated stores.

Field experiments

Field experiments are appropriate in some situations and their use increases realism. Thus, one could experiment with the fluoridation issue in a few cities in one state before trying to extend it to other cities. Different strategies could be examined in different cities. As a practical matter, field experiments are widely used in marketing when new products are tested in certain geographical areas. The disadvantages of the field approach are that the experiment itself may change the outcome of the event that is of primary interest, there is a loss of secrecy, expenses are high, and the other parties in the conflict may act differently during the experiments. The latter behaviour frequently occurs when firms test-market a new product. Another disadvantage is that experiments are not feasible in all situations; for example, could Argentina attack only 5 percent of the Falkland Islands? Or could they try a one-week experimental attack?

Role-playing

Role-playing offers some of the advantages of experimentation while overcoming some of the disadvantages. This section goes into detail about role-playing.

Subjects are given a specific role to play, and they are asked to interact with subjects who have different roles. For example, Busch (1961) described how Lockheed used role-playing to predict outcomes of proposals to its major customers. The nature of the conflict is described, and variations in responses must be possible by at least one party. Perhaps the term 'interactive behavioural simulation' would be more descriptive than 'role-playing'. Nevertheless, most of the research has been done under the label of role-playing.

Research in psychology has demonstrated that role-playing has some validity (see Greenwood (1983) for a review). But this term covers substantially more than that described above. Alternative definitions include opinions surveys where the question is worded, 'What would you do [in a given situation] assuming you had the following role . . . ?' Also, the term 'role-playing' has been used where subjects are informed about the hypotheses and their role before they participate in a laboratory experiment. The same term has also been employed when a subject is asked to assume a role and then to imagine how he would behave in a given situation. Our interest is primarily in what has been called 'active role-playing' because this seems to reflect reality better in conflict situations. For the remainder of this chapter, however, I will abbreviate this and simply refer to 'role-playing'.

Different disciplines use terms other than active role-playing. In political science and in the military, interactive behavioural simulations are called 'games'; in personnel psychology, they are called 'job samples' (or 'work samples'); in law, the term is 'mock trials'; in psychiatry, it is 'psychodrama'; and in sociology, it is 'socio-drama'. The existence of different definitions of the term role-playing, and of different words to mean role-playing, make it difficult to discover the relevant literature. To avoid further confusion, I provide an operational definition of the type of role-playing proposed for predicting the outcome of conflict situations. This definition involves each step in the attempt to simulate the interaction. It is necessary to decide who would be involved ('casting'), how the situation should be described ('describing'), how the role-playing should be conducted ('administering'), and how the results should be interpreted ('coding'). More detail is provided on each step in the following paragraphs.

Casting

It seems desirable that those involved in the role-playing be similar to the people they represent. This would involve background, attitudes and objectives. Interestingly, however, much of the prior research has used random assignment of students to roles, and the results have been described as realistic (e.g., Zimbardo, 1972; Armstrong, 1977). Furthermore, Mandel's review of the research on political role-playing, which he refers to as gaming, led him to conclude that similar results have been obtained whether one used experts or novices in the problem at hand (see Mandel, 1977, p. 614, 617, 624). My advice on casting, then, is to obtain similar subjects if the cost to do so is low; otherwise obtain 'somewhat' similar subjects. Students have been used for most research done to date, and this has been adequate for the most part.

Describing the situation

The description of the conflict situation should include information about each of the participants and their goals, a history of their relationships, the current positions, expectations about future relationships, and the processes that the parties expect to use in resolving their conflict (negotiating on position, negotiating on principle, striking, violence, etc.). Obviously, the descriptions of the situations could be extensive. Consider for example, situations such as the Bay of Pigs incident as described in Janis' book (1982), *Groupthink*.

I suggest using short descriptions, preferably less than two typed pages. The use of simple descriptions and short sessions receives some support from Elstein *et al.* (1978); comparisons of elaborate (high fidelity) simulations of doctor/patient interaction were not superior to simple (low fidelity) simulations in their study. Brief descriptions are also less expensive. Some role-playing simulations have been elaborate and time-consuming. Mandel (1977, p. 625) says that the Pentagon has spent up to $5000 for a single session. However, much role-playing has been relatively inexpensive and based on sessions lasting less than one hour.

The preparation of the situation description requires a good understanding of the situation as well as much care and effort. Pre-testing is needed to ensure that the written description is clear and effective. Small changes in the description might affect the outcome.

The description of the situation can lead to bias, especially in research using retrospective situations. Certain items may be apparent after the fact, and these may favour one or another of the techniques. To guard against unintended biases, it is desirable to use more than one description, and then compare the role-playing outcomes; this adds to the costs, however.

In some cases, it may help to make the surroundings realistic. This might involve having the participants dress appropriately (as in Janis and Mann's (1965) role-play between doctor and patient) or selecting a realistic setting (as in Zimbardo's (1972) prison simulation).

When feasible, the possible outcomes should be specified for the role-players. This will aid in coding the results. Of course, if the alternatives are not obvious, it may be better to leave them open; otherwise an additional source of bias is introduced.

Describing the roles

Role-players should be encouraged to improvise when necessary, in an effort to make the session realistic. Role-players can be asked to act as they themselves would act, given their role and the situation. Alternatively, they could be asked to act as they believe the persons they represent would act. As shown in Kipper and Har-Even (1984), differences in this orientation can lead to substantial differences in outcomes. It is not clear which approach is better.

Administering the session

Lacking evidence that preparation should be extensive, we suggest it be brief (e.g. ten minutes) because this will be less expensive. To help people adjust well to their roles, it is helpful to have more than one person represent a given party; these people can then confer to prepare for their role. Additional time, perhaps ten minutes, should be allowed for this group preparation.

Once the administrator starts the role-play, the players should stay in their roles. They should not step out of their roles to ask questions or to discuss aspects of the case.

Coding

Ideally, each role-playing session should lead to a definite conclusion. This outcome would then be used as the prediction. For example, if a given offer by management to the union would lead to a strike in 9 out of 10 role-playing sessions, one would predict a 90 percent chance of a strike. Sometimes, however, the role-players will not reach a conclusion. In such cases, the participants would be asked to state what they think the outcome of their negotiations would have been.

The above guidelines have been inferred from previous research. To a great extent, however, the guidelines are based on my judgment. It is difficult to

Table 1   Active role-playing procedure for conflict situations

---

Casting
Find subjects 'somewhat similar' to actual participants.

Describing the situation
Furnish brief, but accurate, descriptions. Specify possible outcomes.

Describing the roles
Improvise (for realism).
Stay in role at all times.
Act as the participants themselves would act, or act as the person being played would act.

Administering the session
Hold short sessions (less than one hour).
Allow for a brief preparation (ten minutes).
Prepare a realistic setting (dress, location, etc.).

Coding
Use actual outcome from the role-playing as prediction.
Ask participants to state what the outcome would have been if outcome is not reached.

---

claim that any of the elements in this list are vital to the design. Table 1 summarizes the role-playing procedure.

HYPOTHESES

Our hypotheses on the most accurate forecasting method would favour the use of extrapolation from analogies if ample data were available on many highly similar situations. But for the situations with which we are concerned—large changes—this possibility seldom exists. Lacking such data, we expect that experimentation would be the most accurate. However, experimentation is expensive, sometimes obtrusive, and frequently not feasible.

Active role-playing has a number of desirable features. It is more realistic than all of the above competing methods, except for the field experiment; of particular importance is the fact that role-playing allows for an examination of the interaction among parties. Unlike the field experiment, one can maintain secrecy. Finally, it is much less expensive than the field experiment. In a sense, role-playing might be viewed as a low-cost approach to experimentation.

PRIOR EVIDENCE

As noted earlier, the use of role-playing goes back many years. Goldhamer and Speier (1959) reported that Germany used it in 1929 to plan war strategy. It also has a long history in psychology and law. Despite this, little evidence is available on its predictive validity. Mandel's (1977) review of decades of the use of gaming in politics led him to conclude that no comprehensive systematic review was available. Similarly, little evaluation has been done in the legal profession (Gerbasi *et al.*, 1977). For example, while IBM used a 'shadow' jury to predict the responses of an actual jury in the California Computer Products vs. IBM trial (Cooper, 1977), the IBM chairman, Frank T. Carey, said that no systematic evaluation of this methodology was done, nor were company officials aware of any (personal communication, 12 June 1978).

Kerr *et al.* (1979) stated that few studies in psychology examined the methodology of role-playing and its validity. Greenwood (1983) reached the same conclusion when discussing active role-playing.

To review evidence on the relative accuracy of role-playing for predictive outcomes in conflict situations, I examined the *Social Science Citation Index for the Social Sciences* from 1978 through 1984 (using the terms 'role-playing' and 'socio-drama).' I also wrote to researchers who had published empirical work in this area.

Numerous studies attest to the face validity of role-playing. The evidence suggest that it provides realistic results. For example, in Orne *et al.* (1968), observers could not distinguish between subjects who were hypnotized and those who were role-playing a hypnotic trance. Zimbardo's (1972) simulation of a prison was so realistic that it was terminated prematurely for fear someone might harm a 'prisoner.'

Evidence was sought on comparisons of active role-playing versus other methods. These comparisons could be in either real or contrived situations. Real situations provide higher external validity, but the controls are fewer and the costs are higher. Contrived situations, such as laboratory experiments, may have little relevance to the real world.

Primary interest focused on evidence from 'prospective' studies (i.e., those where the result had not yet occurred). In addition, however, 'retrospective' studies were also examined. Even when it is possible to disguise retrospective events, they present a sampling problem. That is, it makes no sense to select uninteresting and obvious situations. But when selecting interesting cases, it is likely that they are interesting because of unusual outcomes. Because unusual

Table 2 Types of situations in which to assess role-playing

	Retrospective	Prospective
Contrived	★	★★
Actual	★★	★★★★

★ = weak evidence and ★★★★ = strong.

outcomes are typically based on unaided judgment, the use of judgment would be disadvantageous when compared with other methods of forecasting retrospective events. That is, we are saying, 'here is a forecast where judgment did not work.'

The various types of evidence are summarized and rated in Table 2.

Contrived retrospective

Owing to concern over the rights of subjects (Vinacke, 1954), much of it spurred by the Milgram studies of blind obedience in the 1960s, psychologists turned to role-playing as an alternative to deceptive experiments. In doing so, one concern they addressed was whether role-playing would yield results similar to those derived from experiments. Some of these studies involved forecasting the experimental (contrived) outcome.

At first glance, there seemed to be much favourable evidence for role-playing. However, when I considered only the type of forecasting relevant to conflict situations, few studies were left (see Greenwood (1983) for a review). The majority of the studies on role-playing did not involve any interaction. Most did not present an alternative model for comparison. Finally, in some studies, different stimulus materials were used for role-playing than for alternative techniques.

Some evidence did seem relevant, however. Willis and Willis (1970) had subjects role-play an experiment on conformity. They were told the design of the experiment and the hypotheses, and then were asked to respond as if it were a real experiment. While the main effect was similar to that in the actual experiment, an interaction effect was missed. Of course, this result lends itself to alternative explanation (e.g., knowledge of the hypothesis might lead the subjects to respond in a certain way).

In summary, role-playing does seem to provide results that are similar to those from experiments. However, the evidence for this conclusion is weak, and little of the evidence pertains to conflict situations.

Contrived prospective

Kerr *et al*. (1977) conducted an experiment to compare 'real' and 'mock' juries. The 'real jurors' were led to believe that their verdict counted in a case involving an academic violation at a university. On a pre-deliberation questionnaire (in their role, but prior to the enactment of the jury deliberations), 48 percent of the 117 mock jurors concluded that the defendant was guilty; these conclusions might be regarded as 'intentions' to vote. For six-person juries, assuming the initial majority prevails, it may be inferred that 40 percent of the juries would have reached a guilty verdict. However, only 8 percent (1 of 12) of the juries that reached a unanimous verdict concluded that the defendant was guilty. The mock jury results were similar in that none of the ten juries reached a guilty verdict. Thus, role-playing seemed to be superior to intentions, but again the evidence was weak.

Actual retrospective

In a political study known as the East Algonian exercise, Crow and Noel (1965) examined a conflict between a strong country and a weak country. The countries were the United States and Mexico (personal communication from Crow.) The situation was role-played by 96 groups to reach a decision for the Mexican president ranging from 1, a peaceful response, to 11, a warlike response. Historians claim that the optimal decision would have been a peaceful one (a '1' or a '2') and that, in their opinion, this was the obvious choice. However, 57 percent of the role-playing groups reached a 4 or 5, a fairly belligerent response that corresponded to the actual decision. That decision proved to be a bad one for Mexico because it lost Texas. Unfortunately, Crow and Noel (1965) did not report on opinions in the East Algonian exercise. However, if we treat historians' opinions as predictions of the 'right' decision, role-playing led to substantially more accurate predictions of reality.

Armstrong (1977) asked subjects to play the roles of seven members of the board of directors of the Upjohn Corporation. They were told that an unbiased group of medical scientists, after 20 years of study, were unanimously recommending that Panalba, an Upjohn drug with harmful side effects, be removed from the market. The board was given 45 minutes to agree on one of the following five decisions:

(1) Recall Panalba immediately and destroy.
(2) Stop production of Panalba immediately but allow what's made to be sold.
(3) Stop all advertising and promotion of Panalba, but provide it for those doctors who request it.
(4) Continue efforts to market Panalba most effectively until sale is actually banned.
(5) Continue efforts to market Panalba most effectively and take legal, political, and other necessary actions to prevent the authorities from banning Panalba.

Of the 57 groups that played the role faced by Upjohn directors, *none* decided to remove the drug from the market. Furthermore, 79 percent decided to take decision 5. In fact, Upjohn also chose decision 5. (See Mintz (1969) for descriptions of the events in this case.) The role-playing predictions in the Upjohn case differed substantially from the predictions of non-role-players of what they would do in this situation. Only 2 percent of 71 respondents to an interview said they themselves would select decision 5, and over half said they would choose decision 1 (to remove the drug from the market). In opinion surveys, 41 percent of the 46 respondents at a meeting of the Hawaii Economic Association predicted that Upjohn would select decision 5, while 17 percent of 18 students at the Christchurch Polytechnic (New Zealand) predicted such a decision. These results are promising for role-playing.

Actual prospective

Halberstam (1973, pp. 558–560) described a situation where high-ranking officers in the United States military role-played the strategy of bombing North Vietnam. In this role-play, the limited bombing strategy failed to achieve the military objectives for the U.S. Unlimited bombing had some military advantages, but overall it was inferior to the 'no bombing' strategy. Later the decision was made by the U.S. President and his advisers, who had not participated in the role-playing. Their expert opinion on the best strategy was limited bombing; this is widely regarded as a poor decision, since, as predicted by role-playing, the strategy failed.

Since 1908, Washington and Lee University had run mock political conventions to select a Presidential candidate for the party that is not in office. The convention is usually held in early May, about two or three months prior to the actual convention. (A description of the procedure and a summary of the historical results can be obtained from Washington and Lee Unviersity, Lexington, Virginia 24450.) Including the Mondale nomination in 1984, the convention has been correct on 13 of 18 candidates. Public opinion polls have been conducted since 1936; these provide a comparable record of accuracy (Runyon *et al.*, 1971; Gallup Opinion Index for 1972 and 1976; Harris Survey for 1980 and 1984). The candidate who was leading in the poll that was conducted on about the same date as the Washington and Lee convention won the nomination on 8 of 12 occasions. During this period the convention was also correct on 8 of 12 occasions. The two approaches agreed on seven occasions, and when they did, the prediction was always correct.

Borman (1982) found that a battery of tests, one of which was role-playing, was superior to a more traditional battery for predicting success in training for 57 soldiers.

STUDIES ON OPINIONS VS. ROLE-PLAYING

We have obtained additional evidence using actual retrospective and prospective studies. A brief report on some of this evidence was provided in Armstrong (1985). Below, I provide a description of the situations, subjects, experimental treatment, administration, and results.

Situations

Descriptions for each situation were obtained from published accounts. The 'Distribution Plan' and 'Dutch Artists' were actual retrospective situations. One actual prospective situation involved negotiations between owners and players in the National Football League (NFL); we call the situation the 'Football Negotiation'. Two-page background descriptions were presented to the subjects for each of the three situations. In addition, the subjects received a set of closed-ended questions designed to cover the range of possible outcomes.

The 'Distribution Plan' describes a 1961 plan by the Ace Manufacturing Company (actually the Philco Corporation) to sell major appliances in supermarkets. Customers at participating supermarkets would turn in their cash register tapes, and $5\frac{1}{2}$ percent of their total purchases would be deducted from the monthly installment payment for any appliance purchased. The payment of the discount was to be split between the manufacturer and the supermarket on a sliding scale. Philco was interested in predicting whether the proposed plan would be accepted by the supermarkets. (This case was taken from Berg (1970, pp. 87–131).)

'Dutch Artists' is based on a situation faced by the Netherlands government as reported by Newman (1982). Artists in 'Histavia' (the Netherlands) staged a sit-in at the country's major art museum in an effort to gain additional benefits in the form of support for artists who are not able to sell their artwork.

'Football Negotiations' describes the conflict faced by the National Football League's (NFL) Players Association and the owners of the teams. This situation was not disguised because the outcome had not yet occurred. Our information was based on reports published on 1 February 1982 (Boyle, 1982; Kirshenbaum, 1982). No negotiations had taken place prior to this time. The existing contract was scheduled to expire 15 July 1982. The NFL Players Association said they would demand 55 percent of the football clubs' gross revenue to be used for players' wages, bonuses, pensions, and benefits.

Subjects

The 96 subjects were students at the Wharton School, University of Pennsylvania, including 27 undergraduates and 69 MBA students. Fifty-seven percent of the subjects received partial credit for a course taught by the author, while the other 43 percent volunteered their time. No honoraria were paid.

The subjects were asked if they could identify the situation. Only one subject claimed to recognize one of the disguised situations. Results from this pair, in the opinions treatment, were dropped. (Interestingly, that subject's prediction for this case was incorrect.)

Experimental treatment[†]

Subjects were scheduled in two groups of two people each during an 80-minute session. Upon arrival at the testing site, they were randomly paired and given the following instructions:

Today we will be examining decision-making to predict the outcomes of future events involving conflict situations. You have been separated into groups of two. We are going to go through three situations, one at a time. Each group is required to read, understand, and then discuss each situation. Each group is to operate independently.

The order in which the situations were presented was randomized across sessions. Some subjects failed to appear at a few of the sessions. When only three subjects arrived, one of the volunteers was asked to leave and the remaining two subjects were asigned to the 'opinions' group.

With the exception of the no-show sessions, the sessions were randomly assigned to either 'opinions' or 'role-playing'. The treatment for each group is described next.

Opinion sessions

Participants were split into random pairs, based on time of arrival, and were seated at opposite ends of a room large enough so they could not overhear each other. Each pair was given the same situations, one at a time. The following instructions were given:

Please read through the case I've given you. Once you understand the situation, each group should discuss the issues involved. All relevant information is given. Please don't be constrained by what's on the paper. I've given both facts and impressions in the text. It's important to distinguish the two and extrapolate information as needed. Your primary objective is to reach a consensus on the questions. Are there any questions?

After reaching a consensus, they were to choose among the responses to the questions that most closely matched their prediction of the outcome. Although any one situation had a total time limit of 60 minutes, all of the groups were able to complete the situations in the time allotted (80 minutes in all).

[†] Copies of the materials used in the experiments are available from the author.

Role-playing groups

Owing to the time limits, only two of the situations were presented to the role-playing groups. In addition to the background information for these groups, each pair was randomly assigned to the role of one of the two parties in the conflict (e.g. owners or players in the NFL). These roles (available from the author) apparently provided little relevant information beyond that which the subject would have after reading the background information. Our intent was to make the situation sound realistic and to indicate that the person believed strongly in the group's position. We gave the following instructions to each group:

Please read through the case I've given you. You are to take on roles of the individuals involved. Here are your role assignments [pass out roles]. I know some of you know each other, but for now make it in a professional sense. Act as those people in your roles would act; you are making decisions as those people.*† Once you understand the situation and have taken on the roles, conduct a meeting to discuss the situation with your peer. Act as you would act if you were in the role which is assigned.* I've given both facts and impressions in the text. It's important to distinguish the two and extrapolate information as needed. Don't fill out the response sheet I've given you until after the role-playing session. Feel free to use it to focus your discussion. You are interested in global issues and the overall outcome of the situation; don't get bogged down in details and side issues. Improvise as necessary, but do not step out of your role the entire time this session is being conducted. You are to prepare to meet your adversary. You will meet in ten minutes and try to negotiate a conclusion to the situation. Are there any questions?'

After reading and preparation time of no more than 20 minutes, the two pairs met at a conference table in the centre of the room. In the Philco Distribution situation, the role-players were told they were meeting at the supermarket chain's headquarters. For the Dutch Artists, the meeting was held 'in the museum where the artists were conducting the sit-in'. The Football Negotiation was said to be 'in the meeting room of a luxury hotel in New York City'.

The role-play lasted until consensus or until the 60-minute time limit was reached. At the end of the role-play each pair separated and answered questions based on the experience. They were instructed not to mark what they personally thought would happen but, rather, to state the consensus as they saw it. If no consensus had been reached, they were asked to state what

† Unfortunately the role instructions were not clearly specified in this experiment, as shown by the two sentences with asterisks.

they thought would have happened had their meeting been allowed to run to its conclusion. Each role-playing session provided two responses, one from each group. While the two groups interacted during the study, the perception of the outcome was reached independently. Each questionnaire was treated as a separate response. As with the opinion technique, the 'pair' represented the unit of analysis. For the role-playing technique, each pair predicted the outcome of their interaction. (This procedure is expected to overstate the statistical significance of the findings.)

Did the experimental design provide role-players with critical information not given to opinion subjects? To test this, we gave role descriptions to 19 subject pairs (descriptions were identical to those given to role-players except that these were written in the third person). We called this group of subjects 'role-aware'. They were asked to discuss the situation from the perspective of the decision-makers described in the role material.

Administration

Most of the opinion and role-playing sessions were administered by Harry Walker during one week in April 1982. Role-aware sessions were conducted in 1982, 83 and 85. One administrator was present at all times during the sessions. Procedures used for the opinion and role-play groups are summarized in the Appendix.

Results

The relative accuracy of the role-playing and the opinions are summarized in Table 3. Role-playing was significantly more accurate than opinions for the

Table 3 Role-playing vs. opinions in predicting outcomes. (Entries represent predictions by pairs.)

| | | Opinions | | | | |
| | Prediction same as | | Role- | | Role | Statistical |
Situation	actual?	Normal	aware[a]	Total	play	significance[b]
Philco Distribution	No	15	18	33	2	$p < 0.01$
	Yes	0	1	1	8	
Dutch Artists	No	13	4	17	2	
	Yes	1	0	1	2	$p < 0.10$
	No answer	0	0	0	2	
Football Negotiation	No	11	0	11	4	$p \approx 0.10$
	Yes	4	0	4	6	

[a]The role-aware pairs were administered by Lisa Elliott and Elizabeth Schindler.
[b]One-tailed Fischer Exact Test, but overstated due to lack of significance in the role-playing pairs.

Table 4 Actual situations: role-playing vs. opinions

Situation	Conflict between	Percentage of correct predictions (sample sizes)[a]					
		Chance	Opinion		Role-play		
Retrospective							
USA–Mexico	Two countries	18	0	(1)	57	(96)	
Political Conventions	Political candidates	33[b]	67	(12)	67	(12)	
Panalba	Stockholder & consumer	20	34	(64)	79	(57)	
Philco Distribution	Manufacturer and retailer	25	3	(33)	80	(10)	
Dutch Artists	Government & interest group	16	6	(18)	50	(4)	
Prospective							
North Vietnam Bombing	Two countries	33	0	(1)	100	(1)	
Football Negotiations	Employees & owners	33	27	(15)	60	(10)	
	Unweighted average	25	20		70		

[a]The sample sizes represent the number of predictions.
[b]Assuming two leading candidates and 'all others'.

Dutch Artists and the Football Negotiations. Summing across the three situations, opinions were correct on 6 out of 67 of the predictions (9 percent), while role-playing was correct on 16 of 24 predictions (67 percent), ignoring the two no-answer groups.

Additional evidence on the Football Negotiation was obtained from an insurance broker, James Silesky, of Alexander and Alexander in Minneapolis (personal communication). His firm offered strike insurance to NFL players. On 16 April, one player purchased $20,000 coverage for a $1000 premium. According to the agent, this premium was arrived at by 'gut feeling'. It implies less than 5 percent chance of a strike. Our role-playing predictions were significantly different than this market opinion ($p < 0.01$).

A summary of the preceding evidence on actual situations provides much support for role-playing. As shown in Table 4, role-playing was correct for 70 percent of the predictions versus 20 percent for expert opinions (the predictive accuracy of opinions is typical of what one might expect to be obtained by chance).

The importance of interaction

Role-playing provides vivid information to the participants on how they feel about the actions by others—and how the others react to their actions.

Table 5   Opinions vs. role-aware (individual subjects)

	Percentage correct predictions (m)	
	Opinions	Role-aware
Philco Distribution	25 (12)	23 (13)
Dutch Artists	0 (13)	0 (12)

These cycles of action and reaction are difficult for one to imagine without role-playing (or actual experience).

To examine the importance of the interaction, we obtained more data on the 'role-aware' versus the 'opinions only' by presenting the Dutch Artists and the Philco Distribution situations to 25 undergraduates at the University of Canterbury in New Zealand in July 1985. The results, in Table 5, show no difference due to knowledge of the roles. This is consistent with the hypothesis that the interaction is important to the role-playing process. It also suggests that the roles did not add relevant information.

Costs

In addition to examining the accuracy of the predictions, we also examined costs. For the three situations summarized in Table 3, subjects spent an average of 48 minutes for role-playing as against 22 minutes for opinions. Clearly, role-playing is more expensive, as shown by our rough estimates in Table 6. Nevertheless, the potential gains in accuracy should justify the costs in many situations because role-playing predictions can be obtained using only 50 people-hours. If the subjects are not doing the task as part of their job, we recommend that they be given a small honorarium.

Table 6   Costs for role-play vs. opinions (for 10 pairs of subjects)

		People hours	
Task	Personnel	Opinions	Role-play
Preparation	Researcher	17	20
Schedule sessions	Clerical	3	5
Testing	Administrator	2[a]	10
	Subjects	8	15
	Total	30	50

[a]All subjects could be run at one time for opinions.

SUMMARY

From a theoretical viewpoint, role-playing offers advantages over opinions for predicting the outcomes in conflict situations. It facilitates a realistic examination of the interaction among the parties. This is expected not only to improve accuracy, but also to provide a better understanding of the dynamics which, in turn, might lead to the development of new strategies. Prior research provided modest evidence suggesting that role-playing is more accurate than opinions for predicting outcomes. Our experiments added support from two more retrospective situations and one prospective situation. The cumulative evidence from the seven actual situations found role-playing to be correct for 70 percent of the predictions versus 20 percent for the opinions only. The interaction seemed to be a critical element in the superiority of role-playing. However, we have not yet ruled out alternative explanations, and much of the evidence is flawed.

Although role-playing is more expensive than opinions, in absolute terms the cost is small. The apparent gains in accuracy are more likely to be worth the cost for important conflict situations. The substantial improvements possible from role-playing suggest this area to be ideal for further research. Situations where the outcome has not yet occurred are of particular interest because of the bias associated with the selection and description of retrospective situations.

ACKNOWLEDGMENTS

Harry S. Walker and Elizabeth Schindler conducted some of the role-playing sessions. Rod Brodie and Tom Gilmore provided comments on earlier drafts. The Department of Business Administration at the University of Canterbury in Christchurch, New Zealand, provided partial support.

APPENDIX

Opinion test procedure

1. Randomly assign four subjects into groups of two based on arrival (1st person group A, 2nd group B, etc.).
2. Separate into groups to opposite sides of the room.
3. Read general instructions and answer questions.
4. Read opinion instructions and answer questions.
5. Distribute text of one situation to each person.
6. Distribute response questionnaire.
7. Monitor that there is no cross-group interaction and that the group discusses the case before responding.
8. Make sure task is completed in 60 minutes.

9. Ask if anyone recognized the situation and mark their answer sheet if yes.
10. Repeat 5 through 9 for the rest of the situations.
11. Tell the subjects not to discuss situations or test procedure with anyone else, and dismiss with a thank you.

Role-playing procedure

1. Randomly assign four subjects into groups of two based on arrival time (1st person group A, 2nd person group B).
2. Separate groups to opposite sides of the room.
3. Read general instructions and answer questions.
4. Read role-playing instructions, pass out roles, and answer questions.
5. Distribute text of one situation to each person.
6. Distribute response questionnaire.
7. Rearrange the furniture so a table is in the centre of the room with two chairs on either side.
8. Make sure groups prepare to meet each other.
9. Bring groups together at the table when they're prepared (no longer than 20 minutes).
10. Describe where the meeting is held.
11. Allow the role-play to continue for up to 60 minutes or until a consensus is reached or discussion on the event to be predicted ceases. (The time will vary substantially depending on the task.)
12. Separate groups and ask them to force the decision or projected decision into one of the responses on the questionnaire.
13. Ask if anyone recognized the situation and mark their answer sheet if yes.
14. Repeat 5 through 13 for the next situation.
15. Tell the subjects not to discuss the situation or test procedure with anyone else, and dismiss with a thank you.

REFERENCES

Armstrong, J. Scott (1977) 'Social irresponsibility in management', *Journal of Business Research*, **5**, 185–213.

Armstrong, J. Scott (1985) *Long-Range Forecasting: From Crystal Ball to Computer*, 2nd ed., New York: Wiley–Interscience.

Berg, Thomas L. (1970) *Mismarketing: Case Histories of Marketing Misfires*, New York: Doubleday.

Borman, Walter C. (1982) 'Validity of behavioral assessment for predicting military recruiter performance', *Journal of Applied Psychology*, **67**, 3–9.

Boyle, Robert H. (1982) 'The 55% solution', *Sports Illustrated*, 1 February, 30.

Busch, G. A. (1961) 'Prudent-manager forecasting', *Harvard Business Review*, **39**, 57–64.

Cooper, Ron (1977) 'Shadow jury used by IBM at hearings in big anti-trust case', *The Wall Street Journal*, 3 February, 7.

Crow, Wayman J. and Noel, Robert C. (1965). 'The valid use of simulation results', mimeo, Western Behavioral Sciences Institute, 1150 Silverado Street, La Jolla, California 92037.

Elstein, Arthur S., Shulman, L. S. and Sprafka, S. A. (1978) *Medical Problem Solving: An Analysis of Clinical Reasoning*, Cambridge, Mass.: Harvard University Press.

Gamson, William A. (1975) *The Strategy of Social Protest*. Homewood, Ill.: Dorsey Press.

Gerbasi, Kathleen C., Zuckerman, M. and Reis, H. T. (1977) 'Justice needs a new blindfold: A review of mock jury research', *Psychological Bulletin*, **84**, 323–345.

Goldhamer, Herbert and Speier, Hans (1959) 'Some observations on political gaming', *World Politics*, **12**, 71–83.

Greenwood, John D. (1983) 'Role-playing as an experimental strategy in social psychology', *European Journal of Social Psychology*, **13**, 235–254.

Halberstam, David (1973) *The Best and the Brightest*. London: Barrie & Jenkins.

Janis, Irving L. (1982) *Groupthink: Psychological Studies on Policy Decisions and Fiascoes*, 2nd ed., Boston: Houghton-Mifflin.

Janis, Irving L. and Mann, Leon (1965) 'Effectiveness of emotional role-playing in modifying smoking habits and attitudes', *Journal of Experimental Research in Personality*, **1**, 84–90.

Kern, Jeffrey M., Miller, C. and Eggers, J. (1983) 'Enhancing the validity of role-play tests: A comparison of three role-play methodologies', *Behavior Therapy*, **14**, 482–492.

Kerr, Norbert L., Nerenz, D. R. and Herrick, D. (1979) 'Role-playing and the study of jury behavior', *Sociological Methods and Research*, **7**, 337–355.

Kipper, David A. and Har-Even, Dov (1984) 'Role-playing techniques: The differential effect of behavior simulation interventions on the readiness to inflict pain', *Journal of Clinical Psychology*, **40**, 936–941.

Kirshenbaum, Jerry (1982) 'Right destination, wrong track', *Sports Illustrated*, 1 February, 7.

Mandel, Robert (1977) 'Political gaming and foreign policy making during crises', *World Politics*, **29**, 610–625.

Mintz, Morton (1969) 'FDA and Panalba: A conflict of commercial and therapeutic goals', *Science*, **165**, 875–881.

Mixon, Don (1972) 'Instead of deception', *Journal for the Theory of Social Behaviour*, **2**, 145–177.

Newman, Barry (1982) 'Artists in Holland survive by selling to the government', *The Wall Street Journal*, 7 January, 1.

Orne, Martin, T., Sheehan, P. W. and Evans, F. J. (1968) 'Occurrence of post-hypnotic behavior outside the experimental setting', *Journal of Personality and Social Psychology*, **9**, 189–196.

Runyon, John H., Verdini, J. and Runyon, S. S. (1971) *Source Book of American Presidential Campaign and Election Statistics, 1948–1968*. New York: Frederick Ungar.

Vinacke, W. E. (1954) 'Deceiving subjects', *American Psychologist*, **9**, 155.

Willis, Richard H. and Willis, Y. A. (1970) 'Role-playing versus deception: An experimental comparison', *Journal of Social Psychology*, **16**, 472–477.

Zimbardo, Philip (1972) 'The pathology of imprisonment', *Society*, **9** (April), 4–8.

Judgmental Forecasting
Edited by G. Wright and P. Ayton
© 1987 John Wiley & Sons Ltd

CHAPTER 9

Bridging the Gap Between Forecasting and Action

George A. Geistauts *and* **Ted G. Eschenbach**
University of Alaska, Anchorage

IMPORTANCE AND DEFINITION OF THE IMPLEMENTATION PROBLEM

Research on forecasting has been almost exclusively concerned with developing more accurate forecasting methods and with extending extant forecasting methodologies to new applications. Little attention has been paid to the implementation of forecasts or forecasting systems. However, a forecast's value cannot be measured simply by its accuracy; the forecast's impact on decision-making and policy formulation must also be considered. Unfortunately, it is clear that many forecasts have little or no effect on decision-making.

Schultz (1986) summarizes the implementation problem succinctly: 'The simple truth is that, whatever forecasting techniques, models, or systems will prove to be best, organizations will resist integrating any of them into their repertoire of planning and decision-making behavior'. The reasons for this 'resistance to change' include interactions between the perceived accuracy of the forecasting method, the credibility of the forecasters or experts, the relationship between forecasters and users, the internal politics of the users' organization, the users' goals, organizational communication processes, and reward systems.

Forecasts without an impact on policy formulation or on decisions are wasted efforts, and rejected forecasts may even be counterproductive, poisoning the atmosphere for forecasting by creating doubts about judgmental processes and causing decisions to be based on even less correct assumptions about the future.

As a general approach, judgmental forecasting seems to be gaining support. However, implementation is particularly difficult in judgmental forecasting because of certain common perceptions:

(1) There is a desire to base forecasting on science, and science—rightly or wrongly—is associated with mathematical methods and quantification. Thus, judgmental forecasts appear to be less 'scientific'.

(2) Mathematical methods draw upon quantified data and follow a specific procedure, thus leaving an 'audit trail' for examination and replication. By comparison, the steps and data used in a judgmental process are inherently more difficult to describe and often impossible to replicate. (However, proponents of 'bootstrapping' in forecasting and researchers applying artificial intelligence to the design of expert systems would probably argue that the rules used in a judgmental process can be extracted and formulated explicitly.)

(3) As described in Kahneman, Slovic, and Tversky (1982), humans are known to exhibit systematic judgmental biases such as selective perception, illusory correlation, inconsistency, etc.

(4) Human judgment is open to accusations of deliberate bias. Those doing the predicting may consciously slant their predictions to help bring about desired outcomes.

(5) Judgmental forecasts often carry a 'signature'. The forecast may be identified with one or more specific experts, and evaluation of the forecast may be overshadowed by evaluation of the experts' qualifications and personalities.

(6) The judgmental forecast is in potential competition with the judgment of the decision-makers. Judgment is ultimately the stock in trade of decision-makers; therefore, surrender to the judgment of others is a serious matter.

(7) Judgmental forecasting is often viewed as a 'method of last resort' and thus applied in difficult, unstable, and high-risk forecasting situations.

The above factors indicate that decision-makers who rely on judgmental forecasts undertake greater personal risks than do those relying on 'objective' quantitative forecasts. They can be accused of both lacking a 'scientific' basis for their decisions and of poor judgment in selecting those on whose judgment they in turn rely. Even where the decision-maker is unlikely to have to defend the use of a particular judgmental forecast to others, he still has to convince himself that the forecast should influence decisions.

WHAT DOES IMPLEMENTATION MEAN?

The implementation problem is complicated by the fact that there seems to be no single definition of what is meant by the term 'implementation'. For example, does it mean the same thing to say that a forecast had an impact, was useful, or was implemented? Schultz (1984) adopts a definition in which a forecasting 'model that *changes* the decision process will be called "implemented" and a model that both *changes and improves*' the decision process will be called 'successfully implemented'. The underlying rationale for this definition is a focus on improved decision-making, and thus improved organizational effectiveness. However, should improvement in the decision process be measured at the time when the decision is being made or at a later time (in the case of long-range forecasts, at a much later time)? What of the forecast that does not visibly alter decisions, but does improve the internal political position of the decision-maker? What of the forecast that leaks out to opponents of the organization's policies and thus reduces the organization's options?

These questions suggest that implementation must be measured against goals. Because the goals of the forecaster, the decision-maker, the organizational insider, and the organizational outsider are seldom fully congruent, implementation may be measured differently by the various affected parties.

In order to have a working definition we will modify Huysmans' (1970) definition of the implementation of operations research: a forecast can be thought of as implemented if the decision-makers adopt the forecast in essence and continue to use it as long as the conditions underlying the forecast apply. Obviously, the degree of use, and thus the degree of implementation can vary:

—the forecast may have zero or negligible use,
—the forecast may serve only as general background,
—the forecast may be explicitly used in decision-making,
—the forecast may be the decisive element in a decision.

Several other possibilities exist. Although the forecast itself may not be implemented, the *process* of forecasting can still greatly increase learning about the system and its possible future behaviours. Alternatively, the forecast predictions may be rejected, and the rejection itself may serve as an argument for adopting a different view of the future. There is also the possibility of intentional misuse of a forecast in order to influence or justify decisions.

Evaluation and implementation of judgmental forecasts are complicated by the self-altering possibilities of acceptable forecasts with high relevance to decisions. A forecast may be either self-fulfilling or self-defeating, but either case leads to spurious changes in apparent validity. As an example, a Delphi forecast of regional development predicted very poor prospects for agriculture and good prospects for mining. The client, a government agency, responded by placing extra emphasis on agricultural development—attempting to make the agricultural prediction self-defeating—and by establishing a new division of mining—which increases the potential for self-fulfilment of the mining prediction. We consider both predictions to have been 'implemented' despite the radically different effect the agency's decisions will have on their long-term accuracy.

The greater the predictive power of the method or the prestige of the participating experts, the larger this self-altering effect may be. A special case of implementation exists where the experts whose judgment is the source of the predictions are also decision-makers in the system. The self-altering potential of the forecast is strengthened as the process shifts from forecasting into group planning. However, because group planning involves the selection of acceptable futures, its validity is subject to more question by outsiders, and the level of attack on the results and the methodology which produced them may be much higher. Thus a high commitment by decision-makers to implementation may be balanced by external political opposition, and the ultimate degree of implementation may be determined by the organization's political environment.

Finally, a distinction must be made between implementing a specific forecast and implementation of a forecasting method. Implementation of a forecast necessarily requires a one-time implementation of the underlying method, but it does not automatically commit the decision-makers or their organization to long-term use of the method. Permanent implementation of a method generally heightens the degree of risk and places an extra burden on the implementation strategy.

We assume that forecasters want their forecasts to be implemented; indeed, the forecasters' jobs probably depend upon it. Thus we believe that forecasters should be as concerned with implementation as with accuracy. In the balance of this chapter we outline some of the generic considerations that enter into the design of a successful forecasting strategy. We believe that the responsibility for applying this generic framework to a particular forecasting situation is primarily the forecaster's—i.e. the forecaster must design a strategy that produces both accuracy and implementation. Only the assumption of such a dual responsibility will ensure that the technical forecasting input is matched to the capacities and needs of the decision-makers. This does not, however, free the decision-makers from responsible and supportive partnership in the implementation process.

IMPLEMENTATION RESEARCH AND MODELS

Empirical research on forecast implementation is just beginning to develop momentum, and such research on the implementation of judgmental forecasts is almost non-existent. Thus our approach must be primarily conceptual. Fortunately, a substantial body of work has been done on the implementation of operations research/management science (for comprehensive reviews, see Huysmans (1970), Schultz and Slevin (1975), Doktor, Schultz, and Slevin

(1979), Wysocki (1979), and Hildebrandt (1980)) and many of the insights gained appear transferable to the closely related field of forecasting. Additional insights are provided by the emerging literature on the roles of consultants and advisers (Mintzberg, 1980; McGivern and Fineman, 1983; Dror, 1984). Several of the more comprehensive treatises on forecasting have explicitly discussed implementation (Armstrong, 1978; Wheelwright and Makridakis, 1980; Makridakis and Wheelwright, 1982). Ascher's (1978) analysis of the role of forecasting in policy formulation is particularly useful, as is Wenk's (1979) discussion of the political limits to forecasting. Finally, implementation research in turn draws heavily upon the vast body of research on change processes.

The literature provides several interesting approaches to analysing the implementation problem, although none are explicitly focused on implementing judgmental forecasts. Alter (1979) suggests that a set of 'implementation risk factors' which measure deviations from the ideal implementation situation can serve as a useful exercise in identifying implementation stumbling blocks. Eight major deviation categories are identified: non-existent or unwilling users; multiple users and implementors; disappearing users, implementors, or maintainers; inability to specify purpose or usage pattern in advance; inability to predict and cushion impact on all parties; lack or loss of support; lack of prior experience with similar systems; and technical problems and cost/effectiveness issues. Identification and measurement of these factors then can be used as a basis on which to develop an implementation strategy.

Schultz and Slevin (1983) have developed an 'implementation profile' which Schultz (1984) has applied to forecasting implementation. The twelve factors to be considered are: top management support, impact on job performance, the user–forecasting model designer relationship, impact on goal congruence, the amount or degree of change, the forecasting system or model format, the system or model quality, the implementation strategy, cost–benefit justification, implementor resources, decision style, and environmental events. Schultz suggests a 'proactive approach to implementation management' where the general situation is defined and the relevant factors measured. An implementation plan is then developed, an implementation team formed and set to work, and feedback is provided while the implementation is in progress.

Armstrong (1978) suggests a four-step implementation process consisting of finding the problems, agreeing on the problems, generating alternative solutions, and gaining commitment to programmes. The forecasting analyst's role is to be that of a helper to the clients, and client participation in developing the forecasting experiment design is stressed, as is feedback to the clients as the experiment progresses. Finally, both in 1978 and in 1986, Armstrong urges forecasters to 'obtain specific prior commitment from decision makers as to how they will use the forecasts'. A suggested approach for making it easier to obtain the commitment is to cast potential forecasts into scenario formats to make the forecasts more plausible.

Analysis of the published research suggests that the implementation problem can be analysed in terms of three basic measures: *validity*, *credibility*, and *acceptability*. Forecasting research has focused on validity, while implementation research has focused on the other two measures—usually in contexts other than forecasting. Briefly, they can be defined as:

> *Validity*—the inherent correctness, accuracy, or 'truth' of the predictions;
> *Credibility*—the perception potential users have of the forecast's believability or reliability;
> *Acceptability*—the forecast's utility or implementability from the decision- or policy-maker's perspective.

These three measures are only partially related in a hierarchical sense. A forecast with low validity is unlikely to be credible or acceptable, but validity by itself cannot guarantee either credibility or acceptability. The forecasting strategy (research design) must be explicitly based on an analysis of the factors determining credibility and acceptability as well as on consideration of the most effective technique for obtaining valid predictions.

At first glance, validity appears to be a relatively objective technical question, on which the forecaster should be able to speak with considerable, but not necessarily unbiased authority; credibility and acceptability reflect decision-maker perspectives. However, decision-makers will make their own evaluation of validity, and thus all three measures of quality must ultimately be estimated from the perspective of the decision-makers, and not only from the more technical perspective of professional forecasting.

THE FORECASTING ENVIRONMENT

In order to maximize the effectiveness of a proposed forecasting effort, it is useful to visualize it as taking place in an overall forecasting environment. The forecasting environment includes all factors or elements that impact on the forecasting situation, including technical, organizational, and personal elements. Together, these define the 'forecasting problem' faced by the forecaster.

Key individual roles in the forecasting environment include: the experts, the persons whose judgment forms the basis of the forecast; the forecasters, the technical specialists acting as intermediaries in eliciting, summarizing, and presenting the expert judgment; the client, the person or group explicitly contracting for the forecast; the decision-makers, the potential users of the forecast for decision-making or policy formulation; and the stakeholders, all those who may possibly be affected by the forecast. In many cases individuals may play more than one role. For example, in a 'genius' forecast the expert and the forecaster are typically the same.

Frequently, but not always, the clients are also the decision-makers. When this is not so, the implementation problem becomes considerably more complicated, and the forecast may be implemented at one organizational level but not at others. One possibility occurs when higher-level management contracts for a forecast to be used by subordinates in their decision-making. The subordinates, however, may feel that a forecasting approach and its predictions are being imposed on them and that reliance on the predictions may have a negative effect on the quality of their decision process—a decision process for which they will be held responsible but over which they now lack control. A common response is to subtly or overtly reject the forecast. Another possible separation of clients and decision-makers can occur when a lower level of management has contracted for a forecast, but the nature of the predictions makes it obvious that the optimal decisions based on the forecast can be taken only at a higher level of management. There are also instances in which, owing to organizational or personnel changes, clients and decision-makers become difficult to identify. Finally, there is the case of general-audience forecasts in which the decision-makers are presumably the 'public', either directly or through the proxy efforts of their officials; the client in this instance is in effect a sponsor, and the motives for sponsorship are heavily value-laden.

The conceptual model in Figure 1 illustrates the forecasting situation for a fairly complex case in which the client's organization has contracted with an external forecasting consultant. (A specific example is the regional economic development Delphi forecast described at the end of this chapter; what actually corresponded in that study to each element of Figure 1 is shown in parentheses.) The predictions are to be obtained from a panel of experts (former governors, legislators, agency heads, economists, corporate executives), using a forecasting method (Delphi) administered by the consultant forecaster (a university-based team). The experts, through observation of and interaction with the system (the regional economy) whose behaviour is being predicted, obtain the knowledge and insights on which they base their predictions; because of their status or formal position at least some of the experts have a measurable degree of influence over the system, so the potential for self-altering behaviour is present.

Within the client's organization (the department of commerce in the regional government), the client (a division head) has some but not total decision-making power; major influence over the client is exerted by other decision-makers at the client's level (other division heads), by higher management (the governor, the commissioner of commerce, deputy commissioners), and by other internal stakeholders (economists, industry analysts, other

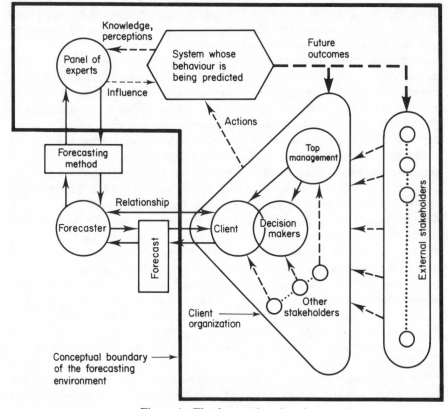

Figure 1. The forecasting situation

officials). There are also external stakeholders (citizens, industry groups, advocacy groups, and legislators). Stakeholders, higher management, and other decision-makers constrain the client's freedom of action—including what forecasts he can accept and act on. (In this case, the commissioner supports Delphi, but the deputy commissioner, an econometrician, opposes judgmental forecasting; the situation becomes complicated as a new commissioner takes office.) Over the course of the forecasting study, a relationship (formal and informal consultation and interaction) develops between the client and the forecasters; this relationship necessarily predates the delivery of the forecast and will significantly influence the forecast's credibility. Interaction between the forecasters and the expert panel also creates a relationship, which the forecasters can consciously manage to increase panellist satisfaction and commitment, thus improving panellist retention and enhancing the quality of predictions. These, in turn, influence the client's perception of forecast quality, and improve acceptability.

As a result of participation on the panel, panellists undergo learning (through the Delphi feedback feature) and their perceptions of the future change; because of panellists' influence over the real system (the regional economy) some alterations of system behaviour may result simply from panellists having been on such a panel. To the extent that the forecast is accepted, system behaviour will also be altered by policy responses to the predictions. (In this case, the forecast provides a more optimistic view of economic development than have other forecasts, and thus gains the interest and support of the commissioner of commerce. Dismal predictions of prospects for agriculture support the commissioner's views of this economic sector, but stakeholder pressures by the agricultural lobby result in continued support of agriculture. Although the forecast has been done for a public agency client, the forecast's effect is diffused by the complex public sector decision structure. Paradoxically, the forecast generates substantial private sector interest.)

Figure 1, and the specific illustration of the model, are representative of the most complex forecasting environments—environments with multiple feedback loops and channels of influence and political pressure. At the other extreme is the forecasting environment where the decision-maker/forecaster applies personal judgment to predict the future behaviour of a system within which he must operate, but which he cannot influence. Most actual forecasting problems will have a level of complexity between these extremes.

In any case, the model helps to clarify the distinctions between the various roles and the differences between the 'decision problem' facing the client organization and the 'forecasting problem' facing the forecaster. In a simple situation the decision problem is the apparent set of choices at the initiation of the forecasting project and the goals of the forecast are clear. The forecast should aid in making the optimum choice, or alter the perceived set of choices, or both. In more complicated situations, the problem is large and complex and the forecast will provide guidance for a myriad of potential future decisions, many of which are not currently imagined.

The forecasting problem thus includes a portion of the decision problem, but the forecasting problem itself is augmented by technical, organizational, and personal elements, which together will determine the success of the forecasting project in terms of validity, credibility, and acceptability.

The forecasting system also consists of concepts, methods, procedures, relationships, and persons. The forecasting system is the forecaster's response (solution) to the forecasting problem, and represents the choice of a particular forecasting strategy.

From a systems perspective, high validity and credibility is desirable, but this may not solve the forecasting problem, or the forecast may not be acceptable to the decision-maker. Identification of the optimal forecasting strategy starts with an analysis of the forecasting environment, and *not* with an initial choice of a forecasting method.

VALIDITY AND CREDIBILITY

Conceptually, forecast validity is audience-independent, suggesting that validity is an objective measure of forecast quality while credibility and acceptability are clearly subjective measures. However, the basic validation dilemma is that although only time can show the extent to which a forecast has revealed the 'truth' about the future, an evaluation of validity must be made at the time the forecast is produced. Both the forecaster and the users estimate validity, but their criteria for evaluating validity may differ substantially.

Professional forecasters commonly approach validation by attempting to demonstrate that the forecasting method being used is valid, and therefore—assuming competent application—the forecast must be valid. Validation through historical analogy is typically supplemented by logical arguments and experimental evidence for the efficacy of the particular judgmental process. This supplemental support for validity may serve more to alter belief in the method's effectiveness than to prove its predictive power in the given situation.

Validation of forecasts based on validation of methodology poses a particularly difficult problem for judgmental forecasting. By their very nature, important aspects of the judgement process are typically not visible nor are the protocols used easily explained. In some forms of judgmental forecasting, such as single-person 'genius' forecasting, the forecasting methodology may not be describable; the 'methodology' thus may appear to consist of little beyond the authority of the person making the predictions. Moreover, while technical factors affecting validity—such as those discussed elsewhere in this book—and past failures can indeed show that a forecast is invalid, past successes and/or a good technical fit between the methodology and the characteristics of the system whose behaviour is to be predicted cannot prove validity. What is established, then, is an argument for validity leading to a sort of perceived or 'pseudo-validity' which the forecaster finds personally convincing and hopes will be convincing to users.

Users approach the validity question from a different perspective, reflecting their typically more limited technical and historical knowledge of forecasting, their concern with the broader problem of decision-making in which the forecast is only one of the elements, and their different personal goals. In evaluating a forecast, validity for users means deciding whether the forecast has sufficient *credibility* to serve as an input into decision-making. With the exception of cases in which there is a deliberate intent to deceive, validity as perceived by the professional forecaster is a necessary but not sufficient condition for achieving credibility.

The user's acceptance of validity is implicitly conditional and utilitarian, as opposed to being an absolute declaration of forecast truth. This pragmatic approach accepts a forecast as valid if it provides adequate guidance for the decision-making situation; under an absolute approach to validity, virtually all long-range forecasting would be impossible and self-altering forecasts would represent insurmountable paradoxes. Thus the pragmatic approach to validity must be taken by those desiring to implement a forecast, but the absolute approach does provide a ready base for those who want to attack the forecast.

In practice, validity is a matter of degree. What we appear to be saying when we declare a forecast to be valid is that it is the best current description of the future available to us, that it provides adequate accuracy or precision for our purposes, and that it has adequate robustness—i.e. that it can sustain reasonable variations from underlying assumptions or presumed data without significantly altering the correctness of the final predictions. We also accept, especially in the case of complex forecasts containing many predictions, the almost hundred per cent certainty that some of the predictions will be wrong.

A tempting way to increase validity arises out of the fact that absolute validity and precision are opposites: for example, a prediction that the world population will grow during the next decade is much more likely to be true than any specific prediction of the numerical magnitude of that growth. However, this decreased precision greatly reduces the usefulness of the forecast. Thus, the degree of precision is typically established by the forecast's intended uses. While accuracy decreases as the time horizon lengthens, so does the need for highly accurate forecasts. The need for robustness can be dealt with through several common approaches, including the explicit statement of critical assumptions, sensitivity analysis, and the generation of alternative scenarios. An important aspect of robustness is the need to consider how self-altering behaviour will be treated; again, the intended uses of the forecast will provide guidelines in this area.

The choices made by the forecaster with respect to treatment of precision and robustness will be important determinants of perceived validity. Other determinants reflect the extent to which validity-reducing problems have been avoided. Is the forecast objective and free from bias; are desires subordinated to predictions; has any group improperly dominated the prediction process; has a significant fraction of experts dropped out; and how have variations in expertise been handled? The perceived validity may also depend on how the forecasting process has treated values, which are dependent on time, country, region, social, and ethnic group. Thus even the underlying question, 'Can/ should these values be modified/predicted?', needs to be addressed.

Finally, validity is of course heavily dependent on the characteristics of the system whose behaviour is being forecast, such as the system's complexity and structural stability, and the length of the forecast time horizon. These are generally beyond the control of the forecaster. The forecaster does, however, choose the best forecasting methodology to match these system properties— although in some cases this choice may be made jointly or by the client. Thus validity and, to a great extent, credibility will be based on the methodology used to generate the forecast and on the specific implementation of the methodology.

The method's credibility is heavily dependent on whether there is a successful pattern of historical use both in similar situations and by similar organizations. Yet a particular application should be distinctive and not appear to be a mechanical application of past principles; judgmental forecasts seem to benefit from the extent to which they can be made interesting. The method itself should be comprehensible, and appear to be both appropriate and logical to the client and/or decision-makers. The implementation should lead to a process that is perceived as objective, where a primary criterion is often the degree of independence exercised by the forecaster and experts. This is the major drawback of internal studies with a significant external audience. Objectivity also requires that the experts clearly separate predictions from desired futures, and obtain a balance of expert viewpoints.

Credibility requires that any forecast group used should appear to have appropriate expertise, and is significantly enhanced by using large groups of widely recognized experts. The inclusion of prominent individuals with significant decision-making authority can also increase forecast credibility. It should be noted that research suggests that moderate expertise and moderate-size panels may be optimal for validity (Armstrong, 1986), and that great expertise or very large panels add little to the accuracy of a forecast. However, while research to substantiate this has yet to be carried out, anecdotal evidence indicates that greater expertise and larger panels do enhance credibility.

Credibility is also enhanced by the professionalism of the forecasters; in fact, to a significant extent, the credibility of the forecast is dependent on the credibility of the forecaster. The forecaster must realize that he is both producing a product and building a relationship. On-time and within-budget delivery of the results, an attractive and understandable report, effective oral presentations of results, and the forecasters' ability to explain both the method and results in language familiar to the client all enhance credibility.

The relationship, and thus credibility, is also enhanced by frequent client–forecaster communication, attention to developing an understanding of the client's decision problem, and a sensitivity to client needs. One of these needs may be client education in forecasting and in the value of the particular methodology being used. Care must be taken not to over-sell the method or promise undeliverable levels of accuracy.

The forecast should be internally consistent, and it should include the underlying rationale for any controversial results. Robustness, early indications of accuracy, and consideration of sensitivity to alternative assumptions enhance credibility.

ACCEPTABILITY

A forecast and the process that produced it may be valid and credible, yet not be acceptable to the decision-makers or to the client. In order to be acceptable, the forecast must be congruent with the decision-makers' needs.

Two of the most important needs of decision-makers are: (1) to preserve the freedom of judgment to choose among decision options, and (2) to preserve their personal reputations for astuteness. Acceptance of a forecast poses a risk to the decision-maker: the more the forecast seems to force a particular decision, the greater the risk and the greater the potential conflict between the forecast and personal and organizational values.

The nature of acceptability is illustrated by Ascher's (1978) analysis of the impact of two forecasts of US resource requirements. *America's Needs and Resources* was prepared under the direction of J. Frederic Dewhurst in 1947 and updated in 1955, and *Resources for Freedom* was the 1952 report of the President's Materials Policy Commission headed by William S. Paley—a well-known broadcasting executive. Both studies covered essentially the same ground, both were 'regarded in academic circles as of roughly equal quality and significance', and both were widely publicized. Nevertheless, even though the Dewhurst report outsold the Paley report by a margin of almost two to one, the Paley report ultimately had a far greater impact.

Ascher finds the explanation for this difference in acceptance in three major differences between the studies. First, 'Dewhurst was a noted scholar, while Paley was rich and famous. The fact that Paley's name adorned the report, and more generally, that the report was a product of a blue ribbon presidential committee, not only provided an inherent attraction, but also clearly signalled the arrival of something important'. Second, the Paley study 'contained a clear message', while the Dewhurst study took the 'approach of converting future needs into dollar equivalents required to meet these needs', and therefore 'was regarded as highly technical and difficult to summarize in terms of *broad* policy implications'. Finally, although the Dewhurst study was difficult to incorporate into broad policy analysis, it nevertheless was 'too specific in presenting forecasts as policy recommendations', while the Paley study 'left its forecasts in neutral form'.

In short, acceptance of the Paley study was enhanced by the greater perceived authority of the forecasters, by the clarity of the report, and by its policy neutrality. The Paley study more effectively met the needs of policy-makers: the greater perceived authority made it easier to defend its use in decision-making, the clarity made it easy to use, and policy neutrality preserved more options for policy development.

While the specific factors which will influence acceptability must be determined on a case-by-case basis, acceptability is likely to be influenced by:

(1) The degree of client and decision-maker autonomy, and the extent of management support.
(2) The number, interests, influence, and diversity of stakeholders.
(3) Organizational values, and relative organizational goal congruence or diversity.
(4) The degree of internal and external politicization of decisions.
(5) The risks and rewards to the client, decision-makers, and stakeholders of potential decisions.
(6) Decision styles and attitudes toward change and planning.
(7) Previous experience with forecasting.
(8) Successful identification of the decision problem.
(9) The suitability, apparent rationality, and historical record of the forecasting method.
(10) The inherent credibility of the experts making the predictions.
(11) The credibility of the forecasters and/or of the forecasting organization.
(12) The professionalism of the forecasting effort and the forecasters.
(13) The communication abilities of the forecaster.
(14) The degree of client and decision-maker involvement in conceptualization and execution of the forecast.
(15) Logistical feasibility and cost–benefit justification of the method.
(16) The apparent objectivity, robustness, and precision of predictions.
(17) The rationale for predictions and relevance to the decision problem.
(18) The clarity of the forecast.
(19) Presentation and dissemination formats.
(20) Timeliness of the forecast.
(21) The degree to which forecast is policy-neutral or supportive of the decision-maker.
(22) The degree to which the forecast builds a consensus, agrees with organizational values, and agrees with other forecasts.
(23) The degree to which the forecast poses a challenge to conventional wisdom—both internal and external to the organization.

DEVELOPING A FORECASTING STRATEGY

In order to enhance credibility and acceptability of the forecast, the forecaster must develop a total forecasting strategy to fit the specific forecasting environment. This requires an explicit analysis of the environment.

Structured interviews and a variety of other systems analysis techniques can be used to obtain a picture of the forecasting environment. Hogarth (1980) outlines a decision analysis approach oriented around judgmental problems, and the implementation profile and other published 'checklist' frameworks are available to guide analysis. But in practice the forecaster is likely to develop a personal approach which involves obtaining answers to a number of key questions. Some generic examples of these questions, based on the acceptability factors outlined earlier, are:

(1) What is the basic decision problem and what decision(s) are required?
(2) What could a forecast do *for* or *to* the client and decision-makers?
(3) How should the concerns of stakeholders be acknowledged?
(4) What is the previous client experience with forecasting?
(5) How can belief in the forecast's validity be increased?
(6) What could increase the client's or each decision-maker's ability to act on the forecast?
(7) What is the consequence of forecast errors and how much sensitivity testing is justified?
(8) What are the logistical limits: time, cost, expertise, procedural, legal?
(9) What trade-offs are possible: breadth vs. depth. accuracy vs. cost vs. time?

After having developed an in-depth understanding of the forecasting environment, the forecaster must select from a number of tactical options the combination that will maximize credibility and acceptability. This selection involves trade-offs, since all options are not simultaneously possible, and may also require some (hopefully marginal) reduction in validity. Some examples of tactical options are:

(1) Using anonymity to decouple the forecast from personalities.
(2) Selecting experts for *both* expertise and prominence.
(3) Using larger panels of experts than required for validity in order to build credibility.
(4) Including experts with opposing values or biases to build an appearance of impartiality.
(5) Asking experts for *both* predictions and value statements.
(6) Using judgmental forecasting as part of an eclectic research programme.
(7) Using multiple scenario approaches that preserve more policy options for the decision-makers.
(8) Educating the clients/decision-makers on the forecasting method.
(9) Actively involving the client/user in the on-going forecasting process through frequent feedback and consultation.

MAXIMIZING CREDIBILITY AND ACCEPTABILITY—A CASE STUDY

Earlier Figure 1 was explained using a large-scale Delphi study. The authors performed such a study for the Alaska Department of Commerce and Economic Development during 1983–84; in the process we had to analyse the forecasting environment and develop a strategic approach (Eschenbach and Geistauts, 1985 and 1986).

Alaska typifies the complex non-linear forecasting environment of developing economies in which human judgment is required for long-range forecasting. The state's dominant industry is oil but, having one-fifth of the US land area, Alaska possesses world-scale resources of gas, coal, hard-rock minerals, timber, and seafood. The development of this potential depends on economic, political, social, and technological factors—many of which resist mathematical modelling.

Our client had decided that a group-based 'Delphi-like' process was necessary. Even given Delphi's imperfections, we concluded that it was the most appropriate method. Our forecasting horizon extended to at least forty years, during which Alaska's economy will change significantly. We had to predict discontinuities, shifts in trends, and even policies to be adopted; clearly a judgmental method was required. The choice then was between individual/genius forecasts (but which one?), institutional/think-tank forecasts, in-house state agency forecasts, and a group forecast. Individual, institutional, and in-house forecasts have all been done in Alaska, but they generally have failed to achieve credibility. That left a group process with Delphi a logical choice. Our task, then, was to adapt Delphi to the Alaska situation in order to produce a study that was both valid and credible.

Delphi embodies many of the elements of reasoned judgment. The multiple iterations, feedback of results, anonymity of predictions, movement toward consensus, and even the Delphi name itself create interest and distinguish it from just another survey. These characteristics would help credibility, as would the fact that Delphi has typically been used to predict events—a critical aspect of long-range forecasting in Alaska. The match between method and the system whose behaviour was to be predicted looked good!

However, to achieve real credibility, the panel had to include many Alaskans with highly recognizable leadership and expertise credentials. As many panel members were themselves strategic decision-makers, our Delphi study to some extent moved beyond group forecasting to encompass group decision-making, which is compatible with Linstone and Turoff's (1975) view of Delphi as controlled group communication. The panel also had to be balanced in expertise, in advocacy orientation, in responsibility areas represented, and in geographic affiliation. Only by deliberately including opposing viewpoints could we achieve the appearance and the substance of objectivity.

The authority and balance criteria required a fairly large panel; this was possible only because Delphi panellists do not meet face-to-face. By avoiding panellist travel we avoided the logistical and cost problems induced by Alaskan distances, and we also increased the participation of leading Alaskans who would otherwise have declined because of tight schedules.

Appropriate expertise for judgmental forecasting is difficult to define. Following Ludlow (1975), we constructed our panel using three broad categories of expertise: decision-makers, technical experts, and advocates. We first identified typical occupations or positions within each category and then identified individuals. Thus we defined a rationale for panel membership, ensured balance between breadth and depth, and minimized the tendency to subtly stack the panel. The final panel included legislators, corporation presidents, native leaders, geologists, economists, political scientists, environmentalists, and former governors.

High panellist retention was imperative for credibility. Meaningful payments to panellists were not possible, and a copy of the final report would be their only tangible reward. A focus on major development issues, emphasis on breadth of coverage rather than simply consensus formation, new topics in each round, and persistent follow-up helped retention. Despite more than 60 pages of questions and feedback, requiring over 800 individual responses, we retained 85 per cent of the panellists. This high panellist-retention rate in turn enhanced both validity and credibility.

In the highly political Alaskan environment where forecasts influence policy, separating predictions from projected desires became a critical problem. While some panellists probably did not maintain the desired separation, panellists were frequently asked both to predict and then to rate desirability of events; both types of responses were included in the feedback and the final report. The panel as a whole did make clear distinctions on many issues; for example, although panellists preferred a policy of economic stability, they predicted that the actual policy would be one of maximum economic growth.

To include the full breadth of 'Alaskan expertise' we could not use written Delphi questionnaires in 'bush' Alaska. Alaska natives (Aleuts, Eskimos, and Indians) are a major political and cultural force, and through their regional corporations they control approximately 90 per cent of the private land. Yet many local leaders would only be comfortable with an oral approach— sometimes not in English. Thus we conducted interviews in five bush villages representing different ethnic groups, geographical regions, development levels, and growth potential. These interviews were linked to the main Delphi process by an interchange of questions and responses.

As a final step in maximizing credibility, the final round focused on the construction of a range of scenarios by concentrating on the most significant events and policies. As panellists had closely linked economic and population growth, population predictions were used to sort individual panellist scenarios into high, medium, and low growth categories. These categories were then used to construct three narrative *group* scenarios, which were internally consistent yet significantly different.

The credibility of the process, and particularly that of the panel, helped increase acceptability. Acceptability was also increased through frequent communication with the client, client review of draft questionnaires, and the formation of an independent 'Delphi Working Group' to critique the proposed research design. The acceptability criterion was also approached through focusing on long-term 'guidance' predictions, rather than on short-term policy prescriptions. Thus the client's prerogatives were preserved, particularly in the official report.

IMPLEMENTATION RECONSIDERED

We are far from having the best answers on implementation, and published empirical research on implementation of judgmental forecasting is hard to find. Yet the importance of the implementation problem cannot be denied. We have drawn on implementation literature in other areas, as well as our own experience, to construct a three-measure framework—validity, credibility, acceptability—for conceptualizing the implementation problem. For those who prefer to concentrate only on the 'science' of forecsting and ignore implementation we would, however, point out that there is a wealth of empirical evidence showing that good forecasts often fail to be implemented!

REFERENCES

Alter, S. (1979) 'Implementation risk analysis', in R. Doktor, R. L. Schultz, and D. P. Slevin (eds.), *The Implementation of Management Science*, Amsterdam: North-Holland.

Armstrong, J. S. (1978) *Long-Range Forecasting: From Crystal Ball to Computer*, New York: John Wiley.

Armstrong, J. S. (1986) 'Research on forecasting: A quarter-century review, 1960–1984'. *Interfaces*, 16, 1, 89–103.

Ascher, W. (1978) *Forecasting*, Baltimore: Johns Hopkins University Press.

Doktor, R., Schultz, R. L. and Slevin, D. P. (eds.) (1979) *The Implementation of Management Science*, Amsterdam: North-Holland.

Dror, Y. (1984) 'Policy analysis for advising rulers', in R. Tomlinson and I. Kiss (eds.), *Rethinking the Process of Operational Research and Systems Analysis*, Oxford: Pergamon.

Eschenbach, T. G. and Geistauts, G. A. (1985) 'A Delphi forecast for Alaska', *Interfaces*, 15, 6, 100–109.

Eschenbach, T. G. and Geistauts, G. A. (1986) *Alaska's Future: Commentary on a Delphi Perspective*, Anchorage: Alaska Pacific University Press.

Hildebrandt, S. (1980) 'Implementation—the bottleneck of operations research: the state of the art', *European Journal of Operational Research*, 6, 4–12.

Hogarth, R. M. (1980) *Judgement and Choice: The Psychology of Decision*, New York: John Wiley.

Huysmans, J. H. B. M. (1970) *The Implementation of Operations Research*, New York: John Wiley.

Kahneman, D., Slovic, P. and Tversky, A. (eds.) (1982) *Judgment under Uncertainty: Heuristics and Biases*, Cambridge: Cambridge University Press.

Linstone, H. A. and Turoff, M. (eds.) (1975) *The Delphi Method: Techniques and Applications*, Reading, Mass.: Addison-Wesley.

Ludlow, J. (1975) 'Delphi inquiries and knowledge utilization', in H. A. Linstone and M. Turoff (eds.), *The Delphi Method: Techniques and Applications*, Reading, Mass.: Addison-Wesley.

Makridakis, S. and Wheelwright, S. C. (eds.) (1982) *The Handbook of Forecasting*. New York: John Wiley.

McGivern, C. K. and Fineman, S. (1983) 'Research and consultancy: Towards a conceptual synthesis', *Journal of Management Studies*, **20**, 4, 425–439.

Mintzberg, H. (1980) 'Beyond implementation: An analysis of the resistance to policy analysis', *Infor*, **18**, 2, 100–138.

Schultz, R. L. (1984) 'The implementation of forecasting models', *Journal of Forecasting*, **3**, 1, 43–45.

Schultz, R. L. (1986) 'A Comment', *Interfaces*, **16**, 1, 105–106.

Schultz, R. L. and Slevin, D. P. (eds.) (1975) *Implementing Operations Research/Management Science*, New York: American Elsevier.

Schultz, R. L. and Slevin, D. P. (1983) 'The implementation profile', *Interfaces*, **13**, 87–92.

Wenk, E., Jr (1979), 'The political limits to forecasting', in T. Whiston (ed.), *The Uses and Abuses of Forecasting*, London: Macmillan.

Wheelwright, S. C. and Markridakis, S. (1980) *Forecasting Methods for Management*, 3rd edn, New York: John Wiley.

Wysocki, R. K. (1979) 'OR/MS implementation research: A bibliography', *Interfaces*, **9**, 2, 37–41.

Part III

Use of multiple regression techniques

Judgmental Forecasting
Edited by G. Wright and P. Ayton
© 1987 John Wiley & Sons Ltd

CHAPTER 10

Social Judgment Theory and Forecasting

Berndt Brehmer
Uppsala University

Human judgment plays an important role in many forecasts, and it is therefore important to investigate the characteristics of judgmental processes so that these forecasts can be evaluated.

Such an undertaking is hampered by the fact that there is no general agreement about what human judgment is: the term is used to denote anything from probability judgments obtained under highly controlled conditions to rather loose statements about what may, or may not, happen in the future.

Psychological research does not provide any unified picture of human judgment either; there is a variety of theoretical approaches to judgment, each with its own definition of the term (see Hammond, Clelland and Mumpower (1980) for a discussion of different approaches to human judgment). A discussion of the role of human judgment in forecasting, therefore, must be made relative to one of these approaches, it is not possible to discuss human judgment in general. This chapter, therefore, concentrates upon one of these approaches, that of Social Judgment Theory, SJT (Hammond *et al.*, 1975; Brehmer, 1979, 1984), and discusses some of its implications for problems of judgmental forecasting.

SOCIAL JUDGMENT THEORY

SJT is intended to be a general framework for the study of human judgment. Despite this ambition, however, it does not cover all of the phenomena that go by the name of human judgment. Perhaps the most glaring omission is that of probability judgment, which is not covered by SJT. SJT is concerned with judgments under uncertainty, but not with judgments about uncertainty.

SJT is based upon Brunswik's probabilistic functionalism (Brunswik, 1952, 1956), and it conceptualizes human judgment in terms of Brunswik's well-

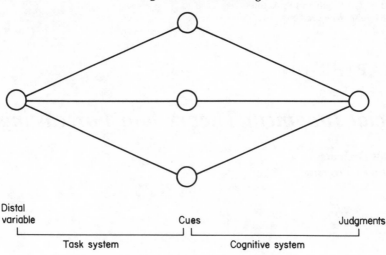

Figure 1. Brunswik's 'lens model'

known 'lens model', see Figure 1. The 'lens model' conceptualizes human judgment in terms of the relation between two systems: a *task system*, which is defined in terms of the relations between a set of cues (which represent the information available to the person for the judgments), and the distal variable (which is what the judgments are about), and a *cognitive system*, which is defined in terms of the relations between the cues and the judgments. In the case of medical diagnosis, to give an example, the cues would be the symptoms available to the physician, the distal variable would be the disease (as assessed by, for example, a post mortem), and the judgments would be the diagnosis. In most applications, the relations between the cues and the distal variable would contain some measure of uncertainty. The systems involved therefore have to be described in statistical terms (see Brehmer, 1979).

In SJT, a complete judgment analysis involves identifying and measuring the cues, the distal variable, and the judgments, and finding the relations among these variables. In many cases, however, the distal variable cannot be measured, and the analysis will then have to be limited to an analysis of the cognitive system. This is the case in forecasting, for example, where the distal variable is in the future, and cannot be incorporated in the judgment analysis.

The 'lens model' clarifies the definition of human judgment employed by social judgment theorists: *judgment is defined as a process of integrating information from a number of more or less uncertain cues into a judgment about some distal state of the world.* Judgment is thus seen as a process involving intuitive statistics, and social judgment theorists often speak of people as intuitive statisticians, using a term coined by Brunswik (1956). This does not mean that social judgment theorists believe that people actually perform statistical analyses when making judgments, but serves as a reminder about the nature of the task facing the person.

The 'lens model' also makes it clear that, because the judgments are about some distal state of the world, they are point estimates of possible states of the world. Judgment is thus seen as a process that provides direct guides to action by computing probable states of the world, rather than as a process that provides indirect guides in the form of probabilities. This is not to say that people cannot, or do not, make judgments about probabilities, only that these judgments are of no concern to SJT. As already pointed out, SJT is concerned with judgments under uncertainty, not with judgments about uncertainty.

THE ROLE OF JUDGMENT ANALYSIS IN FORECASTING

In forecasting, as in any applied context, there are two pressing problems that judgment research should have something to say about. The first is the question of whether one can trust human judgment, the second whether one can improve upon human judgment.

As for the first question, it is not possible to give a categorical answer. Forecasting is about the future, and we cannot know, for a particular forecast, whether the judgments upon which it was based were correct or not until the relevant future state has come to pass. All we can do is to assess the characteristics of human judgment under conditions where we know the outcome, and use these results to form hypotheses about the validity of human judgment in general. A first purpose of this chapter, therefore, is to review research on human judgment conducted within the general framework of SJT, and discuss its implications for the evaluation of forecasts.

As for the second question, we can be a little more categorical. Research on human judgment has revealed a number of problems, and many of these problems can be alleviated by means of judgmental aids. The second purpose of this chapter, therefore, is to describe the judgmental aids that have been developed by social judgment theorists, and to discuss how they could be used to improve judgmental forecasting. But first we have to discuss the problem of how to analyse human judgment.

THE ANALYSIS OF HUMAN JUDGMENT

A basic premise in SJT is that people may not always be able to give accurate descriptions of how they arrive at their judgments. It is therefore necessary to find methods which enable us to infer the characteristics of judgment without recourse to introspective reports. The first problem faced by SJT was to develop such methods.

The basis for the methods employed in SJT is the simple notion that if we know what judgments a person has made and the information upon which these judgments were based, we can always develop a mathematical model which relates the judgments to the information. If we are successful in developing such a model, it will produce the same judgment as the person does when given the same information. The model may then be considered a simulation of the person's judgment processes. As such it has the advantage that it is *overt*, and by examining this overt model we can learn important things about the characteristics of the *covert* judgmental processes.

SJT has opted for linear statistical models as simulation devices (see Brehmer (1979) for a discussion). Under such a model, a person's judgments are described as a weighted sum of the cue variables, i.e.:

$$J = b_1X_1 + b_2X_2 + \ldots + b_kX_k + e$$

where J is the judgment, $b_1 - b_k$ are the weights for the cue variables found in the analysis, $X_1 - X_k$ are the cue variables and e is an error term. Such an equation is usually called a *policy* in SJT.

There are a variety of linear models, but in actual practice, social judgment theorists usually employ multiple regression, because this is the only model that makes it possible to analyse judgment under conditions where the cue variables are intercorrelated. As we shall see, cue intercorrelation is an important feature of a judgment task which must be taken into account in many analyses.

How judgment analyses are conducted

In an actual instance of judgmental analysis, a judge would be presented with a series of cue profiles, and asked to make a judgment about each profile. For example, the profiles may be descriptions of patients, and the judgments may concern how long it patient will need to recover. Some patients would occur twice and form a set of replicates. From these replicates, it would then be possible to obtain an independent estimate of error. When all judgments have been collected, a multiple regression equation is fitted to the judgments. This equation may include non-linear terms and interaction terms. The aim is to find an equation that accounts for all of the systematic variance in the judgments, as estimated from the replicates. When this equation has been found, it constitutes a description of the person's judgment policy.

The characteristics of judgment policies

A linear model provides a description of a judgment policy in terms of five basic characteristics.

(1) *Which cues are used*. This is simply the cues that receive significant weights in the regression analysis.
(2) *The relative importance of the cues that have been used*. This is shown by

the relations among the weights for the cues that have received significant weights in the analysis. There is a certain amount of controversy about which measure one should use here; there are many possible indices of weight in multiple regression. There is evidence, however, that subjects understand the concept of relative importance in terms of relative beta weights (Brehmer & Qvarnström, 1976; Brehmer, Hagafors and Johansson, 1980), so this measure is presumably the most meaningful one psychologically.

(3) *The form of the function relating the judgments to each cue.* A precise description of function form can be obtained, either by adding polynomials to regression equations and assessing their significance, or by transforming the cue values according to some function (if there is some *a priori* hypothesis about a possible function) and assessing whether the beta weight for the transformed cue is significant.

(4) *The rule used for integrating information from different cues.* The basic hypothesis in multiple regression is, of course, that the integration rule is a simple additive rule. Tests for departure for additivity are possible, either by comparing the variance actually accounted for by the regression equation with an independent estimate of error, or by adding cross-product terms to the regression equation and assessing their significance.

(5) *Consistency.* This is indicated by the percentage of systematic variance accounted for by the model. In many analyses, the squared multiple correlation has been used for this purpose, but this is not quite adequate, for the squared multiple correlation is a measure of fit. In the absence of an independent estimate of error, it is not possible to decide whether a low multiple correlation indicates low consistency, or if indicates that the person used a non-additive integration rule, or if there were non-linear cue-judgment relations. Therefore, consistency is best estimated from the correlation between the replicates.

Thus, a linear model gives a description of a judgment policy in terms of a number of intuitively obvious aspects, which correspond closely to how people talk about judgment, with one important exception: consistency. People seem to have no intuitive notion that their judgments may be unreliable in the sense that they contain random error. Yet, this is an extremely important aspect of judgment, and many of the problems associated with human judgment can be traced to this particular characteristic of the judgment process. Therefore it often constitutes the focus of many judgment analyses performed by social judgment theorists.

The problem of subjective cue values

It is important to realize that a multiple regression equation gives a description of a judgment policy in terms of the actual, physical cue values presented to the judge, rather than in terms of subjective cue values. Anderson (e.g. 1971) has pointed out that this makes convincing tests of the nature of the psychological integration rule impossible, for information integration is presumably in terms of subjective cue values, rather than in terms of objective ones. This is obviously correct.

Most recent work in SJT has employed what may be called quasi-subjective cue values. All cues are given in the same metric from, say, 1 through 10, and the subjects are instructed to consider '1' the lowest value of that cue that they can think of (whatever that value may be physically), and '10' as the highest value they can think of (whatever that may mean physically). This is based upon the informal hypothesis that judgment involves the translation of physical cue values into what may be called subjective standard scores. This informal hypothesis has, however, not been subjected to test, and when it is important to know the exact form of the integration rule, it is probably safest to use the analysis-of-variance methods recommended by Anderson (e.g. 1971) which offer a solution to the scale values problem, instead of multiple regression.

A number of recent studies, however, have employed analysis-of-variance procedures in studies of human judgment (see Libby and Lewis (1982) for a review). The results of these studies do not differ from those obtained in studies using multiple regression; the same picture of the judgment process emerges. Thus, the issue of subjective versus objective scale values may not be critical in most judgment studies.

OVERVIEW OF RESULTS AND THEIR IMPLICATIONS

There has been a large number of studies of judgment using the general methods outlined in the section above (not all of them undertaken by social judgment theorists), involving a wide variety of tasks and professional groups. The results from these studies are surprisingly similar, regardless of the nature of the judgment task and subject group, so it seems that we can have some faith in the general picture that emerges from these studies (see Libby and Lewis (1982) and Slovic and Lichtenstein (1971) for reviews). The following results seem to be well substantiated.

(1) Judgment processes tend to be simple. First, they are simple in the sense that they follow additive rules, and second in that very few cues are used (three seems to be a common value).
(2) Judges are inconsistent.
(3) Judges cannot describe how they arrive at their judgments.
(4) There are wide inter-individual differences, even when the subjects are experts with years of experience.

Implications

Each of these findings has important implications, in forecasting as in other contexts where human judgment is used as a basis for decisions. We will discuss each in turn.

Simplicity

Human judgment is often used because other methods seem too simplistic. Indeed, the whole field of judgment analysis emerged from a controversy over the relative efficacy of supposedly simplistic statistical methods and supposedly complex human judgments in the clinical field (Meehl, 1954).

After 30 years of research, we are now in a position to conclude that there is no evidence that human judgment has the complex structure it was supposed to have. Whatever advantages human judgment may have, they are not to be found in any ability to use huge amounts of data, or in any particularly complex form of processing. Clearly, we must expect that human judgment provides a simplistic basis for decisions also.

That this has not been discovered before is presumably due to the fact that people lack insight into how they arrive at their judgments. It has therefore been possible for people to believe that their judgments are complex, just because the information available has been highly complex. In the absence of judgment analysis, it has simply not been possible to evaluate claims that judgments are complex and express some appreciation of the 'totality of the problem'.

Presumably, the simple nature of judgment stems from the general cognitive limitations to which people are subject. This raises the problem of whether people can be aided to process more information in more complex ways. We will return to this problem as we discuss cognitive aids later in this chapter.

Inconsistency

Inconsistency means that there is random error in the policy. Consequently, a single judgment cannot be trusted to express a person's opinion about a matter.

Inconsistency is not simply lack of reliability or measurement error, for it is systematically related to task characteristics, such as complexity and non-linearity (Brehmer, 1979).

One obvious way of getting around the problem of inconsistency is to get multiple judgments from a person. This may not always be feasible, however. A better method is what is known as *bootstrapping* (Dawes, 1971). This involves substituting a person's judgment policy for his or her judgments. The policy produces error-free judgments, and there is evidence (e.g. Goldberg, 1970) that a person's policy actually will produce more valid judgments than the person does because inconsistency has been removed.

Lack of insight

Lack of insight implies that we cannot always trust a person's description of how he or she makes the judgments. For example, the fact that a person claims to have a given cue into consideration (or ignored it) cannot be taken at face value. Only judgment analysis will reveal whether or not a person has taken a given cue into account when making a set of judgments.

Inter-individual differences

That there are wide inter-individual differences suggest that it may often be necessary to use multiple judges to get a reasonably correct basis for a decision. This raises the problem of how one should reconcile differences in judgments, as well as how one should resolve the interpersonal conflicts that may emerge from differences in judgments.

As for the first problem, it is by no means clear that all differences in judgment really need to be reconciled. A few words about this problem may be in order.

What needs to be reconciled?

Two aspects are important in this context. The first has to do with task characteristics, the other with judgment processes.

Task characteristics

In many judgment tasks, the cues are highly intercorrelated. This means that two persons may come up with very similar judgments, despite that they rely on very different cues. This means that even substantial differences in policy may have very little importance in terms of judgments, and that two persons with very different policies may come up with the same recommendation. We will have a case of disagreement in principle, but agreement in practice. Such cases are by no means uncommon. However, if the true intercorrelation structure is unknown, differences of this sort may cause severe problems, especially if the person's discuss their policies without regard for the actual nature of the task to which they must be applied. This illustrates an important issue often overlooked in judgment analysis: that it is as important to know the characteristics of the task to which the policies will be applied, as to know the characteristics of the policies themselves.

Policy characteristics

As noted above, inconsistency is a pervasive characteristic of judgment policies. Lack of consistency can produce disagreement in judgments despite similarity in underlying policies, as well as agreement in judgments despite underlying differences in policies. Only a judgment analysis will reveal the true nature of the agreement or disagreement between two persons, and in the absence of such an analysis it is hard, or impossible, to interpret an observed case of disagreement or agreement between two persons.

Policy conflict

When two persons come up with very different judgments, we face the possibility that there will be conflict. Conflicts caused by judgmental differences have been studied intensely by social judgment theorists, both in the laboratory and in applied settings (see Brehmer (1976a) and Hammond *et al.*, (1977), for reviews).

The results of these studies show that conflicts of this kind are surprisingly hard to resolve, largely because of the nature of the cognitive processes involved in judgment.

In part, the problem of resolving a policy conflict stems from the fact that they are hard to diagnose, as noted above. Without judgment analysis, it is hard to know whether a given case of conflict is caused by inconsistency, or true differences in policy.

However, conflicts are often prolonged because of problems associated with the way in which people change policies. Even when people are willing to change their policies to reach agreement, and make every effort to do so, they may actually fail to reach agreement. Specifically, the process of policy change often produces inconsistency. Because of increasing inconsistency, disagreement stays constant, despite reduction of underlying differences in policy. The persons may not detect this, however, for all they see is the actual disagreement in judgments, and this may lead them to misdiagnose the situation; all a person knows is that he or she is changing his or her policy, and since disagreement is not reduced, it is obvious that the other person is not making any efforts to reduce conflict. This may easily lead to distrust, and makes it impossible to resolve the conflict (see Brehmer (1974) for a demonstration that inconsistency makes it hard for people to understand one another, and Hammond and Brehmer (1973) for a general discussion of the problem).

Discussion is thus no guarantee that conflicts will be resolved, and may actually lead to increased conflict (see Brehmer (1972) for a demonstration).

In part, the problems here have to do with problems in discovering the true nature of the disagreement. This raises the problems of whether people can resolve policy conflicts more readily if they are helped to communicate their policies, and to understand the real relation between these policies by means of some cognitive aid. We will discuss this problem later as we come to the section on cognitive aids.

HOW POLICIES ARE FORMED

SJT has its roots in analyses of clinical judgment (see Hammond (1955) and Hammond, Hursch and Todd (1964) for early examples) and this has had important effects upon how social judgment theorists think about policies and about how they are formed. Thus, social judgment theorists tend to think about policies as cognitive structures that exist as a result of experience with rather well-defined problems. The general problem of how people acquire policies has been modelled upon the task facing a clinical psychologist who gives the same battery of tests to the patients and tries to learn to use the test results to infer the diseases of the patients. The dominating learning paradigm used in SJT—the multiple-cue probability learning paradigm—has been modelled upon this particular clinical situation. While not totally unrepresentative of real world problems, it is nevertheless a limited paradigm, and one that represents a rather pure case of learning to make inferences from probabilistic cues. It will not, however, serve as a general paradigm for how policies come about.

The limitations of the learning paradigms used in SJT, and any other learning paradigm for that matter, are particularly obvious in the case of forecasting, where it will often be the case that the judgment required will concern problems for which the judge has no earlier experience of direct relevance. The policies in these situations, therefore, cannot be learned policies of the kind analysed in clinical judgment. Instead, they must be seen as policies that are constructed on the spot to deal with the problem at hand. In discussing how policies come about, we must therefore not only consider how policies are learned, we must also consider the process of policy construction. For the reasons given above, the discussion of learning can be kept rather short.

Learning policies

As already mentioned, learning studies in SJT have followed the multiple-cue probability learning paradigm (Brehmer, 1979). In experiments in this paradigm, subjects are presented with a series of cue profiles and asked to make judgments about each of them. After each judgment, they receive feedback indicating the correct answer. The learning tasks are constructed in such a way that the multiple correlation between cues and the feedback values representing the distal variable is less than perfect. Thus, the multiple-cue probability learning paradigm is a paradigm for studying how people learn to make inferences from probabilistic cues, and it incorporates the essential features of the clinical situation outlined above.

The results obtained with this paradigm have been reviewed by Brehmer (1979, 1980). They show that when the relations between the cues and the distal variable are linear, the subjects learn these tasks rapidly. However, they do not perform optimally. They are inconsistent; the level of inconsistency is a monotone function of the level of uncertainty in the task. This finding replicates results from studies of clinical inference (Brehmer, 1976b).

When the relations are non-linear, on the other hand, learning is extremely poor (Hammond and Summers, 1972). The differences in learning rate for different kinds of functional rules are explained by differences in the hypotheses that the subjects bring to these tasks (see Brehmer, 1980).

Implications

The results from the learning studies imply that we may have some faith in judgments that are based upon experience, provided that the task is linear, and provided that the experience is relevant to the forecasting task. These conditions are probably best met in short-term forecasting, which requires simple extrapolations. It is unlikely, however, that policies acquired on the basis of experience will have much value in long-term forecasting.

Policy construction

While problems of learning have received considerable attention in SJT, and are reasonably well understood, there has been very little work on policy construction. A full understanding of policy construction would require a theory of how people retrieve information from memory which helps them to decide which cues would be relevant to the task, how they combine information from the cues into an overall judgment policy, and how they implement this policy to make actual judgments. Some first steps towards this goal have been taken in our laboratory in a series of studies. These studies are limited, however, in that they have been concerned only with the problem of how people combine information into a judgment policy and then implement this policy into judgments.

In these experiments, subjects have been given information about the relation between each of a set of cues and the distal variable, and they have then been asked to combine information from different cues into judgments. The results show, that when subjects have no information about how the information from the various cues should be combined, they combine information according to an additive rule (Brehmer, 1986; Brehmer and Qvarnström, 1976, Brehmer, Hagafors and Johansson, 1980). The results also show that subjects interpret information about relative importance in terms of differences in cue-judgment slopes, rather than in terms of variance accounted for (Brehmer and Qvarnström, 1976; Brehmer, Hagafors and Johansson, 1980), and that subjects have problems implementing policies that contain non-linear relations (Brehmer, 1971; Brehmer and Qvarnström, 1976). Finally, the results show that when subjects have information that implies that cues should be combined in a configural manner (they knew that the importance of one cue varied with the value of another cue), they nevertheless combined the information additively (Brehmer, Hagafors and Johansson, 1980).

Implications

These studies constitute a bare beginning, and they concern only limited aspects of the problem of policy construction. The important question of how people decide which cues are relevant, and which cues are not relevant, has not yet been studied. Since knowing the relevant cues is by far the most important aspect of a policy, it is clear that these results do not give much ground for evaluating policies in forecasting. However, a familiar theme emerges from these studies, and this is worth emphasizing. This is the theme of simplicity. Just as we found in the studies of actual policies, we find that the subjects in the policy construction experiments also employ simple additive rules, when the information they have clearly implies a configural combination rule. However, we must not interpret these results to mean that people cannot use non-additive rules. The additive rule may be a common one, but there is evidence that people can use non-additive rules also (see, for example, Brehmer, 1969). To investigate when, and under what circumstances, people use configural rules is an important task for future studies.

COGNITIVE AIDS

The results on human judgment reviewed above show that judgment leaves something to be desired. An important question, therefore, is whether it is possible to find ways of aiding human judgment and alleviate the problems uncovered by research on human judgment.

From the point of view of SJT, and the results obtained within this framework, a judgment aid must fulfil the following three functions.

(1) It must make the judgment policy of a person explicit, so that it can be communicated, and so that the judge can see what the actual characteristics of his or her policy are.
(2) It must allow manipulation of the policy, so that the judge can explore the consequences of various changes in the policy.
(3) It must enable people to compare their policies to help them understand the nature of their agreement or disagreement. It should also enable a person to compare his or her policy with the optimal policy for the task (if this policy is known) to help the person understand how he or she must change to improve the judgments.

A cognitive aid fulfilling these requirements has been developed (Hammond and Brehmer, 1973). The current version is called POLICY, and it has been tried out in a number of contexts, including learning (Hammond, 1971) and policy formation (Hammond *et al.*, 1977).

POLICY is an interactive computer program. It presents a set of cue profiles via a CRT screen or a printer to the subjects and asks for a judgment about each of these profiles.

It then performs a judgment analysis according to the methods described earlier in this paper, and presents the results in graphical form, showing the relative weights for different cues in the form of bar graphs, and the functional relation between each cue and the judgments in the form of a graph for each cue, as well as information about the consistency of the judgment in numerical form. Figure 2 shows some typical displays. It is possible to put in the characteristics of a judgment task, so that the person is able to compare his or her relative weights and function forms to those required by the task, or to have two judges make judgments about the same task, and compare their policies with respect to relative weights, function forms and consistency. Thus,

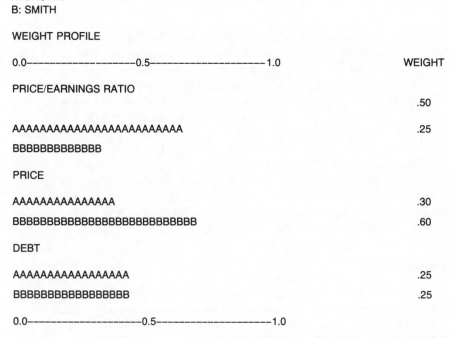

A: BROWN
B: SMITH

WEIGHT PROFILE

0.0-------------------0.5---------------------1.0   WEIGHT

PRICE/EARNINGS RATIO
                                                              .50

AAAAAAAAAAAAAAAAAAAAAAAAAAA   .25
BBBBBBBBBBBBB

PRICE

AAAAAAAAAAAAAAA   .30
BBBBBBBBBBBBBBBBBBBBBBBBBBBBBB   .60

DEBT

AAAAAAAAAAAAAAAAAA   .25
BBBBBBBBBBBBBBBBBB   .25

0.0-------------------0.5---------------------1.0

Figure 2. A printer display comparing two stockbrokers with respect to the weights they employ when making evaluations of stocks

the program can be used both to signal what kinds of changes are needed in a policy to improve judgments, and to explicate the disagreement between two persons. Thus, the program fulfils the requirements that it should make policies explicit, and serve to aid communication of policies, as well as the requirement that it should enable a person to compare his policy to the optimal policy for a task, or to that of another person. These functions would be hard to fulfil without the aid of POLICY, because people have little insight into their policies. Therefore, it may be hard, or impossible, to decide how a policy should be changed to improve accuracy or reduce conflict, or how one should answer questions about one's policy when somebody wants to know how one arrives at one's judgments.

There is evidence that the POLICY program aids learning. Non-linear tasks which cannot be learned on the basis of feedback from a task alone are easily learned with POLICY (Hammond, 1971). However, although there is evidence that conflicts can be resolved with the aid of POLICY (see Hammond *et al.* (1977) for a review), there are actually no controlled studies of the effects of POLICY upon conflict resolution. Consequently, we do not know what it is about POLICY that helps people resolve conflicts, or when POLICY will be useful. More research is needed on this question.

Policy change

Judges can also use POLICY to evaluate the effects of various changes in their policies. Thus, a person may introduce a change in the relative weights that he or she gives to the cues, or in the forms of the functions relating the judgments to the cues by drawing a new relative weight profile on the screen with a light-pen, and evaluate what the effects of these changes would be upon the agreement with another person and the accuracy of the judgments, as well as to investigate what the effects of such changes would be for selected cases that are especially critical for some reason. Such exploration of changes in policy may show that a given form of change, which leads to higher agreement, may not be all that critical in terms of accuracy, or may lead to fewer differences in judgments, compared to the original policy, than the person first thought; and this may well aid policy change and conflict resolution, as shown by Hammond *et al.* (1977).

Implications

The POLICY aid is still in its infancy, and much remains to be done to make it generally useful. The initial results are promising, however, and it is clear that POLICY can fulfil the functions it was designed to fulfil, and that this may lead to improvements in judgment policies, and to a better understanding of one's own policy and that of others.

The policy change option in POLICY may also be a means for overcoming some of the problems that result in simple policies. A policy may have to be simple when it has to be executed in one's head, so to speak. But there is no reason why people should not be able to develop quite complex policies with the aid of POLICY, and then have the computer execute these policies. This may well improve judgmental forecasting by allowing people to overcome the cognitive limitations that keep their judgment policies simple under ordinary circumstances, and it may thus allow them to express what they know about the forecasting task in a better way.

CONCLUSIONS

This chapter has presented some of the results obtained within the general framework of SJT. It should be emphasized that SJT is very much a developing framework, and that our understanding of many important issues, such as that of policy construction, is very limited at present.

The major contribution that SJT can make to judgmental forecasting, therefore, is probably in the methods that it provides for analysing judgmental policies, and in the cognitive aid that has been developed on the basis of the results from these analyses, rather than in specific results and theories about the judgment process. These methods have been found useful in a variety of contexts for understanding and improving judgment and resolving disagreement. There is no reason why they should not be similarly useful for problems of judgmental forecasting.

ACKNOWLEDGMENT

Preparation of this paper was supported by a grant from the Swedish Council of Research on the Humanities and Social Sciences.

REFERENCES

Anderson, N. H. (1971) *Methods of Information Integration Theory*, New York: Academic Press.

Brehmer, B. (1969) 'Cognitive dependence on additive and configural cue-criterion relations', *American Journal of Psychology*, **82**, 490–503.

Brehmer, B. (1971) 'Subjects' ability to use functional rules', *Psychonomic Science*, **24**, 259–260.

Brehmer, B. (1972) 'Policy conflict as a function of policy similarity and policy complexity', *Scandinavian Journal of Psychology*, **13**, 208–221.

Brehmer, B. (1974) 'Policy conflict, policy consistency, and interpersonal understanding', *Scandinavian Journal of Psychology*, **15**, 273–276.

Brehmer, B. (1976a) 'Social judgment theory and the analysis of interpersonal conflict', *Psychological Bulletin*, **83**, 985–1003.

Brehmer, B. (1976b) 'Note on clinical judgment and the formal characteristics of clinical tasks', *Psychological Bulletin*, **83**, 778–782.

Brehmer, B. (1979) 'Preliminaries to a psychology of inference. *Scandinavian Journal of Psychology*, **20**, 193–210.

Brehmer, B. (1980) 'In one word: Not from experience', *Acta Psychologica*, **45**, 223–241.

Brehmer, B. (1984) 'The role of judgment in small group decision making and conflict', in G. Stephenson and J. Davis (eds.), *Progress in Applied Social Psychology*, Vol. 2, Chichester: Wiley.

Brehmer, B. (1986) 'How subjects understand everyday expressions about cue weights'. Department of Psychology, Uppsala University, manuscript.

Brehmer, B., Hagafors, R. and Johansson, R. (1980) 'Cognitive skills in judgment: Subjects' ability to use information about weights, function forms, and organizing principles, *Organizational Behavior and Human Performance*, **26**, 373–385.

Brehmer, B. and Qvarnström, G. (1976) 'Information integration and subjective weights in multiple cue judgments', *Organizational Behavior and Human Performance*, **17**, 118–126.

Brunswik, E. (1952) *Conceptual Framework of Psychology*, Chicago: University of Chicago Press.

Brunswik, E. (1956) *Perception and the Representative Design of Psychological Experiments*, Berkely, Calif.: University of California Press.

Dawes, R. M. (1971) 'A case study of graduate admissions: Application of three principles of decision making', *American Psychologist*, **26**, 180–188.

Goldberg, L. R. (1970) 'Man vs. model of man: A rationale, plus some evidence, for a method of improving on clinical inference', *Psychological Bulletin*, **73**, 422–432.

Hammond, K. R. (1955) 'Probabilistic functioning and the clinical method', *Psychological Review*, **62**, 255–262.

Hammond, K. R. (1971) 'Computer graphics as an aid to learning', *Science*, **172**, 903–908.

Hammond, K. R. and Brehmer, B. (1973) 'Quasi-rationality and distrust: Implications for international conflict', in L. Rappaport and D. Summers (eds.), *Human Judgment and Social Interaction*, New York: Holt, Rinehart & Winston.

Hammond, K. R., Hursch, C. J. and Todd, F. J. (1964) 'Analyzing the components of clinical inference', *Psychological Review*, **71**, 438–456.

Hammond, K. R., McClelland, G. and Mumpower, J. (1980) *Human Judgment and Decision Making*, New York: Praeger.

Hammond, K. R. and Summers, D. A. (1972) 'Cognitive control', *Psychological Review*, **79**, 58–67.

Hammond, K. R., Stewart, T. R., Brehmer, B. and Steinmann, D. O. (1975) 'Social judgment theory', in M. Kaplan and S. Schwartz (eds.), *Human Judgment and Decision Processes*, New York: Academic Press.

Hammond, K. R., Rohrbaugh, J., Mumpower, J. and Adelman, L. (1977) 'Social judgment theory: Applications in policy formation', in M. Kaplan and S. Schwartz (eds.), *Human Judgment and Decision Making in Applied Settings*, New York: Academic Press.

Libby, R. and Lewis, B. L. (1982) 'Human information processing research in accounting: The state of the art 1982, *Accounting, Organizations, and Society*, **7**, 231–285.

Meehl, P. E. (1954) *Clinical vs. statistical prediction: A theoretical analysis and review of the evidence*, Minneapolis: University of Minnesota Press.

Slovic, P. and Lichtenstein, S. (1971) 'Comparison of Bayesian and regression approaches to the study of information processing in judgment', *Organizational Behavior and Human Performance*, **6**, 649–744.

Judgmental Forecasting
Edited by G. Wright and P. Ayton
© 1987 John Wiley & Sons Ltd

CHAPTER 11

Linear Models as Decision Aids in Insurance Decision-making: The Case of Estimation of Automobile Insurance Claims

Danny Samson
University of Melbourne

and

Howard Thomas
University of Illinois at Urbana-Champaign

INTRODUCTION

This study focuses on linear decision models and their use in aiding the insurance underwriter to relate observable policyholder characteristics to expected claims costs and thereby determine realistic insurance premiums. The particular area of application is the insurance of automobiles. Over the years, Ferreira (1974) and others have indicated that insurance companies have developed various strategies (often called 'rating plans') for rating drivers of automobiles. The purpose of such rating plans is to price different risk classes in terms of their accumulated loss experience and design stable risk classification schemes for the efficient management of insurance operations.

As pointed out by Fischhoff *et al*. (1981), formal models can be interpreted as *methods*, whereby the decision-maker is essentially replaced by the model, or as *aids* whereby the model provides information to assist the decision-maker's judgment. In the insurance underwriting application investigated in this study, the linear decision model is interpreted primarily as a decision aid and a decision support system which provides a base judgment about appropriate levels for automobile insurance premiums.

Hogarth (1980) has described the linear compensatory model as a straightforward, comprehensive approach. Hogarth suggests that there are two forms of dependence (which the linear model does not encompass). First, environmental correlation occurs where values of dimensions tend to occur together. Second, interaction effects can occur whereby the actual value of an object is different from the weighted sum of the dimensions.

Linear models have been found to be highly accurate in predicting individual judgments (see Libby and Lewis (1977), and Slovic and Lichtenstein (1971)), and extremely robust in terms of sensitivity to assumptions (Einhorn and Hogarth, 1975; Einhorn, Kleinmuntz and Kleinmuntz, 1979). The linear model is consistent in its treatment of information and comprehensive in its use of information.

Barnett (1983) suggests that linear models can be misused through applying them (e.g. fitting regression parameters) when the relationship between variables are non-linear. He stresses the importance of checking the 'functional form' of relationships and using transformations where appropriate. Johnson and Mai (1979) examined the suitability of linear models in non-linear environments and constructed a distortion index which compares linear and non-linear models.

There are many ways in which the attribute weights of linear models can be set. They can be subjectively assessed as in linear additive utility models (Keeney and Raiffa, 1976) or fitted to observed data using a number of possible criteria. Parsons and Hulin (1982) examined four weighting methods, ordinary and pooled sample least squares, Bayesian regression and equal weighting. Ordinary least squares is the most commonly used method but was found to be inferior to two of the other three methods in Parsons and Hulin's problem context.

Linear models have been widely used in a diverse set of applications. Larcker and Lessig (1983) have found the linear model to be 'generally reliable' (p. 58) in modelling cue importance factors in a stock valuation task. Schepanski (1983) tested the linear model in a task of evaluating the credit-worthiness of business borrowers. In this credit rating study, qualitative tests indicated that the task involved non-linear decision processes; however, calculated tests supported the use of the linear model. This evidence attests to both the robustness of linear models and also supports Barnett's (1983) idea of carefully examining a number of functional forms before making a choice.

Bunn and Seigal (1983) used a linear model to forecast evening electricity loads in Britain based on television-watching patterns. This is a good example of where linear models can be used directly as forecasting models. Linear models have also been extensively used in economic modelling. For example King (1979) used linear demand (consumption) models to predict annual US expenditure.

In researching judgments made by auditors, Libby and Lewis (1977) concluded that linear models successfully predicted their judgments. Slovic and Lichtenstein (1971) also point out that 'the linear model does a remarkably good job of predicting human judgments'. In noting the superiority of linear models to the prediction of decision-makers in graduate school admission decisions, Dawes (1971) suggested that decisions made with the aid of a computer (using a linear model) may be 'less capricious and more valid than those made by the decision maker relying on his own intuitions'.

Linear models, according to Dawes and Corrigan (1974), are also very insensitive and robust to changes in underlying assumptions and can thus reproduce judgments made by more complicated underlying processes with an acceptable degree of accuracy. Therefore, even though the dimensions (e.g. age, sex, area, group, no-claim discount (NCD), etc.) by which an automobile insurance account may be categorized are not fully independent, it would be expected that, as long as departures from independence are not too marked, the linear model is probably a satisfactory representation of the underlying process. By drawing on the results of researchers in the fields of psychology and management, Ashton (1976) presents further evidence supporting the robustness of linear models for decision-making. Slovic, Fischhoff and Lichtenstein (1977) also reviewed a number of diverse field and laboratory settings in which linear models had been successfully fitted. Many of these problem situations (e.g. production scheduling, and graduate student admission decisions) appear to be similar in degree of structure and complexity to the underwriting decision described in this chapter.

INSURANCE UNDERWRITING

The decision regarding whether or not an insurance risk is acceptable for underwriting, or at what price (premium) a risk is acceptable is a judgmental process involving heuristics and decision rules derived from experience and intuition. In some insurance areas, each risk unit is sufficiently different from each other risk unit to make the use of aggregative and associative methods of analysis infeasible. Underwriting decisions in these insurance accounts can be termed as 'nonprogrammed' (Simon, 1971) because of the unique circumstances surrounding each decision and the lack of a data set upon which to base decisions. An example might be the property/liability insurance of dams or nuclear power plants.

'Programmed' underwriting decisions involve the setting of premiums and acceptance/rejection of risk units where relatively large numbers of similar units exist (e.g. automobile or household insurances). In these accounts there are a number of advantages in using appropriate mathematical models to aid the judgment of the decision maker:

(1) Because of the large amount of data the human judge cannot process and use all of the available relevant information. However, an appropriate mathematical model can efficiently summarize the data as specified by the analyst.

(2) The organizational structure of most insurance companies which underwrite motor or household business is such that no single decision-maker can cope with all the underwriting decisions. Hence to ensure a maximum degree of consistency some set of rules or guidelines is appropriate. These guidelines can be derived using mathematical models which incorporate the combined experience of all the firm's (or industry's) underwriters.

(3) Rules which are based on actual experiences (which may be updated to account for changes occurring through time) avoid the random element of human judgment, i.e. the unreliability or capriciousness of the human decision-maker. Research at the Oregon Research Institute has shown that 'bootstrapping', i.e. replacing or aiding an individuals' behaviour with a model based on that behaviour, is a possible approximation 'wherever the true model is monotone in each argument' (Chang and Fairley, 1979).

MOTOR INSURANCE UNDERWRITING

This monotonicity was observed in a large British motor insurance portfolio and in a number of other 'programmed' insurance areas. Hence the regression approach and in particular the 'correlation paradigm' (Bunn and Siegal, 1983) were proposed as possible approaches for modelling the underwriting risk assessment and classification process.

In the present application, linear models were fitted to data on an ex-post basis. The aims of this study were to establish the set of factors which should be included in the risk model and to determine the importance and, hence, the extent that each factor should contribute to the premium calculation.

A number of previous studies have been undertaken in the area of risk modelling in general insurance. Chang and Fairley (1979), Sant (1980) and the SRI report of May 1976 entitled 'The role of risk models in property and liability insurance' provide the justification for using mathematical models, such as the additive or multiplicative form, in risk analysis. Grimes (1971) and Bailey and Simon (1960) have considered class rating and the use of linear models in motor insurance accounts. Gaunt (1978) has reported on the use of information in motor insurance underwriting (through a survey of US insurers). Curry (1964) and Haner (1967) have also studied and reported on a number of risk factors (i.e. characteristics which may be related to risk magnitude). Coutts (1984) has discussed the use of a 'points' system and recognized the limitations of such systems as being inexactness and oversimplification.

A COMPREHENSIVE MOTOR INSURANCE ACCOUNT

The disguised data shown in Table 1 is drawn from a large British motor insurance account. Information on four variables (age of policyholder, level of no claim discount, area in which policyholder lives and group rating of the insured automobile (e.g. family, sports, etc.)) was collected for each policy and each variable was assessed at three levels. Hence each policy was placed into one of 81 cells.

Table 1   Data from a UK motor account and predicted values for claims cost per policy

		Key for each cell	Exposure (number of individuals) Actual claims/policy (£) Fitted claims/policy (£) %(fitted − actual)/actual						
		Age 17–24			Age 25–30			Age over 30		
		NIL NCD	MED NCD	FULL NCD	NIL NCD	MED NCD	FULL NCD	NIL NCD	MED NCD	FULL NCD
Area 1	GP 1	1671 36.44 46.52 27.6	3941 27.17 28.89 6.3	1458 15.98 18.66 16.7	1024 31.15 42.68 37.0	4940 21.70 25.05 15.4	7155 13.92 14.82 6.4	3178 27.72 36.24 30.7	15503 19.01 18.61 −2.1	53928 11.61 8.39 −27.7
	GP 2	2405 47.44 48.99 3.3	6468 23.03 31.36 36.1	3048 18.70 21.13 13.0	1764 40.59 45.16 11.2	9534 24.71 27.53 11.4	18550 17.71 17.30 0.4	5318 31.33 38.72 23.6	34371 19.80 21.09 6.5	190936 12.38 10.86 −12.27
	GP 3	1505 74.5 55.85 −25.0	5760 37.58 38.22 1.7	4240 28.63 27.99 −2.2	1724 60.73 52.02 −14.3	10565 37.74 34.39 −8.87	26368 24.35 24.16 −0.7	4769 48.64 45.58 −6.3	35405 28.44 27.95 −1.7	218233 16.3 17.72 8.7
Area 2	GP 1	1638 38.15 48.72 27.7	2562 27.57 31.08 12.7	1193 20.57 20.86 1.4	1169 32.33 44.88 38.8	5470 23.18 27.25 17.5	6890 17.63 17.02 −3.5	3098 32.34 38.44 18.9	15856 19.22 20.81 8.2	50881 12.92 10.58 −18.1
	GP 2	2286 52.58 51.19 −2.6	5672 32.12 33.56 4.5	2385 23.23 23.33 0.4	2002 39.71 47.36 19.3	10587 25.95 29.73 16.3	17888 18.52 19.50 5.3	5800 38.19 40.92 7.1	32073 21.77 23.29 7.0	186828 14.15 13.06 −7.7
	GP 3	1500 72.80 58.05 −20.2	3498 51.74 40.42 −21.8	3180 28.3 20.19 6.7	1962 69.09 54.22 −20.3	6921 40.87 36.59 −10.4	25573 27.83 26.36 −5.2	5529 56.12 47.78 −14.8	38862 31.92 30.15 −5.5	224061 18.46 19.92 7.9
Area 3	GP 1	1017 35.00 52.86 51.0	2004 31.33 35.23 12.4	530 16.79 25.00 48.9	846 45.62 49.03 7.5	3920 26.37 31.40 19.1	8578 19.34 21.17 9.5	1989 32.12 42.59 31.7	9814 23.75 24.96 5.1	27295 14.36 14.73 2.5
	GP 2	12.95 54.44 55.34 1.6	2804 34.59 37.71 9.0	928 31.68 27.48 −13.2	1486 48.38 51.50 6.4	6480 29.04 33.87 16.6	8083 19.70 23.64 20.0	4056 42.50 45.07 6.0	24822 25.90 27.44 5.9	101099 16.86 17.21 2.0
	GP 3	905 88.83 62.20 −29.9	2626 58.57 44.57 −23.9	1458 48.49 34.34 −29.1	1513 72.77 58.36 −19.8	7429 51.21 40.73 −20.5	12588 32.24 30.51 −5.4	4591 61.72 51.93 −15.8	28497 38.63 34.30 11.2	126937 23.2 24.07 3.75

The linear model which was used is shown in equation (1):

$$y = K_0 + K_1a_1 + K_2a_2 + K_3b_1 + K_4b_2 + K_5c_1 + K_6c_2 + K_7d_1 + K_8d_2 + e \qquad (1)$$

where y = claims cost per vehicle in a cell

and a_1 = 1 for group 1 $\qquad$ a_2 = 1 for group 2
$\qquad\quad$ = 0 otherwise $\qquad\qquad$ = 0 otherwise

$\quad b_1$ = 1 for area 1 $\qquad$ b_2 = 1 for area 2
$\qquad\quad$ = 0 otherwise $\qquad\qquad$ = 0 otherwise

$\quad c_1$ = 1 for nil NCD $\qquad$ c_2 = 1 for medium NCD
$\qquad\quad$ = 0 otherwise $\qquad\qquad$ = 0 otherwise

$\quad d_1$ = 1 for age 17–24 $\qquad$ d_2 = 1 for age 25–30
$\qquad\quad$ = 0 otherwise $\qquad\qquad$ = 0 otherwise

K_i are the regression coefficients for i = 1 to 8

e = error term.

Each risk factor (i.e. group, area, NCD and age) is represented by two binary variables.

This model differs somewhat from Grimes's (1971) method which proposes that the cost of claims, y, on a policy can be expressed by the linear model shown in equation (2):

$$y = \mu + \alpha_i + \beta_j + {}_k + \ldots + e \qquad (2)$$

where μ is the portfolio average and $\alpha_i, \beta_j, \gamma_k$, etc. are adjustment factors (for NCD etc.) about the mean. Grimes's method was adapted to the binary dummy-variable form for two main reasons. First (for computational reasons) the binary form ensures that standard multiple regression packages can be used to find the least squares solutions. Second, the binary form enables statistical significance tests for each of the independent factors to be carried out very easily. Grimes indicates the impossibility of performing such tests with his linear modelling procedure.

A further reason for the use of binary regression arises from the categorical measurement scales adopted for the risk factors. For a factor which is to be represented by X categorical levels, the number of binary regression variables is N, where N is the smallest integer such that $N \geq \log_2(X)$. In the present case, with four independent factors each at three levels, a total of eight binary independent variables were used as shown in Equation (1).

The binary least squares regression model using all of the independent variables yielded the coefficient values as shown in Table 2. The predicted values of claims cost per policy (using these parameters) are shown in Table 1 directly under the actual values.

Table 2   Least squares regression parameters

K_0	24.073
K_1	−9.338
K_2	−6.681
K_3	−6.347
K_4	−4.147
K_5	+27.860
K_6	+10.228
K_7	+10.272
K_8	+6.437

DISCUSSION OF RESULTS

The regression was performed using the University of California BMD statistical package, and each of the 81 cells was given a weighting in the least squares calculation which was proportional to the number of risk units (i.e. the exposure) in that cell.

It must be noted that the data used for this regression is not the raw data on claims cost on a policy by policy basis but is data based on cell averages (and adjusted by a constant factor to maintain firm confidentiality). Hence the considerable variation which exists in claims cost per policy within any cell cannot be addressed by this analysis.

The average deviation of estimated claims cost per policy from actual claims cost per policy was 8.9 per cent (determined as the arithmetic average of the fourth entries shown in each cell of Table 1). These percentage deviations and their varying signs probably resulted from both statistical variation of the data about the underlying cell averages as well as from imperfect fit of the model.

The statistical significance of individual parameters has no practical meaning in this model, since the four rating factors (independent variables), age, area, group and (no-claim discount) NCD status are each represented by two binary variables. Hence the t statistics as calculated by the BMD program are not appropriate as significance measures. Chang and Fairley (1979) use the R^2 statistic to compare the overall accuracy of fit of different models; however, this statistic does not indicate whether individual rating factors are significant (R^2 for this regression was 0.91). The partial F test (Wesolowsky, 1976) is an appropriate test in this case since it can be used to consider the significance of groups of variables, i.e. it can be used to determine whether the inclusion of a variable or group of variables in the set of independent variables causes a significant reduction in the unexplained variation in the dependent variable.

Using Wesolowsky's (1976) terminology:

$$F = \frac{(USS_{y \cdot q - k; j \in K} - USS_{y \cdot q})/k}{USS_{y \cdot q}/(n - m)}$$

where the F distribution parameters are

$v_1 = k$

$v_2 = n - m$, for the numerator and denominator respectively

and where $USS_{y \cdot q}$ is the unexplained sum of squares in y using all q variables.

$USS_{y \cdot q - k; j \in K}$ is the unexplained sum of squares in y when $q - k$ variables are used

$n = $ (number of data points + 1)

$m = $ (number of variables (q) + 1)

The null hypothesis (Wesolowsky, 1976, p. 68) for the rating factors are

$H_0: K_j = 0$ for $j = n, n + 1$ where $n = 1, 3, 5, 7$

against the alternative $H_1: (H_0$ is not true).

Hypothesis 1: $K_1 = K_2 = 0$

The F test is significant at the 0.01 level $(F = 71.3 > F_{0.01})$ i.e. the 'group' rating factor does significantly contribute to the explanation of variance (the null hypothesis is rejected). Similar results for the other rating factors are shown below. Notice that the F tests all indicate significance of the variable pairs at the 0.01 (1 per cent) level.

Hypothesis 2: $K_3 = K_4 = 0$, $(F = 35.9 > F_{0.01})$

Hypothesis 3: $K_5 = K_6 = 0$, $(F = 182.8 > F_{0.01})$

Hypothesis 4: $K_7 = K_8 = 0$, $(F = 35.2 > F_{0.01})$

i.e. all the rating factors were found to be significant at the 0.01 (1 per cent) level since all the null hypotheses were rejected.

Observation of the values of (fitted-actual)/actual percentages (see Table 1) shows that these scaled residuals are most probably not randomly distributed about a mean of zero. As an example, for the 27 'group one' cells there were 23 positive residuals and 4 negative. The chance of this happening at random is less than one in 7000. It is apparent from Table 1 that the minimization of least squares does not lead to the minimization of absolute or scaled deviations of fitted from actual values (as might be expected). However, absolute or scaled deviations often are a convenient measure by which the accuracy of fit of a model may be judged. Johnson and Hey (1972) have provided a discussion of the issue of which sum (i.e. sum of squared deviations or sum of absolute deviations) should be minimized with respect to claim frequency modelling. They found that the least squares method was the more appropriate because of the attractive statistical properties which it possesses as well as the convenience of implementation (on standard computer packages).

The additive model cannot account for any interactions which may exist in the data. When Chang and Fairley (1979) compared additive (no interaction) and multiplicative (fully interactive) models, they found the additive to be slightly better. However, a mixed model would certainly have been better than both of the simple models. A mixed model which was basically additive but with some interaction terms may also improve the explanatory power for the data set in Table 1.

It should be noted that the number of possible second-order interactions is 54 in this case and higher-order interactions may also exist. Therefore, a preliminary sensitivity analysis was carried out to determine the value of including interaction terms in the linear model formulation. This sensitivity analysis attempted to determine whether any of the most important interactions (determined from examination of the percentage deviation figures in Table 1) would have a significant effect when included in the linear model. An illustrative example of a possible interaction is between 'group one' and 'nil NCD' classifications. The nine cells having these characteristics have residuals (i.e. (predicted-actual)/actual percentages) of 27.6, 37.0, 30.7, 27.7, 38.8, 18.9, 51.0, 7.5 and 31.7. With one exception, these differences are all considerably above average, indicating that the model is over-predicting claims in those cells. An additional independent variable in the model could be included to account for this. The significance of this interaction was examined via the specification of an extra variable (called INT1) which has unit value for cells where the interaction effect may exist and zero value elsewhere. Hypothesis 5 was tested as follows:

Hypothesis 5: INT1 = 0.

The partial F test indicates significance at the 1 per cent level ($F = 13.12 > F_{0.01}$). Hence the hypothesis was rejected and INT1 was determined to be significant. The least squares value of INT1 was £13.25 and its inclusion led to a reduction in the absolute value of average (predicted-actual)/actual claims costs per policy from 30.1 per cent to 8.3 per cent (which was very close to the average percentage difference for the whole account) for the nine affected cells.

As a further example, the interaction between 'nil NCD' and 'Age 17–24' was found to be insignificant at the 5 per cent level ($F = 0.25 < F_{0.05}$). As noted earlier, the number of possible second-order interactions is large and higher-order interactions might also exist. These could systematically be estimated using stepwise regression procedures. However, it is likely following the indications from the entire sensitivity analysis procedure that the vast majority of these interaction variables would be found to be not significantly different from zero. In this case, therefore, the increased model accuracy caused by the inclusion of non-linear terms was judged to be of little value in practical terms when compared to the cost in terms of increased model complexity.

IMPLEMENTATION OF RESULTS

A linear model (such as Equation (1)) can predict claims costs for motor insurance accounts, which in turn can be used as the basis for forecasts for the next period (with necessary adjustments being made such as, for example, a trend adjustment for increasing repair costs). Once the forecast for claims cost is made, the gross premiums may be determined by whatever method is deemed appropriate (e.g. by aiming for target loss ratios in each cell). With the British insurance company, premiums were determined by applying a constant mark-up percentage to the claims cost forecasts and then adjusting them in comparison with market rates. In this manner a rating guide designed to be usable by many underwriters, was developed. Claims forecasts also provided a basis for this insurance company to determine and adjust their levels of claims reserves held in anticipation of future claims.

In practical applications, one important test for validating these models is whether they improve the predictions of account managers in estimating future claims, making claims reserving decisions and, ultimately, in setting appropriate premiums. The experience in the British insurance company was extremely positive. Managers seemed both to understand the rationale of the models and to appreciate the value of the outputs and predictions. The utility of the linear model in statistical terms is in its use of the totality of previous experience across the whole account as a basis for estimating claims in each cell. An alternative approach to the use of a model is simply to use the cell by cell experience to predict cell by cell performance. Given, however, the rejection of the null hypotheses in this study (i.e. the significance of the rating factors across the whole account) a claims estimation procedure based on data from only one cell is wasting information (see also Chang and Fairley (1979) and SRI report (1976) for confirmation of this proposition). The critical issue in evaluating the practical use of linear models (or any other) in this application is whether the average cell by cell random fluctuation about the true underlying means is greater or less than the average differences between the fitted model predictions and the actual claims performance of the account. From Table 1 it can be observed that the closest fits were generally obtained in those cells with high exposure (because of the weighting system) and hence the claims performance in these cells (which may individually be statistically credible) are generally quite accurately modelled. The cells with low exposure typically have larger residual values, and generally also have a higher chance of containing claims observations which are not good representations of the true means.

In this portfolio the lowest exposure in a cell was 530 individuals, and without the use of a model, claims prediction would be based on a highly uncertain estimate. Total claims for this cell were fewer than 9000, and this total is highly susceptible to significant variation (e.g. from one large claim).

The strength of the model then lies in its ability to use and relate claims information from the whole account in order to estimate claims where exposure may be very low. In many other accounts examined by the researchers, several cells have exposures of less than 100 individuals (with perhaps fewer than ten claims) and it is impossible to reliably estimate claims based on experience in individual cells in such cases.

USING ASSOCIATIVE, AGGREGATIVE MODELS WITH INDUSTRY-WIDE DATA

A method of further improving cell by cell estimation is to try to obtain industry-wide information and, hence, basic parameter estimation and claims prediction on a much wider sample database. For example, in Britain, an industry-wide data analysis service called 'Standard Table Analysis' is offered by an organization known as the Motor Risk Statistics Bureau and administered by the British Insurance Association. Membership in the bureau is voluntary (rather like membership in the Ratio Analysis service for firms run by the Centre for Interfirm Comparisons) and strict secrecy and confidentiality is assured for each individual firm. Therefore, whilst each individual firm cannot be identified, each subscribing firm gains access to analyses of the aggregate database for all of the subscribing firms.

The Motor Risk Statistics Bureau (MRSB) analysis involves the use of a simple additive model applied to data on claims experience. Basically, the actual claims experience in the analysis period is compared with the 'expected' experience calculated using industry-wide data on actual experience in earlier periods. Expected values are typically obtained for claims frequencies and average claim amounts and the Bureau has found that its simple additive model is satisfactory for most predictive purposes. From time to time the model parameter values change but the underlying additive model appears to be a robust predictive model.

For the individual insurance company the analysis shows, on an industry basis, the differences in claim experience which exist between various levels of any risk factors. Thus, the company can compare its experience with industry norms and averages and determine whether changes should be made in its underwriting practices or portfolio composition.

PREMIUM SETTING USING THE LINEAR MODEL

Premiums set on the basis of the model given in Equation (1) would thus be based on the totality of statistical information available to the firm. In many firms, several individual cells in the matrix have exposures that are too low to be credible as bases for forecasting, thus necessitating the use of a risk model for this reason alone. The use of a risk model also facilitates the production of a relatively simple ratebook for premium calculation. Such a document would ease the calculation burden for insurance managers and external insurance agents by requiring that the premium be calculated according to the sum of a few readily calculated component amounts. This may be much more convenient in an operational sense than having a book composed of many pages of premiums. Revision of rates and of the ratebook also becomes much easier when such a risk model is used. As an example, a relatively simple classification system using six factors, each with four categories would require over 4000 premiums to be tabulated in a representative ratebook given to managers. The same information could be expressed by an additive model using only 19 constants (i.e. 18 parameters). The use of a model makes both premium adjustment decisions and experience rating easier to implement since the adjustments can be made more easily to the model parameters than to the large number of premiums in the ratebook. This would be particularly advantageous where a target loss ratio system is used, i.e. where premiums are set such that:

$$\text{premiums} = \frac{\text{expected claims}}{\text{target loss ratio}}$$

Some insurance organizations make many premium adjustments per annum as a result of claims performance and such decisions could be implemented more easily and at less cost if the adjustments could be made in the form of changes to a few parameters rather than to a large number of figures in the ratebook.

Once a model is established, it can be reapplied periodically, albeit with parameters being modified through time, and used for control purposes to analyse trends in claims within various segments of the account. The model would be useful for indicating which segments of the account are most (and least) profitable. Hence decisions can be made on the basis of objective analyses (of past data) coupled with judgment (regarding future trends) as to which segments of the market are desirable, undesirable, etc., as elements of the portfolio.

CONCLUSIONS

The linear additive model, which has been found to be an adequate model in a number of varying applications, was applied to the rating factors of a comprehensive motor insurance account. The model was a good fit to the data and through the use of partial F tests it was determined that all of the rating factors were significant. The model was fitted via binary regression analytic techniques applied to categorical independent variables. This procedure can also be used to test the significance of interaction variables.

By determining the regression parameters and the significance of the rating factors, the utility of a linear model in this application lies in its use as a basis for forecasting future claims, for premium setting and for controlling the operations of a large programmed insurance account.

Current operational trends in the general insurance industry are to use computer aided systems for premium calculation. These systems generally either involve having agents on-line or else are comprised of insurers sending diskettes for agents to use on micro- or minicomputers. Such systems have made it highly feasible for the information on claims to be efficiently collected and for the premium rating models to be implemented in the form of decision support systems.

REFERENCES

Ashton, R. H. (1976) 'The robustness of linear models for decision making', *Omega*, **4**, 5, 609–615.

Bailey, R. A. and Simon, L. J. (1960) 'Two studies in automobile insurance ratemaking', *Proceedings of the Casualty Actuarial Society*, Vol. XLVII, Part 1, pp. 1–19.

Barnett, A. (1983) 'Misapplication reviews: The linear model and some of its friends', *Interfaces*, **13**, N1, 61–65.

Bunn, D. W. and Seigal, J. P. (1983) 'Forecasting the effects of television programming upon electricity loads', *J. Operational Research Society*, **34**, 17–25.

Chang, L. S. and Fairley, W. B. (1979) 'Private automobile insurance under multivariate classification of risks: Additive versus multiplicative', *Journal of Risk and Insurance*, March, 175–193.

Coutts, S. (1984) 'Motor premium rating', *Insurance Mathematics and Economics*, **3**, 73–96.

Curry, H. E. (1964) 'Refinement of automobile rate and underwriting classes', *Journal of Risk and Insurance*, **31**, 217.

Dawes, R. M. (1971) 'A case study of graduate admissions: Application of three principles of human decision making', *American Psychologist*, **26**, 80–88.

Dawes, R. M. and Corrigan, B. (1974) 'Linear models in decision making', *Psychological Bulletin*, **81**, 2, 95–106.

Einhorn, H. J. and Hogarth, R. M. (1975) 'Unit weighting of schemes for decision making', *Organizational Behavior and Human Performance*, **13**, 171–192.

Einhorn, H. J., Kleinmuntz, D. N. and Kleinmuntz, B. (1979) 'Linear regression and process tracing models of judgement', *Psychological Review*, **84**, 465–485.

Ferreira, Joseph, Jr (1974) 'The long-term effects of merit-rating plans on individual motorists', *Operations Research*, **22**, 5, 954–978.

Fischhoff, B., Lichtenstein, S., Slovic, P., Derby, S. L. and Keeney, R. L. (1981) *Acceptable Risk*, Cambridge: Cambridge University Press.

Gaunt, L. D. (1978) 'Policy and operating techniques in personal automobile insurance', *Best's Review*, March, 16.

Grimes, T. (1971) 'Claim frequency analysis', *JSS*, **19**, part 3.

Haner, C. F. (1967) 'Prediction of automobile claims by psychological methods—a case study in automobile insurance', 1967 Annual Meeting of ARIA.

Hogarth, R. M. (1980) *Judgement and Choice*, Chichester: John Wiley.

Johnson, L. C. and Mai, N. (1979) 'Decomposition techniques: Linear vs. nonlinear models', *Organizational Behavior and Human Performance*, **24**, 60–66.

Johnson, P. D. and Hey, G. B. (1972) 'Statistical studies in motor insurance', *Journal of the Institute of Actuaries*, 1–34.

Keeney, R. L. and Raiffa, H. (1976) *Decisions with Multiple Objectives*, New York: John Wiley.

King, A. T. (1979) 'Estimation of a linear expenditure system for the United States in 1973', *Journal of Economics and Business*, Spring, 190–195.

Larcker, D. F. and Lessig, V. P. (1983) 'An examination of the linear and retrospective process tracing approaches to judgement modeling', *The Accounting Review*, **58**, N1, 58–77.

Libby, R. and Lewis, B. L. (1977) 'Human information processing research in accounting: The state of the art', *Accounting, Organizations and Society*, **2**, 254–268.

Parsons, C. K. and Hulin, C. L. (1982) 'Differentially weighted linear models in organizational research: A cross-validation comparison of four methods', *Organizational Behavior and Human Performance*, **30**, 289–311.

Sant, D. T. (1980) 'Estimating expected losses in auto insurance', *Journal of Risk and Insurance*, **47**, 133–151.

Schepanski, A. (1983) 'Tests of theories of information processing behavior in credit judgement', *The Accounting Review*, **58**, N3, 581–599.

Simon, H. (1971) *The New Science of Management Decision*, New York: Harper & Row.

Slovic, P. and Lichtenstein, S. (1971) 'Comparison of Bayesian and regression approaches to the study of information processing in judgment', *Organizational Behavior and Human Performance*, **6**, 647–744.

Slovic, P., Fischhoff, B. and Lichtenstein, S. (1977) 'Behavioral decision theory', *Annual Review of Psychology*, **28**, 1–39.

SRI Executive Summary Report (1976) 'The role of risk classification in property and casualty insurance', Stanford Research Institute, Palo Alto, Cal., May.

Wesolowksy, G. O. (1976) *Multiple Regression and the Analysis of Variance*, New York: John Wiley.

Judgmental Forecasting
Edited by G. Wright and P. Ayton
© 1987 John Wiley & Sons Ltd

CHAPTER 12

Expert Use of Forecasts: Bootstrapping and Linear Models

Derek Bunn
London Business School

INTRODUCTION

Forecasting for decision-making is now rarely a singular modelling exercise. The latest software packages continue to offer a wider and more diverse range of applicable modelling approaches. The increasing number of specialist agencies, expert consultants and interest-groups offer their own separate predictions and forecasting services. Thus, it is apparent that at least as much judgment may be required in managing and consolidating multiple models to produce a coherent forecast as in formulating the particular structures of the individual models and forecasts themselves.

This chapter will discuss various statistical methods for combining forecasts. This reflects the problem of synthesizing diverse forecasts regardless of whether they are quantitative projections, subjective expert opinions or separate surveys. A case-study will illustrate some of the issues based upon the on-going decision-making context of daily electric load forecasting and planning.

Other chapters in this volume have indicated the value of linear models in forecasting. Lock (Chapter 6) provides a wide-ranging review, going beyond the statistical aspects and covering many behavioural issues associated with group judgment. Samson and Thomas (Chapter 11) provide a detailed account of linear modelling in the case-study context of applied linear regression analysis, with particular regard to the treatment of dummy explanatory variables. Explanatory variables ('cues') in their context are therefore different from the individual predictive variables (forecasts) considered in the models here. Indeed, a regression-based model often provides the basis of one of the forecasts to be combined with other approaches (Box–Jenkins, Kalman filter, individual judgment, etc.). Thus, we can envisage two levels of linear modelling—individual forecasts being based upon a class of linear models of basic causal, or associated input variables (cues) and then a class of linear models for combining several such forecasting models. Why we may wish to nest linear models in this way will be considered in the next section. Also, in a later section, we will discuss the possible case for a third, higher level of linear model controlling the parameters and form of the combining model. In some respects, this corresponds to Chapter 10 by Brehmer, where inconsistency in the 'policies' of judgmental forecasts is identified and the role of linear models for that discussed.

STATISTICAL COMBINATION OF FORECASTS

The idea of combining estimates goes back at least to the work of Laplace in the early nineteenth century, and insights into the statistical efficiency of combined estimates have accumulated steadily ever since (e.g. Edgerton and Kolbe, 1936; Halperin, 1961). Much of the credit, in the statistical forecasting literature, for translating this idea into the use of forecasts has generally been given to the work of Granger and his colleagues, originating in Nottingham in the late 1960s (Reid, 1968, 1969; Bates and Granger, 1969; Newbold and Granger, 1974). In the judgmental forecasting area, combining predictive judgments had been accepted somewhat earlier (see the review by Lock, this volume, Chapter 6) and certainly less controversially. The basic frameworks and issues of decision theory, personal and group coherence, the rational synthesis of information and the modelling of judgment were established topics in the judgmental forecasting area. The *principle* of combining judgmental forecasts was not questioned, only various methods for doing so. The traditional statistical forecasting methodology was still, however, looking to the scientific method, based upon experimentation and the falsification of hypotheses, for principles of rationality. The very *principle* of combining forecasts met with resistance (e.g. Jenkins, 1974) and was seen by many to be unscientific and ad hoc. The gradual acceptance of Bayesian methods, which re-orientated the use of information in models, and decision theory, which provided an alternative rational framework, greatly helped the acceptance of the combining approach. Nevertheless there was still confusion in the use of Bayesian methods of combination, some versions of which were ultimately based upon the ideal of model selection rather than model aggregation (cf. Bunn, 1981).

Within the objective of minimizing the forecast error variance, the efficiency of linear combinations of unbiased predictors was theoretically and empirically well established by the Newbold and Granger (1974) study. Later work tended either to replicate this study (e.g. Winkler and Makridakis, 1983) or provide further case study vindication of the approach (e.g. Reinmuth and Guerts, 1979; Bessler and Brandt, 1981). Overall, the approach of combining forecasts should by now be seen to be well vindicated and no longer especially radical. The current problems are in deciding how the combination should be achieved, and in particular, what is the role of judgment in the formulation. The difference between using an appropriate and inappropriate method of combination can be greater (in mean squared error or MSE terms) than that of the best and worst individual forecasts (see Bessler and Brandt, 1982). The decision-maker's problem is basically how to model and predict the pattern of forecast errors when only a limited 'track-record' of the individual forecast's performance is available.

If a large past history of data is available which also suggests that the pattern of forecast errors is stationary over time, then the parameters of the optimal (minimum variance) combination can be estimated reliably. Thus, following Reid (1969), if f is the $n \times 1$ vector of separate forecasts (unbiased), the optimal combined forecast f_c is given as

$$f_c = (e's^{-1}f)/(e'S^{-1}e)$$

where e is the $n \times 1$ unit vector and S is the $n \times n$ forecast error covariance matrix.

However, if (a) there is only a small data base and/or (b) the error covariance structure is not stationary, then there are robustness problems owing to poor estimation of S. So, several studies have found that more efficient combined forecasts could be obtained by treating the forecast errors as if they were independent. The matrix S would therefore be specified only as the diagonal one of individual forecast error variances. A more extreme response to the robustness problem in attempting an optimal combination is to use impartial averaging (i.e. equal weights of n^{-1}). Clearly, if we have no information on the relative accuracy of our forecasts, we will start off by using this method. However, as a history of forecast errors, or further insight, develops, we would wish to make use of this further information by differential weighting. Ultimately we would seek to implement the optimal combination, when we feel we have enough data to estimate S reliably. This type of evolutionary switching from simple to more parameterized methods of combination, with an expanding database, has been developed and investigated in a series of simulation studies (Bunn 1977, 1981, 1985). One key issue which relates to the relative efficiency of differential weighting methods is the intercorrelation between the individual predictive models. Since this is an important aspect of the case study to be reported later, it is worth discussing, in some detail, the effects of correlation between models. The following section is an elaboration of material in Bunn (1985).

EFFECTS OF CORRELATION

With two unbiased forecasting models, error variances σ_1^2, σ_2^2, and error correlation coefficient ρ the error variance of f_c becomes

$$\sigma_c^2 = [\sigma_1^2\sigma_2^2(1 - \rho^2)]/(\sigma_1^2 + \sigma_2^2 - 2\rho\sigma_1\sigma_2)$$

If we assume that $\sigma_1^2 > \sigma_2^2$, then it can be shown, e.g. Bunn (1978), that $\sigma_1^2 > \sigma_c^2$ unless

(a) $\sigma_1 = 0$; or

(b) $\sigma_1 = \sigma_2$ and $\rho = 1$; or

(c) $\rho = \sigma_1/\sigma_2$

Cases (a) and (b) are degenerate circumstances, but case (c) is non-trivial and quite important. Thus, Figure 1 shows σ_c^2 as a function of ρ for two models with $\sigma_1 = 1$ and $\sigma_2 = 2$. That $\sigma_c^2 \leqslant 1$ for all ρ demonstrates the value of combination over selecting just model 1 ($\sigma_1^2 = 1$), but note the low gain for combining around $\rho = \frac{1}{2}$. Furthermore, when $\rho > \sigma_1/\sigma_2$, the combination is no longer convex with the result that, although the linear weights still sum to one, they will be of opposite sign. Very positive and negative weights can occur, which obviously require careful estimation if the theoretical advantage of σ_c is to be obtained in practice.

Also on Figure 1 we can see the theoretical performance of invoking the independence assumption, i.e. combining the two forecasts *as if* they were independent. Thus, we would have the combined forecast, f

$$f_{in} = (\sigma_2^2 f_1 + \sigma_1^2 f_2)/(\sigma_1^2 + \sigma_2^2)$$

with error variance, σ_{in}, where

$$\alpha_{in}^2 = \sigma_1^2\sigma_2^2(\sigma_1^2 + \sigma_2^2 + 2\rho\sigma_1\sigma_2)/(\sigma_1^2 + \sigma_2^2)^2$$

with $\sigma_1^2 = 1$ and $\sigma_2^2 = 4$, σ_{in}^2 is as plotted. Clearly it is optimal for $\rho = 0$ and only becomes particularly suboptimal in the region of non-convex optimal combinations ($\rho > \sigma_1/\sigma_2$). In general, we can show that $\sigma_{in}^2 \geqslant \sigma_c^2$ with the equality holding only at $\rho = 0$ if $\sigma_1 \neq \sigma_2$. However, if $\sigma_1 = \sigma_2$, then $\sigma_{in}^2 = \sigma_c^2$ for all ρ (since $\sigma_{in}^2 = \sigma_c^2 = (1 + \rho)\sigma^2/2$ when $\sigma_1^2 = \sigma_2^2 = \sigma^2$), as shown by the dotted line in Figure 1.

Thus, as σ_2 decreases to 1, the turning point of σ_c^2 moves closer to 1, giving a smaller region of non-convex optimality and a larger region of approximate linearity in σ_c^2 around $\rho = 0$. Thus, we would expect the independence assumption to perform relatively well when two 'good' forecasts are being combined. Conversely, when one of the forecasts is relatively poor ($\sigma_2^2 \gg 1$), the turning point in σ_c^2 is closer to $\rho = 0$, giving a larger region of non-convex optimality, and a smaller region where σ_{in}^2 is close to σ_c^2. Thus, we might expect the independence assumption to perform less well. Certainly, it has been the case that several writers have suggested that 'poor' forecasts should not be included in a combined forecast (e.g. Bunn (1981) and Dickinson (1973)), even if they do constitute some extra evidence. The reason appears from this analysis to be not so much that, being poor, they contribute little,

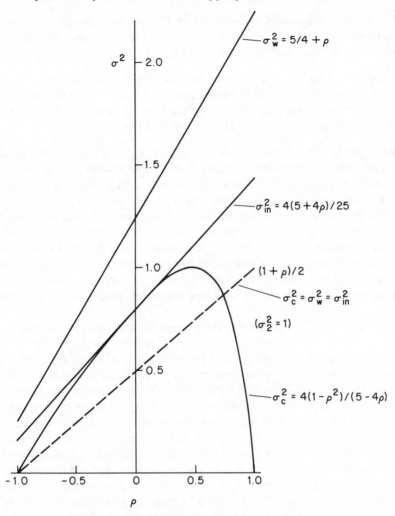

Figure 1. Combined variance of two predictions

but rather that they can undermine the robustness of the combination by 'expanding' the region of non-convex optimality.

Similarly, we can see why several writers (e.g. Newbold and Granger (1974) Winkler and Makridakis (1983)), suggest looking for error-independence between the forecasts to be combined. With poor methods having been screened out, convex combination based only upon the variance estimates can be expected to perform well. However, we should not forget that the very best results will be obtained from combining negatively corre-lated forecasts (e.g. the Hawaiian tourist forecasts in Reinmuth and Guerts,

1979) and that, if ρ can be estimated reliably, even very positive correlations can provide the means to an effective combination. Thus, the following argument in Winkler and Makridakis (1983)

> Suppose that we have three methods and that the correlations among their forecast errors are zero for methods 1 and 2, zero for methods 1 and 3, and one for methods 2 and 3. In this case the forecasts provided by the second and third methods are redundant. . . . (p. 151)

clearly only applies if $\sigma_2 = \sigma_3$, for otherwise a perfect predictor could, in *theory*, be obtained from just methods 2 and 3 and it would be method 1 that is redundant. In practice, however, the inclusion of the dependent method would usually make matters worse because of the estimation problems. Clearly, it is the joint effect of dependence and relative variance that complicates the issue. Thus, for the sake of argument, suppose that for political or other reasons a relatively poor predictor has to be seen to be explicitly incorporated in a composite forecast. Then because this would be driving the turning point of σ_c close to $\rho = 1$, we may well prefer *not* to be looking for independence between this and other predictors in the combination.

The variance, σ_w^2, of combining the two methods with equal weights is also shown in Figure 1. It is clearly never optimal, except as before when $\sigma_2 = \sigma_1$, and is theoretically very suboptimal for high levels of correlation. That it is often advocated in these circumstances points to the difficulty of identifying the best predictor or formulating the optimal combination in many practical situations having a paucity of reliable data. It would seem from our figure that, between knowing nothing (and hence using equal weights) and knowing a useful amount (and hence using differential weights), there is a case for trying to select the singularly best forecasting model. However, as the analysis of Benson and Barry (1982) and the experiments of Bunn and Kappos (1982) provide evidence to the contrary, it seems that robust methods of combination will still yield the most efficient results in these transitional circumstances.

OUTPERFORMANCE PROBABILITIES

It was from this motivation to develop a statistically robust method of combination and one which could readily incorporate judgment on the relative efficacy of the predictive models, that the method of using *outperformance probabilities* was developed (Bunn, 1975, 1977). Simply the combined forecast was defined as

$$f_c = \mathbf{p}'\mathbf{f}$$

where $\mathbf{p}$ is a vector of probabilities, each element p_i representing the probability that forecast f_i will perform best on the next outcome. This pragmatic interpretation of a model probability (a) avoided issues of model truthfulness which are philosophically difficult to operationalize and therefore practically difficult to assess, (b) allowed assessment of **p** as a Beta distribution (or Dirichlet distribution if more than two models are being combined), (c) facilitated a simple non-parametric weighting process based upon a 'track-record' of how many times each model performed best and (d) allowed the issue of outperformance to be judgmental in circumstances where simple error was not an appropriate *ex post* measure of quality. Nevertheless, in situations where 'outperformance' was empirically assessed as absolute forecast error, this method performed well against the optimal, minimum variance method, particularly over small samples, and where the optimal method is sensitive to errors in estimating model intercorrelations. It also performed well against the optimal combination with an Inverted Wishart conjugate prior distribution, which is the obvious Bayesian way to incorporate judgment in the optimizing combination (Agnew, 1985; Bunn, 1977; Clemen and Winkler, 1986).

LINEAR BOOTSTRAPPING MODELS

Research in bootstrapping expert judgment has been reviewed by several authors in this volume and it is therefore unnecessary to repeat those issues in detail here. The key aspect of this work is the general observation that by regressing expert judgmental forecasts on the set of cues (predictive variables) used by the expert, a linear model can be produced to outperform the expert. Thus, the systematic part of judgment is modelled, without, apparently the random assessment noise which degrades expert forecasts. The basic reference is Dawes and Corrigan (1974), and further analytical issues are discussed in Camerer (1981). A lot of published discussion and empirical work has looked at whether equal weighting can be even more reliable than differential weighting (regression or otherwise) and many researchers do advocate, particularly for out-of-sample prediction, the use of equal weights.

Whilst a considerable amount of descriptive insight can be gained in terms of understanding the judgmental performance of experts from bootstrapping models, we have to question its usefulness in forecasting. If we have data on the outcome variables being forecast, we would presumably wish to use these as a basis for model estimation, rather than expert forecasts of their values. We would, in this case, attempt a statistical combination of the optimzing type discussed in previous sections. The case for bootstrapping must therefore lie in cases where the outcome variables are not known, e.g. long-term forecasting, and where the weight of evidence justifies using the bootstrapped model, rather than the expert's judgments themselves.

The effects of correlation, that we discussed previously in the context of optimizing combinations of predictions, have received little attention in the bootstrapping literature, but, in terms of the joint pattern of validities (predictabilities) of the set of predictive cues, are clearly theoretically relevant. That they are also relevant in practice is to be seen in the case study described next.

CASE STUDY FROM DAILY ELECTRIC LOAD FORECASTING

Every day the National Control engineers at the UK Central Electricity Generating Board need to make a variety of forecasts and generation loading decisions from a few minutes to several hours ahead. One particularly important class of such forecasts is produced with a lead time of about 3 hours to support the 'commitment' of generating units to be ready to take up synchronized loads when required. The National Control engineers make such forecasts on the basis of three sources of advice, viz.:

'A'—The sum of the forecast from the seven regional Grid Control Areas.
'D'—The forecast by the Demand Forecasting Section at CEGB headquarters. This is a weather-based regression model.
'M'—An assessment based upon the National Control's 'Multiplier' model, which is a heuristic load-curve based approach.

The forecasts which are recorded by the National Control engineers are expert syntheses of these three input forecasts. Also recorded, later, are the actual peak demands for the periods being forecast.

In this study 246 observations of this data were made for the same time of day forecast (evening peak) over the period August 1982–July 1983. All days for which the data entries showed signs of being adjusted were considered dubious and not used in the analysis.

Table 1 reports the mean forecast error, and standard deviation of forecast errors for the three input forecasts and the control engineers' expert assessments ('C'), in megawatts. Clearly, the control engineers do benefit from the three inputs in terms of reduced error variance. For the mean forecast errors (bias) only that from the Areas is very significant, and the least surprising in this respect as each Area is effectively requesting allocated generation.

In order first of all to investigate bootstrapping, 'C' was regressed upon 'A', 'M' and 'D' both for the full 246 observations and for the first 123 obser-

Table 1

	'A'	'M'	'D'	'C'
Mean	150	77	24	91
Standard deviation	480	465	463	424

Table 2

	Constant	Coefficients			Diagnostics		
		'A'	'M'	'D'	$\bar{R}^2$	DW	F
$n = 245$	3.1	0.32	0.45	0.19	0.89	2.01	674
	($t = 0.3$)	($t = 12$)	($t = 16$)	($t = 7.6$)			
$n = 123$	−1.5	0.32	0.49	0.17	0.89	1.97	518
	($t = -0.2$)	($t = 9$)	($t = 14$)	($t = 5$)			

Table 3

	'A'	'M'	'D'	'C'
'A'	1			
'B'	0.7	1		
'D'	0.7	0.7	1	
'C'	0.8	0.8	0.8	1

vations to facilitate cross-validation, out-of-sample, on the second 123 observations. Table 2 contains a summary of the regression data. The model is clearly stable over the data, despite multicollinearity. The correlation matrix (for both sets of data) is shown in Table 3.

Given the symmetry in correlation structure and the broadly equivalent error variances between the three predictions, equal weights will be close to optimal. Outperformance weights, based upon the relative frequencies of each predictor performing best, would be (0.35, 0.29, 0.36). The bootstrap weights were taken from the regression coefficients, ignoring the insignificant constant term and after normalizing. Table 4 gives the standard deviation of forecast errors for the 'A', 'M', 'D', 'C' predictors, together with 'E' (equal weights) 'O' (outperformance) and 'B' (bootstrapping) combinations over observations 124–246. Although bootstrapping did better than the experts, the reduction in error standard deviation was tiny (and not significant). Furthermore it was also somewhat surprising that (a) bootstrapping did better than the optimizing methods and (b) the combining methods in general only reduced forecast error variance by about 20 per cent over the individual predictors.

Table 4

Method	'A'	'M'	'D'	'C'	'E'	'O'	'B'
Standard deviation	466	436	478	412	410	411	408

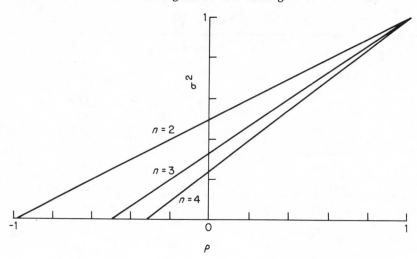

Figure 2. Combined variance of equal-weighting several predictions

Point (b) can be ascribed to the high correlation beween the individual predictive errors (0.7–0.8) and the similarity of their error standard deviations.

Figure 2 shows an analysis of the theoretical combined forecast error variance, based on equal weighting, of 2, 3 or 4 models each with unit error variance and the same correlation coefficients. Note that it is structurally impossible with increasing n to have high, or even moderate negative correlations. In our case, we have ρ approximately 0.75, which according to Figure 2 would give, at best, a reduction of 20 per cent in error *variance*, which is what we observed.

On point (a), it became apparent in examining the data that two policies of composite judgment were being used. Some of the 'N' forecasts were *selected* from 'A', 'M' or 'D'; in all 'A' was chosen 10 per cent, 'C' chosen 25 per cent and 'D' chosen 17 per cent of the time. The remaining 48 per cent of observations were compromise assessments. Thus, there was a policy switching process between *synthesis* and *selection*.

Table 5 gives the forecast error standard deviations for the various methods on the 'synthesis' policy data. This gives a more intuitive ranking of methods 'C', 'E' and 'B'. Table 6 repeats the analysis for the 'selection' policy, which

Table 5

Method	'A'	'M'	'D'	'C'	'E'	'B'
Standard deviation	484	492	447	424	382	403

Table 6

Method	'A'	'M'	'D'	'C'	'E'	'B'
Standard deviation	467	438	475	419	418	415

explains where the earlier counter-intuitive ranking came from. It also suggests that the experts have no real benefit from operating the selection rather than synthesis policy. However, Table 5 does show better performance through synthesis, somewhat vindicating policy switching. There is no reason to believe that the relative efficiency of each predictor is stable from time-to-time (stationary). Thus, special regional effects may be better reflected in 'A', complex weather patterns in 'D' and sometimes 'M' is based significantly upon slightly more recent data. A rule-based model would be necessary to represent this policy-switching procedure. Unfortunately, data was not available in this study to further investigate that aspect.

Overall, however, we must ascribe the near-optimal composite forecasts of the experts, and the lack of significant improvements through linear modelling, not only to the symmetry of variances and high correlations of the input forecasts ('cues'), but also perhaps as credit to their learning, over many years, several times a day, how to use, intuitively, the evidence provided. Compare these results with those of Brehmer (1980) on suboptimal learning from experience.

CONCLUDING COMMENTS

Combining forecasts is a pragmatic response to the failure either to build a comprehensive model of all inputs (which may have insurmountable multivariate estimation problems) or to discriminate effectively the 'appropriate' singular model (through equivocal and insufficient evidence). It is motivated by a desire to use all the information available, but can suffer from being a somewhat confusing agglomeration of different hypotheses. If the purpose of modelling is not just to mine the data for the most accurate aggregate predictor, but provide a basis for testing assumptions and learning about the causality of the future, then a combined forecast may not be so useful.

Bootstrapping continues to accumulate a strong empirical basis for its general use, although its descriptive value should not be confused with the prescriptive value of optimum-seeking methods of combination when outcome data is available. Also, the issue of stability of model structure (the 'policy') should not be taken for granted. Experts may feel evidence warrants model-switching policies, and this would require a bootstrapping model-management procedure to be assessed as a higher level of modelling.

ACKNOWLEDGMENTS

The author would like to acknowledge the help of David Date in collecting the data and the support of A. B. Baker and others at the Central Electricity Generating Board.

REFERENCES

Agnew, C. E. (1985) 'Bayesian consensus forecasts of macroeconomic variables', *Journal of Forecasting*, **2**, 4, 363–376.

Bates, J. M. and Granger, C. W. J. (1969) 'Combination of forecasts', *Operational Research Quarterly*, **20**, 451–468.

Benson, P. G. and Barry, C. (1982) 'On the implications of specification uncertainty in forecasting', *Decision Sciences*, **13**, 176–184.

Bessler, D. A. and Brandt, J. A. (1981) 'Forecasting livestock prices with individual and composite methods', *Applied Economics*, **13**, 513–522.

Brehmer, B. (1980) 'In one word: not from experience', *Acta Psychologica*, 223–241.

Bunn, D. W. (1975) 'A Bayesian approach to the linear combination of forecasts', *Operational Research Quarterly*, **25**, 325–329.

Bunn, D. W. (1977) 'Comparative evaluation of the outperformance and minimum variance synthesis of forecasts', *Operational Research Quarterly*, **28**, 653–662.

Bunn, D. W. (1978) *The Synthesis of Forecasting Models in Decision Analysis*, Basel: Birkhauser.

Bunn, D. W. (1981) 'Two methodologies for the linear combination of forecasts', *J. Opl. Res. Soc.*, **32**, 213–222.

Bunn, D. W. (1985) 'Statistical efficiency in the linear combination of forecasts', *Int. J. Forecasting*, **1**, 151–163.

Bunn, D. W. and Kappos, E. (1982) 'Synthesis or selection of forecasting models', *European Journal of Operational Research*, **9**, 173–180.

Camerer, C. (1981) 'General conditions for the success of bootstrapping models', *O.B.H.P.*, **27**, 411–422.

Clemen, R. T. and Winkler, R. L. (1986) 'Combing economic forecasts', *J. Business and Economic Statistics*, **4**, 39–46.

Dawes, R. M. and Corrigan, B. (1974) 'Linear models in decision-making', *Psychological Bulletin*, **81**, 95–106.

Dickinson, J. P. (1973) 'Some statistical results in the combination of forecasts', *Op. Res. Q.*, **24**, 253–260.

Edgerton, H. A. and Kolbe, L. E. (1983) 'The method of minimum variation for the combination of criteria', *Psychometrika*, **2**, 183–188.

Guerts, M. D. and Ibrahim, I. B. (1975) 'Comparing the Box–Jenkins approach with exponential smoothing', *Journal of Marketing Research*, **12**, 182–188.

Halperin, M. (1961) 'Almost linearly optimum combination of unbiased estimates', *J. Amer. Statist. Assoc.*, March, 36–43.

Jenkins, G. M. (1974) 'Discussion of paper by Newbold & Granger', *J. Roy. Statist. Soc. A.*, **137**, 148–150.

Newbold, P. and Granger, C. W. J. (1974) 'Experience with forecasting univariate time series and the combination of forecasts', *J. Roy. Statist. Soc. A.*, **137**, 131–165.

Reid, D. J. (1968) 'Combining three estimates of gross domestic product', *Economica*, **35**.

Reid, D. J. (1969) 'A comparative study of time series prediction techniques on economic data', Ph.D. thesis, University of Nottingham.

Reinmuth, J. E. and Guerts, M. D. (1979) 'A multideterministic approach to forecasting. L. S. Makridakis and S. C. Wheelwright (eds.), *Forecasting*, North-Holland, pp. 203–212.

Winkler, R. L. and Makridakis, S. (1983) 'The combination of forecasts', *J. Roy. Statist. Soc. A.*, **146**, 150–157.

Part IV

The psychology of scenarios

Judgmental Forecasting
Edited by G. Wright and P. Ayton
© 1987 John Wiley & Sons Ltd

CHAPTER 13

The Use of Mental Models for Generating Scenarios

Helmut Jungermann *and* **Manfred Thüring**
Institut für Psychologie, Technische Universität, Berlin

INTRODUCTION

Who can tell today what information and communication equipment will be available in an average private household in 25 years and what services will be supplied by state and industry? And who dares to forecast seriously what impact such equipment and services will then have on our private lives? Whereas almost everybody expects a general increase in equipment and services, it is not at all clear whether this will result, for example, in an increase or decrease in the social contacts of an individual, in higher or lower intellectual creativity in children, or in greater or less political informedness of citizens. But despite of this uncertainty, or maybe just because of it, there is a broad societal debate about the potential impact of the new information and communication techniques on the lives of present and future generations. And political institutions explore the possible futures to find a basis for taking economic and regulatory actions which are hoped to maximize future benefits and minimize future risks.

The construction of scenarios is one important method of assessing potential long-range technical, economic, political and societal developments— such as the one addressed above. Scenarios are descriptions of alternative hypothetical futures. They do not describe what the future will look like but rather what possible futures we might expect, depending on our actions (or inactions) in the present.

Here is an example of a scenario describing the potential impact of specific technical conditions on one aspect of private life—time spent on watching television—which was developed in a research project funded by the German Federal Government (Jungermann, Fleischer, Hobohm, Schöppe and Thüring, 1986):

It is the year 2010. The so-called BISDN (Broadband Integrated Services Digital Network) has been installed everywhere in West Germany. We take a look at the household of Mrs S., a 65-year-old pensioner living in a big city. The household is also connected to the network. Mrs S. owns a comfortable TV set; she can choose among 30 channels. She also owns a disc recorder for recording programmes. Furthermore Mrs S. can order programmes for recording (copy on demand). Therefore all TV programmes are highly available for Mrs S. and it is very likely that she will spend more time watching TV than a comparable person today.

Generating such scenarios is an increasingly popular method in technology assessment and social impact studies. One reason is certainly that, since the subject of interest is often extremely complex and opaque, little understood and vehemently debated, there is basically no other way than to cut some major paths in the thicket and to forgo any aspirations about prognosis. Another reason might be, however, that the scenario method does not set the boundaries for thinking so narrowly and allows for a moment of speculation. But whatever the motivation behind the use of the scenario method might be, the method requires a very specific use of knowledge that has not yet been studied; sometimes this is called 'disciplined intuition'. Therefore, this kind of intuition cannot yet be controlled by some scientifically justified technique; and, as a result, its products—the scenarios—cannot easily be evaluated in terms of soundness, completeness, or originality. This, then, is the subject of our chapter: What are the cognitive structures and processes used by experts when they explore the future? How might the mind of experts work when they generate scenarios and how could one improve their disciplined intuition?

In the first section of the chapter, we will briefly describe the scenario concept, what technical methods exist for constructing scenarios, and what types of scenarios are to be distinguished. In the second major section we will propose a conceptual framework for understanding the cognitive processes involved in the intuitive generation of scenarios. The core of this framework is the description of retrieval and inference processes based on mental models of causal knowledge.

THE SCENARIO METHODOLOGY

In this section we will describe (1) different concepts of a scenario and the major uncontroversial characteristics, (2) a number of dimensions on which scenario types can be distinguished, and (3) one exemplary technique for constructing a scenario (cf. Jungermann, 1985b). This will provide the basis for our cognitive-psychological analysis of the task of scenario generating in the next section.

The concept

The term 'scenario' is used with various meanings in the literature. However, two definitions are particularly well-known and typical: (a) For Kahn (who introduced the term into the field of forecasting) scenarios are 'hypothetical sequences of events constructed for the purpose of focusing attention on causal processes and decision points' (Kahn, 1965). (b) Mitchell *et al.* (1979), on the other hand, define a scenario as 'an outline of one conceivable state of affairs, given certain assumptions about the present and the course of events in the intervening period'. The difference between the two concepts lies in their emphasis on the course of events between the initial state and the final state. Whereas in Kahn's definition the emphasis is on the explication of the chain of actions and events and their causal relations, the emphasis in the definition given by Mitchell *et al.* is on the depiction of the situation at the time horizon, given certain assumptions about the preceding period. The first concept might be called a 'chain scenario', the second a 'snapshot scenario'.

These and other conceptualizations share, however, several features that more or less constitute the term and distinguish it from terms like, for example, cognitive map (Axelrod, 1976), script (Schank and Abelson, 1977; Abelson, 1981), or plan (Hayes-Roth, 1979):

—A scenario is hypothetical, i.e. it describes some possible or potential future.
—A scenario is selective, i.e. it represents one possible state of some complex, interdependent, dynamic, and opaque affairs.
—A scenario is bound, i.e. it consists of a limited number of states, events, actions, and consequences, or subsets of these categories.
—A scenario is connected, i.e. its elements are conditionally or causally related.
—A scenario is assessable, i.e. it can be judged with respect to its probability and/or desirability.

These features can easily be identified in the little TV-watching scenario we presented in the introductory section. For example, the scenario is obviously hypothetical since it describes some situation 25 years from now. It is selective in that it includes one particular kind of private household, one specific condition of the technical infrastructure, one particular kind of equipment and services, and just one specific impact. Clearly, the situation from which these elements are selected is much richer, but for illustrative purposes this simple picture will do.

Dimensions for classification

Scenarios can be distinguished on a number of dimensions. Ducot and

Lubben (1980) have suggested the following three:

—Exploratory–Anticipatory: Exploratory scenarios are forward-directed, i.e. they start with some known or assumed states or events and explore what consequences might then result. Anticipatory scenarios, on the other hand, are backward-directed, i.e. they start from some assumed final state of affairs and ask for the possible preconditions (events or actions) which could produce these effects.
—Descriptive–Normative: Descriptive scenarios present potential futures irrespective of their desirability or undesirability. Normative scenarios, on the other hand, take values and goals explicitly into account.
—Trend–Peripheral: A trend scenario extrapolates the normal, surprise-free course of events or state of affairs that one might expect if nothing spectacular were to happen or if no particular action were taken. A peripheral scenario, on the other hand, depicts trend-breaking, surprising or unprobable developments.

In terms of this classification, our scenario can be classified as an exploratory and descriptive trend scenario. Unfortunately, the authors of scenarios rarely state, and seem to reflect in the beginning of the construction process, which type of scenario they want to develop and why this particular type is adequate for their purpose. In fact, most scenarios are not of any distinct type at all but represent mixtures of the various types. An explicit consideration of the function the scenario is to fulfil would probably sometimes help the author to develop a more stringent and more appropriate scenario.

Techniques for construction

A number of techniques have been proposed for generating the type of scenarios we are concerned with in this paper. Mitchell *et al.* (1979) use nine features in their description of 18 variants for constructing scenarios. One such feature, for example, is the degree to which relations between scenario elements are newly developed or taken from precanned structures: in an inductive, bottom-up approach, the elements are first generated and then, using matrix and graph theoretical procedures, their relationships are gradually developed; in a deductive, top-down approach, on the other hand, clusters of interrelated elements are used as input for the scenario development. Other features concern the handling of time, the explicitness of probability judgments, and the request of subjective information search.

These features are interesting for comparing construction techniques on a molar level; in the present context, however, it is more interesting to look at such techniques on a more molecular level. One technique has been proposed by the Battelle group (Geschka and von Reibnitz, 1983); it consists of eight steps. (1) The task is defined and structured, the area of interest is specified, and the major relevant features of this area, so-called descriptors, are identified and their present states are assessed. (2) Important external factors and their interrelations as well as their influences on the area of interest are described; interconnected influence factors may form so-called surrounding fields or influence fields. (3) For each field, major descriptors are identified and their present states are assessed; for each descriptor, an assumption is made about its future trend, or, if this is too difficult (the descriptor is then called 'critical') several alternative trend assumptions are made. (4) The consistency of the possible combinations of alternative assumptions regarding the critical descriptors are checked and assumption bundles are identified which include only consistent and probable combinations and which differ clearly from each other. (5) These assumption bundles are combined with the trend assumptions regarding the uncritical descriptors, resulting in a scenario for each field. (6) Assumptions are made with respect to possible interfering events and their probabilities and impacts on the field; their integration in the scenarios may necessitate some revision. (7) The impact of the field scenarios on the area of interest and its descriptors are assessed and respective scenarios are constructed. (8) Strategies are identified which could, depending on the values and goals of the decision-maker, promote or impede developments described in the scenarios.

We have described this technique in some detail because its various steps, though prescriptively formulated, include a number of elements that are also important for a descriptive analysis of the use of knowledge in scenario construction. It is interesting to note that neither this technique nor other techniques explicitly refer to the psychological problem of the intuitive use of knowledge by individuals.

In this section we have explicated the concept of scenarios, we have specified several types of scenarios and addressed the construction problem. We have looked, from a technical point of view, at the kind of knowledge that a person should search for and at the strategy the person should use for retrieving or inferring this knowledge. We will now present a psychological perspective of the task.

A THEORETICAL FRAMEWORK

If we ask a person to generate a scenario describing the impact of future information and communication technology on the private household, what does the person have to do in order to deliver a product like the one presented in the introduction? What is the knowledge used and how is it used? We assume the following steps in the cognitive activity of the person:

—First, the relevant problem knowledge will be activated within the world knowledge of the individual. Which parts are activated and to which degree, depends on the context. For example, a social science expert asked to generate a 'TV-watching scenario' might activate his knowledge about studies on how families spend their free time or about indicators proposed to describe the quality of private life.

—Secondly, a mental model will be constituted on the basis of the activated problem knowledge that includes those elements and relations of the domain which are needed for the specific task. For example, an expert might think of the number of channels, the amount of free time, the purchase power, the size of a household, the need for social contact, the feeling of dependency on technical equipment etc. and try to relate these aspects to each other.

—Thirdly, inferences will be drawn by simulating the mental model in ways determined by the task. For example, if an expert wanted to identify which potential measures were required today to prevent unfavourable effects on social contacts, he might check how the number of unplanned social contacts would possibly vary as a function of the kind and cost of special services like buying food or account managing via home terminals.

—Finally, scenario knowledge is composed by selecting those inferences that seem most relevant, probable, interesting, or whatever the criteria might be. For example, an expert might be most interested in describing potential favourable states of affairs, e.g. the potential increase of intellectual creativity in children through the use of computers, in order to alleviate resistance to their establishment in schools.

Figure 1 shows the assumed stages and the processes that lead to them. We will now describe in more detail these structures and processes as well as some factors that influence the cognitive activity (see also Jungermann, 1985b).

Activation of problem knowledge

The knowledge relevant for building a scenario is part of the 'world knowledge' stored in the individual's long-term memory. Nothing can be activated in memory that is not already there; this includes, of course, the knowledge that many things are not known but that information can or must be gained in the environment.

In cognitive psychology, the storage of knowledge in memory is often conceptualized as an associative network (e.g. Collins and Quillian, 1969; Anderson and Bower, 1973; Norman and Rumelhart, 1975). A network consists of nodes representing concepts, connected by links representing relations between these concepts. For example, the concept 'money' may be related in some memory to the concept 'greed' by a causal relation like 'money induces greed' and to the concept 'Mercedes-Benz' by a conditional relation like 'if you have enough money, then you can buy a Mercedes-Benz'.

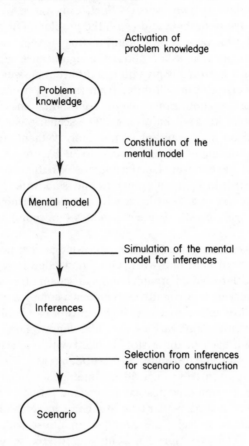

Figure 1. Cognitive structures and processes
relevant for the construction of scenarios

There may be class relations, temporal relations, property relations, and a number of other relations. Since the meaning of a concept is defined through the kind and number of its relations to other concepts, the network is a closed, circular structure. The activation of knowledge is basically conceived as a neurophysiological process: the sensory presentation of some stimulus (e.g. a spoken word) activates the corresponding node in the network, and this activation spreads through the network to other concepts. The stronger the association is between two concepts, the faster and stronger is the spread of activation from one to the other (Anderson, 1977, 1983).

If a scenario is to be generated for some specific area of interest and in some specific context, only parts of the world knowledge are relevant and should be activated. The situation and the task determine largely what these parts are. But we may distinguish two aspects. First, only those parts are evidently relevant which have something to do with the problem. Different answers will be given by different people depending on their expertise and values. For example, if an engineer is asked about the significance of new information technologies, she will probably give quite a different answer than an economist, and the answers of both will differ from the answer given by a politician and a psychologist. Second, causal and/or conditional knowledge is relevant, as opposed to other kinds of knowledge. The scenario construction requires inferences based on causal and/or conditional 'if–then' considerations; for example, if each household will have access to 30 TV programmes in 25 years, then people will have fewer social contacts. Whether a particular causal and/or relation exists in a person's network and is activated, depends again on this person's pre-existing knowledge. In network terminology, then, the relevant knowledge consists of relevant nodes (concepts) and relevant links (relations).

The activation of the relevant problem knowledge does not take place in an entirely unstructured field, however. Our knowledge is organized in many ways. One particular kind of organization is a schema (see Alba and Hasher (1983) for an overview). A cognitive schema is a complex unit of knowledge, based on generalized experiences. A single concept like 'table' may be viewed as a schema that consists of various slots like 'legs', 'plate', etc.; if a specific table is presented, each of these slots is filled with a specific feature which specifies a value on some attribute (e.g. 'wooden legs'). The schema concept also plays an important role in artificial intelligence but it is still open to question whether human schemas have the same properties as postulated in this field. However, one particular type of schema has created great interest in cognitive psychology, namely, the event schema, also called script (Schank and Abelson, 1977). A script represents stereotypic sequences of events, including actions, such as 'dining in a restaurant'. Cognitive scripts work as bundles of expectations about the order as well as the occurrence of events. For instance, the restaurant script consists, on a rather molar level of analysis, of 'entering, ordering, eating, paying, and leaving'. Event schemata represent a very efficient organization of knowledge, facilitating storing, processing, and retrieving information. But the implicit or explicit use of event schemata may also cause mistakes, e.g. incorrect assumptions about some course of events. The elements of an event schema are only probabilistically and not deterministically related, and the reliance on the 'usual', i.e. the schematic course of events, provides pitfalls, although it is generally efficient. For example, Bower *et al*. (1979) found that subjects who had read a stereotypic story and were then asked to recall what they had read, tended toward false recognition of non-mentioned events; they apparently filled their memory gaps with elements that were part of their schema and thus 'should' have occurred in the story. The development and use of schemata is obviously a highly efficient cognitive mechanism; it distinguishes the professional from the amateur. But at the same time it is part of the 'déformation professionelle', hindering professionals from perceiving or imagining the world in a non-schematic way and from understanding other people using their particular schemata. A loss in cognitive flexibility and creativity is the price paid for a gain in cognitive efficiency and parsimony.

The first step in a scenario construction process is thus less trivial than those authors seem to assume who advise experts simply 'to define the relevant components or descriptors'. The activation of problem knowledge within the world knowledge of an individual is influenced by a number of situational and personal factors. Whether a scenario about the impact of information technologies on private life is developed for scientific or political purposes, whether it is generated by experts or lay people, or whether it is built by proponents or opponents of technical progress has an effect on the activation of knowledge for further processing. Such findings should be taken into account when a technique for scenario constructoin is proposed.

Constitution of a mental model

The activated problem knowledge provides the basis for a more focused approach to generating scenarios, i.e. for a more precise selection and combination of those elements in the area of interest which are to serve as descriptors of the states to be explored or which might influence the values these descriptors will take. We assume that a model is constituted from the problem knowledge by mapping the main elements and relations of the domain to be described, and that this model is used for making the required inferences about possible future states of the domain. This model that the expert supposedly forms in the mind will be called a 'mental model'.

The mental model concept was introduced into psychology by Craik (1943) who defined its functions as follows:

If the organism carries a small-scale model of external reality and of its own possible actions within his head, it is able to try out various alternatives, conclude which is the best of them, react to future situations before they arise, utilize the knowledge of past events in dealing with the present and the future, and in every way to react in a much fuller, safer, and more competent manner to emergencies which face it.

This concept has been revived and elaborated in recent years in cognitive psychology (e.g. Johnson-Laird, 1983; Norman, 1983; see also Pitz and Sachs, 1984). Mental models have been proposed as the specific kind of knowledge structures that people use to understand technical devices like pocket calculators (see Gentner and Stevens, 1983), to reason deductively with verbal propositions (Johnson-Laird, 1983), and to judge the probability of events (Thüring and Jungermann, 1986). Surprisingly little has yet been said in the literature about possible forms mental models might take. Thüring and Jungermann (1986) have conceptualized mental models as causal nets, at least for situations which require probability judgments, and have illustrated this idea with two problems, 'environmental catastrophes' and 'energy market', based on items used by Tversky and Kahneman (1983) in their study on the conjunction fallacy. Since the task of scenario building requires the operation of causal knowledge, as was described in the previous section, this conceptualization seems also to be useful for our present discussion. A simple hypothetical mental model of the factors related to the descriptor 'TV-watching time', corresponding to the scenario presented in the introduction, is

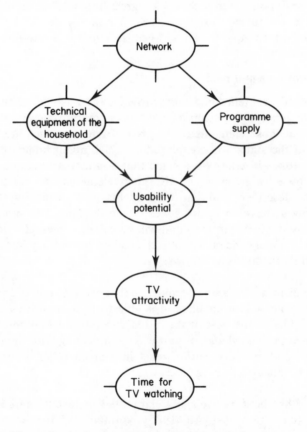

Figure 2. A simple mental model about influences on
TV-watching time

given in Figure 2. If a mental model is constituted for a particular purpose, those variables and relations in the domain are mapped into a cognitive representation which are important for drawing the required inferences.

The resulting mental model is the representation of that part of the problem knowledge that is needed for particular inferences. If the domain is some technical device like a pocket calculator, a mental model may be assumed to be more or less similar to the 'scientific' or 'conceptual' model (Norman, 1983); the focus of research can then be directed on deviations of the mental model from the conceptual model and on the inferences derived from this model. If the domain is some economic problem like the energy market, however, the constitution of the mental model itself becomes a major object of analysis because there is no 'true' model of this domain; rather, there are probably a number of very different mental models which their owners are quite capable to justify. Only after the mental model has been understood can attention be paid to inferences based on this model. Since the scenarios we are discussing describe future situations, and mostly economic or social ones, this second case applies, i.e. there is no 'true' model. It is therefore interesting to look at some factors influencing content and structure of the mental model.

We assume that a person uses two strategies for constituting a mental model. On the one hand, he may retrieve elements, relations, and part-structures from the activated problem knowledge; on the other hand, he may form elements and infer relations from reasoning which are not yet existing or salient in memory.

(a) The constitution of a mental model must begin with retrieving elements and relations from the activated knowledge base. The process is influenced, on the one hand, by factors that generally play a role for all kinds of retrieval tasks. The saliency of information in memory is one such factor, where saliency simply means the strength of pre-activation of an element or the strength of some association between elements. The more salient an item of information is, the better is it cognitively available, i.e. the more easily is it retrieved and becomes a member of the mental model, probably after some evaluation regarding its importance. A number of studies have revealed factors influencing the saliency of information. For example, saliency is strongly influenced by the frequency with which an event has been directly or indirectly observed. For experts, this usually means professional experience, whereas for the public it means report in the media.

A factor more specific for the constitution of a mental model is whether the focus is on facts or values or both. First, if the intention is to construct a purely descriptive scenario, one should expect facts to be activated more strongly and thus retrieved more easily than goals. Second, if the focus is on facts only, we can expect differences among experts depending on their professional background; for example, the mental model of psychologists regarding information technologies and private life in 25 years will probably contain other variables than the model of economists. If the focus is mainly on goals, we can expect differences among experts with differing political viewpoints; for example, the value structures assessed from various stakeholder groups in West Germany for evaluating future energy supply systems differed considerably (Keeney *et al*., 1984), and one can reasonably assume that these value structures reflect basic value differences which would strongly influence the mental model built for constructing scenarios.

Little can be said about the search for and retrieval of causal relations. We might speculate that the process works like this: Assume some element X has been retrieved. This element may be causally related to Y (in memory) either directly or indirectly, i.e. via other elements. If the strength of the causal relation is above some level, element Y and the relation between X and Y will be retrieved automatically; otherwise, Y will not be retrieved (at least not automatically with X) and no relation between X and Y will be retrieved (at least at this moment of the constitution of the model). With these assumptions, the retrieval of substructures can be described as the more or less simultaneous and automatic retrieval of all those elements among which causal relations exist that exceed some associative strength.

(b) Although the retrieval of information from the activated knowledge base may often be sufficient for constituting a mental model, or is at least considered sufficient by its author, the task of describing possible futures sometimes requires, in addition to reproductive cognitive activity, some more constructive, reasoning activity. This is particularly important if no models yet exist, in the literature or in the expert's mind, as for the interrelations among factors in our information technology example. In this case, the expert must go beyond the available information.

One possible strategy is the checking for potential causal relations by searching for 'cues to causality' (Einhorn and Hogarth, 1982, 1986). These authors distinguish four kinds of cues: (1) Covariation of two variables X and Y, (2) the temporal order of X and Y, (3) spatial and temporal contiguity of X and Y, and (4) similarity of X and Y. Whether a causal relation is cognitively established between X and Y depends on the number and strength of cues for such a relation, which may be direct (X causes Y) or indirect, i.e. with intervening variables (X causes A . . . B which causes Y). The stronger the causal connection of the chain of variables is, the more probable is their integration into the mental model. Two assumptions can be derived from Einhorn and Hogarth's analysis (1986) for the strength of the causal connection. First, the longer a chain is, the weaker is its causal strength; this implies that more complex combinations of variables have a lower chance of being used for the mental model compared to simple combinations. Second, the more common and familiar the variables of the chain are, the weaker is their explanatory value; this implies that chains including exceptional and unfamiliar variables appear more attractive and important and thus have a better chance of being used for the mental model than chains with unspectacular and ordinary variables. Both implications are well-known: simple rather than complex, and spectacular rather than ordinary pictures of possible futures dominate the literature. They are easier and more attractive for the author to construct and for the public to conceive.

We have not yet mentioned the knowledge about the strength and form of a causal relation, i.e. the functional relation between two variables in the model. For example, a person might know that, if variable X increases, then variable Y decreases—or, more specifically, that there is a linear inverse functional relation between X and Y. There is also often some knowledge about whether X and Y are deterministically or probabilistically related, and, in the latter case, about how strong this relation is. Obviously, this knowledge is essential for later simulating the model, but at present little more can be said about its activation and use for the constitution of the mental model than what we have said before regarding the use of variables and relations. If there pre-exists some knowledge about the functional relation between two variables, it will probably be activated simultaneously with the activation of the two variables and taken with them into the model. If there is no such knowledge, a person might try to infer it from other information; however, it is more plausible that at this stage only easily available functional knowledge would be activated and that more complicated reasoning processes would be postponed until the particular knowledge is actually acquired in the mental simulation.

The second step of the scenario-construction process outlined in this section consists of the constitution of a mental model, based on the activated problem knowledge, which maps the relevant variables of the area of interest and their causal interrelations. The reproductive as well as the constructive part of the required search, reasoning, and retrieval activities is prone to a number of pitfalls against which a scenario constructor should take precautions.

Simulation of the mental model

The mental model is not a scenario; it is the representation of the major variables and relations in the area of interest. Scenarios are inherent in the model, however, if we define them as possible combinations of values taken by the variables. Let us take the portion of a model given in Figure 2, for example, concerning the time people will spend watching TV in 25 years. Selected variables are 'television time', 'network', 'number of programmes', and 'attractivity of the programmes'. These variables can take various values; for example, 'number of programmes' can vary between 5 and 50, 'programme attractivity' can take the values low, mean, and high, etc. A combination of such values is a scenario; for example, a combination like '5 TV programmes', 'low attractivity', 'BISDN network' and 'low TV-watching time' makes one scenario.

There are as many scenarios as there are combinations of values, but the causal knowledge embedded in the mental model restricts the number of combinations which make sense. For example, if it is assumed in the mental model that some variable X ('attractivity of TV programmes') causes an increase of some variable Y ('TV-watching time')—everything else held constant—then a scenario describing just the opposite effect of X on Y ('high attractivity of programmes but low TV-watching time') would be rather arbitrarily inconsistent with the mental model. It is the function of the mental model that it helps to generate those scenarios, from all possible scenarios, that can be based on and justified from causal knowledge about the area of interest. The use of a mental model for deriving scenarios distinguishes the scientific expert from the science fiction author who is not restricted (but, of course, also not helped) by the structure of a mental model.

But how does a person use the mental model for generating those scenarios that make sense? There is really little known about this process and we can only offer some ideas and draw upon indirect evidence. As a frame, we find it a useful conceptualization that people simulate, or run, their mental model in order to draw the required inferences. First, one variable of the model is selected and a value is specified; then the variable's relations to other variables are searched and those values are identified on these variables which follow from, or are consistent with, the relations. For example, one might select the variable 'network' and specify 'BISDN' as value; this variable may be causally related to the variables 'number of programmes' and 'technical equipment', and the values consistent with the input may be '30 programmes' and 'videophon', respectively. The result of one simulation cycle can be expressed with an 'IF–THEN' statement, in this case 'IF BISDN is installed, THEN 30 programmes'. We will now describe more specifically, though very selectively, the various steps such a simulation process might take and some factors that might influence the process.

(1) First, a variable is chosen from which the simulation cycle can start; let us call this the input variable. Whereas the criteria for this choice are not part of the model, the information for making the choice is taken from it. For example, one might select as input variable the most important variable and use as an index of importance the number of relations a variable has to other variables; the variable which has more relations to other variables than any other variable would then be considered the most important one. Or one might select an action variable (e.g. a potential governmental regulatory decision) rather than an event variable (e.g. the purchasing power of the private household).

(2) Next, a value is specified on the input variable. Depending on context and task, this might be, for example, the most probable or the most extreme

value the variable can possibly take. If a trend scenario is intended (e.g. the future of the automobile), the most probable value would be taken, whereas for a peripheral scenario (e.g. an accident scenario) the most extreme value would be relevant. The output of the first two steps may be conceived as the first part of a production: 'IF variable X takes the value x(i), . . .'.

(3) Then, a search is started from the input variable for other, causally related variables. This is a crucial step of the simulation since there are many possible cognitive search strategies. We distinguish two types of strategies, one concerning the direction and one concerning the specificity of the search.

The first type (described in detail by Jungermann (1985a)) has two variants, a forward- and a backward-directed search strategy. With a forward strategy, a person starts from the input variable, conceived as a cause, and searches for potential effects or consequences; this is a causal reasoning process. With a backward strategy, the input variable is conceived as an effect or consequence for which potential causes or conditions are inferred; this is a diagnostic reasoning process.

The second type has also two variants, a non-specific and a specific search strategy. In a non-specific search, the search starting with the input variable has no specific aim, i.e. no particular output variable is specified; instead, the search proceeds according to probabilistic or other criteria. In a specific search, on the other hand, the output variable of interest is fixed and the search is limited to the path leading from the input to the output variable.

Table 1 shows the four possible combinations of these search strategies. Our characterization focuses on the kind of questions and answers for which each combination is appropriate.

(a) Non-specific forward search: This strategy would apply if the question is, 'What might happen if variable X takes the value x(i)?'. For example, what effects or consequences can be expected on variables like 'technical equipment' and 'programme supply' if the variable 'network' takes the value

Table 1 Combinations of search strategies in the simulation of mental models

	Input as cause	Input as effect
Input variables specified	non-specific forward search	non-specific backward search
Input and output variables specified	specific forward search	specific forward search

'BISDN'? Starting from a specific input variable, the search proceeds successively along all links which emanate from this variable within the mental model without any particular aim.

(b) Non-specific backward search: This strategy would be appropriate if the question is, 'What could produce value x(i) on variable X?'. For example, which events or actions could result in people watching less TV than today? The search proceeds here along all those links which lead directly or indirectly to the input variable X. Techniques like 'brainstorming' or 'nominal group' (Delbecq *et al.*, 1975) suggest non-specific (backward as well as forward) search for information in memory in order to facilitate access to information that might not become available in a more specific search.

(c) Specific forward search: This strategy would help answer the question, 'Which value would result on variable Y if variable X took the value x(i)?'. For example, how much time might people spend watching TV if the BISDN network were realized? The search proceeds along that path that leads from the input variable to the output variable, possibly with intervening variables. Whereas this strategy appears very straightforward at first sight, it actually becomes rather complicated if more than one path emanates from the input variable which—after passing through intervening variables—goes to the output variable of interest.

(d) Specific backward search: This strategy would be used for answering the question, 'Which value on Y could have led to variable X taking the value x(i)?'. For example, what purchasing power of the private household could have produced a rich technical information and communication equipment? The same arguments apply for this strategy as for the forward variants. It seems simple but may be very complicated, depending on the domain and the model of the domain.

All four strategies described can vary with respect to the depth of search. The depth is defined as the number of variables considered in answering one question, i.e. in one simulation cycle. For example, it may take none or many intervening variables to answer the question what effect some value on the input variable X might have on some output variable Y. The non-specific strategies can further vary in breadth, with breadth defined as the number of links emanating from or going towards the input variable. The more links are included in a non-specific forward or backward search, the more comprehensive it is. Breadth and depth are the major characteristics of the complexity of the simulation process. Evidently, simulations of a mental model can easily get very complex, particularly since in 'real-life' problems the number of relevant variables and relations is high. Since the human information processing capacity is limited we cannot expect perfection in the task described.

(4) Finally, a value is assessed on the output variable of interest. As was said for the specification of a value on the input variable, the value assessed depends on the task and on the context; for example, if a peripheral scenario is intended, the most extreme or least probable value would be assessed.

More important, however, is the knowledge of the person regarding the functional relationship between input and output variable (or, in case of a chain of more than two variables, regarding the functional relations between all adjacent variables). This knowledge enables a person to assess that value on some output variable Y that corresponds to the value specified on the input variable. The result of the last two steps may be conceived as the second part of a production: '. . . THEN variable Y takes the value y(i)'.

In many studies a cognitive activity like mental simulation has been suggested to describe and explain how people generate inferences (e.g. Johnson-Laird, 1983; de Kleer and Brown, 1983; Norman, 1983). Particularly interesting in our context is how Kahneman and Tversky (1982) relate mental simulation to probability judgments: 'The ease with which the simulation of a system reaches a particular state is eventually used to judge the propensity of the (real) system to produce that state' (pp. 1–2).

The task seems to require a non-specific backward search. Which states on which variables could produce a particular state on some variable, or particular states on some set of variables? If only few variables need to be considered, the simulation is easier than when many variables have to be searched for, in breadth or in depth. And if the simulation is easy, the probability of the state is judged higher than when the simulation is complicated. Tversky and Kahneman (1983) have provided evidence for this assumption in the so-called 'conjunction fallacy' which they have observed in human inferential reasoning. Their subjects estimated the probability of a conjunction of events higher than the probability of one of its conjuncts if they could establish a causal relation between the events in the conjunction. The conjunction effect has been replicated under various conditions (e.g. Leddo *et al.*, 1984; Locksley and Stangor, 1984). It violates the rules of probability theory according to which the probability of a conjunction can never be higher than the probability of one of its conjuncts. Our approach allows the following interpretation: If a person has to estimate the probability of some event X she might ask which events could produce event X; she would thus apply a non-specific backward search through which a number of potential causes could be generated. But a non-specific strategy is difficult since all links leading to the event must be taken into account; the search is broad and deep. If, on the other hand, the probability of a conjunction of two events X and Y is to be estimated and if one event can be interpreted as a possible cause of the other, then a specific backward search would be sufficient to check whether event Y could possibly cause event X. Since such a strategy is less expensive than a non-specific strategy, it is easier; consequently, a higher probability judgment will be given for the conjunction than for the single conjunct. The mental model approach offers a way not only to explain the conjunction effect but also to predict more precisely under which conditions this effect will be observed and under which not (Thüring and Jungermann, 1986).

The third step of the scenario-building process that we have described in this section is the simulation of the mental model in order to draw the required inferences. The core of this simulation process is the more or less complex pattern of search for effects or causes of some input variable and the assessment of corresponding values on variables which are directly or indirectly related to each other.

Selection of inferences

The simulation cycles of the mental model produce the inferences from which a scenario, or a number of scenarios, are generated. The type of scenario wanted determines primarily the selection of inferences, but other aspects like expectation and desirability can also play a role. We will discuss here only a few possibilities of selecting inferences that we find particularly important and interesting.

(a) Let us first consider the case of a 'snapshot scenario', defined earlier as an outline of a conceivable state of affairs and as a depiction of the situation at the time horizon. As an example, take our interest in the life of a private household in 25 years as effected by information and communication technology. What inferences are needed to construct such a scenario? We assume that a person has run the mental model with certain inputs, i.e. assumptions about values on certain variables, by searching through the knowledge base along causal relations and using the knowledge about the functional relations between adjacent variables. Now, for a snapshot scenario, the variables passed in the course of the inferential process from input to output variable and the inferences drawn about the values they might take, i.e. all the intermediate inferences, are irrelevant. Only the inferred values on the output variables at which the simulation ended, the descriptor variables, are of interest. For our example these might be, for example, the number of social contacts, the time spent on watching television, the feeling of control over technical equipment, etc.

Whereas this restriction of the set of relevant inferences requires no decision, since it is determined by the scenario type intended, the next steps are more difficult. First, a selection can be made among the output variables considered. For example, one might implicitly forget or explicitly exclude variables for which values have been generated that do not differ from the values these variables take in the present, i.e. that do not signal a significant change in the future compared to the present (e.g. time spent on watching TV, due to a ceiling effect). Such variables may seem uninteresting and unimportant for the scenario; they also seem less relevant for considering actions than variables indicating potential dramatic changes. Second, a selection can, and usually must, be made among the various values that the output variable could possibly take. To simplify the discussion we have so far assumed that the simulation results in one value of the output variable; but we have to remember that the person knows that the relation between input and output variables is usually probabilistic and that therefore, given a specific value on the input variable, the output variable can take various values with certain probabilities. Furthermore, these values are not only more or less probable, they are also more or less desirable. These aspects might be used as criteria for the selection of inferences. With respect to probability one might assume that usually the most probable value would be chosen; if, however, a peripheral rather than a trend scenario is intended, values with extreme probabilities would be selected (e.g. a strong decrease in unplanned social contacts). With respect to desirability one might argue that this aspect should not influence the scenario construction at all. But this postulate seems neither from a descriptive nor from a prescriptive point of view justified: Even the experts' attention will often implicitly be drawn to the very desirable or undesirable states of affairs the future might hold for us. And they often should indeed focus their attention on these output values in order to show us the range of potential future risks and benefits (e.g. decrease or increase of social contacts).

(b) Let us now consider the case of a 'chain scenario', defined earlier as a sequence of causally or conditionally related actions and events. For example, we might want to describe how certain information and communication techniques might actually bring about certain effects on private life. For such a scenario not only the final inferences, i.e. the ones concerning the output variables are required but also the variables that mediate the relation between the input and output variable. With respect to the output variable, all considerations made above apply as well, and we will therefore only discuss the selection of inferences as far as intermediate variables are concerned.

The outcome of the mental simulation is here not just one value on the output variable, i.e. the final part of the chain, but a sequence of values on principally all variables that have been passed from the input to the output variable. For example, when the input variable is the technical network structure and the output variable is the frequency of social contacts, intermediate variables might be the technical equipment of the household, the kind and number of available services, the income of the household, etc. Again, not all possible inferences drawn in the mental simulation will be useful for the scenario. First, more than one path may have been inferred leading from the input to the output variable, depending on the search leaving the input variable; a selection must then be made among the various paths. Second, not all intermediate variables will necessarily be chosen for a scenario; the selection will depend on the degree of analytical fineness aimed at, on the perceived importance of links, and also sometimes on the desirability of states of intermediate variables. For example, if the value on the output variable, i.e. the final outcome is very desirable, one might tend to implicitly forget or explicitly leave out intermediate states which are very undesirable, in order to make the whole scenario more acceptable to others. The revolutionary usually does not mention the bloodshed implied by the glorious goal.

These examples must suffice to demonstrate that the construction of a scenario does not end with the constitution and simulation of the mental model but that a further important step determines from which inferences the scenario will finally be composed. This step depends on the task and on the expert performing the task, and it implies, as the other steps described before, many intricate patterns of information processing on the part of the expert. It is obvious that expectations and values play a major role in this process.

The chain type of a scenario is not unlike the concept of a 'cognitive map' proposed by Axelrod (1976). In a cognitive map events are related to each other in two ways: an event either increases or decreases another event. For example, a 'policy of withdrawal' might decrease the 'security in Persia', and this event might increase the 'ability of Persian government to maintain order' (see Figure 3). In terms of our framework, a cognitive map is a path through the model generated in a mental simulation. It is the outcome of a process in which a specific subset of inferences from the set of all inferences is selected and used for representation. The concept of a cognitive map has an intuitive appeal and was one of the first more formal concepts suggested for representing potential realities.

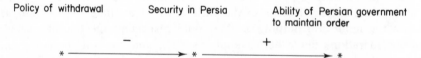

Figure 3. Example of a path in a cognitive map (*Reproduced with permission, from Axelrod (1976, p. 61)*).

The last step in the construction of a scenario described in this section is the selection of those inferences among all inferences produced in the mental simulation which are 'useful' for the scenario. What is useful will depend on the type of scenario intended as well as on other criteria like saliency, probability, or desirability of the inferences.

CONCLUSIONS

The analysis performed in this chapter should have served two goals: on the one hand, to provide an approach to better understanding what actually goes on in experts' minds when they construct scenarios of possible futures, i.e., how their intuition might work; on the other hand, to provide a perspective for designing techniques which help the expert to exploit his knowledge as well as possible and to protect himself against cognitive pitfalls, i.e. for disciplining intuition.

Although our analysis has been guided by recent developments in cognitive psychology, it is evidently neither descriptively nor prescriptively on safe grounds. Theoretical, empirical and technical work is needed to examine certain aspects of the analysis and, most importantly, to validate them in real applications of scenario construction. However, the approach we have proposed offers a framework in which such studies can be placed and linked to each other. It is not supposed to be a theory that could be tested as a whole but rather a heuristic framework that may stimulate future studies.

REFERENCES

Abelson, R. P. (1981) 'The psychological status of the script concept', *American Psychologist*, **36**, 715–729.

Alba, J. W. and Hasher, L. (1983) 'Is memory schematic?' *Psychological Bulletin*, **93**, 203–231.

Anderson, J. R. (1977) *Language, Memory, and Thought*, Hillsdale, N.J.: Lawrence Erlbaum Associates.

Anderson, J. R. (1983) *The Architecture of Cognition*, Cambridge, Mass.: Harvard University Press.

Anderson, J. R. and Bower, G. H. (1973) *Human Associative Memory*, Washington: Winston.

Axelrod, R. (ed.) (1976) *Structure of Decision. The Cognitive Maps of Political Elites*, Princeton, N.J.: Princeton University Press.

Bower, G. H., Black, J. B. and Turner, T. J. (1979) 'Scripts in memory for text', *Cognitive Psychology*, **11**, 177–220.

Collins, A. M. and Quillian, M. R. (1969) 'Retrieval time from semantic memory', *Journal of Verbal Learning and Verbal Behavior*, **8**, 241–248.

Craik, K. (1943) *The Nature of Explanation*, Cambridge: Cambridge University Press.

Delbecq, A. L., Van de Zen, A. H. and Gustafson, D. (1975) *Group Techniques for Program Planning*, Glenview, Ill.: Scott Foresman.

Ducot, C. and Lubben, G. J. (1980) 'A typology for scenarios', *Futures*, **12**, 51–57.

Einhorn, H. J. and Hogarth, R. M. (1982) 'Prediction, diagnosis, and causal thinking in forecasting', *Journal of Forecasting*, **1**, 23–36.

Einhorn, H. J. and Hogarth, R. M. (1986) 'Judging probable cause', *Psychological Bulletin*, **99**, 3–19.

Gentner, D. and Stevens, A. L. (1983) *Mental Models*, Hillsdale, New Jersey: Lawrence Erlbaum Associates.

Geschka, H. and von Reibnitz, U. (1983) 'Die Szenario-Technik—ein Instrument der Zukunftsanalyse und der strategischen Planung, in A. Tlpfer and M. Afheldt (eds.), *Praxis der Unternehmensplanung*. Frankfurt.

Hayes-Roth, B. and Hayes-Roth, F. (1979) 'A cognitive model of planning', *Cognitive Science*, **3**, 275–310.

Johnson-Laird, P. N. (1983) *Mental Models*, Cambridge: Cambridge University Press.

Jungermann, H. (1985a) 'Inferential processes in the construction of scenarios', *Journal of Forecasting*, **4**, 321–327.

Jungermann, H. (1985b) 'Psychological aspects of scenarios', in V. T. Covello, J. L. Mumpower, P. J. M. Stallen and V. R. R. Uppuluri (eds.), *Environmental Impact Assessment, Technology Assessment, and Risk Analysis*, New York: Springer Verlag.

Jungermann, H., Fleischer, F., Hobohm, K., Schöppe, A. and Thüring, M. (1986) *Die Arbeit mit Szenarien bei der Technologie folgenab schätzung*. Bericht für den Bundesminister für Forschung und Technologie, Berlin: Institut für Psychologie, Technische Universität.

Kahn, H. (1965) *On Escalation: Metaphor and Scenarios*, New York: Praeger.

Kahneman, D. and Tversky, A. (1982) 'The simulation heuristic', in D. Kahneman, P. Slovic and A. Tversky (eds.), *Judgment under Uncertainty: Heuristics and Biases*, New York: Cambridge University Press.

Keeney, R. L., Renn, O., Winterfeldt, D. von and Kotte, U. (1984) *Die Wertbaumanalyse: Entscheidungshilfe für die Politik*, München: High-Tech-Verlag.

Kleer, J. de and Brown, J. S. (1983) in D. Gentner and A. L. Stevens, *Mental Models*, Hillsdale, N.J.: Lawrence Erlbaum Associates.

Leddo, J., Abelson, R. P. and Gross, P. H. (1984) 'Conjunctive explanations: When two reasons are better than one', *Journal of Personality and Social Psychology*, **5**, 933–943.

Locksley, A. and Stangor, C. (1984) 'Why versus how often: Causal reasoning and the incidence of judgmental bias', *Journal of Experimental Social Psychology*, **20**, 470–483.

Mitchell, R. B., Tydeman, J. and Georgiades, J. (1979) 'Structuring the future—application of a scenario-generation procedure', *Technological Forecasting and Social Change*, **14**, 409–428.

Norman, D. A. (1983) 'Some observations on mental models', in D. Gentner and A. L. Stevens (eds.), *Mental Models*, Hillsdale, N.J.: Lawrence Erlbaum Associates.

Norman, D. A. and Rumelhart, D. E. (1975) *Explorations in Cognition*, San Francisco: Freeman.

Pitz, G. F. and Sachs, N. J. (1984) 'Judgement and decision: Theory and application', *Annual Review of Psychology*, **35**, 139–163.

Schank, R. C. and Abelson, R. P. (1977) *Scripts, Plans, Goals and Understanding*, Hillsdale, N.J.: Lawrence Erlbaum Associates.

Thüring, M. and Jungermann, H. (1986) 'Constructing and running mental models for inferences about the future', in B. Brehmer, H. Jungermann, P. Lourens and G. Sevon (eds.), *New Directions in Research on Decision Making*, Amsterdam: North-Holland.

Tversky, A. and Kahneman, D. (1983) 'Extensional versus intuitive reasoning: The conjunction fallacy in probability judgment', *Psychological Review*, **4**, 293–315.

Judgmental Forecasting
Edited by G. Wright and P. Ayton
© 1987 John Wiley & Sons Ltd

CHAPTER 14

Judgmental Handling of Energy Scenarios: A Psychological Analysis and Experiment

Charles Vlek *and* **Wilma Otten**
University of Groningen

INTRODUCTION

The organization and policies of industrialized countries are increasingly characterized by long-term, hard-to-avoid and interactive patterns of consequences and effects. The charting of the latter well before they occur is attempted in so-called scenario studies whose intended function is to support strategic decision-making. This is especially revealed in the debate about future energy policies conducted in various countries. The debate originates in two successive 'oil crises' (1973, 1979) and revolves around questions about large-scale energy savings, diversification of source dependence, and the development of new energy technologies such as the operation of nuclear power stations, wind turbine parks and systems for cogeneration of heat and power. Socioeconomic and environmental protection policies and effects are intricately related to a country's energy consumption pattern.

Long-term energy scenario studies focused on Western Europe have been undertaken by working groups of the Commission of the European Communities (CEC, 1980) and the International Institute for Applied Systems Analysis (Häfele *et al.*, 1981; Sassin *et al.*, 1983), respectively. Two particular conclusions of the latter study are: 'that conservation may not be a reasonable way of stabilizing the international balance of demand and supply', and, 'If the EC countries want to achieve a measure of independence . . . , a policy of building up internal supply capacity should be investigated, even at production cost levels well above current international energy prices' (Sassin *et al.*, 1983, p. 9).

In the Netherlands, comprehensive energy scenarios have been developed in 1981–1983 in connection with the adventurous Societal Discussion on (nuclear) Energy Policy (abbreviated SDEP; see Jansen (1982, 1985) and Vlek (1986) for English reports about this 'unique democratic experiment'). The SDEP comprised an 18-month expert-dominated Information Phase ending in the steering committee's Interim Report of January 1983, followed by a six-month nationwide Discussion Phase consisting of several thousand small-group discussions yielding numerous completed multiple-choice questionnaires focused on future electric power generation. The steering committee's Final Report concluded the SDEP in January 1984.

A set of four different scenario studies formed a crucial part of the SDEP's Information Phase. Their aim was to provide SDEP participants with 'no prediction, but a consistent description of a possible future development of the economy, energy consumption and the resulting environmental pollution, starting from certain assumptions about uncontrollable factors (such as oil prices, economic developments abroad, and population growth) and from a package of policy suppositions' (SDEP Interim Report, 1983, Appendix II). Table 1 offers a reduced tabular presentation of the four scenarios each of which forms a mixture of intended actions or policies, and of consequences or effects of either controllable or uncontrollable events.

During the SDEP the four scenarios were made publicly available in four different ways. First, they were fully described and documented separately in low-circulation appendices to the steering committee's Interim Report (1983). Secondly, they were introduced and summarized in a 16-page final chapter of the Interim Report, 50 000 copies of which were distributed throughout the country. Third, the scenarios were schematically presented in a double-page table printed in the 'SDEP Newspaper' published in 500 000 copies made freely available at the beginning of the Discussion Phase. And fourth, essential scenario information was given at the beginning of the 12-item SDEP Questionnaire, when respondents had to indicate their preferred level of total national energy consumption in the year 2000. In fact Table 1 is derived from the relevant question in the SDEP Questionnaire.

Policy decision-making based on long-term scenarios is a relatively recent activity, and the methodology of scenario construction is immature (see Jungermann (1985) for a critical review). Besides, there exists little systematic knowledge about the way complex long-term scenarios are, or could be handled judgmentally (see Renn *et al.* (1985), Biel and Montgomery (1986) for examples). This chapter addresses some of the psychological questions that may be asked, both from a theoretical and an empirical point of view. We will first look at the actual use and evaluation of the four energy scenarios from the SDEP. Next we will take a closer look at the scenario concept itself. After that an experiment will be reported in which eighty subjects studied 'long' and 'short' versions of the scenarios (the third and fourth ways of availability mentioned above) and evaluated them for their plausibility and attractiveness in both a holistic and an analytic manner.

Table 1   A 'short list with title' version of the four scenarios prepared for the Dutch Societal Discussion on (nuclear) Energy Policy

---

Letter Code: A   REFERENCE SCENARIO (RS)

Socioeconomic policy

1. A modest growth of the economy
2. Prosperity will be maintained
3. Employment level will be preserved
4. There will be no radical changes in the general way of living

Energy policy

1. Energy consumption will somewhat increase; energy savings will be stimulated
2. All feasible sources of energy will be utilized, perhaps also nuclear power
3. (no specification on energy prices)

Environmental policy

1. Pollution will be fought when standards are exceeded

Letter Code: B   INDUSTRIAL RECOVERY SCENARIO (IRS)

Socioeconomic policy

1. A recovery of the economy
2. Prosperity may well increase
3. The employment level is not endangered
4. There will be no radical changes in ways of living

Energy policy

1. The growth of energy consumption will not be restricted
2. All feasible sources of energy will be utilized, including nuclear power and renewable energy sources
3. Energy prices will automatically increase under conditions of scarcity

Environmental policy

1. Nature and the environment will be sufficiently protected

Letter Code: C   SHARING OF LABOUR SCENARIO (SLS)

Socioeconomic policy

1. A limited growth of the economy
2. Prosperity will be maintained
3. Employment opportunities will be better distributed through shortening of the working week
4. There will be more leisure time

Energy policy

1. The growth of energy consumption will be moderated
2. All feasible sources of energy will be utilized, including nuclear power and renewable energy sources
3. (no specification on energy prices)

Table 1 (*contd*)

Environmental policy

1. Pollution will be fought, nature will be protected

Letter Code: D   SCENARIO FOR THE PRESERVATION OF
                      ENVIRONMENT AND PROSPERITY (SPEP)

Socioeconomic policy

1. A different development of the economy
2. Prosperity will not decrease, but it will be different in character
3. Employment opportunities will improve
4. The general way of living will change significantly

Energy policy

1. Energy consumption will be strongly slowed down because of limited resources
   and the energy needs of the Third World; energy savings is subsidized
2. Renewable energy sources will be especially developed; nuclear power is
   rejected
3. There will be a levying of taxes on the consumption of energy

Environmental policy

1. The environment will become much cleaner and safer

SCENARIO EVALUATION AND USE DURING THE SDEP

Shortly after their publication at the beginning of the Discussion Phase, an independent Scenario Advisory Committee (SAC, 1983) published a highly critical report on the scenario studies. In it the SAC evaluated them as highly abstract, lacking in an account of socio-political and international factors, devoid of crucial sensitivity analyses, and unclear and non-discriminative with respect to fundamental questions about the possible expansion of nuclear power facilities in the country. Therefore, concluded the SAC, the scenarios had to be handled with great care because their value as a basis for public debate and policy formation was rather limited.

Under lesser time pressure Becker and Van Houten (1984) made a more fundamental evaluation of the SDEP scenarios. These authors agree with the SAC that the scenario methodology is still under development and that it is important to ask what function a scenario is to fulfil before one passes a judgment on it. Becker and Van Houten distinguish projective ('predictive') scenarios from prospective (policy-designing) scenarios and note that all four SDEP scenarios constitute mixtures of these two.

According to Becker and Van Houten (1984) a good scenario consists of (a) a basic analysis of the status quo and its developmental trends, (b) either a projected or a desired image of the future at an adopted time horizon, and (c) a description of developmental processes (whether controllable by deliberate policies or not) by which the status quo is going to be connected to the imagined future. In view of this, and a number of specific criteria derived from it, the authors conclude that the four SDEP scenarios are significantly below level on almost all accounts. Most seriously, as the SAC had already noted, the four scenarios are non-comparable. They significantly differ with respect to the domain of variables covered, the basic assumptions and policy suppositions made, and even the computational models used (different for the SPEP (see Table 1) than for the other scenarios).

During the Discussion Phase of the SDEP the four scenarios were utilized mostly in their reduced tabular format as appearing in the SDEP Newspaper and Questionnaire mentioned above. Many SDEP participants found them difficult to comprehend and to compare, and they doubted their validity. The steering committee itself, too, in its Final Report (SDEP, 1984) seemed to have given up on the scenarios and presented alternative 'fuel packages' for large-scale electric power generation instead. Nevertheless, among people involved in the energy discussion there existed a widespread conviction that the scenarios had offered SDEP participants 'a handle on the future'.

It is worth noting that in fact only two of the four scenarios given in Table 1 appeared to play a major role in post-SDEP policy discussions. While the Government embarked upon a Growth and Diversification Scenario including the construction of at least two new nuclear power plants (which links up best with the Industrial Recovery Scenario of Table 1), the environmental protection movement elaborated, on the basis of the SDEP results, a Decentralization and Conservation Scenario excluding the expansion of nuclear power (linking up with the Scenario for the Preservation of Environment and Prosperity; see De Vries and Dijk (1985)).

The somewhat sad story just told holds several important messages. First, though multi-faceted long-term scenarios may be much in demand by policy-makers, their construction is still problematic. To a large extent the harsh criticisms of the four SDEP scenarios also pertain to the immature scenario methodology available. Second, such scenarios carry the pretence of aiding the structuring, evaluation and decision-making about far-reaching policies. An obvious question therefore is: do they indeed facilitate policy formation so as to eventually lead to insightful and justifiable decisions? Third, to the extent that relevant scenarios do not meet essential criteria associated with their intended role, the actual use of published scenario information may be improper. For example, when the same persons who desire the imagined future also select essential assumptions and policy suppositions to construct the scenario, the latter may easily tend to function as an advertising message whose designers are rather insensitive to the reality value of alternative scenarios. Fourth, it would seem that scenario studies function to bring to the fore and highlight the essential factors of possible future policies, viz. strong developmental trends, major policy objectives, and feasible actions, together with their distinctive sets of potential consequences. Knowing these should be sufficient for effective decision-making.

The first point above raises the question of whether the scenario concept can be defined with sufficient operational precision. The second point calls for empirical research on the way people actually handle scenario information for decision-making. The third point should become less relevant with improvement of the methodology under which scenarios can be properly developed and used according to their intended role. The fourth point is nicely illustrated by the SDEP Final Report ('defer'; 1984) and by the Dutch Government's principal nuclear energy decision ('expand') announced in January 1985. With some effort one could in both documents identify a relatively short list of considerations by which the recommended decision was justified. This is, of course, what one would expect; it seems inevitable for effective decision-making that scenario studies be summarized afterwards in terms of variables to which the decision under consideration proves to be most sensitive. Unfortunately, however, it would appear that scenarios may also be easily summarized in terms of variables to which the responsible decision-maker is known to be sensitive. Human cognitive limitations may not only bring about an effective reduction of complex scenario information, but they may also cause its significant distortion.

A CLOSER LOOK AT THE SCENARIO CONCEPT

Despite the abundant use of the term scenario by many a maker of long-term policies (and most of us are, if only at a personal level) it is difficult to give this concept a precise theoretical definition. In their evaluative paper Becker and Van Houten (1984) circumscribe a scenario as 'a description of the existing state of a society (or part thereof), of possible and/or desirable future states of that society, and of chains of events leading from the existing state to those futures. This circumscription comprises three components, viz. basic analysis, imagined futures and developmental processes' (translated from Becker and Van Houten, 1984, p. 56).

Jungerman (1985), who reviews the essential literature, defines a scenario 'as a consistent representation of the hypothetical development of a system from an initial state to some expected and/or desired final state; analytically it may be conceived as a path in a decision tree' (p. 327).

When could we speak of a 'good scenario'? Becker and Van Houten (1984) list some eight evaluative criteria ranging from presence versus absence of basic analysis, images of the future and developmental processes, respectively, to methodological soundness and substantive relevance for policy-making. Jungermann (1985) cites consistency and plausibility as the two most-mentioned quality criteria of scenarios.

The problem of evaluating scenarios may be better understood if we make the fundamental distinction between individual and social scenarios. From a decision-theoretic point of view a purely individual scenario could be conceived as a path in a (dynamic) decision tree, which sketches an imaginable course of events between an initial decision to embark upon action A, say, and an ultimate 'terminal' consequence at the projected time horizon. The path may go along chance nodes and particular outcomes of uncontrollable uncertain events, and it may also go along later (sub-)decision nodes where conditioned and often corrective actions are selected.

Thus any behavioural scenario is a natural mixture of what Becker and Van Houten (1984) termed projective and prospective scenarios; probabilistic predictions as well as 'utilistic' intentions both play significant roles. Also, any scenario may end in a desirable consequence, or it may end undesirably. To guide individual choice behaviour, scenarios ending in a bad future would be at least as important as scenarios ending in a desired future state. The point here is that it may seem useful to construct scenarios aimed at desired future states of the world, but that rational decision-making in principle pertains to a *set* of alternative initial courses of actions *each* of which minimally involves one, but more likely involves *several* alternative scenarios connecting the initial selected action to the various possible terminal consequences. Thus long-term individual decision behaviour based on scenarios seems a rather complicated affair which is liable to the many possible errors and distortions of human judgment (see Hogarth and Makridakis (1981) for an overview in connection with forecasting and planning).

The latter conclusion applies with even greater force when a set of scenarios pertains to a collective (a community or society) and has been constructed using inputs from various parties. Relatively simple issues like a basic description of the current situation or the delineation of a desirable future state may get rather problematic because of differences in the relevant database and the set of goals used by the different parties.

Potentially the most controversial part of scenario construction, however, would be the modelling of developmental processes comprising both uncertain factors and conditional decisions whose combined probable effects have to be assessed. Here one needs to make plenty of assumptions about the relevance of sets of alternative hypotheses to which probabilities have to be assigned. Also, assumptions are required concerning the feasibility of conditional courses of action and their impact on the set of terminal consequences. Thus there is ample ground for confusion, differences of opinion and enduring controversies among the different parties involved in the construction and evaluation of scenarios whose terminal future states pertain to the interests of all.

Social scenarios naturally tend to be more encompassing than individual ones. The many possible courses of action, or policies, that might lead to a particular future state of the world, as well as the many uncertain factors potentially influencing the nature and desirability of the consequences eventually obtained, make the required scenarios less tractable analytically. The formal definition of a scenario as a path (*one* path) in a decision tree is not easily operationalized under these circumstances and one may have to fall back on less precise and less testable criteria such as comprehensiveness, consistency, plausibility and substantive relevance. The general theoretical question, of course, is whether we could evaluate any branch of a tree representation of a particular decision problem, as, for example, comprehensive, consistent, plausible and relevant enough for a 'good' decision to be taken. The psychologist here would hasten to ask how many 'good' decisions are actually based on simple, *in*consistent and *im*plausible scenarios whose substantive relevance is at best partial to the problem at hand.

In sum, it seems unclear as yet to what extent 'good decision-making' is, or should be, based on elaborate scenarios and how the latter are to be precisely defined in order to be decision-relevant. As long as this state of affairs continues and to the extent that actual policy scenarios contain much more, or less, or something different, than what would be necessary and sufficient for a 'good' decision about the issue under consideration, there is ample room for improper use of the scenarios, and this would even be hard to pinpoint and comprehend.

In the experiment to be reported next, the four (social) energy scenarios of the Dutch Societal Discussion on (nuclear) Energy Policy are used in the way they were summarized by the SDEP steering committee: as a list of feasible policy actions and their long-term effects with respect to the economy, the energy system and the environment.

THE JUDGMENT OF ENERGY SCENARIOS: AN EXPERIMENTAL EVALUATION

The experiment was aimed at obtaining answers to several questions. First, how well is scenario information stored and retained in the user's memory? Second, does a holistic (intuitive) preference ranking of a set of scenarios correspond to a ranking which results from an analytical multi-attribute evaluation, and which specific actions and/or effects are most determinant of the user's overall preference order? Third, which types of actions or effects included in the scenario description are judged relatively feasible or likely, respectively, thus being most determinant of the scenario's overall plausibility? Fourth, is the cognitive handling of scenarios as suggested above related to personal characteristics of the user, such as age, education and political inclination?

These questions imply three foci of experimental attention: memorizability, judged plausibility and subjective attractiveness of (parts of) a set of energy scenarios. These points of interest are investigated under different experimental conditions resulting from the orthogonal combination of three independent variables: (1) quantity of scenario information provided, (2) description of scenarios in list versus story format, and (3) presence versus absence of a scenario label or title.

One hypothesis is that the existence of prior policy preferences, or perhaps a more general political inclination, exerts a significant influence on what is and what is not retained in memory after one has read through the scenario information. Another hypothesis is that a scenario's judged plausibility may be more dependent upon the judged feasibility of the various actions it contains than upon the likelihood of the outcomes of uncertain events or processes over which one has little or no control. A third hypothesis is that an analytical multi-attribute evaluation of a scenario's attractiveness results in smaller differences of opinion among different political groups than an overall holistic rank ordering. With respect to the experimental variables one may hypothesize that listed scenario information is better retained in memory than information presented in story format. One may also suspect that when more information is provided to the user a lower proportion of pieces of scenario information is retained. And one may further suppose that the addition of an informative scenario label or title significantly influences someone's preference order for the four scenarios, especially when little information is provided in story format.

Method

Subjects. Eighty paid volunteers, recruited via an advertisement in the Groningen University newspaper served as subjects in the experiment. They were arbitrarily assigned to eight different groups created on the basis of the three dichotomous experimental variables mentioned above. The proportion of male subjects in each group varied between 30 and 70 and was 34 overall. Average subject age was 22.6 years, varying among groups between 21.2 and 24.3 years. Subjects were spread over 24 different scientific and professional disciplines. The great majority of them had not taken active part in the national (nuclear) energy debate of the early 1980s. Political inclination data will be reported at the beginning of the 'Results' section.

Experimental design. The four energy scenarios of the SDEP, discussed in the first section of this chapter and briefly represented in Table 1 before, were summarily presented to subjects in one of eight different versions. As a set of four, the scenarios were either long (covering about 20 different aspects) or short (8 aspects); they were either presented in list format (as in Table 1) or in story format (see below); and they either were or were not indicated by an informative label (see Table 1) next to a letter code (A, B, C and D) used to identify the scenarios under all conditions. The orthogonal combination of these three experimental variables yielded eight different sets of four scenarios each, to be presented to eight groups of ten subjects each, respectively.

Materials. Each set of four scenarios was described on separate sheets of paper and put in a folder to be presented to subjects. Table 1 above illustrates the *short list* version *with title* of the four scenarios. As an example, the quotation below gives Scenario C (called the Sharing of Labour Scenario, SLS, in Table 1) in its *short* version, in *story* format and *without title* (but with an opening catch-phrase).

> Letter code: C
> 'The consumption of energy should grow less rapidly.'
> When energy consumption grows less fast a limited economic growth is still possible. This will be coupled to a shortening of the working week and a distribution of available work, which will create a greater amount of leisure time. The current level of prosperity will not suffer from this. To provide us with sufficient energy as many different sources as possible must be exploited, including or not including nuclear power. Under the circumstances thus arising it will not be difficult to fight environmental pollution and to protect nature.

The *long* story version of Scenario C took up about 40 lines of text presented on slightly more than one full page, like the other three scenarios in the same set. The long list version of the four scenarios consisted of four lists of about 20 different descriptive aspects ordered under the three categories of socioeconomic (SE), energy-political (EN) and environmental (MI, from the Dutch 'milieu') actions and effects. Each folder containing four scenario descriptions opened with half a page giving the standard conditions valid for all four scenarios, e.g. demographic descriptors, expected technological developments and economic developments abroad. In all conditions the four scenarios of a set were letter-coded A, B, C and D; in the 'title-present' condition the scenario title was added to the letter code (as in Table 1).

For each of four pairs of experimental conditions (long versus short list *and* story with versus without title) there were separate instruction and response booklets dealing with the various judgment tasks in a page-by-page fashion. To facilitate the rank ordering following importance of the selected set of scenario aspects in task (4) below, a set of cards describing the aspects was also supplied to each subject.

Successive judgment tasks. After they had studied the four scenarios for some time subjects had to work successively through basically four different tasks:

(1) Giving an overall holistic ranking of the four scenarios with regard to (a) personal preference and (b) probability of realization, respectively.

(2) Putting the scenarios aside and taking a multiple-choice test in which recognition memory was assessed for about one quarter of all relevant descriptive aspects of each scenario (16 in the 'long', 7 in the 'short' scenario condition). Four variants of this memory test were prepared in which the four scenarios rotated over tested aspects; use of the four variants was randomized over subjects.

(3) Evaluating the four scenarios by means of a Simple Multi-Attribute Rating Procedure (SMART—Gardiner and Edwards, 1975; Edwards, 1977) resulting in a weighted sum of scenario preference scores across the set of aspects selected as 'important'. The presented set of aspects was subdivided in the 'long' ('short') version into 11 (4) SE, 7 (3) EN and 3 (1) MI aspects, respectively.

(4) Judging, under each scenario, the feasibility of specific actions and the conditional likelihood of their predicted effects, again in the 'long' (but not in the 'short') version separately for 7 SE, 4 EN and 2 MI actions, and 4 SE, 4 EN and 1 MI effects, respectively. (One EN action was—after reformulation—also incorporated as EN effect).

Further details of the above tasks will be provided in the 'Results' section of this chapter. The instructional and response booklets were concluded by a set of personal questions concerning, for example, the subject's age, education, profession, and political inclination.

Procedure. Subjects individually worked through their instruction and response booklets in groups of 20 on four different occasions in the second half of November 1985. They were introduced to, and supervised during the experiment by the junior author and a research assistant. Together with subjects' apparent interest in the topic of scenario evaluation this procedure ensured that raw data would be as valid and reliable as one might expect. It turned out that an average of 125 minutes was needed for the 'long story' version of the experiment, and 113 minutes for the 'long list', 90 minutes for the 'short story' and 84 minutes for the 'short list' versions. Thus there seemed to be a story versus list effect on total judgment time; the 'story' version took about 12 and 6 minutes longer on the average in the 'long' and 'short' versions, respectively.

Results

In this section we will successively report on (I) Political inclination and composition of subject groups, (II) recognition memory for scenario information (task (2) above), (III) holistic and analytic judgments of scenario plausibility (tasks (1b) and (4) above), and (IV) holistic and analytic evaluation of scenario attractiveness (tasks (1a) and (3) above). In subsections II, III and IV we will also discuss relationships between dependent task variables and subjects' political inclination. All reported effects have been tested for their statistical significance using multivariate and univariate analyses of variance and some t-tests.

I. *Political inclination and composition of subject groups*

During the Dutch Societal Discussion on (nuclear) Energy Policy (1981–1983) political inclination appeared to be the strongest personal background variable related to variations in scenario preference. The conservative-right mostly preferred an 'economic growth and unlimited energy consumption' scenario; the political left was taken by economic decentralization and conservation of energy policies (cf. scenarios B and D, respectively, in Table 1).

The distribution of political inclinations among the present experimental subjects is given in Table 2. For convenience of analysis and presentation the centre-right governmental parties have been grouped together as well as a small centre-liberal (in the European sense) party and those who said they were politically 'undecided' (who had surprisingly corresponding patterns of judgment).

II. *Recognition memory for scenario information*

Memory for specific scenario information was tested by asking subjects to respond to 16 four-choice questions in the 'long' and 7 similar questions in the 'short' version of the experiment. An example question from the 'long' version is:

According to the Industrial Recovery Scenario the total number of civil servants will . . .
a. be limited to 5000
b. remain unchanged
c. increase by 10 000
d. increase by 50 000.

Table 2   Frequency distribution of political inclination of 80 subjects

Political inclination	Centre-right	'Centre'	Moderate left	Radical left
Dutch labels	CDA + VVD	D'66 + undecided	PvdA	klein links
No. subjects	18	20	20	22

Table 3 Average percentage of errors in
the multiple-choice memory test for 'long'
and 'short' scenario versions

Scenario	A	B	C	D
'Short'	36	34	28	20
'Long'	26	30	43	26

Note. Figures have been rounded to the
nearest integer. Data in each row are based on
judgments of 40 subjects.

The overall mean percentage of errors on the memory test proved to be
significantly lower for scenario D (Preservation of Prosperity and Environment) than for the other three. This may be explained by the novel and
interesting nature of this scenario. Table 3 presents the error percentage for
each scenario separately for 'long' and 'short' versions. The exceptionally
large value for 'long' scenario C (Sharing of Labour) is perhaps due to its
rather unusual and politically uninteresting nature.

No main effects of the experimental variables on the error percentage were
obtained, nor did this percentage significantly correlate with either the
average preference rank given a scenario in task (1a) or the average plausibility rank given a scenario in task (1b). The error percentage also appeared
unrelated to political inclination of subjects.

'Difficult' questions proved to be those requiring numerical responses as in
the example given above, or those that offered the subject the choice among
hard-to-discriminate answers such as when future industrial profits were
presented as possibly: strongly increasing for all, remaining constant for all,
increasing for small companies, and increasing somewhat for all companies,
respectively.

So none of our experimental hypotheses was confirmed regarding effects of
political inclination, amount of scenario information and list versus story
format, respectively, on the memorizability of scenario information.

III. *Judgments of scenario plausibility*

This section reports on the outcomes of two tasks. In task (1b) subjects
were asked to rank order the four scenarios (by laying these out in front of
them) according to probability of realization around the year 2000. Let us
label the results of this judgment 'holistic plausibility'. Task (4) presented
subjects with separate sets of actions and effects under each scenario and
required them to indicate numerically their subjective belief that an intended
action could be carried out ('if all parties concerned do their best') and that a
predicted effect ('given that all intended actions have been carried out')

Table 4   Holistic and analytic plausibility rankings of the four scenarios

| | Holistic | Analytic plausibility | | |
		Action feasibility		Likelihood of effects
Short version	A/C B D	A B C D		A C/B/D
Long version	A B/C D	A/B C D	—SE—	A D B/C
		A/B/C D	—EN—	A C/B D
		A/C B D	—MI—	D C/A B
		A C/B D	—overall—	A C/B/D

Note. Plausibility is ordered from left (most) to right. A / between two scenarios indicates that these are about equally plausible. The number of subjects yielding each rank order is 40. Holistic rankings result from a direct rank ordering task (1b); analytic rankings result from averaged percentage-belief estimates (task (4)).

would eventually occur. We shall label the results of this task 'analytic plausibility'.

Table 4 presents the average rank ordering following holistic and analytic plausibility of the four scenarios (see the short descriptions in Table 1) for the 'long' and 'short' scenario versions. Analytic plausibility is subdivided into actions and effects, and for the 'long' version these are subdivided again into subsets of SE, EN and MI actions and effects.

Given that each rank order in Table 4 is based on raw data from four different groups of subjects, viz. those judging the scenarios in list and story format with and without title, we can make the following observations and conclusions. First, holistic plausibility rankings for 'short' and 'long' scenario versions are in good correspondence and they agree fairly well with 'short' and (overall) 'long' analytic rankings based on action feasibility judgments (column 2). It appeared that the four experimental groups underlying each of the relevant cells in Table 4 are in good agreement with one another. Thus the Reference Scenario A, in fact a rather 'passive' continuation of the status quo, is judged most plausible while the 'environmental' scenario D is definitely judged least plausible, holistically and analytically as far as the feasibility of the implied actions is concerned.

Interestingly enough there are no effects of political inclination on the holistic plausibility ranking; all political parties have an approximately equal rank order overall ('short' and 'long' combined): A B/C D. There are, however, political effects on analytic plausibility based on action feasibility ('short' + 'long'); the intended actions under the Industrial Recovery Scenario B are believed to be significantly more feasible (yielding rank 1 or 2) by the centre-right and centre parties than by the political left (having B on rank 3), and the latter in turn believe the actions under scenario D (which is given rank 4 by *all* parties) to be significantly more feasible than the centre and centre-right do.

A strong and consistent 'title effect' was observed for scenario D ('Preservation of Prosperity and Environment'); although analytic plausibility based on action feasibility was judged low compared to the other scenarios, the overall plausibility percentage average is 58.3 for those 40 subjects given the title, as contrasted with only 43.2 for those judging D without title. Apparently, adding the title to this scenario strengthened its image as (almost) a political programme, a feature which seems less applicable to the other scenarios.

Analytic plausibility rank orders yield a less clear picture when considered by likelihood of *effects* (third column of table 4). In both the 'short' and the 'long' conditions different groups of subjects yield rather different (overall) plausibility rank orders of the four scenarios, which is reflected in the fact that C, B and D obtain rather similar positions (separated by /) in the overall average rank order of 40 subjects. It seems that, although subjects agree about the actions' relative *feasibility* under the various scenarios (column 2 of Table 4), they differ amongst themselves about their *effectiveness* (column 3). This seems to apply exclusively to scenarios B, C and D, all of which imply 'active' changes compared to the Reference Scenario A. The plausibility differences occur mostly with respect to B and D, as one might expect, and they are strongly related to subjects' political inclination. Table 5 shows the approximate reversal of average 'likelihood of effects' percentages for scenarios B and D as one moves from centre-right to radical left in the political spectrum.

For the 'long' scenario condition analytic plausibility has been analysed separately for socioeconomic (SE), energy-political (EN) and environmental (MI) actions and effects. Cells 2,2 and 2,3 of Table 4 give the corresponding rank orders of scenarios according to average belief percentages. Note that for *action feasibility* there is a fair amount of agreement among the three categories, although B is definitely ranked below C (and A) with respect to MI actions as compared to SE and EN. Under 'likelihood of effects' we see the various scenarios obtain rather different ranks following SE, EN and MI. Especially noteworthy is the 'unusual' rank order D C/A B following likeli-

Table 5 Judged likelihood of scenario effects by political inclination

	Centre-right	'Centre'	Moderate left	Radical left
Scenario B	67.2	58.5	50.2	55.9
Scenario D	47.1	57.6	53.5	65.3

Note. The number of subjects corresponding to each column is about 20 (see Table 2).

Table 6 Average percentages of belief in the feasibility of actions and the conditional likelihood of effects under the four 'long' scenarios, separately for SE, EN and MI categories, and in total

	Feasibility of actions				Likelihood of events			
	SE	EN	MI	Total	SE	EN	MI	Total
Scenario A	60	71	71	65	62	61	55	61
Scenario B	60	71	65	64	50	56	47	52
Scenario C	58	71	70	64	48	58	55	53
Scenario D	45	48	39	45	53	50	67	53

Note. Numbers have been rounded to the nearest integer. Total averages are a weighted combination of SE, EN and MI figures, as the latter depend upon different numbers of actions or effects (see the Method section). Each number is based on the judgments of 40 subjects.

hood of environmental (MI) effects (*given* that the various packages of intended actions are carried out). Evidently, scenario D is generally judged implausible for various *other* reasons than the conditional likelihood of its MI (and SE) *effects*.

The peculiar position of scenario D is further illustrated in Table 6 which presents the average belief percentages overall and separately for SE, EN and MI actions and effects. The table clearly reveals that for scenarios A, B and C feasibility of actions is generally judged higher than likelihood of effects (compare 'Total' columns) and that the reverse is true for scenario D. This effect largely occurs through the EN and MI items, perhaps because of their greater specificity compared to the SE items. Clearly, overall (analytic) scenario plausibility is most strongly connected to feasibility of intended actions, except for scenario D where—particularly for the MI items— predicted effects are judged as more likely than the actions aimed at them are thought to be feasible.

Looking at separate actions and effects under the different 'long' scenarios we could spot specific sources of subjects' scepticism, the latter defined as a lower than 50 per cent belief figure. For example, wage reduction of 2 per cent annually until 2000 in scenario B and promotion of public transport at the expense of private transport in D were judged to be less feasible. Also, a decrease in the unemployment rate from 650 000 in 1980 to 200 000 in the year 2000 in scenarios B, C and D was thought to be less likely, as was the decrease by 19 per cent of total energy consumption in scenario D.

IV. *Holistic and analytic scenario preferences*

Tasks (1a) and (3) required subjects to rank order the four scenarios according to their attractiveness and to subject them to a weighted multiattribute utility evaluation, respectively.

Table 7 Average amount of million Dutch guilders allotted as desired investment to the four scenarios in the 'short' and 'long' versions

Scenario	A	B	C	D
'Short'	19	15	30	36
'Long'	11	23	23	44

Note. Figures have been rounded to the nearest integer. Data in each row are based on judgments of 40 subjects.

The *holistic preference ranking* was presented in two parts. First, the subject considered the four sheets of paper containing the scenario descriptions and rank ordered them according to attractiveness on the table in front of him/her. In the second part the subject divided a total of 100 million Dutch guilders over the four scenarios such that each allotted amount reflected the financial investment one would make to promote the realization of each scenario, 'if one had an influential political position'.

The overall average preference orders for the 'short' and 'long' versions as obtained from the two subtasks are in good correspondence; generally, scenarios D and C are most preferred, while A and B are least preferred. Table 7 presents the average amount of million guilders allotted to the 'long' and 'short' scenarios in the second part of task (1a).

Table 8 shows the (obvious) effects on scenario preference of political inclination; the centre-right and both left groups assign radically different preference ranks to scenarios B (Industrial Recovery) and D (Preservation of Prosperity and Environment), evidently the two most controversial ones.

Multi-attribute utility evaluation. Task (3) was performed in three successive steps. First, the subject had to indicate from a presented list of either 21 ('long' version) or 8 ('short' version) variable aspects which of these he or she would select as 'important' for evaluating the four scenarios. As a second step the subject rank ordered the selected aspects from most to least important.

Table 8 Relationship between political inclination and preference rank order of scenarios as obtained from direct ranking

Centre-right	'Centre'	Moderate left	Radical left
B C/A D	C/D B/A	D/C A/B	D C A/B

Note. Preference is ordered from left (most) to right. A / indicates that the two bordering scenarios are about equally preferred. Each rank order is based on data from about 20 subjects (see Table 2) obtained in part 1 of task (1a).

Step three required the subject to consider each selected aspect separately and evaluate each of the four scenarios on it by giving them a grade or 'report-mark' between 1 ('absolutely worthless') and 10 ('excellent'); the meaning of such a scale is highly familiar to anyone having had a Dutch school education. An additional fourth step was computational and was carried out afterwards by the experimenters. For each scenario cross-products were computed of the importance rank given to any aspect and the scenario's report-mark; the set of cross-products for any scenario was then averaged over the subject's (sub-)set of selected aspects. Let us label the latter 'average SMART values', to be considered across subjects.

Note that the above procedure deviates somewhat from the formal SMART technique recommended by, for example Edwards (1977), most notably in the manner of weights assignment which we will keep in mind below.

Selection of 'important' aspects. The average number of presented aspects selected as 'important' was 5.6 out of 8 (70 per cent) and 14 out 21 (66 per cent) for the 'short' and 'long' scenario versions, respectively. No significant effects of the experimental variables on the *proportion* of selected aspects was obtained. Non-selected aspects mostly fell in the SE and EN categories, both more numerous than MI. 'Popular' aspects in the 'short' version appeared to be 'degree of environmental protection' (selected by 38 out of 40 subjects), 'employment rate' (34 subjects), and 'kind of energy sources utilized' (32). The same three aspects proved to be most 'popular' in the 'long' scenario version as well, where they were selected by 36, 39 and 37 subjects, respectively, out of 40. Remarkably unpopular in the 'short' version appeared 'height of energy prices' (selected by 12 subjects, and not presented in the 'long' version), as were 'degree of selective utilization of natural gas' and 'degree to which the business week is shortened' (11 and 12 subjects, respectively) in the 'long' version. The '%' columns of Table 9 reveal an effect of subjects' political inclination on the proportion of SE, EN and MI aspects selected as 'important'. For those familiar with the Dutch energy debate it is not surprising that the centre-right selects more, while the radical left selects fewer SE aspects, whereas the reverse appears the case for MI aspects which are most popular with the political left. Note also that EN aspects are relatively unpopular with the centre-right.

Importance ranking of selected aspects. In the computational SMART procedure the most important aspects are given the highest ranks. We therefore transformed subjects' raw ranking data (1 = 'most important') such that the most important aspect was given a rank of 21 in the 'long', and of 8 in the 'short' version, and we counted backwards as far as necessary to cover all aspects selected by each subject. Given that selected aspects were rank

Table 9   Average proportion (%) and rank of selected aspects for 'short' and 'long' versions taken together, separately for SE, EN and MI categories, as obtained from subjects having different political inclinations

| | Political inclination | | | | | | | |
| | Centre-right | | 'Centre' | | Moderate left | | Radical left | |
Type of aspect	%	rank	%	rank	%	rank	%	rank
SE	79	12	63	10	63	10	59	10
EN	54	11	69	11	61	11	70	13
MI	73	10	92	10	93	12	96	12

Note. All numbers have been rounded to the nearest integer. Figures are based on judgments of about 20 subjects (see Table 2).

ordered, the average rank across all aspects is a direct function of the number selected. Thus we obtained overall average importance ranks of 5.7 and 14.6 for the 'short' and 'long' versions, which is about half-way between 8 and 9-5.6 (the latter being the average *number* of selected aspects) and 21 and 22-14, respectively. Meaningful comparisons among average importance ranks, therefore, can only be made among different kinds of aspects. As is shown in the upper row of Table 11, in the 'long' version MI aspects were ranked highest overall, followed by SE and EN aspects; this was also the case for the 'short' version. The 'rank' columns of Table 9 reveal, for the 'short' and 'long' versions taken together, that this might be mostly determined by the more numerous political left; the order of importance of SE, EN and MI aspects for the centre-right goes against the overall average. Note that the average importance ranks (weakly) follow the pattern of proportions ('popularity') of selected aspects. The relationship suggested by Table 9 also holds for specific selected aspects: those most 'popular' in the selection task were also given high importance ranks, and vice versa.

Grading the scenarios by 'report-marks'. The average report-mark 'over all aspects' given to each scenario in the 'long' version is presented in parentheses in the fourth numerical column of Table 11, yielding the inferred (unweighted) preference order D C B A; the pattern for the 'short' version is roughly the same, yielding D C A B. Both rank orders very well agree with the relative scenario preferences reflected by allotted amounts of investment millions represented in Table 7, and with the direct preference rank order given in the last column of Table 11. As Table 11 shows, scenarios A, B and C are judged lower than 'sufficient' (which would yield a mark of 6) on the average, despite the fact that both B and C are marked as more than 'sufficient' on the SE category of aspects. Scenario D is marked highest overall (7.1) although it fails to reach 'sufficiency' on the SE aspects.

Table 10   Average report-marks given to the four scenarios by the four political
groups

	Centre-right	'Centre'	Moderate left	Radical left
Scenario A	6.4	5.4	5.7	4.7
Scenario B	7.0	5.4	5.3	4.3
Scenario C	6.7	5.9	6.0	5.6
Scenario D	5.4	6.4	7.2	8.3

Note. Each number is based on the judgments of about 20 subjects (see Table 2).

Again, effects of the experimental variables were less pronounced than those of political inclination. Table 10 presents the average report-marks given to the four scenarios by the four different political groups. For each scenario the effects on report-marks of political inclination are highly significant; note that the effects are most pronounced (and opposite) for scenarios B and D. The inferred (unweighted) preference rank orders for the several political parties correspond fairly well with those depicted in Table 8 on the basis of direct rankings.

Average SMART values. An overview of average SMART values (taken across subjects as well as sets of selected aspects) is presented in Table 11. This table only pertains to the 'long' version for which the term 'analytic preference' means the most. First of all, note from the 'over all aspects' column that average SMART values, too, nicely correspond to average direct preference ranks (last column) which we already saw to agree with the average report-marks (in parentheses). The correlation between SMART

Table 11   Average SMART values together with their corresponding report-marks (in parentheses) for the four scenarios, separately for SE, EN and MI categories of aspects (whose average importance ranks are added) and over all aspects together. The last column gives average holistic preference ranks

Scenarios	Categories of aspects			Over all aspects	Holistic preference rank
	SE (14.5)	EN (13.3)	MI (16.0)		
A	78.2	71.7	75.6	76.6	3.2
	(5.5)	(5.6)	(4.7)	(5.3)	
B	99.8	62.7	63.0	82.5	2.8
	(6.9)	(4.9)	(4.1)	(5.7)	
C	94.4	73.2	75.5	84.5	2.2
	(6.5)	(5.6)	(4.8)	(5.8)	
D	84.2	107.8	137.9	103.8	1.7
	(5.8)	(7.9)	(8.5)	(7.1)	

values and report-marks is less when we consider these values by scenario and across categories of SE, EN and MI aspects. This is of course related to the differential importance weighting of these categories. Thus we conclude that the effects of differential weighting of aspects may be unnoticeable overall (cf. the perfect correlation between SMART values and report-marks in column 4), while at the same time it may be clearly visible across the SE, EN and MI component values of the overall SMART average. And thus we see that the scenarios' relative attractiveness can be variously attributed to different categories of aspects. For example, scenario B is judged fairly good with respect to socioeconomic aspects but it receives a very low SMART value on environmental (MI) aspects. Approximately the reverse is true for D which is judged highest on MI aspects. Owing to the differential importance weighting of aspect categories the overall (column 4) SMART preference order of the four scenarios, D C B A, turns out to be a composite of three category-wise preference orders, viz. B C D A under SE, D C A B under EN, and D A/C B under MI aspects. To some extent the different category-wise preference orders reflect the traditional dilemma of economy versus environment (and energy consumption).

Effects of the experimental variables on average SMART values proved to be weak and non-systematic. Political inclination effects on SMART values are very well in line with those on report-marks given in Table 10. Their statistical significance, however, is greatly suppressed, possibly through the introduction of additional statistical noise by the use of importance weights.

Discussion

Let us briefly consider the experimental results in light of the hypotheses formulated at the start of this section. Although the 'interesting' scenario D proved to be memorized (or recognized) more easily than A, C and D, no effects of the experimental variables were obtained on the percentage of errors on the recognition memory test. We did, however, notice that scenarios presented in list format took minutes less to work through than when presented in story format. This suggests that 'listed' scenario information is more easily processed in (working) memory. A major finding of the experimental study is that analytic scenario plausibility mostly depends upon the judged feasibility of the intended actions or policies and is associated less with the conditional likelihood of the predicted effects. This conclusion, however, is not valid for scenario D, the feasibility of whose (unusual) actions was doubted by subjects. There were some (predictable) effects of political inclination on analytic scenario plausibility. Another major finding is that the overall plausibility ranking of the four scenarios, roughly: A C/B D, turned out quite opposite to the overall preference ranking: D C B A. As regards the latter, a fair correspondence was observed between direct preference ranking and analytical preference rating by means of a simple multi-attribute technique. Strong political inclination effects on scenario preference measures were obtained, the political centre-right being most in favour of the Industrial Recovery Scenario B, while the political left cherished the environmental scenario D. Political inclination effects were also observed in the relative popularity of selected judgmental aspects and in their assigned importance ranks. Thus overall scenario preference was concluded to be differentially composed of component preferences with respect to socioeconomic, energy-political and environmental aspects. As one might expect, there were few and non-systematic effects of the experimental variables on scenario preference data. No evidence was obtained about a possibly reduced political 'controversiality' of the scenarios, especially B and D, through the use of an analytical preference composition method.

SUMMARY AND CONCLUSIONS

The four long-term energy scenarios of the Dutch Societal Discussion on (nuclear) Energy Policy have been subjected to both a theoretical evaluation and a judgmental experiment. It appeared that the scenarios fail to meet essential quality criteria such as validity of assumptions, plausibility of developmental processes and comparability with respect to substantive issues such as the nuclear power question itself. Hence their practical use during the societal debate was rather limited. Neither the criticisms nor the low practical value of the scenarios is surprising in view of the immature status of the scenario concept and methodology. A decision-theoretic conceptualization (scenarios as paths in a decision tree) may effectively reduce the potential amount of scenario information and pin the decision-maker down on the essentials. However, for complex multi-attribute scenarios involving various interest groups, the decision-theoretic definition may be analytically intractable.

In the second part of the chapter 'long' and 'short' versions of the four energy scenarios were experimentally investigated for their memorizability, subjective plausibility and attractiveness. The aspect-wise presentation of the scenarios, coupled to an analytic evaluation of their plausibility and preferability, enabled us to pinpoint specific kinds of scenario components either underlying overall plausibility and/or preferability, or particularly sensitive to the effects of subjects' political inclination. Ironically enough, it appeared that the most preferred scenario on the average was judged to be the least plausible, and the analysis suggests that although environmental protection through a wise utilization of energy is highly valued, socioeconomic policies and their predicted effects are believed to be most feasible. These conclusions, of course, should be judged relatively to the method followed and the specific set of scenarios considered.

REFERENCES
Becker, H. A. and Van Houten, D. J. (1984) 'Energie in scenario's'. *Beleid en Maatschappij*, **3**, 55–65.

Biel, A. and Montgomery, H. (1986) 'Scenarios in Energy Planning', in B. Brehmer, H. Jungermann, P. Lourens and G. Sevón (eds.), *New Directions in Research on Decision Making*, Amsterdam: North-Holland.

CEC (Commission of the European Communities) (1980) *Crucial Choices for the Energy Transition*, EUR 6610, Luxemburg: CEC.

De Vries, B. and Dijk, D. (1985) 'Electric power generation options for the Netherlands to 2000; an evaluation of government's and environmentalists' scenarios', *Energy Policy*, **13**, 230–242.

Edwards, W. (1977) 'How to use multiattribute utility measurement for social decision making'. *IEEE Transactions on Systems, Man and Cybernetics*, SMC **7**, 326–340.

Gardiner, P. and Edwards, W. (1975) 'Public values: multi-attribute utility measurement for social decision making', in M. F. Kaplan and S. Schwartz (eds.), *Human Judgment and Decision Processes*, New York: Academic Press.

Häfele, W. *et al.* (Energy Systems Program Group) (1981) *Energy in a Finite World*, Vol. 1, Cambridge, Mass.: Ballinger.

Hogarth, R. M. and Makridakis, S. (1981) 'Forecasting and planning: an evaluation', *Management Science*, **27**, 115–137.

Jansen, J. L. A. (1985) 'Handling a debate on a source of severe tension', in E. Denig the Netherlands', in P. Slaa, W. Turkenburg and B. Williams (eds.), *Risk and Participation*, Proceedings of the Second Conference on Science, Society and Education, Amsterdam: VUA.

Jansen, J. L. A. (1985) 'Handling a bebate on a source of severe tension', in E. Denig and A. van der Meiden (eds.), *A Geography of Public Relations Trends*, Dordrecht: Martinus Nijhoff.

Jungermann, H. (1985) 'Psychological aspects of scenarios', in V. T. Covello, J. L. Mumpower, P. J. M. Stallen and V. R. R. Uppuluri (eds.), *Environmental Impact Assessment, Technology Assessment, and Risk Analysis: Contributions from the Psychological and Decision Sciences*, Heidelberg: Springer Verlag.

Renn, O., Stegelmann, H. U., Albrecht, G. and Kotte, U. (1985) 'The empirical investigation of citizens' preferences with respect to four energy scenarios', in V. T. Covello, J. L. Mumpower, P. J. M. Stallen and V. R. R. Uppuluri (eds.), *Environmental Impact Assessment, Technology Assessment, and Risk Analysis: Contributions from the Psychological and Decision Sciences*, Heidelberg: Springer Verlag.

SAC (Scenario Advisory Committee) (Adviescommissie Scenario's) (1983) *Eindrapport*, The Hague.

Sassin, W., Hölzl, A., Rogner, H.-H. and Schrattenholzer, L. (1983) 'Fueling Europe in the future; the long-term energy problem in the EC countries: alternative R&D strategies', Laxenburg (Austria): International Institute for Applied Systems Analysis, RR-83-9/EUR 8421-EN.

SDEP (Steering Committee of the Societal Discussion on (nuclear) Energy Policy) (1983) *Interim Report* (in Dutch).

SDEP (Steering Committee of the Societal Discussion on (nuclear) Energy Policy) (1984) *Final Report* (in Dutch).

Vlek, C. A. J. (1986) 'Rise, decline and aftermath of the Dutch "Societal Discussion on (nuclear) Energy Policy" (1981–1983)', in H. A. Becker and A. Porter (eds.), *Impact Assessment Today*, Utrecht: Van Arkel. Also available as Heymans Bulletin No. HB-86-784 EX, University of Groningen Institute for Social and Organisational Psychology.

Index

acceptability, 182, 189–190
accuracy, 140
aggregation, 109
  behavioural, 113–116
  mathematical, 116–120
  probabilities, 118–119
  see also group judgments and Delphi
    and role-playing
aleatory logic, 55
ambiguity, 65, 71

base rate, 77
Bayes' theorem, 28, 91, 230, 235
belief bias, 33, 38, 40, 43, 45
belief measures, 72
biases in judgment, 21, 31–46, 49–59,
    70, 139, 178, 254, 261, 272–273
  see also judgmental fallibility and
    heuristics
bootstrapping, 111, 205, 236–239
  see also linear models
brainstorming, 109, 115–116
Brunswik's probabilistic functionalism,
    199

calibration, 21–28, 68–70, 95–99
causality, 113, 246, 252, 256, 258–259
certainty, 33
citation bias, 49
cognitive map, 247, 264
coherence, 12, 19, 28, 88, 230
combining forecasts, 229
computer aid, 99–102, 146, 210–212
conditional reasoning, 34
confirmation bias, 32, 38, 43, 45
conflict situations, 157, 206
  see also policy conflict
conjunction fallacy, 254, 261

consensus, 112
covariance, 231
credibility, 66, 182, 185, 186–189
cross-impact analysis, 92, 102, 147–148

decision analysis, 14–15, 64, 274, 288
decision problem, 185
decision theory, 12–14, 64, 91, 230
decomposition, 92
deductive reasoning, 38
Delphi, 109, 114–115, 129–151, 179,
    183, 191–194
  case example, 191–194
  conventional, 131–132
  differential weighting, 231, 234
  execution, 150, 193
  experts and, 137, 192
  formulation of scenarios, 149–150,
    193
  paper and pencil, 132
  real-time, 132
  reliability, 136–137
  reporting results, 150
  selection of panellists, 149, 191–192
  validity, 136

economic forecasting, 43–44
electric load forecasting, 229, 236–239
energy policy, 267, 268
energy scenario, 267, 268, 274, 288
epistemic logic, 55
equal weights, 234, 235, 237
  see also weights
error variance, 238
evaluation, 179
experts, 25, 28, 137, 158, 161, 180, 183,
    246, 255, 263

291